River of Compassion

Books by Bede Griffiths

The Golden String: An Autobiography

*The Marriage of East and West:
Sequel to The Golden String*

*Christ in India
Essays Toward a Hindu-Christian Dialogue*

*Cosmic Revelation
The Hindu Way to God*

*The New Creation in Christ
Christian Meditation and Community*

*A New Vision of Reality
Western Science, Eastern Mysticism and Christian Faith*

Return to the Center

*River of Compassion
A Christian Commentary on the Bhagavad Gita*

Modern Spirituality Series: Bede Griffiths

River of Compassion

*A Christian Commentary on the
Bhagavad Gita*

Bede Griffiths

Templegate Publishers
Springfield, Illinois

Templegate Publishers
302 East Adams Street
Post Office Box 5152
Springfield, Illinois
62705-5152
217-522-3353
www.templegate.com

ISBN 0-87243-253-X
Library of Congress Control Number:
2001094945

Contents

Introduction

The *Bhagavad Gita* or *Song of God* is a spiritual classic, which, though it comes from the Hindu tradition, belongs not only to Hindus, but to all the world. It is part of the spiritual inheritance of mankind. In calling this commentary on the *Bhagavad Gita* a 'Christian reading', I do not intend to suggest that there was any Christian influence in the composition of the *Bhagavad Gita* – a view which is now generally rejected – or that there is anything specifically Christian about it. I only want to show how it can be a practical spiritual guide to a Christian and to anyone who is in search of a guide on the spiritual path. There are a great many people in the West today, Christian and otherwise, who are attracted to the *Gita* and to other oriental classics, but who have no knowledge of the background of these texts and who need a guidance to help them to understand the bearing they could have on their own lives. This commentary has been written for the benefit of such people, who do not want an academic study of the *Gita*, of which there are plenty, but who want to use it as a practical guide in their spiritual life. We are realising today that no religion can stand alone. We all share a common humanity and need to share the insights of all the different religious traditions of the world. A Christian who is open to the message of the *Gita* will find that it throws new light on many aspects of the Gospel and will see at the same time how the *Bhagavad Gita* gathers a new meaning when seen in the perspective of the Gospel.

In order to study the *Bhagavad Gita*, it will be helpful to place it in its historical context. It is part of an epic poem called the *Mahabharata* which is generaly supposed to have been composed between the fourth century BC and the fourth century AD. The *Bhagavad Gita*, may have been in— troduced about the third century BC. It was the first of various long philosophical discourses to be introduced into the poem. As such, it belongs to what is called *smriti* from the root *smri* meaning 'to remember', which is what we call tradition. It is distinguished from *shruti*, from the root *sr* which means to hear, in other words, revelation.

The *Vedas*, which are the earliest Hindu Scriptures, are considered to be revelation and are usually thought to have taken their present form between 1500 and 500 BC. The *Upanishads* are the last part of the *Vedas* and the earliest ones were written about 600 BC. The *Bhagavad Gita* comes not long after these. It is in a sense a summary of Hindu doctrine because it comes at a crucial moment when several currents of thought, beginning with the *Vedas*, all come together, so that it is a kind of synthesis of doctrine, which gives it its universal character. In a real sense, it can be said that if one knows the *Gita*, one knows the essence of Hindu spirituality. The link between the *Gita* and the *Upanishads* must be understood. It is in one sense a continuation of the *Upanishads*, but something intervened between the *Upanishads* and the *Gita* which really changed the direction of Hindu religion. Hinduism is a marriage of the Aryan Sanskrit religion of the *Vedas* with the religion of the indigenous peoples of India, especially the Dravidians. It was precisely during the time of the Epics, between the fifth century BC and the fifth century AD, that these two movements came together. The *Gita* stands at the confluence of these two movements. What is most important in this development is the devotion to a personal God. In the Vedic understanding of God, of the absolute reality, there are three main concepts: *Brahman*, *Atman* and *Purusha*. *Brahman* is the principle of being, the source of the universe, the immanent presence in the whole creation. *Atman* is the principle of consciousness, the inner consciousness, the Self within every human being; and *Purusha* is the person, the Lord who is the object of worship. The later *Upanishads*, like the *Shvetashvatara Upanishad*, which may be almost contemporary with the *Bhagavad Gita*, are inspired by a popular movement of devotion to a personal god.

In the *Gita* that movement of devotion to a personal God continues but it now takes a very definite form. It is known as the *Bhagavata* movement. Bhagavan is the name for God, the Lord, as an object of worship and around about this time, the fourth century before Christ, a great awakening of devotion to a personal God seems to have taken place. In the *Upanishads* the *rishis* were more concerned with *dhyana*, meditation, and *Brahmavidya*, God realization. But the *Gita* is a response to this popular movement and it takes the form of devotion to a personal God in the form of Krishna. Instead of *dhyana*, meditation, we come to *bhakti*, devotion. *Dhyana* is not lost but devotion comes to the fore.

The author of the *Gita* is unknown but he must have been of extraordinary genius because all religious movements of the time find their place in this work. It was influenced not only by the *Upanishads*, but also by Buddhism and Jainism which carried the rather impersonal philosophical religion of the *Upanishads* even further. In early Buddhism there is no concept of a personal God at all, still less in Jainism. It is also worth mentioning that these religions were part of a movement of the *kshatriya*, the warrior caste, as distinguished from the Brahmins. In the development of the *Vedas*, around 1500 BC, the Brahmin was originally the principal figure. He was the priest who alone could perform the sacrifice. In the *Brahmanas*, which belong to the second period of Vedic religion of about 1200 BC the main concern is with religious ritual and sacrifice. Here the Brahmin, the priest, is naturally in the centre. In the next period, the *rishis* go into the forest, the *aranya*, to meditate and the *Aranyakas*, the forest books, come into being. Then it is no longer the Brahmin, the priest, who matters, as the concern is not primarily with sacrifice but with meditation. The Buddha was a warrior, a *kshatriya*; so also was Mahavira, the founder of the Jains, and with Buddhism and Jainism begins the great movement towards meditation and interior religion. The *Upanishads*, which mark the fourth stage in Vedic religion, are the records of the interior experience of the rishis and form the basis of the mystical tradition in Hinduism. The *Bhagavad Gita* seems to refer to Jainism; it is at least aware of the movement. Also it is influenced at many points by Buddhism and uses several Buddhist terms and concepts, *nirvana* being an example. And of course it continues the mystical tradition of the *Upanishads*.

The influence of the *Bhakti* movement, with its emphasis on devotion to a personal God which began to center on Krishna, is an even stronger contributing factor. It is very difficult to disentangle the whole background of Krishna worship and the unravelling of the strands cannot be done with any certainty. Some think that Krishna was originally a god of the cowherds and that this devotion gradually developed from that. Others, perhaps correctly, say that he was originally a hero. In the *Gita* he appears as one of the supporters of the Pandavas and as a great hero. That again would indicate that the *Gita* belongs to that movement of the *kshatriyas*, the warriors, and Krishna is representative of the warrior caste. On the other hand, there is a mention of a Krishna, son of Devaki in the *Chandogya Upanishad*. A sage refers to Krishna, and gives him certain instructions. It does seem that elements of the instructions which he gives are found in the *Bhagavad Gita*, so there may be a connection between this Krishna of the *Upanishad* and the Krishna of the *Gita*. The probability is that in the development of a cult of this kind, many different influences flow together. There is the cowherd and the warrior on the one hand and the sage on the other and gradually they all come together.

It is interesting that Krishna is always depicted as being blue-coloured. That may mean that he belonged to the indigenous dark-skinned people, which would be an illustration of Hinduism as the marriage of the fair-skinned Aryan people with the dark-skinned Dravidians. Shiva, the other great figure of the Absolute, was originally a non-Aryan. He was a god of the cemeteries, an outcast. Gradually he is taken into the Hindu fold and becomes the God of grace and love. A similar evolution is likely for Krishna. He was originally one of these non-Aryan gods and was taken into Hinduism and identified with Vishnu. Now Vishnu, again, like Shiva, the Rudra of the Vedas, was originally a minor figure in the Vedas. He is generally supposed to have been a sun god. In a famous story which comes into many legends, Vishnu takes three steps and bestrides the whole universe. These are supposed to be the three steps of the sun which rises in the East, takes one step to the meridian and one step to the West thus encompassing the whole universe.

This relates him to the very important figure of Narayana. When an Indian *sannyasi*, or wandering monk, meets another *sannyasi*, he says, "OM Narayana," by way of greeting. Narayana is identified with *Purusha*, the cosmic person in whom the whole cosmos resides and who pervades the whole of creation. Krishna is thus identified eventually with Narayana and with Vishnu as the Lord of the Universe. In the *Gita* all three terms occur.

In Indian sacred art the three-headed figure, the *trimurti*, depicts Brahma the creator, Vishnu the pervader or protector, and Shiva the destroyer and renewer of the universe. For the Vaishnavite or Shaivite that is only a secondary matter. For the one, Vishnu is the Supreme God, for the other, it is Shiva. Krishna was seen as an *avatara* of Vishnu, a manifestation of God on earth.

We come now to another characteristic of the *Gita*. In the *Upanishads* the understanding always was that in order to reach supreme knowledge or wisdom, *jnana*, it was necessary to retire to the forest and to meditate. Only the *sannyasi*, the monk, could attain *moksha*, liberation. Thus the *Upanishads* could only be a religion of a few. What changed everything was the doctrine of the *Gita*, that the householder, living an ordinary life but having *bhakti*, devotion to God, could reach this state of supreme union, not only as well as, but even more easily than the *sannyasi*. For the *Bhagavad Gita*, *sannyasa* is a difficult path for the few; *bhakti* is the normal path for the many. That is why the *Gita* has become a handbook for the Hindu, a kind of New Testament, because it is a teaching for the householder, the man living his ordinary life in the world, married and with children. By his devotion to Krishna, the personal God, he is able to reach *moksha*, to attain final liberation. It is well known that Mahatma Gandhi took the *Bhagavad Gita* as his guide in life. He once said that in all the situations in which he had ever been, the trials, the problems and the conflicts of his life, he had always found consolation and guidance in the *Gita*. It was his stand-by in everything. Very interestingly, he also said, "My one aim in life is to reach *moksha*, liberation, that is to know God. If I thought I could do so by retiring to a cave in the Himalayas, I would do so immediately, but I believe I can find God in my suffering fellow countrymen, therefore I dedicate my life to God in my fellow men." That is why today the vast majority of Hindus, and even the *sannyasis*, think also of this other aspect of serving God in humanity.

Ramakrishna, who was largely responsible for the renewal of Hinduism in the 19th century, introduced the same idea to some extent, and his disciple Vivekananda made it the greatest principle of all. He was a *sannyasi* who organised the Ramakrishna order of *sannyasis* all of whom are dedicated to the service of God and the people. A well-known saying of Vivekananda is, "My God, the poor; my God, the suffering; my God, the oppressed." He sought to find God in the poor, the suffering and the oppressed. That is the doctrine which has come from the *Gita*.

There is no doubt that Gandhi was also deeply influenced by the New Testament, especially the Sermon on the Mount. He had a devotion to Jesus as an example of love and forgiveness, but nevertheless he always based himself on the *Bhagavad Gita*, and the Hindu today still takes it as the base for his understanding of *karma* yoga, conceived as a way of finding God through the service of one's neighbour.

It should be remembered that originally in the *Vedas*, *karma* means ritual work. There is a section of the *Vedas* concerned with ritual, but it was always considered inferior. When Shankara, the great doctor of Vedanta of the eighth century, said that nobody could reach *moksha*, liberation, through *karma*, he was simply saying that ritual will not suffice. After the Vedic period, the idea of *karma* was extended to include moral action in general and then social action.

In the *Bhagavad Gita*, Arjuna is engaged in a great battle and this is his *karma*. He has to work, to do his duty, in order to reach God. The view is that by work, by service, in doing one's duty as a householder, it is possible to reach God. But along with *karma* one must have *bhakti*; the work must flow out of devotion to the personal God.

Finally there is *jnana*, knowledge. Through the service of work, *karma*, and through *bhakti*, devotion, one comes to *jnana*, the knowledge of God. The first six chapters of the *Gita* are concerned primarily with *karma* yoga, the way of work; the next six chapters with *bhakti* yoga, the way of love and devotion, and the last six with *jnana* yoga, the way of knowledge. But these divisions are not at all rigid. The structure is more like that of a musical composition in which a theme is taken up and developed, and then new theme is introduced; then the former theme is taken up again and so a complex pattern of different themes is woven together until all are brought finally into a harmonious and mutually enriching pattern. We must never forget that the *Bhagavad Gita* is a poem and must be read as poetry.

I have used for the commentary the text of Mascaró, published in the series of Penguin Classics. This is by far the most readable version in English and is basically true to the meaing. But it is often rather free, and I have therefore used Zaehner's translation and commentary to correct it where necessary and to give the more exact meaning. I have also referred when necessary to the Sanskrit text and to the translation of Annie Besant and Bhagavan Das. I should also add the great debt which I owe to *The Yoga of the Bhagavad Gita* by Sri Krishna Prem. The author was an Englishman, who lived as a *sannyasi* in India for many years and showed a most profound insight into Indian spirituality both in his *Yoga of the Kathopanishad* and *The Yoga of the Bhagavad Gita*.

This commentary was originally given in the form of talks to the members of our ashram, Shantivanam, in the Tiruchi District of Tamil Nadu, South India. The talks were taped and transcribed and it was owing to the labours of Brother John Sullivan that they were brought into some sort of order. Finally I owe thanks to Dr. Felicity Edwards of Rhodes University, Grahamstown, who undertook to edit the whole work and make it fit for publication.

Chapter 1

The Yoga of Arjuna's Despair

Each chapter of the *Bhagavad Gita* concerns a particular yoga. This first chapter is called "the yoga of Arjuna's despair" and it is significant that the experience of despair is a yoga; despair is often the first step on the path of spiritual life. It is very important to go through the experience of emptiness, of disillusion and despair. Many people do not awaken to the reality of God, and to the experience of transformation in their lives, until they reach the point of despair.

The term 'yoga' is one of the basic words in the *Gita*. It has many meanings but the root of the word is the same as the Latin *yugum* and the English 'yoke'. The normal meaning is 'union' or 'integration' which refers to the goal but it is important to realise that the steps by which we approach union are also yoga. The union is primarily union with God but it involves the uniting or integrating of all aspects of our being.

The text of Chapter 1 begins with two armies drawn up for battle, the Pandavas on one side, the Kauravas on the other. Arjuna is seated in his chariot between the two battle lines.

The occasion of the war has been described by Krishna Prem: "The Pandyas are five brothers who have the right to the throne, but the throne has been usurped by Dhritarashtra, King of the Kauravas and his son Duryodhana. The Pandyas were condemned to go into exile as a result of losing a game of dice. Then on their return from exile, they claim their right to the throne again, but get no satisfactory response. This leads to the Mahabharata, the great war."

From ancient times this battle has been interpreted symbolically; on the two sides of the conflict the Pandavas represent the righteous and the Kauravas the unrighteous. The battlefield is the field of the world and Arjuna represents the human soul seated in the chariot of the body, engaged in the battle of life. The Pandavas, the lawful sovereigns, are the true Self. They have been exiled from the land and their place has been usurped by Dhritarashtra the blind king who is said to have a hundred sons. He represents the selfish ego with the innumerable passions and desires which are its progeny.

The symbolism here is that in the present state of the human being the kingdom has been overthrown and the rightful king exiled. The Self is no longer in control and this false ruler who usurped the throne, the ego, is dominating the human being. Arjuna is in that situation. He sees arrayed on the other side, all his relatives and friends and even his teacher, Drona and his response is, "How can I fight against my own friends?" Again, this is human nature. We are divided against ourselves. Arjuna feels that he cannot fight this battle and in despair he lays down his arms saying, "I will not fight."

At this point, Krishna appears as his charioteer. The imagery here is that the chariot represents the body, Arjuna represents the soul and Krishna the charioteer represents the spirit that drives the chariot. Krishna as the Lord is a manifestation of the spirit within, who now counsels Arjuna as to how to undertake the battle of life. Here right at the beginning we have the main constellation of themes with which the *Bhagavad Gita* is concerned: how to face the battle of life, how the spirit will counsel us, and how each of us will undertake this battle.

The battle, then, takes place in the field of human nature. The spiritual powers in man have been driven into exile and the throne has been usurped by the blind king who represents the ego, which is blind and which has usurped the throne of the soul having driven out the spiritual powers which should be in control.

An interesting point is that the Pandavas were exiled for twelve years in the forest after which they had to remain completely unknown for one more year and only then could they return to claim the throne. This has a deep symbolic meaning. The exile in the forest is similar to the image of going into the desert. The symbolism of the desert is found in many spiritual traditions. The spiritual seeker is driven out of the world, as the Israelites were driven out of Egypt into the desert to wander for forty years. Towards the end of the desert period, a point comes when the powers of the spirit seem to disappear and the powers of matter, or demonic powers, seem to be in complete control. It is characteristic that before great renewal takes place spiritual power seems to be at its lowest ebb and unrightful demonic power appears to be in supreme control. That is precisely the situation here. The Pandavas have been through this 'dark night of the soul' and now, returning to claim the kingdom, they cannot come to an agreement with the usurpers. This is a very significant point symbolising that agreement can never be reached at the level of the human soul because the soul itself is tragically divided against itself.

So on the battlefield Arjuna sees that his enemies are his friends and relatives. There is Bhisma his grandfather's brother and Drona, who is his guru, his teacher, and Arjuna realizes that he is divided against himself. That is the human predicament. In the battle of life, we are divided against ourselves and the point is that there is really no solution to the problems of life on the human level. As long as Arjuna is simply confronting the battle by himself, there is no answer. It is only when Krishna, the Spirit, the Lord, begins to counsel him that an answer can be found. What is demanded of Arjuna, and what is so difficult, is that he has got to fight. He says, "I shall have to kill all these, my relatives and friends." This is the problem. When we are asked to give up the world and to fight against our instincts, passions, and desires, it looks as though there is nothing left and it seems as if one is in a desert.

This highlights one of the perennial problems of spiritual life. We give up Egypt, we give up the world and the pleasures of the senses, we give up appearances and go out into the desert. Our state then is that we have lost the world but we do not seem to have gained anything. That is why Arjuna is in despair. He throws down his arms and refuses to fight because there does not seem to be anything to fight for. Even if he wins he will only have killed all his enemies who are also his friends.

What we all have to learn is that there is no answer on the human level to the problems of human life. As long as it is a question of the human soul, the human body, the human situation, there is no answer to be found and all we can do is throw down our arms and say, "I will not fight!" Only when the Spirit within begins to speak does the answer begin to be found.

The Yoga of Discriminative Wisdom

In Hinduism the fundamental virtue on the way of spiritual wisdom is discrimination, *viveka*. *Viveka* means particularly the ability to discriminate between the real and the unreal. We are living in a world in which the real and the unreal are always intermixed. Discrimination is when we reach the point where we discern eternal reality distinct from, and yet immanent in, the changing reality of everyday experience. *Viveka*, then, is the discernment of the eternal reality within the whole complex of nature and of life. Such discrimination brings freedom. Only when we relate to the Atman, to the eternal and unchanging amid the changes and processes of life, are we no longer bound.

Chapter 2 is introduced by Sanjaya who acts throughout as the narrator. He provides continuity in the discourse between Krishna and Arjuna which forms the substance of the *Gita*.

1. Then arose the Spirit of Krishna and spoke to Arjuna, his friend, who with eyes filled with tears, thus had sunk into despair and grief.

Krishna challenges Arjuna:

2. Whence this lifeless dejection, Arjuna, in this hour, the hour of trial? Strong men know not despair, Arjuna, for this wins neither heaven nor earth.

3. Fall not into degrading weakness, for this becomes not a man who is a man. Throw off this ignoble discouragement, and arise like a fire that burns all before it.

Krishna begins by rebuking Arjuna for his 'lifeless dejection' and 'degrading weakness'. He appeals first to Arjuna's social conscience. It must be remembered that Arjuna is a warrior, a *kshatriya*, whose duty it is to fight in the cause of right. In ancient India there were four castes or *varnas*: the Brahmin or priest, who was the teacher of the law regarding both religion and society, the *kshatriya* or warrior, whose duty it was to defend the law of religion and justice, the *vaishya*, the farmer or merchant, who was responsible for providing the necessities of life, and the *shudra* or worker, who gave his services to the community in all its needs. In its way this was a balanced order of society which has its counterpart in, for instance, the Republic, or 'ideal state', of Plato. The social context of the *Gita* belongs to this feudal order of society and Krishna first of all appeals to this law or *dharma*. It is only gradually that Arjuna rises above this common understanding to the deeper understanding of man's place in the universe. Already, however, he is beginning to doubt the wisdom of this *dharma* and he says:

4. I owe veneration to Bhishma and Drona. Shall I kill with my arrows my grandfather's brother, great Bhishma? Shall my arrows in battle slay Drona, my teacher?

Bhishma represents blind faith, and Drona is the guru, the teacher, who represents religious law and tradition. This highlights the problem of this conflict that there are on one hand the passions, instincts and desires, and on the other the religious traditions, laws and customs of the country. The disillusionment of Arjuna, which is comparable with that experienced by so many people today, is due to the fact that none of these values seem relevant any longer. This is also the situation in the Gospel where there are on one hand the publicans and the sinners who represent human nature following its own desires and instincts, and on the other hand there are the scribes and the Pharisees representing the law and religion. Undoubtedly there is no answer to be found at that level; it is not that one group is right and the other wrong. In the Gospel Christ shows the way which is beyond the conflict, above the values of both the Pharisees and the sinners.

Arjuna on the battlefield finds himself in precisely this conflict:"Shall

I kill with my arrows my grandfather's brother, great Bhishma? Shall my arrows in battle slay Drona, my teacher?" He feels that he is fighting against his own nature and against the institutions and customs of his country. A similar experience is very common today. Many people feel that society as a whole is corrupt. For some it is the capitalist society which is corrupt while others are sickened by political corruption world-wide. Others again are particularly aware of spiritual corruption and the domination of materialism, and tend to lose faith in society as such, wanting only to drop out of it altogether.

5. Shall I kill my own masters who, though greedy of my kingdom, are yet my sacred teachers? I would rather eat in this life the food of a beggar than eat royal food tasting of their blood.

Arjuna would rather become a beggar and drop out of the society than conquer in the battle and be involved in all the sins of that society.

6. And we know not whether their victory or ours be better for us. The sons of my uncle and king, Dhritharashtra, are here before us: after their death, should we wish to live?

The situation is such that we do not really see victory on either side. So often in actual history it is like that. The last two world wars are a good example. It appeared that one side was in the right and the other side in the wrong. In the last war it seemed very evident; Hitler and Mussolini on one side, Britain and America standing for democracy, on the other. But when it came to the actual fight and its outcome at the end of the war, Hitler and Mussolini had been eliminated, but Soviet Russia was on the side of the democracies. The forces that were most contrary to democracy had become its allies. These contradictions arise whenever one tries to answer these problems on this level. Then Arjuna says:

7. In the dark night of my soul I feel desolation. In my self-pity I see not the way of righteousness. I am thy disciple, come to thee in supplication: be a light unto me on the path of my duty.

The "dark night of the soul" is Mascaró's translation. On the whole Mascaró's translation is extremely good but he sometimes uses 'Christian' language, to the detriment of the meaning. R.C. Zaehner has,"My very being is oppressed with compassion's harmful taint", which gives the correct sense. So "dark night of the soul" gives a somewhat particular connotation here but it is meaningful. That is in fact the situation: it is the"dark night" when one cannot see the way of righteousness at all.

8. For neither the kingdom of the earth, nor the kingdom of the gods in heaven, could give me peace from the fire of sorrow which thus burns my life.

Sanjaya takes up the narrative:

9. When Arjuna the great warrior had thus unburdened his heart, "I will not fight, Krishna," he said, and then fell silent.

10. Krishna smiled and spoke to Arjuna — there between the two armies the voice of God spoke these words:

This is an example of Mascaró using language which is evocative of the words of the Bible. It recalls the Book of Exodus when the Ten Commandments were given on Mount Sinai with the opening words, "God spoke these words and said". The original text simply says, "Hrisikesa" — a name for Krishna — "spoke these words in the midst of the two armies." Krishna now takes the problem right out of the sphere of time and out of the human situation as he says:

11. Thy tears are for those beyond tears; and are thy words words of wisdom? The wise grieve not for those who live; and they grieve not for those who die — for life and death shall pass away.

12. Because we all have been for all time: I, and thou, and those kings of men. And we all shall be for all time, we all for ever and ever.

This conveys the very profound understanding that on the human level there is no final answer to any problem. It has to be taken completely beyond the level of the human, beyond time and space and the whole condition of man, to the level of the Atman, the Spirit.

The eternal Spirit is unborn and everlasting and that is Krishna's point.

We have to discover within ourselves this eternal reality. When we have
discovered it we can return and tackle whatever problems arise. Until we
have discovered it and begun to live in it, until we have begun to be
established in that wisdom, we cannot find any answer. Krishna goes on
to say:

13. As the Spirit of our mortal body wanders on in childhood, and youth
    and old age, the Spirit wanders on to a new body: of this the sage
    has no doubts.

This takes us into the question of rebirth or reincarnation. The usual
interpretation is that the soul goes from birth to birth. After death the soul
is reborn in another body. A deeper and more satisfactory understanding,
which is found in a well-known essay of the great Vedanta scholar,
Coomaraswamy, is that it is not the soul that transmigrates at all; it is the
Spirit, the Atman. The one Spirit is incarnate in each person. The eternal
Spirit takes flesh in you and me and experiences in the body and in the
soul of each one of us; it then goes on and experiences in another body
and another life. The whole history of humanity is the history of this one
Spirit experiencing all these different lives and leading all to fulfillment at
the end. That is a possible explanation.

Krishna goes on to say, and this is the practical aspect of it:

14. From the world of the senses, Arjuna, comes heat and comes cold,
    and pleasure and pain. They come and they go: they are transient.
    Arise above them, strong soul.

We are all involved with the world of the senses, pleasure and pain,
heat and cold, sickness and health and so on. As long as we are involved
in that state, we never have peace. This is the sphere of becoming, of change.
But there is something in us which is not of this world, which is not subject
to change, something eternal and this is the Atman, the Spirit. We have
to discover the eternal reality within ourselves and then we can deal with
the senses and the changing appearances of things.

15. The man whom these cannot move, whose soul is one, beyond pleasure
    and pain, is worthy of life in Eternity.

In the *Shvetashvatara Upanishad* there is a parable which illustrates this. There are two birds on a tree; one eats of the fruits (becoming involved), and the other watches (remaining detached). We must keep always in mind when we are reading the *Gita*, that this is the pattern of things. The human being is body, soul and spirit. The soul stands between the body and the spirit and in our normal situation the soul, the *jivatman*, inclines towards the body, towards matter and the senses, towards this world of change, becoming and impermanence, and it becomes immersed in that and loses its way. Repentance, (*metanoia* in Greek), is when the soul changes its mind, changes its attitude, turns back and discovers the Spirit within. Then, instead of being subject to the passions and the instincts, the soul is subject to the Spirit, to the power within, and gains control over the world of the senses and passions. It is not a matter of suppressing them or of their disappearing in some way; it is a matter of learning inner control. So the point is to discover how to be free from attachment, free from our habitual immersion in the senses and passions, and to awaken to the living power of the Spirit within. Then there is a rather striking phrase:

16. The unreal never is: the Real never is not. This truth indeed has been seen by those who can see the true.

Unreal is *asat* and the real is *sat*. This recalls the famous prayer found in the invocation from the *Isha Upanishad*: "From the unreal, lead me to the real. From darkness, lead me to the light. From death, lead me to immortality". The ability to discriminate between the unreal and the real is fundamental in Hinduism. This is precisely what *viveka* is, the discernment of the eternal reality, the Atman, distinct from, yet immanent in, the world of change and process. In relating to this eternal reality we attain freedom. This text does not mean that we are trying to get out of time and space; rather we are trying to see time, space and matter in the light of eternity, of the Atman, the Spirit which is in us. Then we have real *viveka*, real discrimination. Mascaró puts it very nicely:

17. Interwoven in his creation, the Spirit is beyond destruction. No one can bring to an end the Spirit which is everlasting.

In every particle of matter, in every living thing, in every human being, in every human situation, the one eternal Spirit is always present. Ignorance, *avidya*, consists in seeing the appearance of things, the outer form of matter and of man, and failing to see the eternal Spirit, the reality which is within. Wisdom is the discernment of the eternal in the temporal, the unchanging in the changing. In Christian terms we would say that we need to see God in every person and in every thing. God is always present and we are blind to it. Some are totally blind, others get an occasional glimpse of it, but if we were to live as we should, we would always be seeing the eternal reality in very temporal manifestation. God is present in every human situation, in every accident or apparent accident of life. The one truth, the one reality is always there. That is wisdom; that is the Spirit which is everlasting.

18. For beyond time he dwells in these bodies, though those bodies have an end in their time; but he remains immeasurable, immortal. Therefore, great warrior, carry on thy fight.

19. If any man thinks he slays, and if another thinks he is slain, neither knows the ways of truth. The Eternal in man cannot kill: the Eternal in man cannot die.

The great illusion under which we live is to think that when somebody dies the person, rather than the body is dead. It is illusion, *maya*, which comes over us and makes us see the external reality as though it is the Reality, while failing to see the eternal Reality which is present in that situation. Actually, when a person dies we should rejoice and say he is born! He has come to life. He has passed on beyond this *maya*, this appearance of life, to eternal life, to the world of the Spirit. The modern world is intent on preserving the illusion about death. The world believes that death is the end and we must never speak of it; death must be hidden as much as possible and when it takes place, we must remove all traces of it as quickly as possible. We are never allowed to see through the illusion, to see that the death of the body is simply the Spirit within shedding this particular vesture which it has worn for a time. Having reached its term, having experienced in that body, the Spirit is now passing on to a new life beyond death. We choose to live in the illusion.

In that sense, "if a man thinks he slays and another thinks he is slain, neither knows the ways of truth". The idea is that you are not actually killing somebody when you kill him. You are killing his body and setting him free. It may be a great sin to do so because you have no right over the life of another man but you are not killing the eternal in that man. The whole perspective is changed when the eternal Spirit is seen in each person and in each thing.

20. He is never born, and he never dies. He is in Eternity: he is for evermore. Never-born and eternal, beyond times gone or to come, he does not die when the body dies.

Now, we come to a problem which constantly recurs. At this point I would like simply to indicate the nature of the relation between the *Paramatman*, the Supreme Self, and the *jivatman*, the individual self. There are many controversies about this relationship and one often gets the impression that it is simply the one Spirit, the Atman, which is present in each body, while the soul, the *jivatman*, is only an appearance. On this theory both body and soul disappear in the end and only the one Atman remains. But the suggestion which I find most satisfactory is that the relation between the *Paramatman* and the *jivatman* is like that of light to its reflection in a mirror. God is the light which is reflected in the whole created universe. Creation is a reflection, as in a mirror, of the one light. It is reflected in the innumerable different forms of matter and of life. Every human being, each *jivatman*, is a particular reflection of that one divine light and each human consciousness mirrors that divine consciousness. The Spirit that is within us is that eternal light which is shining in my consciousness, in my mind, and which manifests itself through me so that the eternal Spirit is in me and I am in it and that is what never dies.

At the moment of death the body begins to dissolve and the functioning of the psyche ceases. We can no longer think and feel and sense as we do now because the instrument of the body has gone. But the Atman, the Spirit within, is united with the divine Spirit and that remains. At the moment of death, the Spirit takes with it all the experience of the body and the soul. None of it is lost. All that one has experienced in the body and in the soul, in human life, is taken into this experience of the Spirit. The Spirit is the one who experiences in the body and the soul and he takes that experience into himself. If we are living a sinful life, then the spirit, the life in us, is being continually frustrated and our fulfilment at the moment of death is minimal. On the other hand, if we have been following the path of the Spirit as far as we can, then at the moment of death our whole being comes into flower, as it were. All that we have experienced in the body, all our human experience, is gathered into the Spirit and comes to its fulfilment. So the Spirit is the point where the whole human being comes to a head, as it were, the point at which it reaches out and touches the divine, where the Spirit of God meets the spirit of man. That is why when we reach death, the Spirit is set free from the material body, from the whole time sequence, and from the present mode of consciousness, and we enter into the mode of the Spirit and experience the whole of life in its unity.

It is said that at the moment of death, our whole life comes before us. There is some evidence for this; for instance, people drowning or on the verge of death have had the experience of their life coming before them in a flash. All our experience in the body is contained in the Spirit; our whole life is there and at death we experience ourselves as we are in the light of eternity, and so we know ourselves for the first time. That is the point, "that Spirit in us does not kill, that Spirit in us does not die". It is the eternal Spirit in you and in me that never dies. It begins a temporary existence in this body, through the soul, then it returns to its eternal state.

21. When a man knows him as never-born, everlasting, never changing, beyond all destruction, how can that man kill a man, or cause another to kill?

Once that stage of wisdom and spiritual integration has been reached one cannot kill or cause another to kill. One is set free from the whole karmic sequence, Krishna goes on to say. This again is a question of transmigration:

22. As a man leaves an old garment and puts on one that is new, the Spirit leaves his mortal body and then puts on one that is new.

As I understand it, this means that the Spirit in me, having experienced in me and fulfilled its existence in me, has now completed that course, as it were, and the same Spirit now experiences in another body, another soul, and goes on with the whole human history. It is not my individual soul which goes from birth to birth. It is the Spirit, who, having completed his work in me, goes on to another life. My life has now reached its fulfilment in the Spirit.

23. Weapons cannot hurt the Spirit and fire can never burn him. Untouched is he by drenching waters, untouched is he by parching winds.

The aim of asceticism is to realise the Spirit within and then one will not be affected by what happens to the body and what happens to the soul. Or rather, one may be affected, one may feel it, but one will not be overcome by it. And that is what is being aimed at. The point of the *Gita* is not that we try to suppress our senses and feelings, but that we are detached from the senses, feelings and mind, so that we have a clear awareness of what is happening. I would apply that to Jesus on the Cross. He experienced the suffering of the body, he experienced the suffering of the soul, he felt abandoned by God when he cried, "My God, My God! Why have you forsaken me!" (Mk 15.34). Yet the Spirit in Jesus was united with the Father in the Holy Spirit and that is how we should always feel. In all the suffering of the body and of the soul, there is always a presence of the Spirit which remains unchanged, above the conflict.

That is all we can ask of that inner experience; we do not expect to escape pain or suffering, but we should be able to have a center which is not moved, a center which is not affected at all by pain or suffering or anything that happens. As St. Paul said, "I am sure that neither death nor life, nor angels, nor principalities nor things present, nor things to come nor height, nor depth, nor anything else in all creation, can ever separate us from the love of God in Christ Jesus our Lord" (Rom. 8. 38-39). In the Christian view, it is the Spirit, the Holy Spirit, which is uniting itself with our spirit and at that point we are set free from the whole of the conflict of this world.

24. Beyond the power of sword and fire, beyond the power of waters and winds, the Spirit is everlasting, omnipresent, never-changing, never-moving, ever one.

It is wonderful to see how, from all the labour of the rishis, from all their experience in the forest, from centuries of meditation, of discipline, of asceticism and struggle and conflict, they reach that point when they realise the everlasting, omnipresent, never-changing, never-moving Spirit. It is a tremendous achievement of the human Spirit to have reached that point; this was the culmination of the Hindu quest for God.

The Hebrew prophets have another experience of God, quite different, though kindred in many ways. Take Elijah, when he goes to the cave. He sits in a cave and there is thunder and lightning and an earthquake, then there is fire and God is not in the lightning nor in the earthquake, nor in the fire but in a "still small voice", and Elijah "wrapped his cloak about him," we are told, "and went outside". That again, was an experience of God, beyond the fire and the earthquake and the lightning. Beyond all these things, Elijah finds the still, small voice, this inner presence, which is the presence of God and he awakes to the reality.

So, in different situations, the awakening to the reality of the Spirit takes place and it is this that enables us to transcend all the tragedy of human existence. That is what the *Gita* is revealing to us. It is an experience which has come down to us from past ages, and in Hinduism, it reaches its pinnacle at this point.

25. Invisible is he to mortal eyes, beyond thought and beyond change. Know that he is, and cease from sorrow.

The word for invisible is literally the unmanifest, *avyakta*. The idea is that everything in this world, before it becomes visible or manifest, exists in the unmanifest, in Brahman. Brahman is the unmanifest and he is beyond thought, *acintya*. This indicates a major difficulty when we are speaking of Brahman, of the Spirit, the Self: it is always beyond thought. We can use words and thoughts to point towards it but we cannot express it, and all sacred doctrine is of that character. The truth itself cannot properly be expressed. The Spirit, the Self, the ultimate Reality, is beyond words and thoughts and beyond change. We live in the world of impermanence and change, but the world of ultimate Reality is the world of the permanent, the unchanging.

"Know that he is." He does not become. He is not in this world of becoming. He is. It is only when we realize, "He is" that we cease from sorrow. In the *Katha Upanishad* it is said, "How can we speak of him except by saying, 'He is'", *asti*. In the same way in the Hebrew tradition when God reveals himself to Moses, he says, "I am". Those are the only words that can express it. "I am", "He is".

26. But if he were born again and again, and again and again he were to die, even then, victorious man, cease thou from sorrow.

Here we again come to the matter of rebirth and I interpret it as being the Spirit in man which is reborn. It is the Spirit in man that goes from birth to birth. "He is born again and again."

He assumes this body, this soul, in this man. He becomes this man and then when he has finished his experience in you and in me, then he passes on to another birth. It is the Spirit that goes from birth to birth and there is no reason for sorrow in that. Each one comes into being and then passes on.

27. For all things born in truth must die, and out of death in truth comes life. Face to face with what must be, cease thou from sorrow.

This is our human condition. We pass from birth to death and then again there is a passage from death to life. Wisdom consists in realizing that this is our human state and unwisdom is when we think of death as an end, a disaster, a failure, whereas in reality death is a passage beyond. The Spirit in me passes beyond and I, as a human individual, enter into that life of the Spirit and the Spirit himself passes on to another life.

28. Invisible before birth are all beings and after death invisible again. They are seen between two unseens. Why in this truth find a sorrow?

Again, the invisible is the unmanifest, the *avyakta*. The whole creation comes forth in God in the beginning, unmanifest. It is unmanifest in God, in the Word, then it comes into existence, into manifest being. It becomes visible in this world and each one of us experiences this world of manifestation, and then at the moment of death we pass beyond this world again to the unmanifest where we realize God. Perhaps one could quote in this context Wordsworth's "Ode on the Intimations of Immortality from the Recollection of Early Childhood":

> "Our birth is but a sleep and a forgetting;
> The soul that rises with us, our life's star,
> Hath had elsewhere its setting
> and cometh from afar;
> Not in entire forgetfulness.
> And not in utter nakedness,
> But trailing clouds of glory do we come
> From God who is our home.

Wordsworth was a great mystic and had an insight into many of these truths which are found in the *Upanishads* and which have been lost for centuries in our culture. Wordsworth is one who recalls them to us throughout his poetry.

29. One sees him in a vision of wonder and another gives us words of his wonder. There is one who hears of his wonder; but he hears and knows him not.

This vision of wonder exactly expresses the mystery of the Spirit, which is something we cannot express in words and which fills us with awe and wonder. It is what is called the numinous, that which Rudolf Otto called "the idea of the holy." That is what God is; this great mystery. It fills us with wonder and then we speak of it with words of wonder. We hear about it through the *Upanishads*, or the Bible; all sacred scriptures give these words of wonder. But, "we hear and we know him not." The mystery always remains a mystery. In the world we get glimpses of this glory manifesting itself and it fills us with wonder; we are journeying onward towards the fullness when we shall realise and know him as he is.

30. The Spirit that is in all beings is immortal in them all; for the death of what cannot die, cease thou to sorrow.

This is our real being. Each person is a dwelling place of that one Spirit and that Spirit is immortal in each of us. At the moment of birth we come into existence in that Spirit and at the moment of death we pass beyond into that Spirit. What therefore is the reason for sorrow?

The main point that the *Gita* is making here is this understanding of the Spirit, the Atman, and its pervading of the whole creation. The best illustration, I think, is that of the sun and light. The Atman, the Supreme Spirit, is like the sun in which the light is fully present, fully realised. This Supreme Spirit manifests itself in the world, as light radiates out from the sun. Then, the light reflects itself in all the different forms of Nature, in all the different colours: the green of the leaf, the brown of the earth, the blue of the sky and so on, so the one Spirit manifests itself, projecting itself in all the forms of Nature.

Shankara uses this same illustration: just as the sunlight, shining into dirt and mud and filth, is not contaminated, so the one light of the Atman, the Spirit, is not contaminated by matter or by any corruption on earth. That is the basic pattern which we should have in mind. God is light and he manifests himself in creation and in all humanity, and the degree of manifestation depends on the receptivity of the different elements. In the earth, he manifests himself without life; in living things he manifests himself without consciousness; in human beings he manifests himself in consciousness. In the evil man, a man who has turned away from truth, the light is still there, but it is obscured. In the holy man where the light is free from this obscurity, from sin, it reflects itself purely. The aim is that each person should be a pure reflection of the one light. That is the background of the whole of the *Gita*.

The next few slokas are not very important. Krishna appeals simply to our sense of duty. Arjuna is a warrior and it is his duty to fight in a just war.

31. Think thou also of thy duty and do not waver. There is no greater good for a warrior than to fight in a righteous war.

Duty is *dharma* and let us remember that the whole Hindu society was formed on the basis of *dharma*. There are four ends of life in Hindu tradition, *kama, artha, dharma* and *moksha*. *Kama* is pleasure, enjoying oneself. Secondly, *artha* is wealth; it means acquiring wealth and property and so fulfilling oneself and one's family in that way. However, both *kama* and *artha* are controlled by *dharma*. *Dharma* means a man's own duty, his duty in his caste, in his place in life. There are four castes or *varnas*, as we have said, the priest, the warrior, the merchant and the worker, and each must fulfil his function in society; that is the *dharma* of each. Fourthly, there is *moksha*, which is final liberation. This is achieved when one is set free from all bonds of attachment. Krishna now appeals to Arjuna as a warrior to do his duty.

32. There is a war that opens the doors of heaven, Arjuna! Happy the warriors whose fate is to fight such war.

It is a general understanding, that to fight in a just war is a way to heaven. It is very strong in Muslim tradition where it is called the *jihad*, the holy war. Anybody who dies in the *jihad* goes straight to heaven, and Christian tradition had much the same idea right up to recent times. So it is very widespread. But this is appealing to quite a low level of morality and at this point the *Gita* is appealing to the ordinary human understanding.

33. But to forgo this fight for righteousness is to forgo thy duty and honour:
is to fall into transgression.

34. Men will tell of thy dishonour both now and in times to come. And
to a man who is in honour, dishonour is more than death.

35. The great warriors will say that thou hast run from the battle through
fear; and those who thought great things of thee will speak of thee
in scorn.

36. And thine enemies will speak of thee in contemptuous words of ill-
will and derision, pouring scorn upon thy courage. Can there be for
a warrior a more shameful fate?

37. In death thy glory in heaven, in victory thy glory on earth. Arise
therefore, Arjuna, with thy soul ready to fight.

Thus Krishna concludes that level of the argument. Now, for someone
like Mahatma Gandhi as for many people today, that is a very unsatisfactory
kind of prescription because he did not believe in fighting in wars at all,
but this belongs to an older tradition.

In the next verse Krishna goes to a more serious level:

38. Prepare for war with peace in thy soul. Be in peace in pleasure and
pain, in gain and in loss, in victory or in the loss of a battle. In this
peace there is no sin.

This takes the argument back to the transcendent level, where the war
is the battle of life and the conflict is with the powers of evil. This has to
be undertaken with peace; with peace "in pleasure or pain, in gain or loss,
in victory or defeat". This is that 'holy indifference' which, for instance,
St. Ignatius of Loyola advocated and which we will find is one of the basic
principles of the *Bhagavad Gita*. It means complete equilibrium in the face
of all the opposites, the good and the evil, pleasure and pain.

There is a further point of interest here. The word used for "prepare"
yourself for the fight is *yujasva*, from the root *yuj*, which is the same root
as in 'yoga'. Normally yoga means to unite, but an earlier meaning is simply
'to prepare'. One could say that here it means 'yoke yourself' for the fight;

or 'order yourself' for the fight. That is a more limited use of the word, but it leads on to the deeper meaning, which comes in the next and following slokas.

39. This is the wisdom of Sankhya – the vision of the Eternal. Hear now the wisdom of Yoga, path of the eternal and freedom from bondage.

Sankhya and Yoga are both important concepts. Sankhya is the earliest Hindu system of metaphysics. There were six *darshanas* or systems of philosophy. After the period of the *Vedas* there was the period of the Epics, the *Ithihasas*, roughly from 500 BC to 500 AD, and it is to this period that these six *darshanas* belong. The word *darshana* is from the root *drs*, which means 'to see'; "points of view" is how it is sometimes described. These six *darshanas* cover all the realms of knowledge. The first two are the Nyaya and Vaisheshika. The Nyaya is logic. It is important to note that at this stage, about 300 B.C. there was a system of logic in India quite as complete as that of Aristotle, for instance in the West. Logic has always had an important place in Indian philosophy. Second, Vaisheshika is cosmology; that is a philosophy of nature which included an atomic theory. And again, we should remind ourselves that it is at this same time in Greece that Democritus propounded his atomic theory. It is very interesting that at the same time and apparently independently, the Greeks had similar ideas. These ancient systems are not much studied today, but they are important as a basis for philosophy. Then comes the Sankhya and Yoga. Sankhya is the theory of what Aristotle called metaphysics. It concerns the fundamental constitution of the universe. It is based on the two principles of *purusha* and *prakriti*. *Purusha* is Spirit, consciousness; *prakriti* is matter, nature. *Purusha* is masculine and means literally, the male, and *prakriti* is feminine. The whole creation comes into being from the union of the masculine and the feminine. The Chinese call these principles the yang and the yin. In Greek philosophy they correspond to some extent to Aristotle's form and matter, though they are not precisely the same.

When Krishna says, "this is the wisdom of Sankhya", what he means is that this eternal Spirit which he has been describing is the *purusha* of the Sankhya, the Spirit, the consciousness. Now he goes on to describe the Yoga. Yoga is the practical discipline of which Sankhya is the theory. Another translation is: "You have heard the theory; now I will tell you the practice" (Z), and that is, more or less, what it means.

The doctrine of yoga at an earlier stage was that *purusha* is pure Spirit, consciousness, and *prakriti* is matter, nature. As a result of *kama*, or desire, *purusha* has become mingled with *prakriti*, nature. Spirit and consciousness have become confused with matter. The aim of yoga is to separate *purusha*, consciousness, from the body, from matter, and to reach the state of *kaivalya*, of separation, isolation. It is a very limited view but it is interesting, and that was the aim of meditation in the earliest yoga system. In the original yoga systems the intention is to separate the mind, or Spirit, or consciousness from matter and the body. In the *Gita* a much deeper understanding of yoga develops. What the *Gita* conceives as the wisdom of Sankhya is the existence of the one eternal Spirit which is present in everything and which is the basis of all reality, while the path of Yoga is the means of union with this one Spirit, by the integration of the whole personality. That is a much deeper understanding.

40. No step is lost on this path, and no dangers are found. And even a little progress is freedom from fear.

In connection with this freedom from fear Zaehner quotes the *Katha Upanishad* which says, "this whole universe comes from him and his life burns through the whole universe. That Brahman is a great fear like an upraised thunderbolt. Who so shall know it becomes immortal." The idea is that the fear of Brahman moves the whole creation. It is like the fear of the Lord in the Old Testament. This fear is what Rudolph Otto describes as *mysterium tremendum et fascinans*. This mystery of being in the whole creation is something tremendous, something which evokes a feeling of awe, of mystery, of wonder. And the same mystery has a two-fold character both attracting us and evoking fear. The nature of God is both fearful and wonderful. The letter to the Hebrews says, "our God is a consuming fire." There is something terrible in God, but also something infinitely attractive. That is what is meant by the great fear.

41. The follower of this path has one thought, and this is the End of his determination. But many-branched and endless are the thoughts of the man who lacks determination.

The Annie Besant and Bhagwan Das translation speaks of the 'determinate reason'. This is the *buddhi*. Krishna says that the *buddhi*, the intelligence, is single and one-pointed. The *buddhi* is the point of contact with the one Supreme Being, the Atman. The Spirit manifests itself first of all in the *buddhi*, then in the *ahankara*, the ego, and thirdly in the *manas*, the lower reason. Normally, we live in the *manas*, the lower reason, where the one light is reflected in all the variety of nature, and that is where the mind gets distracted. The mind is always moving, always in this discriminating consciousness, going from one thing to another through the discursive reason. This discursive reason is linked to the *ahankara*, the ego, the self-consciousness, but beyond the *manas* and beyond the *ahankara* is the *buddhi*. It is the pure light of intelligence. It is rather like the *nous* of Aristotle, and the *intellectus* of St Thomas Aquinas as distinguished from the *ratio*, the reason. The *manas* is the lower reason which goes from point to point, the *intellectus* is the faculty which grasps first principles and that is what the *buddhi* is. The *buddhi* is the pure intelligence which receives the light and then diffuses it. Everything depends on reaching the point of the *buddhi* where we become *ekagrata*, one-pointed. We must withdraw from the senses which are scattering our attention all around and from the *manas*, the mind working through the senses, and become one-pointed at the point of the *buddhi*; then we are open to the light of the Atman. At this point he says the *buddhi* must be one in its determination; it has got to be fixed on this one point and that is the great aim of Yoga.

If that is not done, the mind is confused. It wanders from one thing to another all the time, always in a state of distraction. One-pointedness is the first principle of Yoga. Krishna then describes the person who has no determination.

42. There are men who have no vision, and yet they speak many words. They follow the letter of the Vedas, and they say: "there is nothing but this."

It is often repeated in the *Gita* and in the *Upanishads* that mere knowledge of the *Vedas* does not do much good. The *Vedas* are the sacred Scriptures and they contain revelation but the mere external knowledge of them is never the final knowledge.

There is a famous story in the *Chandogya Upanishad* where the boy, Svetaketu, goes off at the age of 12 to study the *Vedas*. His father says, "You are a Brahmin by birth, but you are not really a Brahmin until you know the *Vedas*; so you must study." He goes and studies the *Vedas* and at the age of 24, after 12 years of study, he comes back, very proud of himself, very conceited and his father asks him, "Now you have studied all the *Vedas*; can you tell me that by which we hear what cannot be heard, and perceive what cannot be perceived and know what cannot be known?" And the boy says, "No, they never taught me that." What the boy has not understood is the essence of the *Vedas*: that is the Atman, the Spirit which inspires the *Vedas*. One can learn all the *Vedas* without discerning their essence, or study the Bible from beginning to end without knowing the Word of God. Only the illumination of the Spirit enables one to arrive at real knowledge. So with the *Vedas*. One can study all the *Vedas*, but without this insight, this wisdom, one will not understand their inner meaning or discover the truth. So that is why it is said that mere knowledge of the *Vedas* is of no use. Secondly, the *Vedas* are always associated with sacrifice, the fire sacrifice, and the later tradition is that those who follow a ritualistic religion are really always aiming at their own benefit. They are all acting out of desire. They pray for prosperity, for sons, for wealth, for good fortune, or at best, they pray for heaven, for a good reward, for a happy life after death. All these are selfish desires. They may obtain their desires, but they will never be satisfied. They will not get *moksha*, that is, spiritual liberation, because they are still caught in the ego, still desiring self-satisfaction, and therefore Krishna says:

43.   Their soul is warped with selfish desire, and their heaven is a selfish desire. They have prayers for pleasures and power, the reward of which is earthly rebirth.

44.   Those who love pleasure and power hear and follow their words: they have not the determination ever to be one with the One.

The Hindu understanding is that when we seek heaven as the reward of our good deeds on earth, we get our reward in heaven and then we come back to earth again. We have not reached the goal. We have not gone beyond our ego. As long as we are still living in our ego, even in the most spiritual ego, we remain full of desire, which is really self-seeking; we have not reached liberation. So we do not reach this final goal which he describes as *samadhi*. *Samadhi* is the final state of yoga, when we are completely united with the One. This is rather a nice translation therefore, where it says: "they have not the determination ever to be one with the One." United with that One, in *samadhi*, that is the real goal.

45. The three Gunas of Nature are the world of the Vedas. Arise beyond the three Gunas, Arjuna! Be in Truth eternal, beyond earthly opposites. Beyond gains and possessions, possess thine own soul.

We saw that in the Sankhya the two basic principles are *purusha* and *prakriti*. The whole creation comes into being through this union of *purusha* and *prakriti*. *Prakriti*, nature, is made up of three *gunas*, literally 'strands' which are *sattva*, *rajas* and *tamas*. Everything in nature is composed of these three constituents: *tamas* is darkness, heaviness, earthiness: *rajas* is fire, passion, enthusiasm, and *sattva* is light, purity, intelligence. Whether it is in material things or in human beings, these three constituents, are always present. This is the world of the *Vedas*, the world of created reality, not the world of the uncreated Being, of the Atman. Krishna says, "arise beyond the Gunas." One has to go beyond nature to the world of the Spirit. One has to transcend the dualities, the *dvandvas*, pleasure and pain, gain and loss, honour and dishonour. The world of Nature is the world of dualities. There is always this conflict of opposites and only when we get beyond nature, beyond the creation, do we discover the One who is beyond the opposites. That is where, in meditation, we must fix our gaze on the One.

46. As is the use of a well of water where water everywhere overflows, such is the use of all the Vedas to the seer of the Supreme.

This is a verse which has upset many people but which is quite clear. The *Vedas* are revealed Scriptures; they are the most sacred Scriptures for the Hindu and yet it says all these *Vedas* are like a well of water when water is flowing everywhere. When one sees the Supreme, when one reaches the knowledge of the One, of the Word himself, then all the written words become completely secondary or even unnecessary.

That is a common tradition among Hindus. They say a *sannyasi* should be beyond books, that he should have digested all the knowledge in books. We can say the same of the Word of God in the Bible. When we meditate on the Bible, we are trying to discover the Word of God. The Word of God is in all these words, all these images and concepts. Through all those images and concepts, we have to find the Word within ourselves. The Word is experienced within through the Holy Spirit. Then we no longer need all these Scriptures, all these words. Most people will not perhaps achieve that state but still it is very important. So often there is a tendency towards idolatry of the Bible or the *Vedas*, by attachment to the words. In these

sacred Scriptures every word is precious but we can spend our whole life
meditating on these words and never reach the word himself, the Truth
which is manifested in those words.

So that is the idea of this verse — "like a well of water, where water
everywhere overflows, such is the use of all the Vedas to the seer of the
Supreme." That is to one who has the knowledge of Brahman. Zaehner
refers to the same idea in the *Mundaka Upanishad,* where it is said: "Imagining
religious rituals and gifts of charity as the final good, the unwise see not
the path supreme. Indeed they have in high heaven the reward of their pious
actions, but thence they fall and come to earth or even down to lower regions.
But those who in purity and in faith dwell in the forest, who have wisdom
and peace and long not for earthly possessions, those in radiant purity pass
through the gates to the dwelling place supreme, where the Spirit is in
eternity." That is the *sannyasi* who goes into the forest to meditate and finds
the eternal Spirit, the changeless Self.

We come now to the practical doctrine of the *Gita.* Krishna is counselling
Arjuna in the battle of life and the first thing he says is, get beyond the
dualities — good and evil, right and wrong, pleasure and pain, gain and
loss, and discover the Absolute, the Eternal, the One beyond everything,
that Spirit that is in you, in everyone and in everything. That is the main
theme of the *Gita.* In the older theory, the *sannyasi* gradually withdrew
from action. He began by withdrawing from mundane activity and discovered
the Spirit within and then further withdrew until he became completely
detached from everybody and from everything and he withdrew finally from
all action. The teaching of the *Gita* is to detach ourselves from everyone
and from everything, but then, in that freedom of the Spirit, we must be
ready to do what ever is required of us. That is what we are really trying
to learn.

Detachment from the world of the senses, from the activity of the
rational mind, from the *Vedas,* in other words from all scriptures and all
external rituals, is necessary in order to reach this awareness of the Spirit,
the Atman within. But when we reach that Spirit, that Spirit is power; it
is life and intelligence and it is also love. In the light of that Spirit we are
able to act. The Spirit is a dynamic power which inspires us to act, to serve,
to work, and the work done by the Spirit within, so far from binding us,
sets us free. Now Krishna comes to the basic doctrine.

47. Set thy heart upon thy work, but never on its reward. Work not for
     a reward; but never cease to do thy work.

That is the fundamental teaching of the *Gita*. We must do our work, fighting the battle, doing whatever work we are required to do, but without seeking for a reward; that is, we must get rid of all egoism. Naturally, the ego always seeks a reward; whatever it does, it does it for a selfish purpose. If we can remove the selfish purpose, not seek the reward, then our work no longer binds us. That is the basic condition. We will see how the *Gita* gradually develops this theme and deepens it, but the basic understanding is clear here.

48. Do thy work in the peace of Yoga and, free from selfish desires, be not moved in success or in failure. Yoga is evenness of mind – a peace that is ever the same.

Samatva is evenness of mind, equanimity. That is the fruit of yoga. This is a most important principle and it is also very practical. We may have some work to do and it may be good work – say service in a hospital or school or social work but it is most important that we do not do the work for the reward it brings. We must leave the fruit of our work to God, and that means that if we succeed, then we are happy but not exalted by it, while if we fail, we are sorry but not depressed. If one works with the ego, one becomes over-excited with success and depressed with failure and it is that reaction which is wrong. I suppose almost everybody works with some degree of egoism but we can always test the degree of our egoism by the extent of our feelings. If we are really depressed when we fail or if we are very excited when we succeed, that shows our ego is much at work. If one leaves it to God, then one will rejoice in success and feel sorrow in failure but will not be disturbed by it. One keeps that *samatva*, that evenness of mind.

There is a great danger in much of today's activity with people doing social work, seeking to relieve poverty and disease. They feel that everything possible must be done to improve conditions and so they throw themselves into social work and try, for instance, to remove poverty in a certain area. They work hard at it and may meet with some success, but it is equally likely that they meet with failure or come up against insuperable obstacles. If their whole interest in doing the work is in succeeding, they may become terribly depressed and disillusioned and finally perhaps may give the whole thing up. By contrast, the correct way with all the work we undertake, is to surrender it all to God and not to be unduly disturbed by either failure or success. That is the essential condition of any work.

The opposite danger is that if we preach this doctrine of indifference to results, it may sound as if work is of no importance and encourage others to work half-heartedly, but that, of course, is a misunderstanding. The point is to put one's whole heart into the work and do all one can, and then the whole thing is surrendered to God and if it fails, one is not overcome by grief. This was also the teaching of St. Ignatius which he called 'holy indifference'. There is a famous story of St. Ignatius: he was asked, if the pope were to abolish the Society of Jesus, (as happened later on), what would he do? Ignatius said that after half an hour's meditation, he would accept it with complete equanimity. That is wisdom.

49. Work done for a reward is much lower than work done in the Yoga of wisdom. Seek salvation in the wisdom of reason. How poor those who work for a reward!

The 'yoga of wisdom' is *buddhi* yoga or "spiritual exercise of the soul, or integration through the soul" (Z).

This, I feel, is the main principle in the work we do. The work must come from the inner center of our being where we are united with God. Then the work is meaningful and fruitful and the results achieved will not disturb us. But if the work is simply done for itself, as it frequently is, then it is just as likely to do harm as to do good. So work done for reward is much lower than this yoga of wisdom, *buddhi* yoga. Seek salvation then in this *buddhi* yoga.

50. In this wisdom a man goes beyond what is well done and what is not well done. Go thou therefore to wisdom: Yoga is wisdom in work.

Another translation is, "united to the pure reason of the buddhi, one abandons here both good and evil deeds. Therefore cleave thou to yoga" (B & D). This translation is a little difficult. 'Going beyond' suggests that we discard both good and evil work and it can lead to misunderstanding, but the basic idea is that good and evil belong to the dualities, the *dvandvas* and the good in this sense is always a limited good. As long as we are seeking limited good and limited evil, we are not reaching the goal; we have to go beyond all limited goals to reach the One beyond. In that sense we go beyond good and evil. But it can have a very dangerous interpretation and it often has. There are those who say that the yogi, if fully emancipated, can do anything and it will not be sin. He is above good and evil. There was a very interestng sadhu, a South African, who came to our ashram many times. He was a remarkable man who at that time had been a sadhu for 12 years. He was at first very much respected by all the Hindu devotees but he had this theory that once you have reached pure consciousness, you were freed from all moral restraints. He would say, "I do not see why I should not kill somebody if the spirit moved me; I would be right to kill that person". This is really the way Nietzsche's thought is often understood. Most of the sadhu's Hindu devotees began to leave him. It is a sort of perversion which easily comes in. The higher one gets, the more serious are the perversions which come in and that is why they always say that the yogic path is like a razor's edge. One reaches a point where one can very easily fall from the highest to the lowest. It is a very common experience. The same applies with sensuality. There are some yogis who say they are completely free to enjoy themselves with women. It does not affect their Atman. They have reached the level beyond, so they can enjoy themselves. But that is not the meaning here. It is simply a question of getting beyond the duality of good work and bad work, beyond all limitations.

Now we come to this interesting phrase: "Go therefore to wisdom: Yoga is wisdom in work", or as it can be translated, "skill in action". Yoga is skill in action. There is a beautiful illustration of this in one of the stories of Chuang Tzu. In China there was a famous butcher who cut up his meat with an axe. He said he had never had to sharpen his axe in 17 years. The blade was absolutely perfect after all those years, because every time he used it, the blade always went exactly between the joints of meat and it never hit on any hardness which would blunt it. So he would cut the meat up with a marvellous swing of his axe and everything fell apart perfectly. The Emperor heard about this feat and came to see him and asked him how he managed to cut up the meat like that. And the butcher replied, "I first meditate on the Tao. I bring my mind into harmony with the Tao, and then act spontaneously, from the Tao within, not from my own effort". The Tao is the order of nature, the rhythm of the universe. The man had put himself in tune with this universal rhythm. That is skill in action. That is perfect yoga — when our actions are perfectly attuned, perfectly harmonious, perfectly spontaneous. Another example is Zen in archery. There is famous book by a German who went to Japan to study Zen in archery, to learn how to release the arrow from a bow in the proper way. He studied for six years. Every time he tried the master would say No! He was always putting his ego into it, pushing the arrow in some way. Only after six years, he suddenly took aim and the arrow simply flew from the string and he felt himself to be one with the arrow and the mark. Then the master said "Now you have learned". That is the perfect art, to be able to be completely calm, still within. The action flows from within in harmony with the order of nature. If all actions were like that, we would all be perfect.

But, in fact, the ego enters into everything we do, good or bad. One finds that often with very efficient people. They are very good at administration and at all kinds of organization but they may be terribly demanding, difficult people to live with. It is all done through the ego. On the other hand, there are some people who can manage a big business or hospital or do complex work and they seem always to be in control of everything, yet never push themselves forward. Everybody feels that they are being supported by them. That again is yoga in action. This is the great art: "Go therefore to wisdom. Yoga is skill in action". The translation is not too accurate. It is literally yogaya yujyasva, 'yoke yourself to yoga'. Unite yourself fully because yoga is skill in action. When we are fully one, the action is perfect. As long as there is any division in us, there will be conflict is our actions. Krishna concludes this portion of his discourse with the following verses:

51.   Seers in union with wisdom forsake the rewards of their work, and free from the bonds of birth they go to the abode of salvation.

These wise men who are controlled and integrated, who are *buddhi yukta* — united in their *buddhi* — who have renounced the fruit of work, these will be freed from the bondage (Z). These are free from the bondage of this world and they go to the abode of salvation, or literally the region that knows no evil. The word is *anamaya*, the painless region.

52.   When thy mind leaves behind its dark forest of delusion, thou shalt go beyond the scriptures of times past and still to come.

Most scriptures are bewildering, and the *Vedas* are very bewildering. There are many different currents of thought in them and by this time a lot of conflict and confusion had arisen, just as in the case of the Bible. Many sects have built themselves up on the Bible; the Bible can confuse one as much as anything in the world. So when bewildered by all these scriptures, "go beyond the scriptures of time past and still to come." Scripture is *shruti*, what has been heard, in other words, revelation. The idea is that one is no longer depending on any kind of revelation from outside but is rather united totally to the Spirit within.

53. When thy mind, that may be wavering in the contradictions on many scriptures, shall rest unshaken in divine contemplation, then the goal of Yoga is thine.

"When thy mind shall rest unshaken in divine contemplation" — literally, "stands motionless and still, immovable in *samadhi*". *Samadhi* is one of the four higher stages of Patanjali's Yoga. There is *pratyahara*, separation from the senses, recollection, withdrawing yourself; *dharana*, the concentration of the mind on one thing; *dhyana*, when meditation is a continual flow of the mind towards one point, the continuous adherence to the One: and finally, *samadhi*, absorption, when we are totally united with the One. That is the final stage. That is the stage of contemplation, when the soul, once bewildered by scriptures, stands motionless and still. This stillness, the still point, is *samadhi*. "Then the goal of yoga is thine". The word 'yoga' can have many senses. Eventually, it comes to mean the state of union. Yoga essentially is union, but the steps by which we approach it are also yoga.

Zaehner points out that there are four or five meanings to the word 'yoga'. First of all, it is practice as opposed to theory, Sankhya. Secondly, he likes to describe it as spiritual exercise. Yoga is a *sadhana*, spiritual practice. Then it is the control or integration that comes about through spiritual exercise; then as a result of that, it is the sameness, the indifference, the equanimity; and finally, when perfect control and harmony has been found, it is the skill in performing work; it is the yoga in action. That is the fullness of yoga.

We now come to a very important section. It describes the man of steady wisdom, *sthita prajna*. Arjuna asks:

54. How is the man of tranquil wisdom, who abides in divine contemplation? What are his words? What is his silence? What is his work?

The word for contemplation here is *samadhi*; it can be translated 'steadfast in contemplation', 'fixed in *samadhi*'. *Samadhi* is as near as can be to what we mean by contemplation. Contemplation is the experience of God. Mere meditation is a human effort, being the discursive movement of the mind reflecting upon God, whereas contemplation is the experience of God uniting us with Himself.

Krishna describes this man of wisdom in a text which has become a classic of spiritual wisdom and a summary of the teaching of the *Gita*.

55. When a man surrenders all desires that come to the heart and by the grace of God finds the joy of God, then his soul has indeed found peace.

"By the grace of God finds the joy of God" is more a paraphrase than a translation. The literal version is far more interesting. It is, "when a man abandons all desires of the heart and is satisfied in the Self by the Self" (B & D). That is so much more meaningful, because the whole teaching of the *Gita* is to learn to live within our heart, our inner Self and when we abandon all the desires of the heart- all the progeny of *kama*, the instinctive desires, that is — then we discover in the inner depth of our being our Spirit, which is the Spirit of God in us. Actually I think it comes to the same thing as the peace of God and the joy of God, as Mascaró translates, but it is an altogether different terminology and background. In order to reach this state the first thing is to overcome desire. Desire, *kama* is the great obstacle. *Kama* can be translated egoistic desire, but it involves the whole of the desire nature. The human being is said to have three bodies or sheaths (*koshas*). There is first the *sthula sharira* the physical body, then the *sukshma sharira*, the subtle body, and finally the *manokosha*, the mind, or the mental body. The subtle body is sometimes called the desire-body and it is from that that we have to be free. It is not a question of suppressing these desires; we have to be totally free from them. As long as we are being moved by this desire nature, we will always be enslaved to our own feelings, our own appetites, our own ego. When these desires are abandoned, then one is satisfied in the Self by the Self, then one is called 'stable in mind' *prajna pratishtita*. Untranslatable, it is a beautiful phrase. He has 'steady wisdom', as Zaehner calls it. That is to say, a wisdom, an understanding, an attitude to life which is firm, steady, constant in all situations.

56. He whose mind is untroubled by sorrows, and for pleasures he has no longings, beyond passion, and fear and anger, he is the sage of unwavering mind.

The same idea is found here: untroubled by sorrow, with no longing for pleasure. Pleasure and pain are the dualities. Everybody is running after pleasure, everybody is trying to avoid pain. Until we get beyond these spontaneous reactions, we will never get any peace. Pleasure is followed by pain. It is the realm of endless opposition.

The ideal is that we are neither disturbed by sorrow, nor attached to seeking pleasure in any way. That is extremely important, to be free from pleasure-seeking. It does not mean that we despise pleasure. Every pleasure is taken as it comes, but we do not grasp it and we do not pursue it. When we run after pleasure, then we may get something of it but immediately we get a reaction of pain. We have to be "beyond passion and fear and anger". These are the three basic emotions. In Sanskrit, they are *raga, bhaya* and *kroda*. *Raga* is passion or desire, *bhaya* is fear and *kroda* is anger. There is the same division in St. Thomas Aquinas who described the three basic emotions as: *concupiscentia,* desire, *ira,* anger and *timor,* fear. Those are the basic passions and they have to be stilled. As long as we are moved by concupiscence, this longing for pleasure, we are not free. The first instinct of a baby is the instinct for pleasure, for the warmth and the comfort of the mother's breast. When it feels deprived of these things, it gets angry. The crying of the baby is an expression of its anger. All of us have been through this; we have sought pleasure and become upset or angry when deprived of it. Some people go through life like that, like babies, seeking their pleasure and very angry if anybody tries to deprive them of it. Together with desire and anger there is fear, because as long as we are seeking pleasure and getting upset when we are deprived of it, we are always afraid that our pleasure will be taken away. We are perpetually in a state of emotional disturbance and that is disastrous. The man of steady wisdom is beyond these disturbances.

57. Who everywhere is free from all ties, who neither rejoices nor sorrows if fortune is good or is ill, his is a serene wisdom.

The secret of this 'serene wisdom' is to be free from 'ties', to be unattached. This does not mean that we do not feel pleasure or sorrow, or that we are unaffected by success or failure, but that we are not disturbed by the one or the other. We must be detached from our ego, our 'self', so that we accept both pleasure and pain, success and failure, with equanimity.

58. When in recollection he withdraws all his senses from the attractions
    of the pleasures of sense, even as a tortoise withdraws all its limbs,
    then his is a serene wisdom.

The example of the tortoise who withdraws his limbs when aware of
danger is a common illustration. The senses must be under control. We
are free to enjoy ourselves, but the senses must always be under control
so that they can be withdrawn from their objects when necessary.

59. Pleasure of sense, but not desires, disappear from the austere soul.
    Even desires disappear when the soul has seen the Supreme.

61. Bringing them all into the harmony of recollection, let him sit in
    devotion and union, his soul finding rest in me. For when his senses
    are in harmony, then his is a serene wisdom.

The only way to overcome this tendency is to bring the senses into
the harmony of recollection. This is the work of yoga. Yoga is union. It
is union between the mind and the senses, but deeper still, union between
the soul and the Spirit. The *Gita* here introduces the concept of *bhakti*,
devotion to a personal God, as the means by which the soul is united with
the Spirit and this will become one of the main themes. The senses have
to be 'yoked' in harmony and then the soul by its love and devotion, can
find rest in God.

62. When a man dwells on the pleasures of sense, attraction for them
    arises in him. From attraction arises desire, the lust of possession, and
    this leads to passion, to anger.

63. From passion comes confusion of mind, then loss of remembrance,
    the forgetting of duty. From this loss comes the ruin of reason, and
    the ruin of reason leads man to destruction.

The opposite course is now described. From the pleasure of the senses
rises attraction, then desire, then lust and anger, then confusion of mind
and finally the ruin of reason. Reason is the *buddhi*, the faculty of
discrimination, the power to discern between good and evil, the 'voice of
conscience'. When this is lost, man is brought to destruction.

64. But the soul that moves in the world of the senses and yet keeps senses in harmony, free from attraction and aversion, finds rest in quietness.

It is very important to recognise that it is not a question of suppressing the senses. The soul moves in the world of the senses but is neither attracted nor repelled by them.

65. In this quietness falls down the burden of all her sorrows, for when the heart has found quietness, wisdom has also found peace.

More literally, "in him whose heart is peaceful reason soon attains equilibrium" (B & D). The word for peace or tranquility is *prasanna*, so the thoughts are *prasanna*. That is very beautiful for although the basic meaning is 'tranquil', it can also mean 'transparent'. Thus *prasanna* is complete transparency; one is completely open and true. Another meaning of *prasanna* 'is 'inner peace'. In one who has found this, the *buddhi* the inner mind, stands firm. In the next verse there is a beautiful progression.

66. There is no wisdom for a man without harmony, and without harmony there is no contemplation. Without contemplation there cannot be peace, and without peace can there be joy?

Those are the stages of perfection. There is no wisdom for a man who is not integrated, *yukta*. To one who is not integrated there is no contemplation. The word is *bhavana*. Zaehner thinks that it means development, growth, but others translate it as meditation or concentration. I think we can take it as contemplation. Without contemplation there is no peace; without peace, how can there be joy? For St. Paul the fruits of the spirit are these: love, joy, peace. It is precisely the same doctrine.

67. For when the mind becomes bound to a passion of the wandering senses, this passion carries away man's wisdom, even as the wind drives a vessel on the waves.

This is the opposite course, when one is swept away. It is important to realise that when we are carried away by the senses and feelings, we are being dominated by unconscious forces in our nature. That is always the problem; unless we have this inner control, we are simply a prey to unconscious forces which are always working in us. Once we have established the inner control, then we are no longer subject to them.

68. The man who therefore in recollection withdraws his senses from the pleasures of sense, his is a serene wisdom.

69. In the dark night of all beings awakes to Light the tranquil man. But what is day to other beings is night for the sage who sees.

This is a very famous verse which is often quoted. When this outer world of the senses becomes dark, then the inner light awakens and one is in the light. On the contrary, when the outer world is dominant, that is night for the sage. So it is really the opposite of what it appears. Another translation is, "What for other men is night, therein is the man of self- restraint awake — when other folk are awake, that is night for the sage who sees" (Z). Zaehner has an intersting comment on what it means to see, *pasyate.* It means to see the truth, and he ennumerates twelve examples of seeing, all from the *Gita.* Seeing the Self, seeing the Highest, seeing inactivity is action, seeing all beings in the self, seeing all beings in God, seeing that Sankhya and Yoga, theory and practice, are one, seeing Self in self, seeing Self in all beings, seeing God everywhere, seeing the self as not being an agent and seeing self in transmigration. These are examples of this seeing. The sage who sees the truth does not depend on the outer senses. He depends on the light within. When the outer senses are all active, then there is darkness within. When the outer senses are dark, the inner light shines more clearly.

Now another beautiful verse which expresses again this idea of the senses:

70. Even as all waters flow into the ocean, but the ocean never overflows, even so the sage feels desires, but he is ever one in his infinite peace.

Or "as the waters flow into the sea full filled, whose ground remains unmoved, so too do all desires flow into the heart of man and such a man wins peace, not the desirer of desires" (Z). The Sanskrit is *kama kami,* the man who is a desirer of desires. This is very important because it is not saying that we give up all desires but that we are free from all desire for desire, all attachment to desire. It is not that we do not feel desire. Desires flow into us as the waters flow into the ocean, but we are not attached to them and we are no more disturbed than the ocean is by the waters.

Things flow in and flow out and we are not disturbed. If we are running after them grasping and seeking, then we are carried away. That is the *kama kami*, the man who is attached to his desires.

71. For the man who forsakes all desires and abandons all pride of possession and of self reaches the goal of peace supreme.

The literal meaning is much deeper than "pride of possession". It is *nirmame nirahankarah*, free from the thought of 'I' and 'mine'. A much better translation is: "who does not think I am this. This is mine" (Z). Zaehner, has a good note on that, showing that this is strictly Buddhist doctrine according to this the concepts of 'I' and 'mine' are illusory. Neither the body nor the mind, nor the senses, nor feeling, nor perception, nor consciousness, nor anything associated with life in this world can be described as 'I' or 'mine'. This is also the great intuition of the *Upanishads*. The 'I' is our inmost being and in no way can our body, our senses, our feelings or our mind be the true 'I'. They are our instruments while the true 'I' according to the *Upanishads* is the eternal Spirit: I am this Being within. It is the identification of the Self with the body, the feelings and the senses, that is the great illusion. When we withdraw that projection, then we discover our real self.

72. This is the Eternal in man, O Arjuna. Reaching him all delusion is gone. Even in the last hour of his life upon earth, man can reach the *nirvana* of Brahman — man can find peace in the peace of his God.

Here is another example of Mascaró giving a Christian sense to the text. The last phrase, expressing the same thought in Christian terms, is a paraphrase. The text reads simply: "The *nirvana* of Brahman", In the same way "the eternal in man" is literally "the state of being fixed in Brahman" (Z), *Brahmi sthitih*. When one has freed oneself from desires and no longer has a thought of the 'I' or 'mine' then one awakes to reality, to truth, to real being. And that is to be *Brahmi sthitih*, standing in Brahman. "Standing there, even at death, he goes to the *nirvana* of Brahman" (Z). *Nirvana* is a Buddhist concept and literally means 'blowing out'. It is the blowing out of the flame of life. Buddhism often appears to be a very negative religion and the question has often been raised as to whether it should be called a religion at all, since it negates so many things which are considered fundamental. There is no God, no soul and none of those things which we think are the essence of religion. The Buddha's method was negative. He said free yourself from attachment. For him the root of all evil was *tanha*, attachment, clinging: clinging to the senses, clinging to your feelings, clinging to your thoughts, clinging to your ego. Release yourself from all these things and when all this has gone out, has been blown out, is finished with, when there is no longer any becoming, then you pass over to the peace of *nirvana*. This sounds purely negative but when one reads the text, one sees that *nirvana* is full of bliss. It is a state of absolute bliss. Actually *nirvana* is experienced when one is totally freed from the ego and from the appearance of things, when one has realised reality or truth. That is why "the *nirvana* of Brahman" is a phrase of great beauty. It gives the positive as well as the negative aspect. *Nirvana* is the blowing out, the end of this flux, this change, this illusion; and Brahman is the reality, the truth, the being to which we attain.

The *Gita* does not go any further at this stage. It says nothing more about the personal God. There is just one mention of the personal God as we have seen; otherwise it is a doctrine of self-realization, but nothing beyond. As it goes on, it develops the idea of the *nirvana* of Brahman and shows how it is actually union with the personal God.

Chapter 3

The Yoga of Action

Chapter three of the *Gita* begins with a very pertinent question. Arjuna, faced with a battle, has put his arms down and said, "I will not fight." Krishna's argument first of all was to raise Arjuna's mind above the battle and above this life altogether; to set before him the aim of realising the eternal Being, the eternal Spirit which never dies and is never born. The way to reach this awareness of the eternal Reality and to find joy by the Self in the Self is, as we have seen, by detachment. This is freedom from attachment not only to the senses and to the passions but to the mind itself.

Arjuna quite naturally questions Krishna.

1. If thy thought is that vision is greater than action, why dost thou enjoin upon me the terrible action of war? The word for vision is *buddhi*, which is better translated wisdom or discrimination.

2. My mind is in confusion because in thy words I find contradictions. Tell me in truth therefore by what past may I attain the Supreme.

Krishna's response is very relevant to the whole question of the relation between contemplation and action, as it is known in the Christian tradition.

3. In this world there are two roads of perfection, as I told thee before,

43

O prince without sin: Jnana Yoga, the path of wisdom of the *Sankhyas*, and Karma Yoga, the path of action of the Yogis.

To these two paths Krishna later adds the third path of *bhakti* Yoga. But at the moment the question is between *jnana* or *buddhi* yoga, the yoga of wisdom or discernment, and *karma* yoga, the yoga of work. How do we reach the Supreme? Is it by wisdom alone, by meditation alone, which would be the *jnana* path, or rather is it by action, by *karma?*

4. Not by refraining from action does man attain freedom from action. Not by mere renunciation does he attain supreme perfection.

The illusion is to think that if we can only get away from the world, from all these disturbances, to some quiet place, we will solve all our problems. But Krishna, like many another teacher, shows that such escapism achieves nothing. Mere renunciation, leaving works undone with a negative attitude, will not lead to the attainment of the Supreme.

5. For not even for a moment can a man be without action. Helplessly are all driven to action by the forces born of Nature.

Actually it is an illusion to think we can ever be without action. We breathe, and breathing itself is an action. The body is in action, the whole world of nature is activity and we are in this world of activity. We will never be without action of some sort. Even if we retire to a cave, we still have to eat. Many *sannyasis*, like the monks in the desert, experience this as one of the most difficult problems they have to face. Many people go to a solitary place to live alone, to be free from all cares and distractions, and then they discover that a great deal of time is taken up with getting their daily food. Everything has to be done for themselves so they have to find their rice or bread if somebody does not bring it to them. So much of the time is spent just getting provisions, cooking, washing and cleaning up afterwards. By contrast, those in community have the whole thing done for them. They can go to have their meal and then go away without any problems. So it is often highly illusory to suppose that by giving up action we are going to achieve the state which we are is seeking. Then Krishna says very wisely:

6. He who withdraws himself from actions, but ponders on their pleasures in his heart, he is under a delusion and is a false follower of the Path.

The great danger is that a person will retire into solitude to meditate and then spend all his time thinking about the world he has left, and what he has renounced, and what he would like. When all these things are going round and round in his head he is more attached to the world than when he was actually engaged in it. The same kind of problem arises in fasting, where one of the difficulties is to keep from thinking all the time of what one might be eating, and what one is giving up, or of what one will be eating the next day when the fast is over. The external action leads nowhere at all; it is the interior attitude of the mind which is all-important.

7. But great is the man who, free from attachments, and with a mind ruling its powers in harmony, works on the path of Karma Yoga, the path of consecrated action.

The fundamental teaching of the *Gita* is freedom from attachment, *asakta*, as the essential condition. As we saw at the end of Chapter 2 this means freedom from all attachment to the senses, passions, thoughts and the whole activity of the mind. "With a mind ruling its powers in harmony", that is, controlling the senses by the mind, "perform your work." So the path is simple but fundamental, the path of work without attachment. If the mind is unattached, at peace, unified and integrated, then the action is a sacred action.

So Krishna concludes:

8. Action is greater than inaction: perform therefore thy task in life. Even the life of the body could not be if there were no action.

Without eating, without breathing, without some sort of action, bodily life cannot be sustained. Action is necessary to man, but action is to be done in a spirit of detachment and inner freedom.

9. The world is in the bonds of action, unless the action is consecration. Let thy actions then be pure, from the bonds of desire.

The background of all this is of course, the idea of *karma*. Krishna is

arguing against the view that *karma*, action, binds the soul. The basic Hindu
belief is that every action has its inevitable consequences, good or evil. Anyone
doing either a good or an evil action, is going to be bound by those
consequences. Therefore many would say, stop acting. An extreme form
of this doctrine is the Jain belief that all activity should gradually cease.
According to Jain philosophy each person is a *purusha*, a pure spirit. In
innumerable lives *purusha* has fallen into the bonds of *karma*, action, being
bound by this world and his own passions. The aim of the Jain monk was
to free himself from all action. The strategy was gradually to withdraw from
worldly activity, then from all intellectual activity and finally from all physical
activity. He would gradually eat less and less until, at the last stage, he would
let the body drop off by no longer eating at all. That was the Jain way
of perfection and although it sounds terribly negative, the Jains were a very
artistic people and were great humanists. They copied ancient books and
wrote many very important works themselves. They also did wonderful
painting and sculpture and many of the caves in India to which Jain monks
retired are decorated with beautiful carvings and paintings. There is a famous
shrine at Sravan Belgola in Karnataka where there is a statue sixty-five feet
high of a naked figure of a man standing upright with his arms at his sides.
It is only among the Jains, it seems, that one finds such a figure of primeval
man standing naked, absorbed in contemplation. The story is told of one
Jain contemplative who at times was so absorbed that ants would come
and build a nest all round his legs. Once the ants built a nest right over
the top of his head and he remained in contemplation until he was completely
submerged by the ant hill.

These Jain monks really did take the call to detachment literally. They
retired to caves in the hills and there, when they felt that their time had
come, they died. When they had finally rid themselves of all *karma*, the
effect of all past deeds, and when they had cleansed themselves completely,
then they were ready to drop the body and attain *kaivalya*, that is, a state
of spiritual 'isolation' and perfection. In its way this is a beautiful idea but
it is not for everybody. The fundamental demand is "let thy actions then
be pure, free from the bonds of desire," not simply give up action.

Krishna now takes the argument a stage further. It is not only necessary
to detach yourself and to work without a reward, but also your action has
to become a sacrifice.

10.   Thus spoke the Lord of Creation when he made both man and sacrifice:
      'By sacrifice thou shalt multiply and obtain all thy desires.'

Actually the phrase is: "Let this be to you the cow that yields the milk of all that you desire." The word is *Kanadhenu*, the cow that gives all you desire. A very profound idea which was universal in the ancient world, is that the law of life is sacrifice. It appears in the *Vedas*, and the basis of the whole Vedic system is that everything comes from, and must return to, the creator. Sacrifice is the law of the universe. There is a coming forth from the creator into the world and a returning again. Man has to perform this rite of return, and the sacrifice is that act by which he restores things to God. In making everything over to God by sacrifice, man is fulfilling the law of the universe and he, correspondingly, is himself fulfilled. He receives by this practice, the milk of all that he desires; in other words, all his desires are met. So sacrifice is not primarily negative. We tend to think of sacrifice as giving up something, but that is really only a preliminary aspect. The deeper meaning is that we take whatever it is out of our own use and make it over the God. And so an action becomes sacred when it is consecrated to God, the word sacrifice coming from *sacrum facere*, literally, 'to make sacred'. Sin is precisely the opposite, for sin is appropriation, taking things out of the hand of God and making them our own. That is the universal sin. There is always the tendency to take things as though they were our own, as though they belong to this world only and have no relation to the divine. This taking everything out of the realm of the sacred is one of the basic sins of the modern world.

In an Indian village everything is related to the sacred and nothing is done without some sacrifice. For instance, at the ashram, if we are building a house, a hermitage or any other buildings, the Hindu craftsmen will come along and the first thing they will do is choose an auspicious day and hour. When the time comes for work to begin, they are all there for the blessing, ready to consecrate their work. They will not begin any work without that. When the work is coming to its fulfillment, when they have doors and windows and everything made and the building is ready to be completed, there is another blessing because man can neither begin nor complete his work without God. Before putting up a building it is customary to consecrate the land and to place the house in relation to all the directions of space. The builder also relates himself to the cosmos. He is establishing himself in the cosmos, in relation to God, in relation to the gods, (that is, the cosmic powers), in relation to his neighbours and to everything. Building is a total act and therefore it is totally consecrated. Even in what we would think are profane actions of life, such as a meeting of a weavers' co-operative society in a village, the sacred is not neglected. Every meeting begins with a prayer and when the account books are produced, before they can be used, sandal wood paste is put on all the corners. Even the account books are consecrated!

Such practice is fully in accordance with the ancient idea that everything must be related to the world beyond, to the Infinite. In the modern world, since the Renaissance, everything has been progressively taken out of the sphere of the sacred. A king used to be a sacred person, this being symbolised by his crown and by the ceremony of coronation. It was the same with a Rajah. Today a prime minister and a president are completely secular people; there is nothing sacred about them at all.

For us in the West today a house is profane whereas in medieval Europe, for instance, every village had its sacred places. There would always be a church in the middle of the village. But in a modern suburb very often there will not be a church at all. The sacred has been eliminated as far as possible. Of course where the sacred had become an obstacle to progress, desacralisation was advantageous. People can be so obsessed with all the rituals and taboos of religion that they are unable to do normal work. That was Nehru's point of view. Nehru was an agnostic and he experienced religion in India as an obstacle because whenever he wanted to do anything, there was some sacred custom to prevent it. It was forbidden in Hindu tradition to slaughter a cow and therefore there were millions of old cows which were no good to anybody, eating food and wasting the land. That is another aspect and although one must see both sides, it is disastrous to take everything out of the sacred altogether. Ultimately everything has to be related to the One, to the Truth, to the Reality beyond and that is the function of sacrifice.

11. 'By sacrifice shalt thou honour the gods and the gods will then love thee. And thus in harmony with them shalt thou attain the supreme good.'

The gods, of course, as we have already mentioned, are the cosmic powers which in the Christian tradition are known as angels. We have to relate ourselves to the whole cosmos. That is why in the Indian rite of the Mass we have eight flowers which we place at eight different points around the offerings, representing the eight points of the compass, the eight directions of space. In this way the Mass is understood to be offered up at the centre of the universe. Every sacrifice has thus to be related to the Centre. When entering a Hindu temple the devotee relates himself all the gods, that is, the powers of the cosmos. First of all, on entering by the gateway he venetates the statue of Ganesh, the elephant-headed god, whose function is to remove obstacles. A coconut is broken in front of him and that means the breaking of the ego, the outer self, signified by the hard outer shell, so that the inner self, the white substance, the sweet milk of the divine life within, is revealed. And then, after asking for the obstacles to be removed from his mind so that he is open to the godhead, the devotee goes around to all the different shrines relating himself to the cosmic powers until he comes to the inmost shrine where the formless God resides. All the other gods 'with form' are manifestations of God but at the centre is the *lingam*, which is the sign of the formless deity, God 'without form', who dwells in the centre of the heart. The devotee relates himself to the cosmic powers until he comes to the inner centre of all and worships in the sanctuary within. That is the symbolism of temple worship. Not all Hindus are aware of the symbolism. Many go to the temple because they want some favour in this world, a bride or a job or success in business, but there are always those who realise the deeper meaning.

12. 'For pleased with thy sacrifice the gods will grant to thee the joy of all thy desires. Only a thief would enjoy their gifts and not offer them in sacrifice.'

If you offer sacrifice, you put yourself in harmony with the universe and therefore reap the benefit of it. Your life is in harmony and in it there will be peace and joy. "Only a thief would enjoy their gifts and not offer them in sacrifice." To take food without recognising it as a gift of God is to appropriate what is not one's own. In Christianity there has long been a tradition of saying grace before meals, though it is becoming rare today. This is a way of acknowledging that food is a gift of God. Eating and drinking are dependent on the providence of God. We give thanks for the food we are about to receive. In the Hindu tradition, a banana leaf is placed before each person who then sprinkles water round it, to make a sacred space, to purify that space. At the offertory of the Mass in the Indian rite, we first of all purify the altar and the surroundings by sprinkling water around it, making a sacred space. In the same way when we receive our food we make a sacred space. The food comes from God and it is going to feed our life. Eating becomes a sacrifice for it is the offering of the food in the fire of the stomach to the Spirit within. That is the meaning of eating and drinking. Conversely, to take the food without offering sacrifice is to be a thief, taking God's food, God's gift, and appropriating it for oneself. Nearly everybody today commits this theft when they eat, in failing to recognise that the food comes from God as part of cosmic order. That failure is the essence of sin.

I read a story some time ago about a little girl who was taken out into the country and for the first time she saw flowers growing wild. She said to the person with her, "Do you think God would mind if I picked some of His flowers?" I think that is a very beautiful attitude of mind. Flowers are a gift of God and if we pick them we are taking what belongs to God. In ancient times no one would ever cut down a tree or kill an animal without a sacrificial offering. They would sacrifice saying to the tree, "We're sorry; you're a beautiful tree and we recognise it, but we've got to offer you."

That is the principle of sacrifice which was universal in all ancient cultures, as in the ancient Christian world.

Then Krishna says:

13. Holy men who take as food the remains of sacrifice become free from all their sins; but the unholy who have feasts for themselves eat food that is in truth sin.

The holy man is supposed to eat what remains over from the sacrifice. It is a common custom for the devotee to go to a temple to worship, and be given as *prasad*, a gift from God, the food that has been offered. But others who just eat to enjoy themselves, "eat food that is in truth sin." This is a tremendous truth. When we eat food just to enjoy ourselves, we eat sin!

Now there follows a description of the process by which the food we eat comes from God.

14. Food is the life of all beings, and all food comes from rain above. Sacrifice brings the rain from heaven, and sacrifice is sacred action.

We all live on the fruits of the earth, and for those fruits we depend on the rain. The rain comes from God; it is a gift of God. We work the earth and plant and tend the plants, but ultimately we depend on the rain, so the food comes from above.

"Sacrifice brings the rain from heaven," the idea being that when we sacrifice we put ourselves in harmony with the cosmic order and then God will give his rain. This was also an Old Testament understanding as, for instance, in Leviticus 26:3,4 where it is said, "If you keep my commandments and do all that I have commanded you, then I will give you rain from heaven and abundance of corn." If we are in harmony with God and with the cosmic law, then we will be cared for.

This sense of harmony is evident among the pigmies of Central Africa, as Colin Turnbull relates in his book *The Forest People*. The pigmies live entirely in the forest and from the forest; the forest is their home. They know it through and through, every animal and every plant in it, and their whole life is integrated with the life of the forest. They have confidence that if they respect the forest, the forest will support them. They have to obey the law of the forest because if they do not they will suffer. If someone does something he ought not to do, with regard to animals or a tree or anything, he is severely punished. "The forest is good", they say, "the forest will support us." It is a very deep principle, which again, we have largely lost. Our idea is that we have to conquer nature. The colonization of America is a good example. The pioneers drove west, conquering nature, exterminating the Indian tribes, and later, bringing bulldozers and tractors, they brought the whole land under control by a mechanized system of farming. It was very successful but we know now the price which had to be paid.

Working in harmony with nature, offering one's work as a sacrifice, makes all the difference. The same idea exists in other cultures. In China there was the custom that once a year, in Peking, the Emperor offered a sacrifice in the temple. The prosperity of the people was felt to depend on that sacrifice. The Emperor, who was considered to be the Son of Heaven, was putting himself in harmony, in subjection, to the Law of Heaven, and if the Emperor was in harmony, then the people would be too. If the people were in harmony, the earth and all its riches would be also. Thus the whole of the cosmos would be in harmonious inter-relationship. But if at any level, either the Emperor or the people started breaking those laws in their attitude to the earth, then the whole harmony of creation would be disturbed. That is largely what is happening in the present day. Being ignorant of the necessity for harmony, and using every effort of science and technology to dominate the earth, we are producing powers of destruction which could destroy the whole earth.

A Taoist text, quoted by Zaehner in his book *Concordant Discord*, illustrates this. There was a gardener in China who had a beautiful garden and one day somebody came to him with some clever technical device to make his gardening easier. To this the gardener's response was, "It is not that I do not know all about your device but I would be ashamed to use it." His gardening was done according to the law of nature, in harmony with the Tao, for China was built upon the idea of the Tao, the harmony and inter-relatedness of everything in the cosmos.

We, however, have given way to all these clever devices which make things easier and enable us to get things done more quickly. For instance, it is the custom in India today to use artificial manures for the coconut palms. The result is a better crop for a few years but the earth is gradually impoverished and the environment poisoned. If, however, the soil is built up gradually over the years with organic matter the yield at first will be less but a permanent enrichment of the soil will be achieved.

15. Sacred action is described in the Vedas and these come from the Eternal, and therefore is the Eternal ever present in a sacrifice.

The word here translated as Eternal is Brahman. "From Brahman work arises and Brahman is born from the Imperishable" (Z). It seems clear that this is one of the very early uses of the word Brahman. Brahman originally meant the Vedic mantra, the prayer offered at the sacrifice, and this seems to be the meaning here. So sacred action comes from the sacred word of the *Vedas*, and these come from the Eternal, the Imperishable. Whenever this offering is made, those who sacrifice relate themselves to the Eternal and the Eternal is present in their sacrifice.

16. This was the Wheel of the Law set in motion, and that man lives indeed in vain who in a sinful life of pleasures helps not in its revolutions.

Dharma chakra is the wheel of the law. If we are living according to *dharma*, then we are in harmony with nature and everything goes well. "And that man lives indeed in vain who in a sinful life of pleasures helps not its revolutions." That is the idea of the Buddhist prayer wheel. In turning the prayer wheel Buddhists understand that they are helping to turn the wheel of the law. This is not merely superstition; it is a gesture by which they try to relate themselves to the harmony of the universe as opposed to all those gestures which, being done just for pleasure or for profit, disassociate us from the harmony of the universe.

Having shown the real meaning of sacrifice, Krishna now goes back to his main theme.

17. But the man who has found the joy of the Spirit and in the Spirit has satisfaction, who in the Spirit has found his peace, that man is beyond the law of action.

The word for Spirit is Atman. A more literal translation is, "the man who rejoices in the Self and with the Self is satisfied and is content in the Self, to him verily there is nothing to do" (B & D). The basic theme is that all actions should come from the Spirit within, from the inner Self. Everything we do is to be related to the Source of Life, to the Source of truth, and because of this all our action is true and harmonious; all our action is done according to the law of nature. That is the ideal.

18. He is beyond what is done and beyond what is not done, and all his works he is beyond the help of mortal beings.

This is a little obscure. "In work done and work undone on earth, he has no interest. . . no interest in all contingent beings. On such interest he does not depend" (Z). It sounds rather as though the *Gita* is going back on what was said and some interpreters find contradiction here, but I think it is true to say that in the *Gita* there are different, and even opposing, traditions that have been brought together and not fully harmonized. One doctrine will be brought out and then it will later be corrected with another. The impression is certainly given here that if one is living in the Self, one will not need to do anything. It even says, "there is naught he needs to do" (B & D). But Zaehner translates, "he has not interest in any contingent being. On such interest he does not depend." Zaehner's interpretation is nearer to the truth. The man who has realized the Self is not bound to do any work. His work comes from the inner freedom of the Spirit. He is not interested, in the sense that he is not attached to anything. Living in detachment, he is free to work and free not to work, as the Spirit calls him; that is what the *Gita* really teaches. The point comes out in the next verse.

19. In liberty from the bonds of attachment, do thou therefore the work to be done: for the man whose work is pure attains indeed the Supreme.

Zaehner sums up the argument. "Conform your work to the world process, the cosmic order of which you are a part. But do not take pleasure in worldly things. Take pleasure in the immortal Self alone, which will make

you independent of the work you have to do. Therefore detach yourself
from any interest that binds you to what you do. And do it because as
I, Krishna, am about to tell you, that is precisely what I, who am God,
do." That is a point which is developed a little later. In acting like this,
one is doing what God himself does.

20. King Janaka and other varriors reached perfection by the path of action:
     let thy aim be the good of all, then carry on thy task in life.

King Janaka is a *kshatriya*, a king or rajah, who appears in the *Upanishads*
as a man who sought perfection. He is a warrior saint, rather like St Louis,
the French king, a warrior who reached spiritual perfection and he is taken
here as an example of one who is made perfect by work. "Let thy aim
therefore be the good of all," the welfare of the world, *lokasya samgraham*.
It is important to recognise that Self-realisation has a universal value.
Whatever work is done in that spirit is done for the good of the whole
world. This is a truth which is as intrinsic to Christianity as it is to Hinduism.

21. In the actions of the best men others find their rule of action. The
     past that a great man follows becomes a guide to the world.

This is very true and was clearly shown in India, for instance, by the
example of Mahatma Gandhi, who became a model for all India to follow.
Now Krishna refers to himself, the Lord, as an example.

22. I have no work to do in all the worlds, Arjuna — for these are mine.
     I have nothing to obtain because I have all. And yet I work.

Krishna speaks in the name of the Creator: he has no work to do. He
is not bound by anything in the world. He is completely fulfilled in himself
and yet he works. That is both the Christian and Hindu tradition of the
creation of the world. It does not come forth from God out of necessity.
God did not have to create it. In Hindu thought creation is said to come
from the *lila*, the play, of God or as we say from the love, from the overflow
of goodness — *bonum diffusivum sui*, as Bonaventure calls it. There is an
energy in love that wants to share and that, rather than through any kind
of necessity, is why the world comes into being.

23. If I was not bound to action, never-tiring, everlastingly, men that follow many paths would follow my path of inaction.

God sets this example to the world, of always working. In the Gospel Jesus says, "My Father worketh hitherto and I work" (John 5:17). He was aware of himself as continuing the work of his Father. It is the work not only of creation but also of redemption and of restoration. "If I were not bound to action, never tiring, everlastingly, men that follow many paths would follow my path of inaction." The *Gita* claims that this *karma* yoga, the path of action, is following the example of God himself who, working without any attachment or bond at all, in total freedom, is always at work in the world.

24. If ever my work had an end, these worlds would end in destruction, confusion would reign within all: this would be the death of all beings.

25. Even as the unwise work selfishly in the bondage of selfish works, let the wise man work unselfishly for the good of all the world.

26. Let not the wise disturb the mind of the unwise in their selfish work. Let him, working with devotion, show them the joy of good work.

That is a practical and realistic point of view. It is useless merely to tell people to work without attachment but when they see the example of doing work with devotion and the joy which it brings, they will be convinced. The word 'disturb' which Mascaró uses in "let not the wise disturb the mind of the unwise" is literally 'to split', 'to divide the mind', *buddhi bhedam*. *Bhedam* is difference, *buddhi* is the mind. It implies that the mind is naturally single, undivided, and to split it is to dissipate it, to destroy it. Literally it is what is meant by *schizophrenia*, from the Greek *schizo*, to split and *phren*, the mind. So the man of unwise mind is divided and has lost his inner integrity. He is what St. James calls "a man of double mind" (James 1:8 and 4:8). We are all to some extent double-minded in this way. We have a split in our minds and we are trying to restore the mind to its original unity and integrity by means of yoga. Thus, "Let him encourage all manner of works himself though busy acting as an integrated man" (Z). The word for integrated is *yukta*, that is, yoked, or united. Now Krishna introduces another idea.

27. All actions take place in time by the interweaving of the forces of Nature; but the man lost in selfish delusion thinks that he himself is the actor.

28. But the man who knows the relation between the forces of Nature and actions, sees how some forces of Nature work upon other forces of Nature, and becomes not their slave.

This idea, which derives from the doctrine of the Sankhya, is that all the activities of nature come from the forces of nature, from *prakriti*. Purusha is spirit, consciousness and it is inactive. That is why Kali is sometimes represented as dancing on the prostrate body of Shiva. Shiva is pure consciousness. He is spirit and is inactive and perfectly still, while the whole activity of nature comes from *prakriti*. The argument is that all these forces of nature are at work in you and me and we must not think "I am the doer." It is actually all these forces which are working in us. Now this can be confusing for it can be taken to suggest that we can be completely inactive, simply suspending all activity and allowing the forces of nature to go on. At this point it must be remembered that there are different currents in the *Gita*, and this, the Sankhya doctrine, is only one of them. Further on the *Gita* amends this doctrine. The old doctrine, which was the source of so much asceticism was that the Spirit is detached; it is pure consciousness and has nothing to do with *prakriti*, with nature, with action. This, as we have seen, is the view of the Jains. In this view the aim of life is to detach oneself totally from the world of action, from nature, leaving the body to be ruled by the forces of nature, while the spirit, purusha, remains completely separate, isolated, *kevalam*. That obviously is a very inadequate doctrine and it is also dangerous because it can lead to schizophrenia, the split or divided mind we have discussed. But the doctrine of the *Gita* and the later Vedanta is far deeper. Both the *Gita* and the later Vedanta accept that there are all the forces of nature on the one hand, and that on the other hand there is a power of consciousness which has to be detached from the forces of nature. But above nature and above consciousness is the Lord who is at work in nature and who works also in our consciousness. When we unite ourselves with him we can be in harmony with all of nature and not be disturbed by it. So the text does not mean that we have to separate ourselves from all activity.

29. Those who are under delusion of the forces of nature bind themselves to the work of these forces. Let not the wise man who sees the All disturb the unwise who sees not the All.

Many people think that when they are obeying the forces of nature, their instincts, appetites, desires, and ambitions, they are masters of their destiny and are conquering the world. In actual fact such people are simply being driven by the forces of the unconscious. This is seen in many world leaders like Hitler or Mussolini, who were driven by the forces of nature and were puppets in the big world machine. The wise man is not deluded by all these forces for he has separated himself from them. Many people on the other hand are simply enslaved by the forces of nature around them and are being driven by them all the time.

"Let not the wise man disturb the unwise." We should not go about upsetting people. The Hindu ideal is that the wise man does not go about trying to change people. He lives his own life in inner purity and does all his actions without attachment. He is thus an example to others without deliberately disturbing them.

Now comes the third stage. Firstly, we act seeking no reward; secondly, we make the action a sacrifice, a sacred action; thirdly, we relate it to the Supreme, we surrender to God. So Krishna says:

30. Offer to me all thy works and rest thy mind on the Supreme. Be free from vain hopes and selfish thoughts, and with inner peace fight thou thy fight.

"Offer to me all thy works," that is, to Krishna, to the Lord. So far, it has been: do your work in harmony as a *yukta*, an intergrated person. This is the ideal of *buddhi* yoga, the yoga of wisdom. Now the third stage is added where all work is to be surrendered to the Lord, in a spirit of *bhakti*, devotion. This will become one of the main themes of the *Gita*.

31. Those who ever follow my doctrine and who have faith, and have a good will, find through pure work their freedom.

"Whatever men shall practise this my doctrine, firm in faith, not cavilling, they too will find release from work" (Z). This is clearer, release from work, *karma*, meaning, of course, deliverance from the bondage of work.

32. But those who follow not my doctrine, and who have ill-will, are men blind to all wisdom, confused in mind: they are lost.

33. 'Even a wise man acts under the impulse of his nature: all beings follow nature. Of what use is restraint?'

This is a curious verse. Mascaró puts it in inverted commas, suggesting that it is an objection put in, because by itself it is a little strange. The argument of the *Gita* has been that nature goes on with her works, but that wise man, being detached, is able to free himself from this bondage of nature. Now this sloka, "Even a wise man seems to act under the impulse of his nature. All beings follow nature. Of what use is restraint?" appears to be an objection from the other side. The next sloka makes it clearer.

34. Hate and lust for things of nature have their roots in man's lower nature. Let him not fall under their power: they are the two enemies in his path.

"In all the senses, passion and hate are seated, turned to their proper objects. Let none fall victim to their power, for these are brigands on the road" (Z); or, as Mascaró translates, "These are the two enemies on the path". So passion and hate, attraction and repulsion, *raga* and *dvesa* are the two enemies. We now come to a very well-known saying which is of great importance.

35. And do thy duty, even if it be humble, rather than another's, even if it be great. To die in one's duty is life: to live in another's is death.

That, of course, rather supports the caste system, where everyone has his own duty in life and must keep to it. But we should not really despise that, because it was a traditional doctrine in every religion that man has his own state of life. The Anglican Book of Common Prayer, for instance, says, "Do your duty in that state of life in which it has pleased God to call you." One should always remain in one's state of life. People today are very much against that. The idea of this rather hierarchical society was that everyone had his place, and one can even say of the caste system, that though it had many abuses, everybody had a place. Even the sweeper, the untouchable, had his place and he had his support. The society could not do without him and therefore he had to be supported. So there is a kind of justice in it and this was certainly the common understanding. Everyone, the priest, the warrior or the worker, should remain in his own *dharma*, each person doing the work to which God has appointed him. We are too much inclined to think that everybody should try to climb to the top and that makes for a very competitive order of society. Although there is something to be said in favour of the other system, the ideal lies somewhere between the two.

Now we come to a still more important passage where Arjuna asks:

36. What power is it Krishna, that drives man to act sinfully even unwillingly, as if powerlessly?

That is a very common feeling which is also expressed by St. Paul in his letter to the Romans when he says, "I do not do the good I want, but the evil I do not want, that I do" (Rom. 7.19). There is something in us that makes us act sinfully, even unwillingly, as if powerlessly. Today, I think we are much more aware of that. We recognise that we are driven by unconscious forces which cannot be controlled. Sometimes sin is conscious, but so often we are not fully aware of what we are doing and we are even driven by these unconscious forces to act unwillingly, as if we had no power to resist.

Krishna answers Arjuna's question:

37. It is greedy desire and wrath, born of passion, the great evil, the sum of destruction: that is the enemy of the soul.

Desire is said to be the most radical evil. There may be Buddhist influence here, for the Buddha thought that *tanha*, clinging to things and to people, is the root of all evil and that it is the result of egoism.

38. All is clouded by desire: as fire by smoke, as a mirror by dust, as an unborn babe by its covering.

39. Wisdom is clouded by desire, the everpresent enemy of the wise, desire in its innumerable forms, which like a fire cannot find satisfaction.

In a sense it is desire that drives everybody, the desire for pleasure, for profit, for wealth, for company, for friendship, for things good and evil;

there is this tremendous drive in our natures. As we have seen, it is not the desire itself that is wrong, but the uncontrolled desire that simply drives without reason, and then obscures wisdom and creates confusion.

40. Desire has found a place in man's senses and mind and reason. Through these it blinds the soul, after having overclouded wisdom.

These are the three basic faculties of the soul, the senses, (*indriyas*), the *manas*, and the higher reason, the *buddhi*. So all our faculties are obscured by desire. This is very close to what Freud meant by libido. *Kama*, or libido, is the underlying passion which unconsciously dominates everything we do.

41. Set thou, therefore, thy senses in harmony, and then slay thou sinful desire, the destroyer of vision and wisdom.

"Therefore restraining the senses, strike down this evil" (Z). The text does not say that one must kill this desire, but this sin. It is the negative power of sin, the destroyer of wisdom, that must be killed. That is the real cross. The ego nature has to be crucified, killed, before the mind and the whole being can be set free. It is the root evil, "the destroyer of both vision and wisdom". There are two words here: *jnana* which means knowledge or wisdom, and *vijnana* which indicates division and signifies discriminating knowledge. *Jnana* is one-pointed knowledge, or divine wisdom. *Vijnana* is rational, discursive knowledge or discernment. The very powers of understanding are destroyed.
      Then there is a nice passage which is reminiscent of the *Katha Upanishad*.

42. They say that the power of the senses is great. But greater than the senses is the mind. Greater than the mind is Buddhi, reason; and greater than reason is He − the Spirit in man and in all.

The word for 'He' is simply *Sah*, meaning the 'Self', the 'Spirit'. The ultimte reality is often not named. Instead it is called simply *Tat* or *Sah*. The *Katha Upanishad* says, "Beyond the senses is the mind, *manas* beyond the mind is the intellect, buddhi and beyond the intellect is the *mahat*, the universal cosmic mind, beyond the *mahat* is the *avyakta*, the unmanifest, and finally beyond that is the *purusha*, the person. He is the Supreme".

43. Know Him therefore that is above reason; and let His peace give thee peace. Be a warrior and kill desire, the powerful enemy of the soul.

It is important to notice the need to go beyond the higher reason, the *buddhi*. The *buddhi* is the faculty by which we go beyond our senses and beyond our mind, the *manas*, and then we have to go beyond even the *buddhi* to reach Him — the One who is above reason, "and let His peace give thee peace." The literal translation is "restraining self by the Self". We only learn to control ourselves by this inner Self. The great illusion is to think that the ego can control the body and the senses and everything, and many people are trying to make progress on that level. In ordinary asceticism people try to control the body, denying the passions and desires, and to control the imagination and the mind; but all the time the very power by which they are trying to control all this is precisely the one that needs to be controlled and of course they cannot control that. This kind of attempt at control merely leads to being more and more rooted in the ego. Only when we go beyond our ego, beyond ourself, will this power of grace, or however we describe the Self within, afford this control. That is also the Christian idea; only through grace can we be delivered from the powers of our own nature. It is a gift of God. The lack of control that we have over ourselves is the essence of the notion of original sin. We are in a state which we cannot get out of by ourselves, and therefore we need redemption. Something has to come into human nature from above it, and it is that alone which can release us and set us free. So the process is one of going beyond the mind to the Self that is within.

"Be a warrior and kill desire, the powerful enemy of the soul." That gives a deeper sense to the whole discourse. We notice that the external battle has been left behind. At the beginning Arjuna is represented as being engaged in an external battle, but the real battle is internal. His fight is against the enemy of the soul; to destroy desire is the real object, not to destroy enemies on the battle field. To kill the enemy within, the force which is killing the true Self.

Chapter 4

The Yoga of Partial Knowledge

In this chapter there is raised the subject of the *avatara*, which in Christian terms is conceived as incarnation. By partial knowledge is meant knowledge of sacrificial action of which the avatara is an example.

Krishna begins by saying:

1. I revealed this everlasting Yoga to Vivasvan, the sun, the father of light. He in turn revealed it to Manu, his son, the father of man. And Manu taught his son, king Ikshvaku, the saint.

2. Then it was taught from father to son in the line of kings who were saints; but in the revolutions of times immemorial this doctrine was forgotten by men.

3. Today I am revealing to thee this Yoga eternal, this secret supreme: because of thy love for me, and because I am thy friend.

It is said of all ancient doctrines that they come down from the beginning of time. Yoga is said to be primeval in the sense that it is passed down from the beginning. That is why in the Hindu tradition there is the practice of going to a guru. The guru has been initiated by another and that line of initiation, in theory, goes back to the beginning. There is great truth in the notion that none of these things are invented by man and that they come originally from God. "Every good gift and every perfect gift comes from above, from the Father of Light," as St. James says (James 1.17). Here Vivasvan represents in a mythological sense the sun, the Father of Light and Manu is a sort of Adam or primeval man. In the Hindu story of the flood, Manu is like Noah. This is a typical example of the tendency to trace everything back to the beginning. Just as the Jews trace all their laws back to Moses, and Moses received them from God, so the Hindus trace all their laws back to Manu, and he received them originally from Brahman. Everything is traced back to the source from which it comes in a line of descent. Very often the doctrine is said to have been obscured and forgotten, and then it is renewed.

Modern man has the opposite idea, tending to think that everything progresses, from very immature beginnings to a more and more perfect state, so that twentieth century man feels that he is the crown of humanity, of history and of all creation. For the ancients the opposite was true. For them the first man, Adam, or Manu, was supreme and thereafter it was a matter of a gradual descent or decline. For instance, in the Book of Genesis, all the patriarchs from Adam to Abraham are described as living for several hundred years, but when it came to Abraham, he only lived for a hundred and twenty years, while Methuselah's lifespan was nearly a thousand years; so the more ancient people lived longer and had the greater wisdom.

In Hindu chronology there are four *Yugas*, or Ages. The Golden Age was in the beginning when man was nearest to God, when according to Hindu tradition he was standing on four legs. Then in the Silver Age he was standing on three legs, in the Bronze Age he was standing on two; and now we are living in the Iron Age, the *Kali Yuga*, when he is standing on one leg and everything is about to collapse. So there are two opposite points of view, each with its own validity. We tend to think that we are gradually progressing, while the ancient traditions hold that there is a transcendent wisdom which is eternal and has been with man since the beginning. We progress in knowledge and understanding, but not in this essential wisdom. This is a wisdom which Krishna is now revealing to Arjuna. It is a revelation. He reveals it to him "because of thy love for me and because I am thy friend." The word he uses is *bhakta*. This word is used for the first time here, and it is a key concept. The root of *bhakta* is *bhaj*. It originally seems to have meant 'to share in', 'to participate in' and then 'to participate through affection'; and so it had various meanings, but by the time of the

Gita it had come to mean 'love and loyalty', as Zaehner translates it. It is a devotional love, not a passionate love. It is a devoted love which is constant and firm. So Arjuna is the devotee of Krishna who is going to reveal this Yoga to him. Arjuna now questions Krishna:

4. Thy birth was after the birth of the sun: the birth of the sun was before thine. What is the meaning of thy words: 'I revealed this Yoga to Vivasvan'.

Krishna has appeared as a warrior, a hero in the battle; how can he say he was born before the sun? Krishna explains:

5. I have been born many times, Arjuna, and many times hast thou been born. But I remember my past lives, and thou has forgotten thine.

This introduces the idea of reincarnation. I am always hesitant about the idea of reincarnation as it is commonly understood, as the individual soul passing from one body into another. A deeper view of it may be as I have said that there is one Self which is manifested in all humanity. But while most of us are only aware of our own individual self with some little background beyond, those who have deeper knowledge are able to realise their relationship with the generations who have gone before. Those with the most profound insight would realise their place in the whole history of mankind.

The Buddha said he had experienced all his former births. It is a sign of intuitive wisdom to know not only one's isolated individual self, but oneself in the history of humanity. It may be compared with the words of Christ, "I say unto you, before Abraham was, I am" (John 8.38). Christ is the Word of God, who unites all humanity in himself. This Word of God is manifested in the whole universe and in all humanity, and each of us participates in some measure in this one Word, the Self of all. A Jungian analyst once told me that he thought that just as the embryo in the womb recapitulates all the stages of evolution, from protoplasm through fish and animal to man, so every human being in the womb recapitulates all the stages of human development from the first man up to the present. So we all have the past history of humanity within us. If we can know ourselves through and through, we can know humanity. The man of wisdom, the Buddha, the enlightened one, has the knowledge of humanity within himself. Christ of course, is precisely man who "knew what is in man" (John 2.25). As the Word of God, he has the fulness of the knowledge of man within himself. In that sense, a man of wisdom knows all his past births; he knows all the past of humanity.

6. Although I am unborn, everlasting, and I am the Lord of all, I come to my realm of nature and through my wondrous power I am born.

This is a very well known verse describing the *avatara*. The word for 'wondrous power' is *maya* – Zaehner translates it as 'creative energy'. Now *maya* is the word which, in its later development, is usually translated 'illusion', but originally it meant something more like magic power. It is the power which creates, the power which produces. It can be used for a magician who creates some illusion and that is how it gradually acquired the sense of illusion. But in the earlier stages it is much more simply a manifestation of power, therefore it is the power in creation. In the *Shvetashvatara Upanishad* it is said that *maya* is the created world and the creator is the *mayi*. Here it still has that sense. *Maya* is material nature, *prakriti*, and he who controls it is the *mayi*, the mighty Lord.

Zaehner quotes Shankara, who says, "Vishnu's maya is essentially the three constituents of nature by whose compulsion the world goes round." So the *maya* of Vishnu is the phenomenal world. There are two stories about Vishnu and his power of *maya* that are very instructive. They are told by Zimmer in his *Myths and Symbols in Indian Art and Civilisation*. In the first one the sage Narada was talking to Vishnu and he asked Vishnu to explain his *maya*, this mysterious power. Vishnu told him to go into the water of the lake next to which he was sitting. So he plunged into the water, and when he came up he found himself in a different situation altogether, and as a woman, rather than a man. The woman (really Narada) was the daughter of a king, and was duly married to the son of a neighbouring king, and then had several children. After a time there was a quarrel between her husband and her father and a great battle took place in the course of which both her father and her husband were killed. Both bodies were placed on the funeral pyre and she, as a devoted wife, threw herself into the flame of the pyre. At that moment she came up out of the water and there was Vishnu sitting on the shore of the lake. All this had taken place between the time Narada had plunged into the water and the time he came up again. The idea is that all human life, all these adventures we have, are all simply passing moments in the *maya* of Vishnu. In the other story Vishnu told Narada to go and fetch him a glass of water. So he went along to a village and found a house where he was met by a beautiful girl with whom he fell in love. He was taken to her house and the family approved of him. Arrangements were made and they married and in due course had three children. The village was a small one set in a valley. One day there was tremendous rain and the whole village, including Narada's house, was flooded. He tried to escape with his wife and children. He set off through the rushing water with one hand supporting his wife and holding two children with the other hand, and the third child on his shoulder. As he moved, he stumbled and the child on his shoulder fell off into the water. In trying to catch hold of this child he lost the other two, and his wife also was swept away. At this moment he came up out of the water and there was Vishnu saying, "Have you brought me that glass of water which I asked for?" It is a wonderful perspective of human time and the eternity of God. Only in India could you have a story like that.

Now the famous verse:

7. When righteousness is weak and faint, and unrighteousness exults in pride, then my Spirit arises on earth.

8. For the salvation of those who are good, for the destruction of evil in man, for the fulfilment of the kingdom of righteousness, I come to this world in the ages that pass.

The phrase "my Spirit arises on earth" is a paraphrase. The word is *srajami* and the root *sri* means to create, to project. I project myself, I create myself, I am born. This introduces the idea of the *avatara*, that is, the 'descent' of God into the world. We should remember that there were ten *avataras* or incarnations of Vishnu, and that Krishna was only one of them. The ten *avataras* have been popularised today in many plays and films. In the tradition Vishnu comes first of all as a fish, then as a tortoise, and then as a boar, after that as a man-lion, and then as a dwarf, and then as a hero, Parasurama. The supreme *avataras* are Rama and Krishna, plus the Buddha, who was introduced at a later date. And finally Kalki, the *avatara* who comes at the end of the world. Modern Hindus often interpret this in terms of the evolution of the world. They would say that Vishnu appeared as a fish when the world was still under water. As the land was emerging from the waters he came as a tortoise. When the land had fully appeared, he came as a boar. Then as animals developed into man, he came as a man-lion, half animal, half man. After that he came first as a dwarf, then as a full-grown man in the hero, the warrior, Parasurama. When man had reached the highest level of righteousness and wisdom, he appeared as Rama and Krishna. The Buddha was added when Buddhism was absorbed into Hinduism. Finally comes Kalki to bring the world process to an end. These are the ten *avataras* of the classical tradition, but some of the *Puranas* mention twenty or even forty.

Hindus today tend to say that every age has its *avatara*. Many gurus proclaim themselves to be *avataras*. The most renowned one at present is Satya Sai Baba who claims to be the supreme *avatara* beyond Jesus, Buddha, Krishna, Rama and all the others.

There are obvious resemblances to the Christian idea of incarnation, and while we should not neglect what there is in common, we should also see what is different. First of all, the whole background of the concept of the *avatara* is mythological. The tortoise and the fish, the boar and the man-lion are mythological figures. Even Rama and Krishna are only semi-historical. There may have been a historical Rama and Krishna, but they are more like Hector and Achilles or Agamemnon, the heroes of the Greek epics. Probably such beings existed, but many of the stories that have grown up around them are legendary. The same is true of Rama and Krishna; they have a mythological background. Secondly, the concept of the *avatara* belongs to cyclic time. The ancient world, India certainly, and Greece also, conceived time as moving in cycles. There is the Golden Age, the Silver Age, the Bronze Age and the Iron Age, but as soon as things have got to the very limit of the Iron Age, the *Kali Yuga*, a new cycle begins and a Golden Age comes round again. The world comes out from Brahman, goes through all these stages and in the end returns to Brahman, and then once again everything comes forth. In this way the whole creation is seen as moving in cycles with no beginning and no end.

Moksha is liberation from this endless cyclic existence, this wheel of time, this *samsara*. Being caught in the wheel of *samsara*, the good would always decline into evil, and the evil return again to the good. From this arose the concept of *moksha*, meaning liberation from the whole cycle of time, the final liberation. The theory of rebirth also derives from cyclic time; one is born again and again in an endless cycle of births and deaths. The only way out is *moksha*.

Now the Hebrew-Christian revelation introduced a new understanding into this, namely that time is in progress towards an end, an *eschaton.* We talk about eschatology. The Hebrew revelation does not derive from a mythological conception of the cosmic order. The concept of cyclic time belongs to the cosmic religion, since nature always goes in cycles. Spring is followed by Summer, and then Autumn and Winter, and then returns again. The sun rises and sets; the moon waxes and wanes; people are being born and dying, and life goes on. The cosmic religion is thus cyclic in its view of time. By contrast, the religion of Israel concerns God's revelation not in the cosmos but in history, and this is constantly emphasised in contemporary Biblical studies. The Bible is the record of God's revelation in history, and specifically in the history of Israel, beginning with Abraham, Isaac and Jacob. The pattern was revealed in the deliverance from Egypt under Moses and the establishment of the kingdom under David. All this is God's revelation in the history of that particular people and that history is gradually coming to a head, a fulfilment. In the New Testament — when the time had been fulfilled, as the Gospel says — Jesus was born in historical time and crucified under Pontius Pilate. Paul says, "It was his purpose in the fullness of time, to bring all things to a head in Christ" (Eph. 1.10). Monsignor Knox, in his translation of that verse, puts it very nicely, saying, "To give history its fulfilment, by bringing all things to a head in Christ."

The *avatara* is distinguished from the incarnation in belonging to cyclic time and to a mythological world and in manifesting itself again and again. With the *avatara* there is no fulfilment of history, no sense that this world of space and time is not simply to disappear but to come to its fulfilment. The Christian understanding is that God is working in history and though there is a mythological background to the Old Testament, the story becomes more and more historical as time goes on. The Books of Samuel and Kings, for instance, are historical books based on contemporary records and when we come to the New Testament everything centres on the historicity of Jesus who was born under Augustus and crucified under Pontius Pilate. The incarnation in Christ is situated in history at a particular point of time and, in bringing everything to a head, it reveals the purpose of history. So the differences between incarnation and *avatara* are principally that the incarnation is historical, that it has finality, that it reveals the purpose of history and brings history to its fulfilment. That in turn makes a great difference in our understanding of human life.

In the Hindu tradition the avatara is conceived as a play, a lila of God.

All creation is a play and human life is a play of God. Though there is something to be said for this view, it is obviously inadequate. When you think of all the terrible suffering in the world and the agonies which people endure, it is not enough to say that God is playing with them. The crucifixion is not a play at all; it is totally different. The idea of the New Testament is that human history has a meaning and a purpose. We were born not merely to take part in a play but each one of us has his own place in the plan of God, which is working towards a final culmination. Each life has a unique meaning. That purpose and meaning of history and of life are revealed in the historic person of Christ, in the historic events of his life and death and resurrection. That is the doctrine of incarnation.

There are other points which could be made, but these are the most fundamental. Many people would say that the difference is that in Christ, God became man, but I find that very difficult to argue. From all the evidence, Krishna is God becoming man, but not God becoming man in a unique, historical way, as a unique person bringing fulfilment to human history.

With regard to the origins of the story of Krishna there are two theories. One is that there was originally a local god who was confused in the course of time with a hero of that name and gradually the concept of the *avatara* developed. The other, which may be more correct, is that he was originally a hero in the earliest strata of the *Mahabharata* and this hero became deified and recognised as God. The same thing happened with Rama. It has been proved to everybody's satisfaction that in the earlier books of the *Ramayana* he is simply a hero, and then later he becomes a divine person when the later books were added. This is a common process. When a hero arises, devotion to him develops, and then all his deeds are magnified and gradually the idea emerges that he is a manifestation of God. Then, as in the case of Rama and Krishna, he becomes identified with God. To a Hindu devotee, Rama is God. Mahatma Gandhi is a good example of this faith. Rama was simply the name of God to him. The last words he uttered were, "Ram! Ram!" — "God! God!"

Now we come to a key passage on the whole question of work.

9. He who knows my birth as God and who knows my sacrifice, when he leaves his mortal body, goes no more from death to death, for he in truth comes to me.

Mascaró gives, "He who knows my birth and my sacrifice", but actually the word for 'sacrifice' is simply *karma* — my birth and my action, that is, my work in the world, which, in a deep sense, is sacrifice. The goal is to know the Lord and to know his action in the world. This is where Shankara is very unsatisfactory. For him, the problem was that if Brahman was active in the world, he would be bound by that action, since *karma* always binds. Therefore because Brahman could never be bound by anything, Brahman does not act in the world. It only appears that he acts. Since there is no real action of God, in order to reach God you must go beyond action, beyond *karma*. But the *Gita* has the much more profound view, that God is eternally inactive and yet He always acts. We begin to see that here is the key to the whole poem. The action comes from one who remains unmoved in Himself. So this action of God in the world can be interpreted as a sacrifice. So far liberation has been perceived as a *nirvana* of Brahman, which is a state of emptiness, a changeless state. Now it is developed a stage further. To reach that state is to come to Krishna, the personal God.

Zaehner sums up the argument rather well at this point. He says, "By meditating on Krishna's incarnation and his deeds, both as God and as man, one comes to know the God that acts", which he compares with the Lord of history in the Christian tradition. Secondly, as if to restore the balance, the ascetic idea of detachment and contemplative wisdom is again proclaimed, and finally the idea of *bhakti* is introduced. In this way, the *Gita* proceeds gradually, step by step, introducing one theme, then another, then taking up the first theme again, as in a musical composition. This is one of the more important features of the *Gita*. So the theme of devotion is introduced here, "He comes to me", Krishna says. It is not merely knowing Brahman; he comes to the Lord.

10. How many have come to me, trusting in me, filled with my Spirit, in peace from passions and fears and anger, made pure by the fire of wisdom!

This is a further point. Men who are free from passion, fear and anger, the three basic passions already considered — *raga*, *bhaya* and *krodha* — become pure. Here we encounter two very interesting words, *manmaya* which Mascaró translates as "filled with my Spirit", which is not a bad translation but literally it means "filled with me". a very strong phrase. Then *mam upasretah*, "taking refuge in me". "Filled with me and taking refuge in me". Here the two paths of *jnana* and *bhakti* come together with *karma*, and this is a very important development. There is *karma*, the action of freeing oneself from passion, fear and anger, then *jnana*, "made pure by wisdom", and finally *bhakti*, "taking refuge in me". "They come to my mode of being," as Zaehner translates it. They come to my being, they participate in the being of God.

11. In any way that men love me, in that same way they find my love: for many are the paths of men, but they all in the end come to me.

That is a marvellous phrase and important words are introduced. The word for love is *prapadante*, and *prapatti* is the word used for total surrender to the Lord. So "in whatever way men love me" means "surrender to me". "In that same way do I return their love." Here is the word *bhajami*, from the same root as *bhakti*, and that is interesting. *Bhakti* is our devotion to God, but also God has this devotion to us. Zaehner translates, "I return their love", that is, I give my love to them. We saw that the word *bhakti* means 'inhere in', 'attend on', or 'belong to'. So the Lord is saying, "I attend on them, I inhere in them, I belong to them."

"For many are the paths of men, but they all in the end come to me." This is again very profound. The idea is that the one Lord is present everywhere, drawing everybody by different means. In the past this doctrine was held in a very exclusive sense, but now we see it in an inclusive sense. Christ is the word of God, the salvation of God, which is offered to all, which is present everywhere, and by whatever way anybody approaches the Lord, in faith, in love, in hope, he has been drawn by the grace of God in Christ. Krishna says, "Whatever path they take, they all come to me." The Buddhist will say the same. For the Buddhist the Buddha nature is in all men and all have to discover it in themselves. That is salvation; the light of grace is present in everyone.

12. Those who lust for earthly power offer sacrifice to the gods of the earth; for soon in this world of men success and power come from work.

This is yet another theme. Another way of translating it is, "Desiring success in their acts, men worship here the gods; for swiftly in the world of men comes success engendered by the act" (Z). The word used for 'desire

of success' is *siddhi*. *Siddhi* means perfection but it comes to mean particularly
the powers which come through yoga, or psychic powers. It means also
'power in the world', so those who seek the *siddhis* worship the gods, and
the gods, remember, are inferior. They are not the Supreme. If we worship
the powers of nature, we get those powers; if we worship money or power
or prestige, then we get our reward from them. "Swiftly comes reward in
that way." If we want these things, we can have them. As Jesus says in
the Gospel, "I say unto you they have their reward" (Matt. 6.5). It is a
sign of failure in the spiritual life to stop short with worldly success. Those
who seek success may achieve it, but they get nothing more.

13. The four orders of men arose from me, in justice to their natures and
     their works. Know that this work was mine, though I am beyond
     work, in eternity.

These orders are *varnas*, which are often called castes, but this is a little
misleading. *Jati* is the word for caste. The *varnas* are the four estates of
life — the priest, the warrior, the merchant and the worker. Zaehner translates
the last sentence as, "Of this I am the doer and yet I am the changeless
one." This is the teaching of the *Gita*. Krishna is the Lord; he is the creator,
the doer of all things. He creates all the differences among men and yet
he remains changeless in himself. Zaehner points out how Shankara interprets
this passage. He says, "From the empirical point of view, the point of view
of maya, God is the only agent and therefore in accordance with the law
of karma, which binds the agent to and by what he does." And therefore
Shankara says, God cannot be active in this world at all. It is only an
appearance. But the *Gita* has a much deeper view. God acts in all this world;
he is present in every action, the evil as well as the good, and yet he is
not affected by those acts. He remains changeless in himself. Zaehner quotes
a beautiful saying from the *Isha Upanishad* "Unmoving, swifter than thought,
the gods could not seize hold of Him as He sped before. Standing, He
overtakes others as they run. He moves and He moves not. He is far, yet
He is near; He is within this whole universe and yet He is without." That
is a deeper view, a view which can only be expressed by paradox.
     So the four orders of man rise from this work of God. These four orders
are an ordering of human society. Human society needs an order of priests
and an order of warriors, of statesmen; it needs an order of merchants, of
farmers and finally an order of workers. It is not degrading to be a worker;
each has his own place.

14. In the bonds of work I am free, because in them I am free from desires. The man who can see this truth, in his work he finds freedom.

More literally it is, "works can never affect me. I have no yearning for their fruits" (Z). Do not grasp at the fruits of action. This is the first condition. Whatever work is done, we should not grasp at the fruit; we are not seeking the fruit, we are not seeking a reward, our ego should not be involved in it. That is how God acts in the world: in perfect freedom and without any idea of a reward or anything. "Whoso should know that this is how I am, will never be bound by works" (Z). Once we learn to work as God works, we are free from all bondage of any kind.

15. This was known by men of old times, and thus in their work they found liberation. Do thou therefore thy work in life in the spirit that their work was done.

In the West we tend to consider the future as the ideal, whereas the tendency until recently was to put the ideal in the past. In fact the ideal is not really in time at all. It can be projected into the past or into the future, but best of all is to realise that the eternal reality is here and now. Then it is as valid to look back as to look forward.

Now Krishna goes back to the main theme.

16. What is work? What is beyond work? Even some seers see this not aright. I will teach thee the truth of pure work, and this truth shall make thee free.

There was obviously great controversy going on as regards the question of *karma*. *Karma* originally meant 'ritual'. Shankara rejects all work of this kind for the *sannyasi*, the monk. All work binds, therefore he should not do ritual work. A pure *sannyasi* will not usually perform any rituals. Many do so today, but the strict *sannyasi* will refrain from all ritual action. When he takes *sannyasa*, he takes off his Brahmin tuft and his Brahmin thread and undergoes a funeral rite. He no longer belongs to society and the ritual action which belongs to society is not his. He is completely free from all work.

17. Know therefore what is work, and also know what is wrong work. And know also of a work that is silence: mysterious is the path of work.

18. The man who in his work finds silence, and who sees that silence is work, this man in truth sees the Light and in all his works finds peace.

We come now to one of the key phrases in the *Gita* and one of the most enlightening which, unfortunately, Mascaró translates very strangely. There are times when Mascaró is ingenious and really brings out the sense, but he is sometimes too free. The literal translation is, "He who sees inaction in action and action in inaction, he is wise among men" (B & D). The idea of action in inaction is found in the Chinese concept of *wu wei*, or active inactivity. In Taoism, that is the key to all life. The *Tao Te Ching* says that the power which is the first principle of all creation is eternally inactive, yet it leaves nothing undone. This is paradoxical but the meaning is clear, that every action has to come from an inner centre of quiet and peace. We act through the body and the body is controlled through the mind, and the mind is active. But both body and mind are to be controlled from an inner centre of reality which is perfectly inactive and still.

It is a state of concentration, of stillness at the center. The inner being is perfectly still, perfectly harmonious, perfectly integrated, united with God; and then from that inner stillness all action flows. Then the action is harmonious according to the law of God, and to the law of nature. That is "action in inaction". It is something that is largely lost today. This is why the world today is so filled with activity, with the 'work ethic', as it is called in America. It is activity which has no fundamental rest. Once we let action take over, then all that is said about *karma* is true. We are bound by our actions. This is what has happened with the whole industrial system; it cannot be controlled. It has released forces which simply control men, reducing them to slaves of the machine. We have to be rooted in the beyond if we are to have any peace or justice or harmony.

Since the Renaissance the tendency of the West has been to eliminate systematically that beyond, to make science and reason control everything, with the aim of having 'man' in control of the universe. But the result is that he is completely subject to the law of *karma*. The inevitable forces of nature will drag him down. He cannot escape it. The only escape, as the *Gita* is teaching us all the time, is to free ourselves from the body, from the mind, above all from the dominion of the scientific mind, and discover the centre of peace within. Then we have active activity, "action in inaction". The Sanskrit phrase is *karmani akarma. Karma*, action; *akarma*, inaction. Inaction in action, or worklessness in work.

19. He whose undertakings are free from anxious desire and fanciful
thought, whose work is made pure in the fire of wisdom: he is called
wise by those who see.

"Free from desire". *Kama*, that is always the critical thing. Important
also is freedom from *samkalpa*, which Mascaró translates as "fanciful
thoughts". The word means 'conscious, deliberate motives'. It is the mind
with its self-centred motives which is the obstacle all the time. "Whose works
are made pure in the fire of wisdom." "The fire of wisdom" is a beautiful
phrase and the idea is that we have to burn everything up in that fire. We
have to burn up the mind and its "fanciful thoughts", and then from that
inner purity we attain to wisdom. Zaehner quotes from the *Isha Upanishad*:
"Into the deep darkness fall those who follow action, into deeper darkness
fall those who follow knowledge." It seems contradictory but by knowledge
is meant the lower knowledge of the mind. The person who acts without
knowledge, ordinary knowledge, is blind; but the person who acts with
no more than limited empirical knowledge is more blind. That is perfectly
true. The person who acts ignorantly is blind, but he can get out of it. The
person who thinks he is right and is acting with scientific precision, in a
limited way, is in serious trouble, not to say beyond redemption. Such a
person will not admit any limitations in his or her scientific thinking and
therefore can never get free. That is the kind of knowledge which has to
be burnt up.

20. In whatever work he does such a man in truth has peace: he expects
nothing, he relies on nothing and ever has fulness of joy.

Zaehner says, "When he has cast off all attachments to the fruit of works,
ever content, dependant on none, though he embarks on work, in fact he
does no work at all." That is the point. When we have cast off all attachment
to the fruit of work, then we have this inner contentment. "He expects
nothing, he relies on nothing, and he ever has fulness of joy." In other words
he works, but the work does not disturb him in any way. That is what
this means. We can be at peace in the midst of work.

21. He has no vain hopes, he is the master of his soul, he surrenders all
he has, only his body works: he is free from sin.

I do not think that it is correct to translate here, "only his body works".

A better translation is, "He only does such work as is necessary for his body" (Z). He works for the needs of his body but not more. Besant and Das translate it, "performing action by the body alone" but this is less satisfactory than Zaehner's translation.

22. He is glad with whatever God gives him, and he has risen beyond the two contraries here below; he is without jealousy, and in success or in failure he is one: his works bind him not.

"He is glad with whatever God gives him" is a little more than the text says. It is, "content with whatever he obtains without effort" (B & D). He takes things as they come. He is beyond the contraries, that is, the *dvandvas* the dualities. That is always the need. If we are always going after pleasure, always avoiding pain; always seeking success, trying to avoid failure; always seeking for health and prosperity, always avoiding ill-health and poverty, we are between the dualities. When we go beyond them, then we have no envy, no jealousy and we are the same in success and in failure. He who works in that way is not bound. He is perfectly detached, he has freedom. In the next verse this theme is worked up to a climax.

23. He has attained liberation: he is free from all bonds, his mind has found peace in wisdom, and his work is a holy sacrifice. The work of such a man is pure.

"His work is a sacrifice." That is what God's work is. All God's work is self-sacrifice, self-emptying. We had this before, if we make every work a sacrifice, eventually it is God that is doing it through us. Work is a sacrifice and "all action melts away" (B & D). It means that his works are burnt up in the fire of wisdom. There is no longer anything to hold him.

24. Who in all his work sees God, he in truth goes unto God: God is his worship, God is his offering, offered by God in the fire of God.

Here we have a wonderful verse which has vast implications. This is often sung as a grace before meals. It is:

Brahm'arpanam, brahmahavir brahm'agnau brahmanahutam;
Brahm'aiva tena gantavyam brahma karma samadhina.

Mascaró's translation christianises it a little by using the word 'God' for Brahman. Literally it is: "The offering is Brahman's, Brahman is the thing offered by Brahman in the fire of Brahman," – a most mysterious verse. It is interesting to reflect that this can be read as an exact description of the Eucharist in the Christian tradition. In the Catholic understanding of the Eucharist, Christ is at once the victim who is offered in sacrifice, the priest who offers the sacrifice, and his sacrificial love is the fire which consumes and transforms the sacrifice. Zaehner translates, "The offering is Brahman, Brahman, the sacrificial ghee (butter) is offered by Brahman in Brahman's fire." On this principle every genuine sacrifice is totally an action of God. So ultimately it is all one reality. The whole creation is a work of sacrifice, the one Eternal Being offering himself in us.

It reminds us of the *Purusha*, the primal man from whose sacrifice the whole creation came into being. The whole creation comes from the sacrifice that was made in the beginning, and thus every particular sacrifice is a participation in the one eternal sacrifice.

The *Gita* now gives various examples of sacrifice, the exterior and the interior sacrifice, the sacrifice of the senses and of the breath.

25. There are Yogis whose sacrifice is an offering to the gods; but others offer as a sacrifice their own soul in the fire of God.

26. In the fire of an inner harmony some surrender their senses in darkness; and in the fire of the senses some surrender their outer lives.

It is a little obscure. A better translation is, "Others offer their senses in the fire of self-restraint" (Z).

27. Others sacrifice their breath of life and also the powers of life in the fire of an inner union lighted by a flash of vision.

"Lighted by a flash of vision" in Sanskrit is *jnana dipiti*, which Zaehner translates as "kindled by wisdom".

28. The others, faithful to austere vows, offer their wealth as a sacrifice, or their penance, or their practice of Yoga, or their sacred studies, or their knowledge.

These are all different ways of offering sacrifice. Everything in life can be made a sacrifice and offered up to God.

29. Some offer their out-flowing breath into the breath that flows in; and their in-flowing breath into the breath that flows out; they aim at *Pranayama,* breath-harmony, and the flow of their breath is in peace.

Pranayama is the sacrifice by which one gains control of the breathing.

30. Others, through practice of abstinence, offer their lives into Life. All those know what is sacrifice, and through sacrifice purify their sins.

31. Neither this world nor the world to come is for him who does not sacrifice; and those who enjoy what remains of the sacrifice go unto Brahman.

32. Thus in many ways men sacrifice, and in many ways they go to Brahman. Know that all sacrifice is holy work, and knowing this thou shalt be free.

The teaching of the *Gita,* therefore, is that we should make all our work a sacrifice and that whatever work we do, it should be offered to God. By making that sacrifice we become free. This is reminiscent of St. Augustine's definition of sacrifice as any holy work which is offered to God.

33. But greater than any earthly sacrifice is the sacrifice of sacred wisdom. For wisdom is in truth the end of all holy work.

"Better than the sacrifice of wealth is the sacrifice of wisdom" (Z), *jnana yagna.* That means that one makes an offering of all external actions to the spirit within, to this inner centre which is the presence of God, the presence of the Holy Spirit, the divine wisdom within. In this way all exterior actions are interiorised and become expressions of the inner life of the Spirit.

34. Those who themselves have seen the Truth can be thy teachers of wisdom. Ask from them, bow unto them, be thou unto them a servant.

In the Hindu tradition it is the *jnani,* the man of wisdom, who alone is the guide to true life. It is not earthly wisdom, it is the knowledge of the Self, the knowledge of the Spirit, the knowledge of the Truth within. Those who have that knowledge can impart it to others. That is the function of the guru.

Another way of translating this is, "Learn thou this by discipleship, by investigation and by service" (B & D). That is, one should go to a teacher and have reverence for him, one should question, and seek knowledge and also serve him. Those are the ways in which one comes to this knowledge. It is not an academic knowledge which can be acquired by study, but knowledge which demands a change in life style — an attitude of humility, of receptivity and of self-surrender.

35. When wisdom is thine, Arjuna, never more shalt thou be in confusion; for thou shalt see all things in thy heart, and thou shalt see thy heart in me.

A more literal translation is, "Thou shalt see all things in thyself, and thyself in me." There is an important development of thought here. In the *Upanishads* it had been said that one must find all things within one's Self, that is, in the inner Spirit, which is one with the Spirit of the universe. But here Krishna goes a step further and says that one must find the Self in him, that is to say the inner Self or Spirit has to be seen as the presence of God within.

36. And even if thou wert the greatest of sinners, with the help of the bark of wisdom thou shalt cross the sea of evil.

It is important to recognise that this wisdom does not merely enlighten the mind, but purifies the heart and thus delivers from sin.

37. Even as a burning fire burns all fuel into ashes, the fire of eternal wisdom burns into ashes all works.

The fire of wisdom burns up the sinful nature. That is the significance of the ashes which according to Hindu custom are smeared on the forehead. The idea is that one has burnt up one's lower self; the ego has been burnt up and the ashes represent the purified self.

38. Because there is nothing like wisdom which can make us pure on this
     earth. The man who lives in self-harmony finds this truth in his soul.

More literally, "He who is perfected in Yoga, 'self-harmony', finds
wisdom in the Self." Yoga brings one into this state of harmony or union,
uniting body and soul with the inner Self, and the inner Self with the Self
of all beings.

39. He who has faith has wisdom, who lives in self- harmony, whose faith
     is his life; and he who finds wisdom, soon finds the peace supreme.

Or, "A man of faith, *shraddhavan*, intent on wisdom, *jnana*, his senses
restrained, wins wisdom. And wisdom won, he will soon come to perfect
peace, the *param shantim.*" Starting with faith and restraining the senses,
one aims at *jnana*, wisdom, purity and simplicity of mind, and when that
is won one comes to perfect peace.

40. But he who has no faith and no wisdom, and whose soul is in doubt,
     is lost. For neither this world, nor the world to come, nor joy is ever
     for the man who doubts.

This is a rather grim prospect for many people who have no faith at
all but it must be taken in its context. After all, as Tennyson said, "There
is more of faith in honest doubt than in all the creeds." There is a form
of belief by which one just accepts things on trust without any real
discernment and then, when one begins to doubt and question that, one
goes through a period of disbelief, which arises out of an awareness of the
limitations of blind faith. Then through the questioning one comes to genuine
faith, to the experience of that which lies beyond, and that is the state of
wisdom.

41. He who makes pure his work by Yoga, who watches over his soul,
     and who by wisdom destroys his doubts, is free from the bondage
     of selfish work.

Or, "Let a man in spiritual exercise (that is yoga) renounce all works,
let him by wisdom dispel all doubts, let him be himself" (Z). The last phrase
is striking, *atmavantam* — possessing the Self, ruled by the Self; though
it has also been translated as being 'watchful over the self'.

42. Kill therefore with the sword of wisdom the doubt born of ignorance that lies in thy heart. Be one in self-harmony, in Yoga, and arise, great warrior, arise.

This whole discourse is still being addressed to Arjuna on the field of battle and Krishna has now shown him the way to fight the battle of life without being involved. It is no good giving up the fight, and it is equally no good going into the fight while simply surrendering to passions and desires. By setting oneself free from the body and its passions and from the mind's activity and by attaining to this *jnana*, this wisdom, this awareness of the Self within and then by being established within that Self, one recognises the Lord dwelling within the Self. Surrendering to him, one is able to act from that centre, from that wisdom, and all one's actions, being done without any desire for a reward, have no binding force at all; there is no egoism in them. They simply flow from the Self, from the Spirit within and eventually they are a work of God in us.

That is the real goal. No action is perfect until it reaches the state where we can say "I am not the doer; God is working in me." Only that is perfect action, and that is actually inaction. The inner self is totally surrendered and the action is not coming from the self. It is coming from God.

Chapter 5

The Yoga of Renunciation

The *Gita* now goes into the question of the relation between contemplation and action. There has long been a debate in Christian tradition as to the relative value of the contemplative and the active life, which is a close parallel to the question which is raised here.

Arjuna asks:

1. Renunciation is praised by thee, Krishna, and then the Yoga of holy work. Of these two, tell me in truth, which is the higher path?

The question is put in terms of *sannyasa* and *yoga*. *Sannyasa* means renunciation and implies giving up work in order to obtain wisdom by contemplation. Yoga is used in the sense of work or activity.

Krishna replies:

2. Both renunciation and holy work are a path to the Supreme; but better than surrender of work is the Yoga of holy work.

The teaching of the *Gita* is quite clear in this matter. Better than *sannyasa* which renounces work is that yoga which does work without attachment. The common view was that the *sannyasi* should give up work altogether to live in pure contemplation. The question is which is best, the life of the contemplative who does no work, lives in communion with God and engages in no activity at all, or that of the person who enjoys union with God and at the same time engages in activity. The *Gita* favours the latter position. But as we will see, it is not at all easy to answer the question raised in the previous chapter as to what exactly should be the relation between the inner self and the action in the world.

3. Know that a man of true renunciation is he who craves not nor hates; for he who is above the two contraries soon finds his freedom.

True *sannyasa* is not giving up work or action. It is freedom from desire and aversion, the two basic causes of attachment. To be the same in pleasure and pain is the real *sannyasa*. If we are perfectly detached there is no work we may not do. *Sannyasa* is above the contraries of pleasure and pain, good fortune or ill. That is the deeper teaching of the *Gita*.

4. Ignorant men, but not the wise, say that Sankhya and Yoga are different paths; but he who gives all his soul to one reaches the end of the two.

Sankhya and Yoga later developed into two separate systems of philosophy, but here Sankhya is simply equivalent to contemplation and Yoga to action and we see that they are not really different. If we are totally detached, 'surrendered' to the Lord, as Krishna will say later on, then we are able to act freely and with perfect understanding and we are not bound by our works. So "ignorant men but not the wise say that Sankhya and Yoga are different".

5. Because the victory won by the man of wisdom is also won by the man of good work. That man sees indeed the truth who sees that vision and creation are one.

"Vision and creation": the terms are *sankhya* and *yoga* which may be better translated 'contemplation and action'; so "he who sees that contemplation and action are one, he who sees that sees indeed". He is the man of real wisdom.

That is the clear teaching of the *Gita*. The ideal is to live in the world, to serve, and at the same time to be one with God, having the inner peace,

the *buddhi yoga*, the yoga of wisdom. But as we will see there remains a
problem.

6.   But renunciation, Arjuna, is difficult to attain without Yoga of work.
     When a sage is one in Yoga he soon is one in God.

Literally "he is one in God" is 'He comes to Brahman'. It is hard to
attain this renunciation without the practice of *yoga*. The sage, the *muni*
that is, the man of silence who is *yoga yukta*, who is yoked and integrated
in yoga, 'comes to Brahman'; he is united with God. "He soon comes to
Brahman". That is, he comes to the final goal.

The path of *sannyasa* is difficult without work. At the time of St.
Benedict there was much discussion in Christian circles as to which was
better, the common life or the solitary life. This was the subject of a great
debate in Western monasticism. In the early Christian tradition, as in the
Indian, there was a theory that the monk, the perfect contemplative, should
live in solitude and silence and prayer without ceasing, only united to God
and not doing any work at all. That was held to be the ideal. But that is
a very difficult state to attain, as the *Gita* says. In the Christian tradition,
though intent on prayer and silence, the solitary monk came to be occupied
in some simple work like basket-weaving, and so was saved from the dangers
of a life without any work at all.

St. Benedict, in legislating for the monks in the West still upholds the
solitary life as the ideal. But the monk had first to be trained in the monastery,
in community life, where he had to live and work with others. Only then
was he fitted for the "solitary combat of the desert" as St. Benedict calls it.

So in the Christian tradition there is the same problem – and in the
Eastern Church in particular, the pure contemplative, the solitary monk,
has always been held to be the ideal. Even now in an oriental monastery
the ideal is the monk who, having been through the community life goes
on to live as a hermit. Staretz Silhouan who lived on Mount Athos as a
hermit in the last century is a perfect example of this.

In the West, the followers of St. Benedict apart from the Cawaldolese
who have preserved the cremitical life, have gradually eliminated the hermit
ideal, and the common life with work is considered the typical monastic
life. But we have often gone to the other extreme. Thomas Merton used
to complain that at his own monastry, Gethsemani, the whole monastery
revolved around the making of cheese. The monks were earning their living

by cheesemaking and this tended to dominate the whole life.

This is a problem in many monasteries today. If there is a large community of, say, fifty or sixty monks, they need to be supported by some kind of industry. In my own monastery in England we had a farm and a pottery, and both of these tended to absorb the time and attention of the monks, taking them away from prayer and the normal life of the monastery. In the end, both were handed over to lay people so as to have the monks free for their proper work of prayer. So the problem is always there: how to reconcile contemplation and action. Once we take up some activity, whether it is work in the monastery or some work outside like a school or a parish, we tend to get absorbed in the work and the inner life of prayer declines. Yet the *Gita* shows us that there is an answer. It is possible to work in such a way that not only does the work not distract us from prayer but it actually becomes contemplation in the true sense, that is, an activity of God within. That is the teaching of the *Gita*.

So renunciation, *sannyasa*, without work is difficult, whereas the "sage who is *yoga yukta*", who is integrated with *yoga* in a practical way "soon comes to Brahman".

7. No work stains a man who is pure, who is in harmony, who is master of his life, whose soul is one with the soul of all.

"He becomes the self of every creature" (Z), that is to say, every creature becomes himself. The individual Self is at one with the Self of every other being. That is one of the goals of yoga and of Vedanta and of the *Gita* as a whole. We find the same ideal expressed in the *Isa Upanishad*: "Who sees all things in the Self and the Self in all things". That means that we enter into the inner centre of our being and at that centre we realise that we are one with all people and with all things. This is the essential vision. People often mistakenly think that persons who are engaged in meditation, in looking inwards, are leaving the world, separating themselves from the world, getting isolated and self-centered. In fact the exact opposite is the case. The more we are integrated with our inner centre the more we are open to others and to the whole of creation. The person who is totally integrated and totally one with that inner centre is one with creation, with humanity and with God. This is the final stage. To become the centre of all being. To become aware of this essential oneness in the whole creation and in every being. That is the goal.

The next point is that work done in a spirit of detachment is seen to be exemplified in God. He works in the whole world. The Lord is present and active in the whole creation. When things go wrong in this world, it does not affect God. God is compared to the sun shining on the whole earth. The light enters different kinds of receptacles, undergoes various experiences, and is broken up into diverse refractions, what Goethe called the 'Passions of Light'. The light suffers all kinds of 'passionate' experiences but the light itself is not affected by it.

The next slokas are important.

8. 'I am not doing any work', thinks the man who is in harmony, who sees the truth.

9. For in seeing or hearing, smelling or touching, in eating or walking, or sleeping, or breathing, in talking or grasping or relaxing, and even in opening or closing his eyes, he remembers: 'It is the servants of my soul that are working.'

Now here we begin to come upon a problem. The ideal is to work from the centre of the person, but what is the relation between the inner self, which is at peace and in harmony, and the activities of the senses and the mind? There is one view which suggests that we are completely detached from our work. This view holds that although the body, senses and mind are working, we are not working; we remain totally detached and indifferent. In fact there are three ways in which this activity can be understood.

One is that all the activity of the world comes from nature, from *prakriti*. This was the view of the old Sankhya system. Nature here includes the mind. The senses, the mind, and even the intelligence, the *buddhi*, are all part of nature, and it is these that are working. But *purusha*, the person, the inner consciousness, the spirit within, is perfectly inactive and is the witness, not involved at all. That is a sort of dualism. We encountered the same view in the previous chapter: that one can keep oneself in that state of inner detachment and let the body function on its own. This is a very common view in Hinduism.

The second view is that of Sankara. According to him all the work of nature, *prakriti*, is ultimately *maya*. It has no ultimate reality. If we are involved in it, it is real to us, but if we wake up to supreme wisdom, *paravidya*, and realise Brahman, then we realise there is no activity at all. It is pure illusion, it is like a mirage. All activity in this world is ultimately unreal. The only object of life is to get beyond all activity. That is why in that tradition, the pure *sannyasi* does not do any work. He must reach the state where all work ceases except for what is unavoidable; for instance, he has to eat a minimum amount of food to keep the body going. They say of the *jivan mukta*, the one who has realised salvation or liberation while still alive, that he has nothing to do. He simply survives here and looks on, but there is nothing he can do.

Implicit in this view of Sankara is that all the activity of this world is ultimately purposeless. It is a very strong belief in the Hindu tradition that this world ultimately has no meaning. This belief derives from the cyclic view of life. The world comes out from Brahman and there is activity, and then it goes back to Brahman. There is no meaning or purpose in it. The wise man allows this to go on. He lets the work of nature go on in him, thinking and acting and doing, because his body is still involved in the world. But he is completely detached from, and indifferent to, the whole process.

There is a third view beyond these two which is that the world and all activity is a *lila*, a play of God. This was the view of Ramakrishna. The great mother is playing, and all that goes on in this world is her play. By itself that is hardly satisfactory for it means that all the suffering of the world is ultimately meaningless. The concept of *lila* however, can also be interpreted in the way towards which the *Gita* is working and which the modern Hindu certainly supports, namely that this *lila* of God has a meaning and a purpose. In this view God is not merely at play but is purposefully active in the world. That seems to be the deeper meaning of the *Gita*, though it is not held quite constantly.

This is consistent with the Christian understanding of the activity of God. The Crucifixion reveals that suffering is redemptive. The sufferings of this world have a meaning and a purpose and lead to a final fulfillment. God assumes the sin and suffering of the world into his own being, redeeming it and bringing it to fulfilment. On the other hand, many Christians tend to be too involved in history, in work, in service to suffering humanity, and so tend to lose sight of the other side of it. There is a sense in which all this world is passing away and we have to fix our gaze on that which lies beyond. The Hindu, on the other hand, does not realise sufficiently the reality of the human person, of his sufferings, of his destiny, and that this life has an ultimate purpose. It is not just a *lila*, a play. So what is important is to find an equilibrium, realising the values of this world, of time and history, but seeing them in the light of eternity. It is always so difficult in one's own life to find this balance. Either we give too much importance to what we are doing, as though everything depends on that, or we give too much importance to prayer, to the world beyond, in New Testament terms, to eschatology.

In the New Testament, the early view was that Jesus was to return at any moment. The *parousia*, the second coming of Christ, was expected at any time so that everything that was done in this world was very relative. St. Paul advised, "Those who are married, let them be as though they were not married. Those who buy in the market as though they did not", and so on. The world was a sort of temporary phase which they had to carry on with while they were waiting for the *parousia*. It was only after some time that the church began to realise that the world was going to last much longer than they had anticipated. Perhaps it is only today that we are realising the full importance of life in this world. Right through the Middle Ages it was something one had to endure; one had to do one's best, one had to do one's duty, waiting all the time for the world beyond. Now we have gone to the opposite extreme. Many say there is no world beyond. We have got to find everything in this world, we have to find our fulfilment now. So we are always swinging between these two poles. We have to find an equilibrium. There is no simple answer; each person has to find the balance within himself. This is one of the places where Hindu and Christian have to meet together and work together. We must learn from one another. That is the secret.

10. Offer all thy works to God, throw off selfish bonds, do thy work. No sin can then stain thee, even as waters do not stain the leaf of the lotus.

Mascaró translates Brahman as 'God'. It is a little misleading, because it has not got that fully personal aspect at this stage. Zaehner translates more literally, "ascribing his works to Brahman", the supreme reality. "No sin can stain thee even as waters do not stain the leaf of the lotus." This is a famous Buddhist image. In fact all of this portion, and particularly what we are coming to, is very Buddhist in its language and in its understanding.

Zaehner quotes from the Buddhist scriptures: "Just as a lotus born of water, grown up in water, passing up above the water, is not stained by the water, so is the Buddha: though he has grown up in the world and conquered it, yet he is not stained by the world." So also the *Chandogya Upanishad* says: "As water does not stick to a lotus leaf, so do not evil deeds cleave to the man who knows this." In Christian terms the idea is expressed in the phrase "being in the world but not of it."

11. The Yogi works for the purification of the soul: he throws off selfish attachment, and thus it is only his body or his senses or his mind or his reason that works.

Now here another problem comes up. Even if we say that we are to work, to be active, still the idea remains — and this again we find in Christian monasticism — that the work is done for self-purification. It was particularly common in the early monastic tradition. If good works were done, it was for the monks' self-purification. There was little interest in other people. If we serve patients in a hospital, we may not be interested in the patients, but simply in our own purification by means of the work done. That can be a very dangerous standpoint. The *Gita* is saying that one is working for the purification of the Self; the body, the mind, and the senses go on working but the inner self is completely detached from the whole process and is not really concerned. Here then is a problem. The motive Krishna gives for doing the work is really only that it is our *dharma*, duty. Why does Arjuna have to fight? Because he is a warrior and because this is a righteous war. It is the duty of a warrior to fight in a just war. Therefore do your duty, whatever it may be. It is your *swadharma*, your own duty, according to your caste, to do your service in the world. You do it with complete detachment, without feeling the work has any real meaning or purpose in it. You are purifying yourself and you are going to get your own eternal reward, but not in this world. This again is a common view in the Hindu understanding. The world has no ultimate purpose in it. It is all a cyclic movement. It all goes round and round. It was the Hebrews who brought the idea that the world is moving towards a goal and that there is a purpose in it. Even so, it is very difficult to believe that much of the work done in the world is meaningful.

For a person working in a factory, in mass production, for a clerk in business, or for most people in fact, this is the only attitude they feel they can adopt. The attitude is: I have got to earn my living. I do this work for eight hours a day because it is my duty, but I keep my mind completely detached from it. I have no interest in it at all and in fact I dislike the whole

concern, but I keep my mind free, and I try to live a human life outside
my work. That is a very common attitude. I think that it is also fairly general
in the Christian tradition, along with the idea that we do our work as a duty.

In the past people did their work, whatever it was, for the glory of
God and for the salvation of their souls, but were not really interested in
changing the human situation. Even today that accusation is made. We build
schools and hospitals which keep the present social system going but we
do not enquire whether that system itself is not essentially unjust, so that
a great deal of work is being put into perpetuating an unjust social system.

There are those who say that we should come out of our institutions
and change the structure of society, perhaps joining the Marxists in total
revolution. In the Christian context the idea of bringing about change is
expressed by saying that in Christ God becomes incarnate, enters time and
history, and changes the course of the world. This world has a force in
it now which is directing it towards a final fulfillment and in the world
we are working for the Kingdom of God. That is a vision common to many
modern Hindus and many modern Christians.

Again it is a question of where the emphasis lies. Nowadays the emphasis
is more and more on actual change in this world; changing ourselves, changing
society and making a more human life. In doing this it is understood that
we are working with God. This was the concern of Mahatma Gandhi. He
felt that traditional spirituality tended to be too directed towards oneself,
its aim being to become completely detached and to live a pure and holy
life in devotion to God, while the world was left to go on its own way.
For Gandhi it was of crucial importance to change the world.

In this understanding one is working with God for the evolution of
the world, for the change of humanity toward a final goal. But there is
a danger also in this point of view. If we think too much about changing
this world, we can become terribly frustrated because even where a new
social order is instituted, as in Soviet Russia, China, or elsewhere, although
some improvement may have been made, after a few years the same problems
arise in a new form and others present themselves, so that in the end things
are a good deal worse. So we begin to ask what is the point of all this?
Even though our work is to change the world for the sake of the Kingdom
of God, we have also to be always looking beyond. As Jesus said, "My
Kingdom is not of this world." So a balance is needed as we endeavour
to hold these two opposites together in a living, harmonious tension. Precisely
how to do that is one of the main problems of life.

"So his body, his senses and his reason works". We would say rather that his inner spirit works through his body, his mind and his reason. The question is how to keep the mind in this inner purity and awareness of God and yet accomplish effectively the work we have to do. We should recognise that there are two faculties in the mind, the intuitive and the rational. It is held that one side of the brain is intuitive and unitive while the other is rational, discursive, discriminative, analytical and dividing. These two faculties should work together.

When the rational mind takes control it tends to divide up and disintegrate everything it deals with and this is largely what happens today. Everything is seen in parts so that reality is fragmented and the unity is missed. Alternatively, if the intuitive mind is functioning alone it has no discrimination. It is blind and unitive, embracing everybody and everything without discernment or discrimination. That tends to be a weakness of the East. People in India often confuse everything in a vague unity which misses the point. What should be happening is that the intuitive and the rational should be working together. When there is complicated scientific or medical work to do we should be unified in ourselves, in our inner being. Our intuitive mind is working through all the faculties, however actively we may be engaged with our hands, our brain and so on. Behind every movement there can be inner intuitive vision.

The *Gita* rather suggests that the spirit is detached and the senses and mind are working, but ideally it should be the Spirit itself, God himself, who is working in us to achieve these things. We only function fully when we are totally surrendered, body, mind, soul and every faculty, to this inner power, which is the Spirit of God. So that is the real goal, and in work done like that we are both totally surrendered to God, doing the will of God, and totally active in all our members and faculties.

That is the example given in the life of Christ. He is totally surrendered to the Father, at one with the Father and yet he is totally involved in the work he has to do in the world, his preaching and healing, and the sacrifice of his life.

12. This man of harmony surrenders the reward of this work and thus attains final peace: the man of disharmony, urged by desire, is attached to his reward and remains in bondage.

That is the first stage, to surrender the reward. There must be no working for egoistic motives.

13. The ruler of his soul surrenders in mind all work, and rests in the joy of quietness in the castle of nine gates of his body: he neither does selfish work nor causes others to do it.

Mascaró says he does no 'selfish work' and that conveys the meaning but it may be closer to the text to say that he has really renounced all work. He is sitting quietly in the inner sanctuary, allowing other people to work, but he is not engaged. Yet it is also possible to interpret it as no selfish work, and that would convey a deeper meaning. We have always to distinguish between an indifference which just looks on and allows things to take their course, and an indifference which is surrender to God and wills the work of God in the actual action in which one is engaged, and that makes all the difference.

14. The Lord of the world is beyond the works of the world and their working, and beyond the results of these works; but the work of Nature rolls on.

Here is the same problem. It is going back to the Samkhya view that the work is being done by nature. *Purusha*, the Spirit, is not doing anything. He is only looking on. The *Gita* is trying to get beyond that, but here it is still using that kind of terminology. According to this theory the Spirit is simply the witness looking on and the work is done by nature.

15. The evil works or the good works of men are not his work. Wisdom is darkened by unwisdom, and this leads them astray.

This suggests, again, that the Lord is not concerned with either our good works or our evil works. We may commit sins, but he is not affected by them, and equally we may do good works and offer them to him, but he is not affected by that. Again it is a not uncommon view. Even Sankara would say that. He says that all the good works of religion, sacrifice, alms-giving and so on, though they are good for purifying the soul and although they lead towards liberation, yet they have no ultimate value in themselves. God is not pleased with good works any more than he is annoyed with evil ones. That is the course of nature. We have to go beyond good and evil.

That is a very disconcerting view. This, I feel, is where the idea of Brahman, the Supreme Being, the pure Spirit, pure consciousness, is insufficient. Either the world is regarded as *maya*, illusion, or else it is *lila*, just a play. But it is a new idea that the Lord is concerned with the world, the world of his creation, that he has a purpose in the world, and that ultimately the purpose is love. That love is the motive of the whole creation and of all human activity, and that love is fulfilled through human work in the sense that the love of God is fulfilled in us when we work according to love. This is what is revealed in the Gospels. Although a similar idea of love is current in Hinduism it does not have the same force as in the Gospel. The Gospel brings a new perspective in making this motive of love fundamental and supreme.

Many will say that part of the reason why India is in such a state today is because of this traditional religious doctrine. Pandit Nehru and others felt it strongly. For centuries the idea was that this world does not really matter, and if people are dying on the streets of Calcutta, or anywhere else, that is their *karma* and the work of nature goes on. The important thing is to get beyond it all. This is why there is so much neglect and indifference of the wrong kind and why Mahatma Gandhi reacted so strongly in trying to bring in the idea of serving God in the poor and the suffering. This idea has been widely accepted, and the Hindu today shares with the rest of the world a much greater consciousness that there is a purpose in history, and that we are working out that purpose. The people today are building up India as a nation. It is a work in which we are all engaged. The wise man today will be concerned with that work. But all the same, one still finds that it is very difficult in the Hindu tradition to get people to work seriously. There are examples like the Ramakrishna order which is a remarkable achievement. They have modelled themselves in many ways on the Church and have schools, colleges and hospitals which are run on the same lines as Christian institutions. But in government institutions the tendency is to regard the work as a job which one does to earn money, to keep the family going and make one's way in the world, without their being any serious concern for the work itself. However, change is coming and leaders are trying to make people realise that the service of the country is part of one's *dharma*. Here again, it is important that the Christian and the Hindu should be working together. The Hindu tends to be defensive because Christians have been so militant and aggressive in the past, thinking that they alone were right and everyone else was in error. Naturally Hindus reacted negatively against that and are therefore now not very willing to come together and to cooperate. But cooperation will come as both Christian and Hindus grasp the insight that each needs the other.

16. But those whose unwisdom is made pure by the wisdom of their inner
    Spirit, their wisdom is unto them a sun and in its radiance they see
    the Supreme.

"But some there are whose ignorance of self is destroyed by wisdom"
(Z). Their *ajnana* is destroyed by *jnana*. This is beautiful for it is like the
sun, which, it is said in a rather difficult phrase, "illumines that highest one".
More literally it is "In them wisdom shining as the sun reveals the supreme"
(B & D). That makes better sense. By this wisdom, by this insight, we realise
the real meaning of the work we are doing. It is coming from God and,
as we surrender it to God, we shine with the light of God within.
    The next verse is striking.

17. Their thoughts on Him and one with Him, they abide in Him, and
    He is the end of their journey. And they reach the land of never-
    returning, because their wisdom has made them pure of sin.

This translation is a little misleading in using 'Him', rather than 'It'.
It should read, "Thinking on That", and "merged with That". The Hindu
often speaks of ultimate reality in impersonal terms. It is just 'That'. Literally,
the *buddhi* or inner intelligence, is focussed on 'That', the 'Atman', the essential
self. Established in 'That' and journeying towards 'That', the goal is 'That'.
"They go along the path from which there is no return". They do not come
back to this world again. They have gone beyond, finally.
    I think if we put it in the context of Christian thought it becomes clearer.
If we think of God as the ultimate, as pure consciousness, we may get the
idea that we simply separate our consciousness from this world, trying to
unite it with God, and share that pure consciousness. On the other hand,
if we think of God as love and our aim is to be united with that being
which is pure love, then it is a dynamic force. Love is dynamic, so that
when reaching the goal, we are in the power of love, and that directs our
life and activity, sending us out to serve, to work, and to do whatever God
wants. He may want us to stay in a cave, and that is one way of loving
God, but equally He may want us to work in a slum. So it makes a great
difference if the ultimate reality is conceived as love, and not merely as
consciousness. Towards the end of the *Gita* the idea that God is love is
emerging. That is the supreme achievement of the *Gita* in Hinduism and
it is also the central focus of the Gospel.

The ultimate reality is love; it is a dynamic force which creates and sustains the world. It is this that descends on the apostles and sends them out to preach and to heal, and to transform the world. What drives them is *agape*, the love which is God himself in Christ. This makes a motive for action which is rather different from that of the Hindu. At the same time the danger for the Christian is that he plunges into activity and gets so absorbed in it that he loses the inner equilibrium, the harmony, the purity of heart which the *Gita* teaches. It is that that is our real work. We have to learn in the midst of activity to have this equilibrium, this purity of heart.

18. With the same evenness of love they behold a Brahmin who is learned and holy, or a cow, or an elephant, or a dog, and even the man who eats a dog.

The characteristic of this wisdom is that it leads to *samatva*, evenness or equanimity. Such a person sees God in everyone and everything, not only in a sacred person like a Brahmin or in a sacred animal like a cow or an elephant, but also in a dog which, because it is a scavenger, is considered unclean, as is still more a man who eats a dog.

19. Those whose minds are ever serene win the victory of life on this earth. God is pure and ever one, and ever one they are in God.

The translation, "The victory of life on this earth" is a little free. Literally it is, "They have overcome the process of rebirth", that is, they are beyond the world of becoming. They become one with Brahman who is free of all imperfection and ever the same. Here again 'God' is Brahman, which signifies the impersonal or transpersonal state of the Godhead.

20. The man who sees Brahman abides in Brahman: his reason is steady, gone is his delusion. When pleasure comes he is not shaken, and when pain comes he trembles not.

The man who 'sees Brahman' is the *Brahma-vid*, the knower of Brahman. This is the highest form of knowledge when one is 'established' in the absolute reality.

21. He is not bound by things without, and within he finds inner gladness. His soul is one in Brahman and he attains everlasting joy.

In the Sanskrit it is *Brahma-yoga-yukta-atma*. The *Atman*, the self, is *yukta*, joined by *Yoga*, with *Brahman* or ultimate reality. When this goal is reached he finds unfailing joy.

22. For the pleasures that come from the world bear in them sorrows to come. They come and they go, they are transient: not in them do the wise find joy.

The pleasures that come from contact with the senses are said to be *dubkha yonaya*, that is, they have a womb of sorrow within them. This is an example of Buddhist language and ideas which were assimilated into the *Gita*. Here we have the familiar Buddhist idea that all pleasure brings pain with it and the more you seek pleasure the more you are pursued by pain. That was the Buddha's fundamental insight: ultimately everything is *dubkha*, everything is unsatisfactoriness, and it is necessary to go beyond the whole world of opposites in order to achieve inner peace. Our whole mind and our whole being must be set on *nirvana*, the state beyond the senses and the feelings, beyond our present mode of consciousness. So he says of pleasures, "They come and they go, they are transient; not in them do the wise find joy". If they have a beginning, they have an end and therefore one is never going to have satisfaction in them; one must go beyond.

23. But he who on this earth, before his departure, can endure the storms of desire and wrath, this man is a Yogi, this man has joy.

Desire and anger, *kama* and *krodha* are the two basic passions in human nature. The aim is not to eliminate desire and anger but to be unmoved by them. The storm must be endured, it comes and it passes away, but one remains constant beneath it.

24. He has inner joy, he has inner gladness, and he has found inner Light. This Yogi attains the *nirvana* of Brahman: he is one with God and goes unto God.

Such a person has joy within and light within. Instead of being tossed about in the outer world, he finds the light within. The phrase '*nirvana* of Brahman' is of great interest. *Nirvana* is the final state in Buddhism and it is often thought of as a negative state, in the sense of being the absence of all life. Zaehner, however, has an interesting description of it based on the Pali text, where he says that, literally, it is a blowing out of the fire of life, the fire of *tanha*, that is, craving. This leads to that peace or equanimity which is so characteristic of Buddhism. It is the cooling of the desires that brings about health and the Buddha is described as the surgeon who makes health possible. In the Buddhist idea, there is no human self, every human being is a coming together of *skandas*, which are elements. These elements come together and produce this body and this mind and this experience and then as the body disintegrates, so the soul disintegrates. There is ultimately no body and no soul, only a continual movement of energies, coming together and disintegrating. In this world nothing is permanent; only beyond the world of flux is it possible to experience peace and joy. This is the condition of wisdom and enlightenment. Although this state is completely negative as regards the present mode of consciousness, it is actually positive in the sense that it is final fulfilment. *Nirvana*, then, as Zaehner says, is certainly extinction of life as we know it, but is also a state of liberation, of spiritual freedom, uninhibited by space, time or causation. The Buddha compares it to a level and charming countryside, or the scent of a flower. This freeing of transcendent reason and wisdom from the bondage of passion and hatred is compared to a man observing oyster shells and fish in limpid water. It is seeing things as they really are *sub specie aeternitatis*.

So that is the meaning of *nirvana* in Buddhism. But the *Gita* enlarges this conception by speaking of the "*nirvana* of Brahman". This is described as *Brahma bhuta*, that is, becoming Brahman. This is also a Pali phrase which is very common in Buddhist texts. It is described as the state of being without craving, appeased, cooled, experiencing joy, with the self become Brahman. As a result of there being no self one simply merges into Brahman. There is no ego, there is no self left at all. The *Gita* would say that the Self, the Atman, is then one with Brahman. When one reaches Brahman one enjoys a state of timelessness, of pure equanimity and pure enlightenment. That is to become Brahman; to share in the being of Brahman, which is very much what in Christian terms is meant by sharing in the divine nature. As the letter of St. Peter says, "we are made partakers of the divine nature" (2 Pet. 1.4). As usual, Mascaró translates Brahman as God. "The Yogi attains the *nirvana* of Brahman, he is one with God and he goes unto God". That is a Christian rendering, but the sense is fundamentally the same.

25. Holy men reach the *nirvana* of Brahman: their sins are no more, their doubts are gone, their soul is in harmony, their joy is in the good of all.

In this final state the soul is set free from sin and doubt, that is, from all the dualities, and what is even more significant, its 'joy is in the good of all'. The final state is not one of isolation but of universal love or compassion, *karuna*. *Karuna* is also one of the basic virtues in Buddhism.

26. Because the peace of God is with them whose mind and soul are in harmony, who are free from desire and wrath, who know their own soul.

The "peace of God" is again the "*nirvana* of Brahman", the state of transcendent bliss, and this arises when "they know their own soul", that is, they know the Self, the inner Spirit in which man is united with God.

All these things go together. As one is freed from passion, anger and desire and as the mind becomes controlled, one reaches the state of inner stillness. At the same time the real self, which controls the body, the mind, and everything else, makes itself known. When that Self is known, one becomes one with Brahman.

From a Buddhist point of view there is no Self, one simply becomes Brahman, one becomes that Reality. The Buddha said not to inquire or to try to rationalise it. Simply follow the path and you will reach that state, and then you will know all about it. In the *advaita* of Shankara there is much the same idea that ultimately this world, the Self in this mode of experience, is unreal. When Brahman is reached you know reality, you are that Reality; as expressed in the famous saying, the Mahavakya: Thou art That.

That can perhaps be interpreted from a Christian point of view in the light of the text of Genesis where it says that man is made in the image of God. That is the traditional Christian view and it can be interpreted as the Fathers explained it, that each person is like a mirror in which God is reflecting Himself. Our being comes from God and is in God and yet it is distinct from God. Each one is a unique mirror of the infinite.

There is a beautiful poem of Guru Amardas, the Sikh saint, in which he makes exactly the same point. The Sikhs have a very profound idea of a personal God. It says that when your self-will is destroyed you discover yourself as the image of God. God is in you and you are in God. This is the point where the human spirit becomes one with the Spirit of God. It is important to understand that this is a dynamic point. We are not normally fixed and still. We are in a state of flux and we are trying to bring our mind and our will to that point where we are fixed in the Spirit and at that point of the spirit we are open to the Holy Spirit, to the life divine, to Brahman. That is to experience Brahman, to become Brahman, without ceasing to be ourselves. We become a perfect mirror of the Absolute. From a Christian point of view there is no loss of self but rather the realisation of the Self in the One, in the Eternal.

27. When the sage of silence, the Muni, closes the doors of his soul and,

28. resting his inner gaze between the eyebrows, keeps peaceful and even the ebbing and flowing of breath; and with life and mind and reason in harmony and with desire and fear and wrath gone, keeps silent his soul before final freedom, he in truth has attained final freedom.

This is a perfect description of Yoga and is one of the earliest texts concerning Yoga. The *Yoga Sutras* of Patanjali belong to the fifth century after Christ and this is the third century before Christ. In the *Katha Upanishad* and also in the *Svetasvatara Upanishad* there are somewhat earlier descriptions of yoga.

"When the sage of silence, the Muni, closes the doors of his soul". That is always the first thing. It is called *pratyahara* and is a withdrawing from the outer world and centering on the inner self.

"Resting his inner gaze between the eyebrows". It is said that one should train the mind by focussing on some particular point, such as one of the *chakras* which are the centres of psychic energy, of power and of life in each of us.

In Kundalini Yoga there are seven chakras or centres of psychic energy. The divine energy is said to be concentrated at the base of the spine in the form of a serpent, and has to be drawn up progressively through each of these centres. The first centre, at the base of the spine, is called the *Muladhara*. Above this there is the sex centre called the *Swadhistana*, and this is the centre of procreative life energy. Above this, at the level of the navel, is the *Manipura* which is the centre of emotional life. Then comes the heart centre, the *Anahata*, and this is the focus of the will and the affections. Beyond this is the throat centre, the *Vishuddha*, where the power of speech and music and poetry are centered. Higher again is the *Ajna* chakra at the point between the eyebrows, and this is the seat of the pure intelligence and the centre of light. This is the point between the eyebrows mentioned in the text of the *Gita*. Finally there is the thousand-petalled lotus, the *Sahasrara*, at the crown of the head. All these energies come to a head in this lotus which opens on the Divine Light. This is where the whole person comes to flower, as it were, and reaches perfection.

The Virgin Mary is depicted in India as seated on a lotus like the Prajna paramika, the supreme perfect wisdom, in Makayana Buddhism. She is the mother in whom divine wisdom, which in India is conceived as the Divine Mother, comes to flower.

"Keeping peaceful and even the ebbing and flowing of breath". That is *pranayama*. There are many forms of breath control but the simplest and the most fundamental is to keep the ebb and flow peaceful and even. This is a practical yoga: the doors of the senses are closed, the mind rests at the point between the eyebrows, and the breath is kept even and steady.

"With life and mind and reason in harmony". These are the three powers of the soul. The life is the *prana*, the energy entering the body with the breath; the mind, the *manas*, is the lower mind which works through the senses, while the reason is the *buddhi*, the pure intelligence, or the *nous* of Greek philosophy. When all are in harmony, the whole person is integrated, *yukta*. Yoga is never a suppression of anything; neither of the body, nor of the passions, nor of the senses, nor of the mind. It is a bringing of the whole person into harmony, into a perfect order.

"With desire and fear and anger gone". When it is said that the three basic passions are gone, the meaning is that they come under complete control, being transformed from negative into creative forces. There is nothing in our nature which may not ultimately be transformed.

One should never attempt to suppress, for instance, anger. Anger can be a good thing, because anger is the force whereby one resists evil. We need that force but it can be very dangerous when it gets out of control. So also desire is very basic to our nature. We cannot live without it, and ultimately the desire is for God. Even fear is necessary; we need to be afraid, to have a warning mechanism when things are hostile to us. We need these basic passions but they must all be under the complete control of the inner Self.

"Keeps silent his soul before final freedom, he in truth has attained final freedom". That is, he is liberated, he has attained *moksha*. The phrase used is *moksha parayana*, literally, 'journeying towards *moksha*', or liberation. Liberation consists of perfect equilibrium and freedom. Mircea Eliade entitles his book on yoga, *Yoga, Immortality and Freedom*. That is total freedom, including freedom from death itself, and that is the goal of the perfect yogi.

29. He knows me, the God of the worlds who accepts the offerings of
men, the God who is the friend of all. He knows me and he attains
peace.

So far we have been using the language of Buddhism and of yoga without
any mention of a personal God at all. But in this last verse the teaching
of the *Gita* is that this final state of *moksha* or liberation, centres on the
personal God.

"He knows me and he attains peace". Here the Gita *opens* up the
somewhat impersonal world of Brahman and the *Atman* to the reality of
the personal God. Zaehner translates, "Knowing me to be the proper object
of sacrifice and mortification", *yajna* and *tapas*. This means that all *tapas*
and *sadhana*, spiritual discipline, and yoga, are being done ultimately for
him, "the great Lord of the worlds and the friend of all creatures" (Z).

Here is the teaching of the *Gita* which is also the teaching of the
Upanishads. When one reaches the true Self, the *Atman*, the very centre
of one's being, one also reaches Brahman, the very centre and ground of
the whole creation; and that *Atman*, that Brahman, is the Lord and is an
object of love and worship. So the whole of this yoga finally flowers in
worship and love.

This implies also a respect for the creation in which the Lord is present.
Ramakrishna gives the impression, which is so common in Hinduism and
even in certain forms of Christianity, that the spiritual path is always going
beyond this world, until we eventually reach a state of *samadhi* when there
is no more activity of any kind. He says that at first we are *bhaktas*, we
worship God, we sing songs to God, and we praise the Lord of Creation.
But as we go further the soul is lost in God and does not remain in the
body for more than twenty-one days. It simply passes beyond.

This attitude also appears in Abishiktananda's book, *The Further Shore*.
The urge to be always going beyond is one aspect of Hinduism. The perfect
man is one who has simply gone beyond this world. He has no further
concern with the world at all. It is an aspect of the Christian ideal of the
monk who, beyond all community life, has gone into solitude and is only
engaged in prayer and waiting for death when he finally reaches his
consummation. We should not reject that ideal altogether for it is an aspect
of life and of *sadhana*. It is one direction in which the spiritual life moves,
in the freeing of ourselves from attachment to the world, to the body, the
senses, the feelings, the imagination, the mind, and the will; and also the
freeing of ourselves from all human contacts and from all human society,

become one with God in this ultimate depth of our being.

However the journey does not necessarily stop there, because the God whom we reach at this point is the God of the whole creation, the God who creates and redeems humanity and the cosmos, and who is a God of love. Therefore when we reach that state we enter not merely into pure consciousness, but also into pure love. That love then completely fills our life; it may, and usually does, direct us to some kind of work or service. This ultimate spirit is a dynamic power; it is the Holy Spirit which is love. When we surrender ourselves to it we surrender ourselves to a love which then compels us and may drive us in any direction to whatever work we have to do.

That is the way by which one can escape from the dilemma of simply being taken out of this world. From the Christian point of view it is fundamental that the life of the Spirit is not simply a way of escape from the world. People often say that it is selfish to be simply seeking one's own salvation and then to pass beyond. Each religion, each tradition, has felt this problem. In Buddhism it is noteworthy that the early Hinayana or Theravada tradition was simply intent on reaching *nirvana*. The *arahant* is the perfect man who has reached *nirvana* and has passed beyond.

Then at about the time of the *Bhagavad Gita*, there was the *bhakta* movement of devotion to a personal God, which later spread all over India. In Buddhism this led to the conception of the *bodhisattva*, who, when he is reaching his goal, makes a vow not to enter into *nirvana* until all sentient beings have been liberated.

Here the great compassion of the Buddha comes into play. The Buddha himself, instead of passing beyond and entering *nirvana* after his enlightenment, devoted himself to the liberation of the world. For the rest of his life he preached the *Dhamma*, the path of liberation. So the *bodhisattva* is the holy man who is devoted to the salvation of the world. This compassion of the *bodhisattva* is portrayed in the beautiful figures on the walls of the caves of Ajanta. Buddhism thus has a profound sense of compassion and of service. Similarly in Hinduism there is the path of pure *sannyasa*, of going beyond, but equally there are the saints of Hinduism, the *bhaktas* who rejoice in the love of God. Even Shankaracharya, though he was a great *advaitin*, wrote hymns in praise of God. Having profoundly experienced the One beyond all duality, he spent his life in propagating the doctrine of *advaita* or non-duality, which led to the renewal of Hinduism. He went all over

India and established maths or monastic centres at the four corners of India, so that this doctrine might be spread everywhere.

The two elements are always there and in any spiritual life it is essential to keep this balance of the opposites. On the one hand we are being carried beyond everything to God alone, beyond the whole creation, while on the other hand the very power of God, the Spirit of God moving in us, directs us towards love and towards service. Every Christian and every religious person is called to this pure contemplation, to realise God, but each one has her own gift, her own charism, which calls her to serve the sick or the poor, or to teach or to preach, or to write books, or whatever it might be; but it should come from this depth of self-realisation, God-realisation. It should not come from the level of the three lower chakras. There is always the danger that we just work from an ordinary human level; we have some prayer and some spirituality to sustain our work, but without going any deeper. But the deeper one goes in the vertical direction towards God the more one should be able to go out in every horizontal direction towards humanity. Jesus is the perfect example. He lives in communion with the Father and is totally one with the Father; in this bliss of Oneness he is totally open to the whole humanity. He surrenders his life totally for the world.

A distinction is often made between a lower *bhakti* and a higher *bhakti*. The former is simply singing songs and loving God in a rather sentimental way, and that is fine as a beginning, but there is also a higher *bhakti*. That is the love which engages the ultimate depth of the soul. St. John of the Cross describes it as an experience of love which is actually God himself loving in us. It is not our love any longer. The love of God has taken possession and he is living, acting, and moving in us. That is the final fulfilment and that divine love can send us in any direction. We are simply in its hands. It is not for us to decide what we are going to do any longer. That for me is the final answer, and I think the *Bhagavad Gita* is moving all the time towards that position.

There is a strong tradition of this in Hinduism, but the conflict is never quite resolved as to whether the perfect man is the one who leaves the world, or who is at the service of the world. Perhaps one cannot resolve it.

The debate continues between contemplation and action, the debate already indicated in the work of St. Thomas and St. Bonaventure. The question was whether the final state is the 'vision of God' by knowledge, by the intellect, as St. Thomas held, or whether it is the 'love of God', which is centered in the will. St. Bonaventure said that perfection is in the love of God and knowledge results from that. St. Thomas says that perfection is in the knowledge of God and it is from that that love results.

Perhaps one can respond to the dilemma by saying that there is a depth of the soul in its encounter with God in which knowledge and love are so intimately one that they cannot be distinguished.

Chapter 6

The Yoga of Meditation

The sixth chapter continues the previous theme and develops it further, revolving round the question of the relation between contemplation and action, or in the *Gita's* terms, between Sankhya and Yoga. Sankhya is the contemplative discipline and Yoga the practical discipline.

Krishna is speaking:

1. He who works not for an earthly reward, but does the work to be done, he is a Sannyasi, he is a Yogi: not he who lights not the sacred fire or offers not the holy sacrifice.

The point here is that the essence of *sannyasa*, renunciation, is renunciation of the self. It is not a renouncing of action or external things; it is a matter of inner renunciation. The man who works without attachment, free from any self love is a true *sannyasi* and also a yogi. This means that contemplation and action are one. Contemplation is freedom from all attachment, so that one adheres to God, to Brahman. In the *Gita* it gradually becomes clear that this means adhering to, and living in, the personal God. This brings freedom from all attachment and from all desire of reward, and in that freedom one does one's work. That is always the teaching: do not seek the fruit of your actions. This is the true meaning of both *sannyasa* and yoga.

"Not the man who builds no sacrificial fire and does no work" (Z). The word for "no work" is akriya, which can mean no work in the ordinary sense but here more probable means no holy work or ritual. That was the ancient idea of the *sannyasi* and it still remains today. A *sannyasi* does not build a sacrificial fire for he has given up all ritual. The Hindu *sannyasi* is not supposed to perform any ritual. He is not a priest. This is important also for Christian monks. It has always been recognised that the priesthood is completely secondary in the monastic ideal, and should never be identified with it. The monk is essentially not a priest. He may undertake a priestly duty for a specific purpose in the monastery or elsewhere, but it is not an essential part of his vocation, because the priesthood is a specific service to the community and the monk as such has no particular ministry or work to do.

In the Hindu tradition, before initiation into *sannyasa*, the disciple, if he is a Brahmin or of high caste, removes the sacred thread and undergoes a funeral ceremony. This is like the Christian monastic profession where the monk lies prostrate in the sanctuary, as a symbol of his total self-sacrifice. Formerly he used to be covered with a black pall to show that he had died to the world. The *sannyasi* renounces all worldly attachments, all family bonds, all caste. He is free from all bondage to the social order. This led to the idea, as we have seen, that the *sannyasi* is beyond work. Work binds and if he continued to work he would be in bondage of *karma*. Therefore he does no work. The *Gita*, however, teaches that he should do his work, but that he should do it without attachment, not seeking any reward and offering all he does as a sacrifice; then he is a true *sannyasi*.

2. Because the Sannyasi of renunciation is also the Yogi of holy work; and no man can be a Yogi who surrenders not his earthly will.

This is the test. The word for earthly will is *samkalpa*. Zaehner translates this as 'purpose', but I think Mascaró's version is better. The earthly will is the egoistic will; therefore without renouncing his "earthly will" no one can be a yogi. The essential need is the renunciation of the ego, of the self. The ego, when it is centred on itself, is the root of all evil for it then becomes the principle of self-will. He who renounces all self-will is a true *sannyasi*. That is the essence of *sannyasa*.

3. When the sage climbs the heights of Yoga, he follows the path of

work; but when he reaches the heights of Yoga, he is in the land of peace.

More literally it is, "For a sage who is seeking Yoga, action is called the means; for the same sage when he is enthroned in Yoga, serenity is called the means" (B & D). This is very close to the idea of the early Christian monks: that all action is a preparation for contemplation. That was the common understanding; the active life belongs to beginners and consists in the life of virtue, humility, patience, charity. All this is a preparation for the life of contemplation, when one is no longer in need of such activities. That is one theory and it is very strong in the Hindu tradition also. The *sannyasi* is beyond action altogether; he is in pure contemplation. But the *Gita* is suggesting a different view which is much more profound, namely that when the *sannyasi* has reached this spiritual perfection, he is then free to act in any way that God may call him.

He surrenders himself totally to the divine, to Brahman; then he is free to act from the principle of the Spirit within, and not from his own ego, not from any self-will.

4. And he reaches the heights of Yoga when he surrenders his earthly will: when he is not bound by the work of his senses, and he is not bound by his earthly works.

So when there is no attachment to sense or to activity, through the earthly will, then he is a true yogi and also a true *sannyasi.* It is very important to realise that ultimately the yogi and the *sannyasi* are one and that for both it is a matter of being free from all attachment. The doctrine of the *Gita* leaves one free to act. That is why Mahatma Gandhi could take the *Gita* as the guide for his life. Total service of humanity is compatible here with total surrender to God.

So the two ideas are there. The one is that action is preparation for contemplation, and that in contemplation there is no action left and all is quiescence. The other idea which the *Gita* is putting forward, though it does not always make it clear, is that action leads to contemplation and that contemplation involves perfect detachment which enables one to act freely according to the law of the spirit within.

That is the theme of those first four verses.

Now we have three very interesting verses on the Self, or Atman. The word self has two senses. It can be written with a small "s" or with a large "S" and it is often difficult to distinguish between its two meanings. Zaehner makes no distinction and says, "Raise the self by the self, let not the self droop down, for the self's friend is the self indeed, so too is the self the self's enemy." Mascaró has:

5. Arise therefore! And with the help of thy Spirit lift up thy soul: allow not thy soul to fall. For thy soul can be thy friend and thy soul can be thine enemy.

Here, then, are the two senses of the word Atman. The first is the *jivatman*, the individual self, or soul. That includes the senses (*indriyas*), the mind (*manas*), the ego (*ahankara*) and even the intellect (*buddhi*) is included in this lower self, although that is also the point where we can go beyond ourselves. That is the lower self with a small "s". But beyond this lower self there is the higher Self, which is actually the true Self and is the Self of our striving. The verse then could be read in this way: "With the help of your Spirit, (that is the higher Self), lift up your soul (the lower self). Allow not your soul to fall. For your soul (your lower self), can be your friend, it can also be your enemy."

The soul stands between the *Paramatman*, the supreme Spirit, and the world of the senses, the passions, and of activity. It can always choose either to turn towards the world and the body, and to live according to the law of the world and the body, or to turn to the Spirit within and live by the law of the Spirit. Zaehner points out that it is almost exactly the same as St. Paul's description of the Spirit and the flesh in the letter to the Romans. "Those who live by the flesh set their minds on the things of the flesh, but those who live by the Spirit set their minds on the things of the Spirit" (Rom. 8.5). According to St. Paul to live by the Spirit is to live by the Holy Spirit within and to live by the flesh is to live by one's natural feelings; the one he calls the natural man, the other the spiritual man. The one is the *anthropos psychikos* that is, the man of the soul (*psyche*); the other is the *anthropos pneumatikos*, that is, the man of the Spirit (*pneuma*). So in St. Paul, Spirit is exactly equivalent to the Atman and the psyche or soul to the *jivatman*.

The Spirit is the point of meeting between God and man. That is where human destiny is always resolved, at that point where we are in touch with God and with the world. We are either turning towards God and being illuminated, and receiving the power of the Spirit of God, or we are turning towards the world and gradually getting alienated from the Spirit. It becomes a little clearer in the next two verses.

6. The soul of man is his friend when by the Spirit he has conquered his soul; but when a man is not lord of his soul then this becomes his own enemy.

Zaehner has more literally, "Self is the friend of the self of him whose self is by the self subdued". The soul is our friend when that soul has been subdued, controlled by the higher Self. Where Mascaró translates, "is not lord of his soul", the word is *anatman*, meaning the man who has no self, or as Zaehner translates "the man bereft of self". This is a very subtle point. Our real Self is the Spirit and when the body, the mind, and the soul, the *psyche*, are all under the control of the inner Spirit, then we are considered *yukta*, we are integrated. At that point we are realized and are at one with the Spirit which is also the Spirit of God. At that point the Spirit of God meets the Spirit of man. That is our state of unity. On the other hand, when the soul withdraws from the Spirit, it creates the illusory self. What people imagine to be their real self is usually their outer personality. They may identify with either their ego or their persona, their outer self, the latter being even more limited, and hence more illusory, than the ego. Neither the ego nor the persona are our real self. But worse, both the ego and the persona mask or hide the true self — persona literally means a mask. To get through those outer superficial layers of personality and to discover our true person is only possible if we are seeking God. Otherwise we have no real self. We are trying to be a self outside God, outside the Spirit; that is, we are living an illusion. All of us do this to some extent.

Zaehner gives a second version in which he uses the words 'carnal self' for the lower self, and that is exactly the mediaeval sense. The lower self was the carnal self. "The carnal self is the friend of the spiritual self of him whose carnal self is subdued by spiritual effort, but for the man bereft of spiritual self, the carnal self will act as his enemy." The carnal self, which includes what we would call 'soul', and which on this view transmigrates, can be lost or destroyed. One can be eternally alienated from the centre of one's being. Such a person is, as Zaehner says, literally *anatman*, bereft of self. In Christian terms, he is lost. Zaehner quotes from Thomas Merton. "Hell can be described as perpetual alienation from our true being, our true

Self, which is in God." That is the essence of evil, to be separated from our true self, our true being, which is found in God.

7. When his soul is in peace he is in peace, and then his soul is in God. In cold or in heat, in pleasure or pain, in glory or disgrace, he is ever in Him.

Or, better, "the higher self of the soul which is subdued and quietened, is wrapped in ecstasy" (Z). Another translation is, "The higher self of him who is self-controlled and peaceful is uniform in cold and heat, pleasure and pain, as well as in honour and dishonour" (B & D). The word for the higher self here is *paramatman*. This raises a problem. Ultimately, there is only one Self, the Supreme Self, which is manifested at different levels of reality. First of all, the *Paramatman*, the Supreme Self, can be conceived as beyond all word and all thought. It is the ultimate transcendent mystery. Secondly, the Atman can be conceived as the source of all reality, the source of all creation, of consciousness and of human existence. Thirdly, the same Atman can be conceived as indwelling in each person, each thing. In each one of us the One, the Supreme Spirit, is dwelling. That Supreme Spirit dwelling in me is my higher Self. These three senses are fundamental. The absolute Supreme, beyond everything, the *Parabrahman* or *Paramatman*, then the Brahman or Atman as the source of everything, the creator Spirit, and then the Atman or Brahman manifested in every person in every thing, the indwelling Self. That is my higher Self and it is ultimately one with the Supreme.

"When this self is subdued and quietened" (Z). The word for 'quietened' is *prasanta*. It can also mean transparent, but tranquil is better. The word for the soul that "is in God" is *samagita*. It is the same root as in *samadhi*. Shankara translates it as 'concentrated', 'gathered into the Self'. So this soul is subdued and tranquil and gathered into unity. It is a state of perfect, integrated unity. The root of *samagita* is from *sama* which means same, so that we could translate, "Such a soul, in cold and heat, in pleasure and pain, in honour and disgrace, is always the same." It has sameness, equilibrium. It is essential to grasp this vision of the One; that is the key to everything. To realise the one Self, who is manifested in the whole creation and in every human being, is the whole aim of life and when we do that, we know ourselves in God, and God in us.

8. When, happy with vision and wisdom, he is master of his own inner life, his soul sublime set on high, then he is called a Yogi in harmony. To him gold or stones or earth are one.

"Happy with vision and wisdom" is literally, "Content with *jnana* and *vijnana*". *Jnana* is the word for wisdom; it is the higher wisdom, and *vijnana* introduces the element of duality. It is more 'discriminative knowledge'; so 'unitive knowledge' and 'discriminative knowledge' one could call it, wisdom and discernment.

Then there comes a most interesting phrase, *kutastha*, which Zaehner says means literally 'standing on a peak'. *Stha* is 'standing'; *kutha*, 'on a peak'. It can be translated as rock-seated (B & D), unshakeable, but Zaehner illustrates it beautifully from the *Mahabharata* which he quotes: "Once you have crossed this, you will be freed from every side, clean, knowing yourself as pure; firmly relying on the highest part of your soul, the buddhi, the highest intelligence, you will become Brahman. You will have transcended all defilements, yourself serene, immaculate, as one standing on a mountain, *parvata stha*, surveying those beings still living on the plains. Now you are standing still and looking down from above on everybody on the plain." He gives another quotation from the *Mahabharata*: "As a man standing on a high rock might look on men living in the plains, so does he who has scaled the battlements of wisdom look down on folk of little wit who mourn for men who do not need their mourning." And then again: "Among men preoccupied with their affairs, involving duty, pleasure, and profit, who are all the time being carried off by the flood of time, you will stand as one standing on a peak."

"He is a Yogi. To him gold or stones or earth are all one." This is a familiar illustration. Ramakrishna used to take gold in one hand and earth in the other and contemplate them until he realised they were the same. The idea is that all, ultimately, is Brahman. There is one Reality which is manifest in the earth, and in gold and precious stones. There is one Spirit in everyone and everything. The aim is to see the one Reality in every manifestation. One has to see God in everyone and everything and to recognise that the good is present in the midst of evil. That understanding, it is true, can be dangerous. Although the *Gita* generally avoids it, it sometimes gives the impression that it does not matter whether a person is good or bad. There is a kind of indifference which takes no notice of any differences at all. Everything is of the same value. Among many Hindus there is a tendency to think that. Many Hindus like to say that all religions are the same. In a certain sense this is true because the same Spirit is present in all religions. It is, however, manifested in different ways. The differences are important and one should appreciate them. Simply to think that gold and earth are the same is valuable in one way. It can free one from the terrible attraction to gold and aversion to mud and dirt. But one should also be able to discern the difference; Brahman is manifesting in different ways in the world. It is like the story of the disciple who was taught by his master that all is Brahman. One day he was going along the road when an elephant broke loose and was charging towards him. He just stood there, looking at the elephant, saying to himself, "All this is Brahman. Nothing can happen to me." The elephant took him up in his trunk and threw him off by the side of the road, where he was picked up unconscious. They brought him back to the guru and the man complained to him, "You said all is Brahman. I thought the elephant was Brahman — how can this hurt me?" The guru replied, "Yes, but the mahout who was riding the elephant was shouting to you to get out of the way, and he also was Brahman."

God is speaking to us through everything and we have to discern the presence of God in every situation. That is the difficulty of learning the will of God. It is coming to us from so many different directions and the discernment of the Spirit is to discern what is the will of God for me here and now in this concrete situation. So that is the meaning of seeing gold or stones or earth as the same.

9. He has risen on the heights of his soul. And in peace he beholds relatives, companions and friends, those impartial or indifferent or who hate him: he sees them all with the same inner peace.

This habit of looking on things with equanimity applies also to human relationships. We have to learn to look on friends and enemies in the same way. This, of course is equally the teaching of the Gospel: "Love your enemies. Do good to those who hate you" (Matt. 5:44). This is the most challenging teaching that we can encounter in any religion; it is the acid test of one's detachment.

Now in verse 10 we come to the beginning of a series of verses or slokas on yoga. The *Yoga Sutras* of Patanjali, which is the classical text on yoga is usually considered to be comparatively late but of course it is building on a long tradition which goes back at least a thousand years before. We find a first references to Yoga in the *Katha Upanishad,* (about 500 BC) and in the *Shvetashvatara Upanishad* which is perhaps a little later (about 400 BC). This is one of the key passages on yoga in the *Gita.*

10. Day after day let the Yogi practice the harmony of soul: in a secret place, in deep solitude, master of his mind, hoping for nothing, desiring nothing.

What Mascaró translates as "practise the harmony of soul" is literally "let him be yoked in Yoga," that is, integrated in yoga. Then he says that he should sit in a place apart. It is helpful to practise yoga in a place which is free from disturbance. Many people find it helpful to have a special place where they can sit. It is said that if possible, you should always use the same place, as it gradually acquires associations which give it a sacred quality. Although of course this is not essential, it can help.

The next point is that he should be 'master of his mind", that is, having "his thoughts and self restrained" (Z). Yoga is defined by Patanjali in the first sutra as *citta vritti nirodha,* the cessation or the restraint of the *vritti* — the movements, of the *citta* — the mind.

"Hoping for nothing, desiring nothing." This is equivalent to *aparigraha,* one of the five *yamas* or restraints in the yoga system of Patanjali: the others being not to kill (*ahimsa*), not to steal (*asteya*) to observe chastity (*brahmacharya*), and to speak the truth (*satya*). *Aparigraha* means "not grasping" which is the equivalent to the command "not to covet" in the Old Testament. "Hoping for nothing" really means not having any earthly hopes; it does not necessarily exclude spiritual hope.

11. Let him find a place that is pure and a seat that is restful, neither too high nor too low, with sacred grass and a skin and a cloth thereon.

I remember once a yogi came to our ashram and told us that one should always sit for meditation in the same place and that if possible one should have a kusa mat, a deerskin and a cloth They should never be moved and should be kept very sacred. That custom originated from this verse in the *Gita.* In practice the kusa grass is made into a mat, a deerskin is placed on it and then a folded cloth is put on top of the deerskin. Not only is this traditional; it also helps to insulate the body from cold and damp. It is very important to notice that in yoga one is trying to attain a state of complete harmony. This is very different from the Christian tradition of the Fathers of the desert. Their aim was to conquer the flesh by watching, fasting, and bodily mortifications. I think we must remember the historic circumstances which led to this. They probably found these disciplines necessary but it had a very bad effect on the Christian tradition of asceticism. The result is that many people reject asceticism altogether. "Well, if asceticism is like that," they say, "then it is not for me." But yoga is the exact opposite. Yoga is perfect control without any strain. One should never force oneself. In doing the *asanas*, postures, there must never be strain. One exercises a steady pressure and gradually the muscles relax and control comes, but without any strain. So yoga involves attaining complete control, but in perfect harmony. As the *Gita* says a little later, "Yoga is not for him who eats too much or for him who eats too little, or for him who sleeps too much or for him who sleeps too little." It is the middle way which is more difficult than either of the extremes.

12. On that seat let him rest and practise Yoga for the purification of the soul: with the life of his body and mind in peace, his soul in silence before the One.

More literally: "There let him sit, and make his mind *ekagrata*, one-pointed" (Z). That is one of the key words in the understanding of meditation. Every thing has to come to a point. That is what is meant by *dharana* in Patanjali's yoga system, concentration on a point. One can take a point outside, or keep it within, but ultimately of course the point is the centre of one's whole being; the inner Self is that point. It is not in space or in time. It is a point without any dimension. One is focussing on that. "With his mind one-pointed, let him restrain the action of his thoughts and his senses" (Z). When one has restrained the senses, one must restrain the thoughts. They are much more dangerous than the senses. The senses are not so hard to control, but the thoughts are like wild horses. So the *citta*, the mind, must be controlled. And "let him . . . practise yoga," *yunjyad yoga*, which is literally, let him be 'yoked in yoga'. Let him unify himself in this unity of yoga. Then a further point which is always stressed in yoga:

13. With upright body, head, and neck, which rest still and move not; with inner gaze which is not restless, but rests still between the eyebrows;

In the *asana* of meditation the head, neck and spine should all be straight. Actually sitting on a chair or a stool is perfectly all right as long as the head and neck and spine are kept upright. When the head, the neck and the spine are in straight line an inner harmony is felt and the central rhythm of the body is established. For those who can do it the lotus posture is ideal for then the whole body is said to be perfectly balanced and in perfect equilibrium. One is then perfectly centred in oneself and in the world around. Zaehner translates the next phrase : "Fix your eyes on the tip of the nose." This is one interpretation of this technique. The other is that which Mascaró gives, that the gaze should rest between the eyebrows, that is, in the *ajna chakra*, one of the seven chakras or centers of energy. The *ajna* is the centre of light, of intelligence. At this point one becomes sensitive to the whole cosmic order, to the intelligible order of the universe.

In the next verse we move to a new point of view. So far we have been following the ordinary course of yoga, and now the main theme of the *Gita* is introduced, that of devotion to a personal God.

14.   With soul in peace and all fear gone, and strong in the vow of holiness, let him rest with mind in harmony, his soul on me, his God supreme.

The 'vow of holiness' is *brahmacharya*, a word which is often translated as chastity, but it has a much deeper meaning. The term means literally 'moving in Brahman' or as we might say 'dwelling in God'. It is precisely this that is implied in the vow of holiness, *brahmacharya*. Zaehner translates the last words of the sloka, "his thoughts on me, intent on me." The Sanskrit is *macitto* and *matparah*, literally 'me-thinking', 'me-intent'. This is a wonderful example of how the *Gita* works. It is trying to integrate the different systems of Yoga and Sankhya into a new doctrine which centres on Krishna as the personal God. For Christians this is extremely valuable, because it shows how we can integrate yoga, and Buddhist methods of meditation, and the metaphysical doctrine of Vedanta with its concepts of *purusha* and *prakriti*, and relate them all to the person of Christ.

Zaehner remarks on this: "In the next stanza, we are told that Krishna is the single object of meditation. There is a great difference between chapters five and six. In chapter five there is no reference to the personal God until the very last stanza. In chapter six on the other hand, this God obtrudes Himself every more insistently until *nirvana* itself is shown to have value only in that it subsists in Him."

15. The Yogi who, lord of his mind, ever prays in this harmony of soul, attains the peace of *nirvana*, the peace supreme that is in me.

   This is an example of the use of Buddhist terminology. *Nirvana* is the Buddhist term for the extinction of desire, the end of all becoming, the end of all change and transience. *Nirvana* is the going beyond. The Buddha simply spoke of this state beyond and taught the way to reach it, but he would never describe *nirvana*. *Nirvana* can ony be known by experience. But the *Gita* wants to show that this *nirvana*, this state of perfection, of stillness which is also joy and peace, is found in Krishna, the personal God. The peace of *nirvana*, the peace that passes all understanding, is found in God. And so Krishna coins a beautiful phrase, "The *shanti*, the peace, of *nirvana* is *mat samstham*, resting in me." *Nirvana* is in Krishna, in God. The path of yoga is raised to a new level and we are now introduced to the experience of a personal god.

16. Yoga is a harmony. Not for him who eats too much, or for him who eats too little; Not for him who sleeps too little, or for him who sleeps too much.

17. A harmony in eating and resting, in sleeping and keeping awake: a perfection in whatever one does. This is the Yoga that gives peace from all pain.

   This is what makes yoga a really practical discipline today, and a real guide in life. There is always this middle way. Aristotle speaks of virtue as the mean between two extremes, and the Buddha teaches the Middle Way. St. Benedict's Rule is precisely the middle way for the monk, rather than the extreme of either indulgence of asceticism. The integrated man is the man who knows the point of equilibrium between extremes. He it is who is always *sama*; he always remains the same between the pairs of opposites.

18. When the mind of the Yogi is in harmony and finds rest in the Spirit within, all restless desires gone, then he is a Yukta, one in God.

   'One in God' is Mascaró's interpretation of what a *yukta* is. The interpretation is correct but the word 'God' is not in the text. Mascaró often paraphrases in that way, which is usually legitimate because the text often needs interpretation. A *yukta* is a person who is integrated and unified, and to be integrated in this way is to be 'one in God.'

The next verse gives a beautiful image, the meaning of which is very profound. It is a perfect image of the state of the soul of one who has reached the inner peace, the peace of *nirvana*.

19. Then his soul is a lamp whose light is steady, for it burns in a shelter where no winds come.

These few verses contain the basic doctrines of yoga as found in the *Gita*. It is a most practical doctrine. The *Gita* is bringing the whole doctrine of yoga and of samkhya, of discipline and doctrine, into relationship with a personal God. It opens the way to a new understanding. The same process is also found in the *Upanishads*. They begin with Brahman, the mystery of being and realise more and more that this mystery of being is the Atman, the inner Self. They reveal that the human self is one with the Supreme Self, the Being of the whole creation, and then, as it develops in the *Upanishads*, this Atman, this Brahman is seen to be *Purusha*, the personal God, the Lord, who is an object of worship.

Finally in the *Gita* the personal God becomes an object of love so the whole process gradually unfolds. I think we can properly speak of this process as revelation. R. de Smet, an authority on Indian philosophy, spoke of the "holy history of India". It is really remarkable how one can see this new understanding, this conception of a personal God coming to light a little before the time of Christ. I think that it is a movement that took place in many parts of the world, not simply in Israel. There was an advance both in Buddhism with its idea of the *bodhisattva* and in Hinduism with the idea of a personal God as the embodiment of love and compassion, these developments taking place at about the same time. We realise that God is revealing himself in many ways, not only to Israel, but to India, to China, and to primitive people also. The question arises as to how Christ is related to all this. We can say that Christ is the Word, the Self-revelation of God, and as such is present in all genuine religion. This Word is present in Hinduism and Buddhism, gradually revealing his personal character. In Jesus this process reaches a climax and the personal character of God is finally revealed.

20. When the mind is resting in the stillness of the prayer of Yoga, and
by the grace of the Spirit sees the Spirit and therein finds fulfilment;

The one Self is manifesting, expressing himself, in each one of us and
the aim of yoga is to restrain the senses and the mind so that one enters
into the inner Self and becomes aware of the supreme Self dwelling within.
A more literal translation is, "Seeing Self by Self in Self" (B & D). This
is a beautiful expression of the goal of yoga, "to see the Self in the Self
by the Self." It is to discover the Self, the *aramatman*, the ultimate Ground
of Being, as dwelling, as manifesting himself 'in' one's own Self, and this
can only be done 'by' the Self. It is only God acting in us who can reveal
the indwelling Presence and enable us to realise the ultimate unity of being.
This can be interpreted in terms of the Christian doctrine of the Trinity.
The Father is the *Paramatman, Parabrahman*, the ultimate Ground of Being
beyond word and thought. The Father reveals himself in the Son, the Word,
the Self-expression, Self- manifestation, of the One. And this Self-revelation
of the Father in the Son is made known by the Holy Spirit, the Self-
communication of God, the power or energy of the Spirit, acting in the
depths of the human being, in the spirit of man, and enabling him to recognise
the indwelling presence of the Spirit within. It is this ultimate mystery of
being which is being revealed in different ways in the different religious
traditions.

21. Then the seeker knows the joy of Eternity: a vision seen by reason
far beyond what senses can see. He abides therein and moves not from
Truth.

The translation is rather free. More literally, "He finds a supreme delight,
which reason can grasp beyond the senses" (B & D). Reason here is the
buddhi which is able to grasp, to experience, the supreme joy. The *buddhi*
is the higher mind and it is at this point that we know the Self. "Established
therein he moves not from reality" (B & D). Established in that, one is cen—
tred in reality, in *tattva*, or 'thatness'. The senses convey a reality to us but
it is as though through a mirror, through the changing phenomena of the
universe; only when we get beyond the senses and beyond the *manas*, the
mind, which is still determined by the senses, do we see Reality as it is.
The intellect, the *buddhi*, sees through beyond the senses to the real. The
yogi does not move from the Reality once established there. Zaehner quotes

the *Katha Upanishad* in regard to this: "This is the Self, deep-hidden in all beings, the Self that shines not forth. Yet it can be seen by men who see the subtle things by means of the buddhi." The *buddhi* pierces through the outward appearance, through the senses, through the outer mind and discovers the inner reality. That is the state when we know the truth.

22. He has found joy and Truth, a vision for him supreme. He is therein steady: the greatest pain moves him not.

Zaehner makes an interesting point here. "He wins the prize beyond all others, or so he thinks. Therein he stands firm unmoved by any suffering." What is meant by this is that when one reaches this point of the *buddhi* and the mind no longer moves, one is in touch with reality, becoming fixed and firm. This is the 'stable state' of Brahman. The Stoics also had this idea that the mind becomes perfectly firm and is no longer moved by the senses. They say that Epictetus had his legs sawn off and went on discoursing on philosophy while it was happening. The Stoic was not moved by the senses at all. Zaehner shows how though this is a great achievement, there is something far beyond it, when beyond this steady state of Brahman one discovers a deeper reality. The yogi feels that when he has reached that state, then he has reached the goal, but in fact there is something much more profound which he still has to find.

23. In this union of Yoga there is liberty: a deliverance from the oppression of pain. This Yoga must be followed with faith, with a strong and courageous heart.

Now this again is very Buddhist. Literally, it is, "He should know that this is what is meant by Yoga, the unlinking of the link with suffering and pain" (Z). *Samyoga* is the linking together with suffering and *viyoga* is the unlinking. *Duhkha* is the Buddhist word for the whole human experience. It means sorrow, suffering, pain, unsatisfactoriness. The starting point of the Buddha's teaching was that "all is suffering, all is impermanent, all is unreal," without a substance, without a self. The Buddha said, when you realise that the whole transient reality which appears to your senses and to your mind is pain, is unreal, then you discover the reality which is beyond and that brings perfect joy. That is the heart of Buddhist teaching.

He sees that yoga consists in "the unlinking of the link with pain" (Z).

Duhkha – sorrow, suffering, pain, unsatisfactoriness

It may well be that nearly all suffering is due to the reflection of the mind on pain. Pain is in the nerves and senses. But why we suffer is because the mind reflects on the sensations of the nerves and senses. If we do not reflect on the pain, we do not suffer. There is enough evidence of that. A good example is the soldier during the first world war who had his arm shot off. At first he went on running, completely unaware that anything had happened and it was only when he looked and saw it that he began to suffer. A better instance is what happens in yoga. It is possible to withdraw the mind from the body so as not to feel at all, and an advanced yogi can do this. Swami Brahmananda was one of the disciples of Ramakrishna and it is said that a disciple of his once had a carbunkle on his neck which was very painful. The doctor said it would have to be cut out. The disciple was not prepared to have an anaesthetic, so he refused the operation. His guru, however, insisted that he be operated on but said that instead of having the anaesthetic he should withdraw his consciousness from his body. So the disciple went into the operating theatre and on asking how long the operation would take was told that it would take about twenty minutes. So he withdrew his body consciousness for half and hour and did not feel anything. I suppose that when he returned to normal consciousness he would have felt it. One can have the same experience with toothache; because we think about it all the time, it can be agonising; but if one can withdraw the mind from it, or even if some distraction comes and the mind is carried away, then one simply does not feel it any longer. So this is an important lesson. To "unlink the link with pain" to unlink that to which our mind has become linked, that is the art of yoga. The mind has become linked with the senses, with the feelings with the body. Yoga is the unlinking, the separating, the detaching of the mind from the body, and when that happens, one is no longer a slave to one's feelings.

24. When all desires are in peace and the mind, withdrawing within, gathers the multitudinous straying senses into the harmony of recollection,

Zaehner translates: "Let him renounce all desires which spring from the will." The word is *samkalpa* which is best translated 'will' or 'purpose'. So all desires which spring from one's own human will must be renounced, "all of them without any remainder" (Z); nothing must remain over. "Then let him restrain in every way by the mind alone the senses' busy throng" (Z). The mind must control the senses. In the *Katha Upanishad* the human being is compared to a chariot. The soul is seated in the chariot; the chariot is the body, the horses are the senses, and the reins are the mind. When the senses are uncontrolled, they are like the vicious horses of a bad charioteer; but when they are controlled by the mind, they resemble well-trained horses and the chariot can proceed harmoniously. We must make every effort then to control the senses by the mind.

25. Then, with reason armed with resolution, let the seeker quietly lead the mind into the Spirit, and let all his thoughts be silence.

Mascaró's translation, while being poetic, does not bring out the meaning. More literally it is, "Little by little let him gain tranquility by means of reason controlled by steadiness" (B & D). The aim is to bring the mind to the point of the *buddhi* where it is steady, stilled and controlled, instead of wandering about through the senses. The whole problem of yoga is that the mind naturally goes from one thing to another; it is always wandering. The question is how to bring it to one point — the single point where it becomes steady and controlled. "By the soul held fast in steadfastness, he must make the mind subsist in the self" (Z). The *manas*, the lower mind, must be brought under the control of the Self. In the *Katha Upanishad* the faculties are described as the senses, (*indriyas*), the mind, (*manas*) and the intellect, (*buddhi*). And so it goes on to say that the yogi must bring speech under the control of the mind. Speech, by which one goes out of oneself and communicates with others, must be brought under the control of the mind. The *manas*, the mind, must be brought under the control of the intellect, the *buddhi*. Finally the *buddhi* must be brought under the control of the Spirit, the Atman. It is a gradual bringing of all the faculties back to their centre and bringing them under control at their centre. Here the *Gita* is describing exactly the same process. The *buddhi* is made firm and strong and controls the *manas* and the *manas* and the *buddhi* together are standing firm in the Atman, the true Self. Coming to rest in the Self "he must think of nothing at all" (Z). On reaching that point, thinking stops. We have said that the purpose of yoga is *citta vritti nirodha*, cessation of the movements of the mind. But when one is not thinking, it does not mean that one is not intelligent. Pure intelligence is very active in pure awareness, but there is no movement of thought.

26. And whenever the mind unsteady and restless strays away from the Spirit, let him ever and forever lead it again to the Spirit.

In mental prayer or meditation the mind keeps wandering. We keep bringing it back, and it wanders again and we bring it back again; and so it goes on, maybe for months and years, until at last the mind becomes stabilised. Whenever the fickle mind roves around or wanders, the soul will bring it back and subject it to the Self. The teaching of the Greek Church Fathers was very similar. They used to say, "Let him lead the thoughts from the head to the heart and keep them there." The thoughts go roving around in the head, but if we bring them down into the heart, that is, the centre of the person, there they come to rest.

27. Thus joy supreme comes to the Yogi whose heart is still, whose passions are peace, who is pure from sin, who is one with Brahman, with God.

When his mind is still, *sukha*, the highest joy, comes to him. The passionate side of his nature, his *rajas*, is at peace. He is free from all stain. Stain signifies impurity. He is freed from sin and then he becomes Brahman, *Brahmabhuta*. He becomes one with Brahman. That again, according to Zaehner, is a Buddhist phrase. When one goes beyond the senses, beyond the flux of things, one becomes Brahman. One realises the still state of Brahman, the state of purity, of peace.

28. The Yogi who, pure from every sin, prays in this harmony of soul soon feels the joy of Eternity, the infinite joy of union with God.

Mascaró again translates Brahman as God, as in the previous verse he paraphrased, "who is one with Brahman, with God," but the distinction between God and Brahman is retained by Zaehner. God is the personal God, and Brahman is the impersonal aspect of the Godhead. It is important to maintain this distinction.

What Mascaró translates as, "the infinite joy of union with God" is better translated by the wonderful phrase, "with unbounded joy he attains the touch of Brahman" (Z). *Brahman-samsparsam* is the touch of Brahan, the touch of the infinite. Zaehner makes a very good point here. He says, "How is it, one may ask, that the fully integrated soul which has already 'become the Brahman' can attain to the 'touch of Brahman' or to 'union with Brahman'? The answer would seem to be that this process of integration presses and concentrates all that can be 'saved' in the human personality into its timeless centre, the Self, described in the *Upanishads* as 'more minute than the minute'. This process of integration causes the same personality, now liberated, and free from all the bonds of earthly life, to make 'contact' with everything else that shares this quite different mode of being."

Once we reach this inner point where we seem to be isolated, we suddenly discover ourselves to be in communion with everyone and everything. Zaehner goes on, "This is Brahman's saving touch which brings unbounded infinite joy. It is the touch of which the Buddhists know nothing. Yet it is the most real of all, the 'union of opposites' – that of the point without magnitude, the human self, and of the utterly unmeasured and unmeasurable, the inconceivably great." It is the paradox of the Self, which is more minute than the minute, and yet greater than the great, vaster than the vast. It is that point where one expands into infinity. So Zaehner says, "by the maximum concentration of all that is in us into the infinitely small, the timeless Self, one finds that this nothing is, nevertheless, conformed to infinity." Although Zaehner doubts that this is a Buddhist experience, this emptiness which is total fulfilment is, as I understand it, very much the Buddhist experience of nirvana in the Mahayana tradition. Zaehner continues, "It can almost be said that when this process of integration reaches its goal, there is an explosion. The self bursts asunder and finds itself utterly available to Brahman's saving touch. One seems to be concentrating one's self, separating from everybody and getting more and more isolated, and then on reaching that point, one suddenly explodes and realises: 'I am at one with the whole of creation, with all humanity.' " This interconnection and interpenetration of all things, which is now revealed, is not what the classical Sankhya had conceived. This is something new, although it was already present in the *Upanishads*. There is a beautiful passage in the *Chandogya Upanishad*, which speaks of this experience of Brahman, how "He is myself within the heart, smaller than the grain of rice, a barley-corn or a mustard seed or a grain of millet or the kernel of a grain of millet." Likewise in the Gospel, the Kingdom of Heaven is compared to a grain of mustard seed. It is the tiniest thing in the world. It has no dimension at all. Yet it is "greater than the earth, greater than the air, greater than the sky, greater than all these worlds." Then the *Upanishad* concludes; "All works, all desires, all sense, all tastes belong to it. It incompasses all the universe, does not speak and has no care. This my Self within the heart, is that Brahman. When I depart from hence I shall merge into it. He who believes this will never doubt." When one goes beyond the senses and the mind, at that point the whole world is rediscovered but in a new dimension.

One is no longer subject to the senses; one is completely free but can use and enjoy them to the full. So all senses, all tastes, all desires, all works, are found there but in a totally new way.

29. He sees himself in the heart of all beings and he sees all beings in his heart. This is the vision of the Yogi of harmony, a vision which is every one.

More literally, "He sees that Self abiding in all beings and all beings abiding in the Self, and everywhere he sees the same" (Z). That is this final vision – on finding the Self, one finds all things, all creation in that Self. Again it is a kind of circumincession, or mutual interpenetration. The fullest reality of all is realised within. Some people imagine that when one is meditating, one is getting more and more isolated and separated from the world, and that in a sense is true. There is separation on the level of sense and even on a psychological level. But if one reaches the depth of reality then one rediscovers the whole creation in its depth, in its centre, in its unity. Then one finds all things in one's Self. This is a very common idea in the *Upanishads*. Again Zaehner has a very nice comment, "The man who is fully integrated and made one, becomes aware of something that is other than himself, in the one case, this touch of 'contact' with Brahman, in the other, a Person who stands behind and supports the timeless peace of *nirvana*." In the next verse we will see how when one sees all things in the Self one "sees all things in me", as Krishna says, that is, in the personal God. Zaehner continues, "To make contact with Brahman is to resume contact with everything. Detaching oneself from outside contacts, (*sparsa*) has been replaced by contact (*samsparsa*) with the omnipresent Brahman and through Brahman with all things but in a new dimension, a new light. Thence by detaching himself from all things he becomes Brahman, he sees 'self in self', he sees himself solely and simply as immortal, eternal, beyond time, One; but 'contact' with Brahman as other than himself transforms the vision from one of completely static en-stasy into one of all comprehending ec-stasy. The cosmos flows into him and he flows into the cosmos, the unity remains but there is boundless diversity too." This is an insight of immense importance. The ultimate reality is not a static, undifferentiated unity, but a unity in which all diversity is contained. It is not simply a concentration into one but in the one we rediscover all. That is the vision of God. In God everything is present, every grain of sand, every movement in time and space, every form of consciousness — everything is there but in a totally new way, rediscovered in the One.

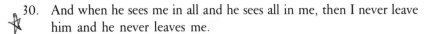

30. And when he sees me in all and he sees all in me, then I never leave him and he never leaves me.

What we are discovering is that these three concepts, Brahman, Atman and Purusha, or the personal God, are all ultimately identical. They are the one reality realised in different ways. When that one reality is seen manifested in the whole creation behind all the phenomena of the senses, we call that reality Brahman. When that one reality is seen in ourselves as the root and ground of our own being, the principle of our own life and consciousness, we call that reality Atman. And when we see that one reality, that one Self as an object of worship, as the Lord, Isha, then we know it as a person, as *Purusha*, in the relationship of love. So there can be an awareness of the universal cosmic being, the Brahman; an awareness of the Self, the Atman, the ground of our own being and consciousness; and there can be at the same time, an awareness that this Brahman, this Atman, is the Lord who is worshipped, the *Purusha*, the Cosmic Person, with whom there is a relationship of love. And that is what the *Gita* is concerned to bring out, the ultimate reality of love. So we not only enter into this new universe of communion with the creation and communion with humanity, but we discover the Person of God at the heart of the universe. "He sees me in all and he sees all in me, then I never leave him and he never leaves me." The *Gita* is here giving the same message as the Gospel. For the Christian, Christ is the personal aspect of God, the person in whom the universe finds its ultimate meaning and who reveals himself as love.

31. He who in the oneness of love, loves in me whatever he sees, wherever this man may live, in truth this man lives in me.

Actually the word is *bhajati* which is from the same root as the word *bhakti*. It had various meanings but at this time it had come to mean devotion or love. All this reminds one of St. John's gospel, "If anyone love me my Father will love him and we will come to him and make our abode with him" (John 14:23). This is what is meant by 'circumincession' in the Trinity. The son is 'in' the Father and the Father is 'in' the Son; the Father shares the nature of the Son, the Son shares the nature of the Father, but they are not simply identified. There is a living relationship, an absolute unity and yet distinction within the unity. The being of the Godhead is differentiated in the Son, or Logos, who is his Self-manifestation, and returns to unity in the Spirit, who is his Self-communication in love. The same process takes place in us when we reach Brahman, when we reach God. We do not discover a pure identity of being, a sort of isolation, but a wonderful intercommunion, an experience of being in relationship, an experience of love. 'Unity in distinction' is the teaching of the Gita.

Zaehner has a long note here. In the *Isha Upanishad* there is a very strange passage which is not easy to interpret. It says: "Into blind darkness enter they who revere the uncompounded. Into darkness blinder still go they who delight in the compounded. So from wise men have we heard who instructed us therein." The meaning of that seems to be that there is a unitary being in the universe which is the compounded — the universe itself is this compound; and the uncompounded is that which is beyond the universe, which sustains and holds it together. One is blind if one only sees the compounded, in other words nature and material reality; but it is also not enough to know simply the uncompounded, the spiritual reality apart from nature. For beyond the material and the immaterial is the Person who embraces the whole.

This verse then, "He who is in the oneness of love, loves me in whatever he sees, wherever this man may live, in truth this man lives in me," parallels the Christian conception of creation in Christ. St. Paul says, "In Him and through Him and for Him all these things are created and all things stand together, consist, in Him" (Col. 1: 15-17). To live in Christ is to find Christ in all men, in all things, and to find all men and all things in Him, in the one Person who sustains the whole universe.

32. And he is the greatest Yogi he whose vision is ever one: when the pleasure and pain of others is his own pleasure and pain.

"By analogy with the Self, he who sees the same everywhere, be it pleasure or pain, he is considered a perfect yogi" (Z). There are two possible interpretations of this verse. One is that when we see this one Self everywhere in everything, we are alike in pleasure and in pain. But a deeper meaning which even Sankara seems to hold, is that we feel the pleasure and pain of others as our own. Both Sankara and Ramanuja give this a humanitarian sense and say that by analogy with oneself one sees that what is pleasant and painful to oneself must also be pleasant and painful to others, and one should therefore refrain from harming them. That is a very common Hindu idea. They often say, you are myself, therefore your pain is my pain, your joy is my joy." This experience can lead to a very deep sense of solidarity. But the problem of the movement of the mind remains and Arjuna is troubled by this. He expostulates to Krishna:

33. Thou hast told me of a Yoga of constant oneness, O Krishna, of a communion which is ever one. But, Krishna, the mind is inconstant: in its restlessness I cannot find rest.

Here the word used is *cancalatva,* which means restlessness, wandering, or fickleness.

34. The mind is restless, Krishna, impetuous, self- willed, hard to train: to master the mind seems as difficult as to master the mighty winds.

"For the mind is fickle, (*cancalam*): impetuous, (*pramathi*), exceeding strong: how difficult to curb. As difficult to curb as the wind" (Z). That is the experience of all who try to meditate. The mind has a terrific hold, it is always active and one cannot control it except by the grace of God. Krishna replies:

35. The mind is indeed restless, Arjuna: it is indeed hard to train. But by constant practice and by freedom from passions the mind in truth can be trained.

Though ultimately only the grace of God can control the mind, it is our responsibility to discipline it by "constant practice"; perseverance is the essential requirement in the practice of yoga. It has to be done day by day, week by week, year by year, until the mind is brought to the 'still point' where it is open to the grace of God.

36. When the mind is not in harmony, this divine communion is hard to attain; but the man whose mind is in harmony attains it, if he knows and if he strives.

There is always a co-operation between the human will and divine grace. We have to strive continually and yet to know that only the grace of God can enable us to succeed.

Arjuna is still troubled and asks Krishna:

37. And if a man strives and fails and reaches not the End of Yoga, for his mind is not in Yoga; and yet this man has faith, what is his end, O Krishna?

38. Far from earth and far from heaven, wandering in the pathless winds, does he vanish like a cloud into air, not having found the path of God?

39. Be a light in my darkness, Krishna: be thou unto me a Light. Who can solve this doubt but thee?

It is quite a practical problem. One starts meditation and one is neither in heaven or on earth. One does not reach the state of equilibrium which is being sought and one is no longer at home in the world. One is in a sort of suspended state between God and the world. It can be a very unpleasant state. So what happens to that man?

Krishna reassures and encourages Arjuna:

40. Neither in this world nor in the world to come does ever this man pass away; for the man who does the good, my son, never treads the path of death.

If he is simply a 'doer of good works' he will never tread the path of death, so Krishna gives Arjuna courage.

41. He dwells for innumerable years in the heaven of those who did good; and then this man who failed in Yoga is born again in the house of the good and the great.

This again is the idea of reincarnation; if in this life you do not attain to this yoga, to this union with God, the ultimate, you still have a reward for all your efforts. The reward is in heaven but you must come back again to earth. In the Hindu tradition heaven is the highest created state but it is not the final state of uncreated being beyond. So one eventually comes back to this world. A Christian would say that by the redemption in Christ, our good works become the means by which we transcend the world but we reach the ultimate goal by his grace and not by our own works.

42. He may even be born into a family of Yogis, where the wisdom of Yoga shines; but to be born in such a family is a rare event in this world.

43. And he begins his new life with the wisdom of a former life; and he begins to strive again, every onwards towards perfection.

There is a very strong belief that if you advance on the spiritual path in this life, when you are born again you start your new human life at the level you previously attained. An example of this is the Tibetan tulku who, although he has attained enlightenment, is born again in this world in order to serve while retaining the achievement he has reached in his former births. He examplifies the idea of the *bodhisattva* in Buddhist tradition.

44. Because his former yearning and struggle irresistably carries him onwards, and even he who merely yearns for Yoga goes beyond the world of books.

45. And thus the Yogi ever-striving, and with soul pure from sin, attains perfection through many lives and reaches the End Supreme.

46. Be thou a Yogi, Arjuna! Because the Yogi goes beyond those who only follow the path of the austere, or of wisdom, or of work.

"Higher than the mere ascetic is the yogi and higher than the man of wisdom (*nanayogi*), and higher than the man of works (*karmayogi*). Be thou then a yogi, O Arjuna!" (Z). The *Gita* puts the yogi above the ascetic, that is the man who does *tapas*, above the man who has wisdom or knowledge, the *jnani*, and also above the man of works. The yogi is the one who has attained to the perfect integration of being in the inner Self, in God. This means that union by grace with the personal God is the highest state because then whatever work one does, or whatever devotion or knowledge one possesses, it is derived from this source. The yogi in this sense is one who does not depend on himself at all, but has reached total union with God. This is made clear in the next verse.

47. And the greatest of all Yogis is he who with all his soul has faith,
     and he who with all his soul loves me.

Here the highest yoga is described as the yoga of faith and love. One
can see here how the *Gita* has brought all these elements together; the
Buddhist idea of transcending the world of the senses and the passions and
reaching that still state of *nirvana*; the yogic idea of becoming Brahman,
of becoming one with the inner Self, in perfect integration, in the still point
of one's being; and then going beyond that to the faith and love which unites
us with the Personal God beyond.

That is a view of yoga which is also totally Christian. It integrates the
whole person and it culminates in faith and in love. All the great religious
traditions are trying to help one to reach this inner centre of one's being
and to discover this inner peace, this perfect joy. How that is discovered
depends on one's faith and on one's love. If one simply has a philosophical
understanding a very deep experience may be attained but it is not the same
as if one has faith and becomes integrated in the love of God. Different
experiences lead to different ways in which the experience is described. The
Buddhist *nirvana* and the Hindu *moksha* are not the same, nor are they
the same as the Christian vision of God. So the Buddhist, the Hindu, the
Muslim and the Christian are all experiencing the ultimate Reality but
experiencing it in different ways through their own love and through their
own traditions of faith and knowledge. There are obviously various degrees
as well. There is a tendency to say that when one reaches the supreme state
everything is the same and that there are no differences any more, but I
do not think that that is true. In a sense the experience of the ultimate
truth is different for each person, since each person is a unique image of
God, a unique reflection of the one eternal light and love.

The whole argument of this chapter culminates in this conception of
faith and love as the ultimate means of realisation. Everything depends on
whether one is motivated by faith and love. Many simple people in every
religion have faith and love and reach final realisation by the grace of God,
but they have not learned to meditate. They have not learned to integrate
the personality in its inner center. Having faith and love, they stop short
of achieving inner integration. Others, on the other hand have a deep
integration but if it is without faith and love, it remains an imperfect state.
With some yogis, there is a deeply concentrated state above pain and pleasure,
but there may be very little love in their nature. The perfect man is the

one who has both integrated his personality in its inner center, in the Self, and who, in that inner centre of his being, opens himself to the 'touch of Brahman', to the action of divine grace, allowing himself to be transformed by love.

Chapter 7

The Yoga of Knowledge

This and the following five chapters are all concerned with the revelation of Krishna, the personal God. The previous chapters have led up to this point, with the method of yoga, the stilling of the senses and the passions, and attaining freedom from fear; then the stilling and concentrating of the mind and finally the integrating the self in its inner centre. In chapter six we came to the stage where, on reaching that point of stillness and integration, there is an opening onto the whole mystery of God. At this point the personal God reveals himself and the Gita now takes up this theme.

1. Hear now, Arjuna, how thou shalt have the full vision of me if thy heart is set on me and if, striving for Yoga, I am thy refuge supreme.

The first words are *mayi asakta manah* which means your mind must be attached, *asakta*, to me. The doctrine up to now has been to be detached; detached from the senses from the mind and from everything. Now it is said that the mind must be attached to God. That is the only proper object of attachment; one must be detached from everything else and attached to God alone. "Practising yoga take refuge in me, *mad-asrayah.*" Ultimately this is a detachment from the ego, the lower self, and a surrender to the supreme Self, who reveals himself as a personal God.

2. And I will speak to thee of that wisdom and vision which, when known, there is nothing else for thee to know.

Again, we have *jnana*, wisdom, and *vijnana*, discriminative knowledge. A better translation would be, "I will teach you that wisdom and knowledge which when you know there is nothing further to be known." This is an idea found also in the *Mundaka Upanishad* "What is that which being known everything is known?" The whole point is that as long as we have discriminative knowledge alone, we are going from one thing to another and there is no end. Science is endless for there is always something more to be discovered, but when we reach intuitive or unitive knowledge, when we know the One from which the many proceed, then there is nothing further to be known. That is the final knowledge. It is all-inclusive and total.

St. Thomas Aquinas quotes Boethius, who describes eternity as *tota et simul*, it is total and simultaneous. Everything is known together in its totality and in its unity. Our problem is that we see everything in space and time, everything is divided in space and moving in time, but in God, the totality is there without any division of space, and the unity is there without any movement of time. The whole is concentrated in this fulness, and that is the knowledge beyond which there is nothing to be known.

3. Among thousands of men perhaps one strives for perfection; and among thousands of those who strive perhaps one knows me in truth.

This can be rather disquieting as it seems that the chances of knowing God are rather slim, but perhaps it should be added that by the grace of God the truth may be attained even without striving. The word for perfection is *siddha*. This word is often used of the powers of yoga. The *siddhis* are preternatural powers acquired in yoga. Many may strive for perfection through tapas, through methods of concentration, yet of all those who strive as ascetics, as yogis, only one may come to "know me", who is the Supreme, who is the end of all yoga.

Now we move on to the revelation of Krishna, the personal God, as the Creator manifesting in the whole creation, and this is the main theme of the *Gita* which is broached for the first time here. Krishna says there are two forms of his nature; the visible and the invisible.

4. The visible forms of my nature are eight; earth, water, fire, air, ether;
   the mind, reason, and the sense of 'I'.

These are the eight *tattvas*, the eight constituents of nature, according
to Sankhya doctrine on which the *Bhagavad Gita* relies. In the early philosohy
of the Samkhya there are always five elements: earth, air, fire and water,
plus ether or space. Then beyond the five material elements, the ether being
a sort of passage to the immaterial, are the three constituents of human
nature: the *manas*, the *buddhi*, and the *ahankara* which are the mind, the
intuitive intelligence and the sense of 'I'. It is important to notice that the
mind and intelligence belong to the lower nature. But we must not forget
that the One is always manifesting himself on all these different levels. The
whole material universe is one aspect of his manifestation, and the human
being with its mental powers is another.

5. But beyond my visible nature is my invisible Spirit. This is the fountain
   of life whereby this universe has its being.

There is an important point here which Zaehner interprets very well.
Krishna speaks of his higher nature as, "Nature developed into life by which
this world is kept in being." The phrase is, *jiva*-bhuta. *Jiva* is life and it is
often translated as soul, but every plant or tree has a *jiva*, a life principle.
So this is "my nature which is *jiva*-bhuta," 'become life', or is the 'life-element'.
Zaehner interprets this as being what is known as the *mahat*. The concept
of the *mahat* is a very important one which appears first in the *Katha
Upanishad*. There the vision of nature, beginning with the senses, the mind
and the intelligence, (the *indriyas*, *manas* and the *buddhi*), is developed. The
buddhi is the higher intelligence in man, the point where man is open to
the beyond. But beyond the *buddhi* is what is called the *Mahat* which literally
means the 'great', and that is explained as the cosmic order or the cosmic
intelligence. Zaehner makes it clear that there are two levels in which
Brahman manifests. There is the whole material order which goes up to
the *buddhi*, and then there is the spiritual order, beginning with the *mahat*,
the cosmic order. It is also what Plato called the intelligible world, the world
of the gods, and in Christian tradition it is the world of the angels. Beyond
the material world, including the human intelligence, there is a whole spiritual
world, the cosmic order, consisting of the cosmic intelligences, the cosmic
powers, the *devas* or the angels. St. Thomas Aquinas, and the Christian

tradition generally, believed that the whole material creation is a kind of reflection of the spiritual creation and is ordered by it. The whole creation is ordered by the angels. Newman used to think when he was a boy that there were angels present all around him, and many have had a similar experience. Some people have the power to see spirits in nature.

There is a place called Findhorn, up in the north of Scotland, not far from Pluscarden Abbey, where I was living before I came to India. Some years ago a group of people came to this very barren stretch of land by the sea and what started happening there through the group appears to be a good example of communication and co-operation with the realm of the devas or angels. One woman in the group is a kind of medium and she is able to see the spirits of nature, the spirits of the trees and plants. When the group moved in and began to cultivate the land, they did everything according to the instructions of the spirits. The result was that they turned this wasteland into one of the most fertile places in Scotland. People came from all over the country to see the luxurient vegetables, flowers and trees growing on every side. The woman consults the trees and plants as to what they want and where the would like to be planted, and as a medium she interprets these messages as coming to her from the angels. It is becoming increasingly common now to realise that there is a psychic world beyond the physical world. In the West, however, although it is studied in parapsychology, still relatively few people are aware of it. Here in India most people, at least in the villages, live in this psychic world. For instance, we sold a cow recently to a devout man in the neighbourhood. He came along to take her and to my surprise – although I should be used to these things – he insisted that he had first of all to garland the cow with flowers. Then he had to have incense, to incense her, then I had to put the rope over her neck. Only then could he take her. And he had to remain until it was dark. He could not take her earlier because she might be affected by the evil eye. She would be very sensitive to it. All these are psychic elements of which we are normally unaware and regard as mere superstition. For us, to sell a cow is a commercial deal, but for these rural people a cow is a sacred animal; she has a psychic, as well as a physical nature and one should be sensitive to it. It is becoming common knowledge that if one plays music to cows they give their milk better, and plants seem to grow better when they are tended with love.

There are three levels of existence, the physical, the psychic and the spiritual and we should be very careful not to confuse the spiritual and the psychic. The psychic is not spiritual; it is neither good nor bad. It can be good and it can be bad. Magicians and sorcerers deal with the psychic aspect of things, but it can also be controlled by the power of the Spirit.

So what is called the *Mahat* is the cosmic order from which the life of all nature comes. The whole physical world is enveloped, as it were, in the psychic world. Sri Aurobindo, a great philosopher of modern India, has shown the place of the psychic world in the whole order of being. He said that one can learn to study the psychic world as accurately as the physical world. It is a completely ordered cosmos. It manifests, for instance, in dreams and one can learn to observe one's dreams until the dreams become completely orderly. So this psychic world is real and has an intelligible order. It is much more difficult to observe than the material world because one can only apprehend it through the psychic or subtle senses and through a subtle intelligence which in the West generally has, until recently, been almost completely lost. We have developed the gross senses and the gross mind and we are so completely absorbed in these that we think that that is all there is. But beyond the gross level are the subtle senses and the subtle mind. These both belong to the psychic world which envelops the whole cosmos.

6.   All things have their life in this Life, and I am their beginning and end.

More literally, "To all beings these two natures are as a womb (a *yoni*)" (Z). The whole of nature is regarded as the womb in which the Divine Lord plants His seed. That is also an idea of St. Augustine who spoke of *rationes seminales*, the 'seminal reasons'. These are the seeds of the Word which are implanted in nature, in *prakriti.* They originally come from the womb or root of nature, the *mula prakriti* and are gradually evolved into the whole order of nature.

"Of this whole universe, the origin and the dissolution am I" (Z). God Himself, the Supreme, works through these two natures, through the physical nature and through the psychic, through the natural order and through the angelic or divine order. Later, in Chapter 14, Krishna says, "Great Brahman is to me a womb and in it I plant the seed." There the term Brahman is used in an unusual sense for the whole order of nature. In that order of nature, Krishna, the God, plants the seed.

7.   In this whole vast universe there is nothing higher than I. All the worlds have their rest in me, as many pearls upon a string.

The idea of a *sutra*, a thread, is very common. It is said in the *Brihadaranyaka Upanishad*, "Do you know that thread upon which the whole of this world is strung and the one who holds the thread, the ruler within who holds the thread," that is, the God who is within? He holds the thread and it is a beautiful idea that all the universe is strung on that thread. Another aspect of it also comes in the *Brihadaranyaka Upanishad*. Gargi, the wife of Yajnavalkya — it is very important that women join in all these debates — asks Yajnavalkya, her husband, what is that in which all this world is woven like warp and woof, and he goes through all the elements of nature and the world of the gods until he comes to Brahman. Brahman is that in which the whole of creation is woven. It is the same idea that ultimately, beyond the material world, beyond this whole psychic or cosmic order, is Brahman, the absolute Reality. The whole universe is strung on him. But in the *Gita* an advance is made on this when it is realised that this Brahman, this ultimate Reality, who is the source and the ground of the whole creation, is the personal God.

Krishna then goes on in a very poetic passage to speak of himself as in everything. This has a pantheistic flavour, but it would be wrong to limit the meaning to that.

8. I am the taste of living waters and the light of the sun and the moon. I am OM, the sacred word of the Vedas, sound in silence, heroism in men.

We would say that everything comes from God; all being is from God. We are also willing to say that God is in everything, but we hesitate to say that God is the being of everything. What Krishna is really saying is, "I am in the water, in the fire, in the earth, in everything," and I am the living principle in everything. "I am the taste, the flavour" (Z), the *rasa*. *Rasa* is a beautiful word, meaning the flavour of food and drink, and then in music or art the quality of whatever it is, that one savours. "The taste of the living water" is the taste of God in the water. We lose sight of all these other levels of reality. We bring everything down to the chemical level. Water is H_2O. We know its chemical composition and then we think that we know what water is, and that there is nothing more to know. But on a deeper level of understanding water reveals the whole mystery of life. It quenches the thirst, it feeds the plants, it makes everything grow, it contains the whole power of life in itself. Then beyond that is the presence of God in the living water, in its taste, in its movement and its clarity. The whole mystery of being is present in every flower, in every plant, every piece of earth. St. Francis referred to the water as his sister. Science denies this aspect of things; it is concerned only with what can be measured. It is not wrong to separate the material aspect of reality, of water, earth, air and fire, and examine them simply chemically and physically. But then we should not go on to think that the other aspects have disappeared and that matter is all. That is the mistake. We may examine as much as we like, and such investigation brings much greater understanding, but we have to remember that beyond the material is the whole psychic world, and beyond that is the living God. We should be able to retain and experience all these levels of reality.

"I am OM, the sacred word of the Vedas." OM is the original word and it is very close to the 'Word' in St. John's gospel; from this 'Word' all sounds come, all words come, all language comes, all truth comes. It is said that the *Vedas* are the elaboration or manifestation of that word and the *Vedas* are said to be *nitya*, eternal, and *apauruseya*, without any human author. They are the original word, the OM, being manifested.

9. I am the pure fragrance that comes from the earth and the brightness of fire I am. I am the life of all living beings and the austere life of those who train their souls.

The last phrase is rather complex. It is literally the "asceticism of the ascetic", the *tapas* of the *tapasvi*. *Tapas* is the word for asceticism, discipline; it includes the whole spiritual effort, and an ascetic is called a *tapasvi*, that is, one who practises ascetism. It is important to realise that our ascetic effort is itself the work of God in us.

10. And I am from everlasting the seed of eternal life. I am the intelligence of the intelligent. I am the beauty of the beautiful.

"I am the bija," that is the seed; it is a key word. *Sanatanam bijam* means eternal seed, *sanatana* being another important word. *Sanatana dharma* is the name that Hindus give to Hinduism. The word Hinduism is an invention of the Western people. Actually it was the Persians who first used the word Hindu to describe the people who lived around the river Indus and then the religion of these people became known as Hinduism. Many Hindus strongly object to this, however, and the only word they use to describe their religion is *sanatana dharma*, the eternal law. *Dharma* is the law, the cosmic order, and their religion is the expression of this eternal law.

"I am the primeval seed of all contingent beings" (Z). The Word of God is the seed from which everything comes and Zaehner rightly translates it 'primeval'. Then Krishna says "I am the *buddhi buddhimatam*," the intelligence of the intelligent — the *buddhi* is the pure intelligence — and the *tejas tejasvinam*, the splendour of the splendid.

11. I am the power of those who are strong, when this power is free from passions and selfish desires. I am desire when this is pure, when this desire is not against righteousness.

St. Thomas says that all being is good and all evil is a defect of being. That is his basic principle. So God is in the goodness and the being of everything but is not in the defect; he is not in the absence of being, or the negation or privation of being. Sin is described as the privation of being, a lack of what is due. It is not positive; evil has no positive being. It has a very positive effect, of course, but it is not positive in itself. It is a lack of being.

So God is in all that is good and he is the effective power of all that is good. He is present in the evil but he is not the effective power of evil since evil in itself is not anything positive. Evil is a misuse of a power that is good. "I am the power in the powerful — such power that knows neither *kama*, desire, nor *raga*, passion." Those are defects in our power. When we are consumed by desire and passion, our energy is deflected. It is not pure, it is not concentrated. There is this power in our nature which is essentially good but when we seek to appropriate that power and use it to indulge our own passion and desire, then we corrupt the power and it becomes evil, although the power itself is good. Every power we use for evil is essentially good. The power by which a murderer stabs his victim is essentially good. The energy which goes with the act is good but the intention of the mind and the will in the act is evil because it is defective. Zaehner translates, "Desire (*kama*) am I, in contingent beings, but such as does not conflict with righteousness." The desire is good in itself, but when the desire becomes egoistic and conflicts with *dharma*, with what is right and good, it becomes a force of evil.

There is a wonderful passage which Zaehner quotes from the

Mahabharata here, which is very illuminating. It is spoken by desire, *kama*. "I cannot be slain by any being, by any being whatever, since he is wholly without the means. If a man should seek to slay me, putting his trust in the strength of a weapon, then do I appear again in the very weapon he uses. If a man should seek to slay me by offering sacrifices and paying all manner of fees, then do I appear again as the 'self that dwells in all actions' in moving things. If a man should seek to slay me by the Vedas and the ways of perfection then I appear as the 'stilled, quiet self' in unmoving things. If a man should seek to slay me by steadfastness, then do I become his very nature, unaware of me though he is. If a man should seek to slay me by ascetic practice, strict in his vows, then do I appear again in his very ascetic practice. If a man should seek to slay me, wise and bent on liberation, then do I dance and laugh before him as he abides in the bliss of liberation." This egoistic desire pursues us whatever we do. If we are trying to lead an ascetic life, then we become proud of our asceticism and are dominated by egoistic desire. If we are seeking by ascetic practice steadfastness in yoga we become attached to our steadfastness in yoga. This selfish attachment obstructs every spiritual endeavour. Even our love of God is prompted by selfish desire and only becomes pure when freed from egoism. Everything is corrupted by this *kama*, this egoistic desire. Even desire for liberation itself can come from an egoistic desire, whereas liberation is essentially freedom from the ego. The ego corrupts everything we do right through to the very end. We cannot escape it; the grace of God is the only thing that can free us from it. That is the only way, and then Kama itself becomes transformed into the pure energy of love.

12. And know that the three Gunas, the three states of the soul, come from me: peaceful light, restless life, and lifeless darkness. But I am not in them: they are in me.

These three *gunas* are the constituents of which the world is woven. We have mentioned them before; they are the constituents of all nature — *tamas*, darkness, the earthly element; *ragas*, fire or energy; and *sattva*, purity or light. In a human being *tamas* is dullness, sloth; *rajas* is enthusiasm, courage; and *sattva* is intelligence, purity. So those are the three constituents of nature but God is above all these constituents. He says, "I am not in them but they are in me." This idea is developed later on but it is important to observe it here because of the problem of pantheism in Hinduism.

Hinduism is often said to be pantheistic but the *Bhagavad Gita* makes it clearer than anywhere else that it is not so. Krishna has said, in the previous slokas, that he is in everything and now he is very careful to balance this, because one might think that by being in all things he is somehow modified by them. So he says, "They are in me but I am not in them." They are in me because they are completely under my control. But I am not involved in them, or dependent on them. He is very careful to show that he is totally free. So this is clearly not pantheism.

Now we come to the question of *maya*.

13. How the whole world is under the delusion of these shadows of the soul, and knows not me though for ever I am!

The 'shadows of the soul' are the three *gunas*. The whole universe, that is, nature, *prakriti*, is composed of these three *gunas* and we are all under the spell of these powers of nature, not realising that they all depend on something, on someone beyond. This is what *maya* is. It comes from the root *ma* which means to measure. We find it in so many words like the word matter, that which is measured. It is the root also of the word moon, the moon being that by which the months are measured; and of *mens*, the mind which is the measure of all things. *Maya* is thus the measuring element in nature.

14. My mysterious cloud of appearance is hard to pass beyond; but those who in truth come to me go beyond the world of shadows.

Mascaró here translates *maya* as my 'mysterious cloud of appearance'. This is one aspect of it. It may also be translated 'creative power' (Z). *Maya* is both the power which creates or 'measures' the world, and the world that is thus measured. Later it gets the meaning of illusion and it is very often translated as illusion, but *maya* is really nature considered as the manifestation of God. If we see nature alone and do not see God in it, then we are under an illusion. Then maya is deceiving us. But when we see God through that *maya*, then the *maya* becomes the means by which we know God. It depends on our point of view. This whole created world is a manifestation of God and if we only see that manifestation, and do not see God behind it, we are under an illusion. The world itself is then illusion. But when we see rightly that the world is simply a veil through which God is manifesting Himself then it becomes the means to know God.

That is the whole problem. Either the world is a sign and a means by which we realise God or it becomes a blanket which hides God. Everything turns upon whether we make this world into an illusion or whether we make it into a sacrament, a sign of God. "All this is my creative power. Whoever shall put his trust in me alone, shall pass beyond this *maya*," as Zaehner translates it. Once we put our trust in God, we go beyond the *maya*, and are no longer deceived.

15. But men who do evil seek not me: their soul is darkened by delusion. Their vision is veiled by the cloud of appearance; their heart has chosen the path of evil.

Those who do not put their trust in God, are deluded and deceived, their wisdom is destroyed by this *maya* and they cleave to an *asura*, an evil power. There are two orders of spiritual beings, the *devas* and the *asuras*. The *devas* are the gods, the spirits of light, and the *asuras* are the demons, the spirits of darkness. In almost every tradition there are these two orders, the cosmic powers of good and evil. They represent the subtle or psychic forces in the universe. If we ignore the presence of God and the spiritual powers in the world around, we become subject to the demonic powers. This is what has happened in the world today. By science we simply know the material world, that is, the material aspect of reality, and we mistake this world for the only reality there is. Then, without realising it, we become subject to demonic forces which are present in matter, in nature, and in the unconscious. Thus science and technology, which are essentially good in themselves, become the means for creating nuclear weapons which can destroy humanity and devastate the whole earth. This is the result of being under the delusion of *maya*, of matter, and being driven by the forces of the unconscious.

Science thus becomes demonic, because it is not controlled by the Spirit. It is simply the human mind exerting itself to its fullest extent on matter, but unconsciously coming under demonic powers.

16. There are four kinds of men who are good, and the four love me, Arjuna: the man of sorrows, the seeker of knowledge, the seeker of something he treasures, and the man of vision.

17. The greatest of these is the man of vision, who is ever one, who loves the One. For I love the man of vision and the man of vision loves me.

The 'afflicted', the 'man who seeks wisdom' or the 'man who strives for gain', each in their different way want something from God, as Zaehner puts it. The afflicted man wants relief, the man seeking wisdom wants wisdom, the man seeking wealth wants wealth. But the man of vision who has wisdom and who is integrated is seeking God in himself. This is the difference: first of all we seek God for something we can get from him; only later do we discover that God himself is what we want.

18. These four kinds of men are good; but the man of vision and I are one. His whole soul is one in me, and I am his Path Supreme.

"All these are noble but I hold the wise man, the *jnani*, as my very self" (Z). It is a beautiful phrase: he says *atma eva*, I consider him as myself. The wise man has united himself to God. He is one with him in love and God is his very self.

19. At the end of many lives the man of vision comes to me. 'God is all' this great man says. Such a spirit sublime how rarely he is found!

The phrase 'God is all' is literally 'Vasudeva is all'. Krishna is God incarnate manifesting himself as the son of Vasudeva. Such a 'spirit sublime' is literally a Mahatma. Mahatma is the great Self. There are different words for these great souls which are used very interestingly in India. Gandhiji was always called Mahatma, the great soul. Aurobindo was Mahayogi, the great yogi. Ramana Maharishi was the great rishi, the Maharishi and Tagore was Gurudev, the divine guru. Ramakrishna was Paramahansa, the supreme swan, the bird who takes flight to the infinite. Each is different and the people are very acute in the way they discern the different spiritual characteristics.

20. Men whose desires have clouded their vision, give their love to other gods, and led by their selfish nature, follow many other paths.

This relation of the one God to the many gods is fundamental in Hinduism. The many gods are the powers of nature, the powers of heaven and earth, the power of wealth, the power of money, political power; all these are the gods. But wisdom consists in seeing that all these are only aspects of the One Being. This is the authentic Hindu vision. All these devas are names and forms, *nama* and *rupa*, of the One Being, who has no name and no form. He manifests himself in all these powers and may be worshipped in and through them; idolatry and superstition consists in worshipping the powers apart from the One. That is polytheism. But the Hindu doctrine strictly speaking is always that the devotee is worshipping the One through these powers or gods. This is not to say that many Hindus are not idolators. They may forget the One. Take the worship of Lakshmi, the goddess of wealth. If one considers wealth as coming from God, the One Supreme, then it is perfectly legitimate to ask for that, but if one worships wealth in itself, Lakshmi herself, then one is an idolator. Who is to judge who is the idolator? There is the same problem with Christian worship. If St. Anthony gives someone what she wants, does that person understand that it is God who acts through St. Anthony or does she think simply that St. Anthony is giving it to her? Once she begins to think that St. Anthony gets things for her, then she makes St. Anthony a god, expecting him to give her this and that; she becomes an idolator.

That is a danger in all religion. That is what the Protestants feel about the worship of the saints. That is why Judaism and Islam insist on the worship of the one God alone. But the worship of the one God under different forms is not necessarily wrong, and so also prayer to the saints can be justified. Yet the danger is always there. A murder took place when I was living in Bangalore; a man killed seven people. They were lying in bed and he killed them one after the other. He only wanted one of them really, but he disposed of them all. I was told that for two or three weeks before the murder he had been praying and sacrificing to the goddess Kali to give him the power to do this. There are similar stories of robbers in Italy who used to pray to the Madonna to give them a good outcome. That is always the danger when you separate the creature from the Creator.

I always like the story of the young man who was studying theology in Rome, puzzling over the arguments for the existence of God. He was staying in a lodging and the housekeeper there saw him puzzling over this all the time and asked what was troubling him. He said he was studying the question of the existence of God. "Ah," she replied, "what does the existence of God matter, when we have the Madonna?"

21. For if a man desires with faith to adore this or that god, I give faith unto that man, a faith that is firm and moves not.

Any genuine faith in any god or any holy person is given by God. That is the idea of it. Faith itself is always a response to an inner light, a recognition of the presence of God, whatever form it may take.

22. And when this man, full of faith, goes and adores that god, from him he attains his desires; but whatever is good comes from me.

This is the essential Hindu understanding, that all good comes from God alone, whatever may be the form under which he is worshipped.

23. But these are men of little wisdom, and the good they want has an end. Those who love the gods go to the gods; but those who love me come unto me.

Worship of lesser gods is always limited. They can give only created goods, while only the uncreated Good can satisfy the soul. If you worship something less than God, you will have your reward, but only those who worship the one God come to him in the end.

24. The unwise think that I am that form of my lower nature which is seen by mortal eyes: they know not my higher nature, imperishable and supreme.

The lower nature is the five elements and the human mind. So the unwise, the people without *buddhi*, without spiritual intelligence, will mistake this world of the senses and the mind for the reality. They do not realise the higher nature which is being manifested through the lower. "They know nothing of my higher nature," the *parambhavam* which is changeless and supreme, *anuttamam*.

25. For my glory is not seen by all: I am hidden by my veil of mystery; and its delusion the world knows me not, who was never born and for ever I am.

Krishna says, "I am concealed by my *yoga maya*," and there are various interpretations of this term. Zaehner speaks of 'the creative power of yoga'. Creation is like a sort of yoga through which God manifests himself. He says, "My creative power and the way I use it." *Maya* is this power, the power of God through which the creation comes into being. The yoga is the activity, the action of that power, 'the way I use it'. But notice that *maya* does not mean delusion except in this sense: when we mistake this world, this *maya*, this nature, for reality, for the ultimate reality, then we are deluded and then *maya* becomes an illusion. When we see it as the work of the divine and see the divine shining through it then, on the contrary, it is means of union with the divine.

"I am not revealed to all; this world, deluded knows Me not − the unborn and the changeless" (Z). Behind the changing world is the unchanging reality; behind all that is born, behind all that is made, there is the unborn and the unmade.

That is the essential truth, that is wisdom, that is *jnana*; and illusion or ignorance, *aparavidya*, is mistaking the outward form of the world and the appearance of the senses for the ultimate reality. That is the great illusion. It is very like being at the cinema and imagining that what one is seeing is reality. That is what most people do. This world is like a cinema show. We see the movie and we think that is the reality; then at death, the lights go up and we realise what has been happening, we know the truth. We see the reality behind the show.

26.   I know all that was and is and is to come, Arjuna; but no one in truth
      knows me.

This ultimate mystery is not known. Our knowledge is of things in space and time; we do not normally know that which is beyond. 'Known' means known by the *buddhi*, the mind, but when one gets beyond all the faculties, then one can have an experience of that which is beyond and which is not known in the ordinary sense.

27.   All beings are born in delusion, the delusion of division which comes
      from desire and hate.

"By the delusion of the pair of opposites" (B & D). The word for delusion here is *moha*. The cause of this delusion is that we are always being attracted by the senses to what is pleasant and averted by the senses from what is unpleasant. We get a delusive view of reality based on our own emotions. That is the central unreality of the world — that we see everything distorted through our own emotions, our desires, our fears and our anxieties. This is the delusion coming from the *dvandva*, the dualities. It is only when we go beyond the dualities and discover the One, that we know truth as it is. Then we are freed from desires and hates and fears and everything else.

28. But there are men who do what is good, and whose sins have come to an end. They are free from the delusion of division, and they worship me with all their soul.

"Their sins have come to an end." Sin is essentially attachment. It is the attachment of the ego to the world, whereas freedom from sin is freedom from that attachment. There are some who have gone beyond sin, or rather, "whose sin has come to an end."

"Doers of what is good and pure: released from the confusion of duality, (the *dvandva*), love and worship Me" (Z). Confusion comes from the 'dualities', good and evil, pleasure and pain. Truth is beyond the dualities.

29. For those who take refuge in me and strive to be free from age and death they know Brahman, they know Atman, and they know what Karma is.

"They will come to know what Brahman is in its wholeness, as it appertains to the self, the whole mystery of works" (Z). There is a series of Sanskrit terms, *adhiyatman, adhidaivam, adhibhutam*, and Zaehner says that all these are adjectives and that they qualify Brahman, although most translations take them as though they were nouns. What this sloka really means is that they will know Brahman in all his manifestations: Brahman manifested in the Self, the *adhiyatman*, Brahman manifested in the cosmic order, the world of the gods, the *adhidaivam*, and Brahman manifested in nature, the *adhibhutam*, which is here referred to as 'Karma', the law of nature. So Brahman is the One manifesting at all these levels and that is the One that we are seeking to know.

30. They know me in earth and in heaven, and in the fire of sacrifice. Their souls are pure, in harmony, and even when their time to go comes they see me.

More literally, they know the Brahman manifested in the creation, or contingent being, (the *adhibhutam*), in the world of the gods, the cosmic order, (the *adhidaivam*), and also in the sacrifice, (the *karma*). God is manifested in the whole cosmic order and in the cosmic sacrifice. The whole cosmic order rightly understood, is a sacrifice. The Purusha, the primeval Person, offers himself, sacrifices himself, and the whole creation comes into being through the sacrifice of Purusha. The whole creation is sustained by this sacrifice of Purusha which is represented in the Vedic sacrifice, and Krishna is the cosmic Person, whose sacrifice sustains the world. This can be seen as a foreshadowing of the Christian conception of Jesus as the "Lamb slain before the foundation of the world" (Rev. 13:8), whose sacrifice on the cross redeems the whole creation.

Chapter 8

The Yoga of Imperishable Eternal

In this chapter Krishna teaches Arjuna to know the two paths, the path of light and the path of darkness, and how to attain the highest end, the Eternal. The chapter also gives an insight into the structure of the universe according to the *Gita*. Brahman is the supreme Reality, known in the *Upanishads* as the *akshara*, the imperishable, the ground and source of all existence. Zaehner makes the point here, however, that in the later *Upanishads* like the *Shvetashvatara Upanishad*, as later in the *Gita*, the personal God is said to be above the imperishable (cf 15.18). This marks a refinement in understanding of the nature of reality. At first the supreme Reality is conceived as pure being and pure consciousness existing in perfect bliss, *saccidananda*, but its personal character is not fully realised. In the *Gita* it is gradually revealed that this absolute Reality is also the absolute Person, the *Purushottama*, who is the principle not only of being and knowledge but also of love. The Atman is the supreme Reality, the Brahman, manifesting himself as the spirit in man.

Arjuna asks Krishna:

1. Who is Brahman? Who is Atman? And what is Karma, Spirit Supreme? What is the kingdom of the earth? And what is the kingdom of Light?

2. Who offers the sacrifice in the body? How is the offering made? And

when the time to go comes, how do those whose soul is in harmony know thee?

Krishna replies:

3. Brahman is the Supreme, the Eternal. Atman is his Spirit in man. Karma is the force of creation, wherefrom all things have their life.

4. Matter is the kingdom of the earth, which in time passes away; but the Spirit is the Kingdom of Light. In this body I offer sacrifice, and my body is sacrifice.

Brahman is the supreme reality. Atman is its manifestation in man. *Karma* here is used of the activity of God in nature. The *adhibhutam*, which Mascaró translates the 'Kingdom of earth', is the manifestation of Brahman in the material world, and *adhidaivatam*, which Mascaró translates the 'Kingdom of light', is the manifestation of Brahman in the world of the gods, the *devas*, who are literally spirits of light. The world of the gods is called *Purusha*, which Mascaró translates 'the spirit', because all the gods are but manifestations of the one Cosmic Person.

Finally, Brahman is manifested in the sacrifice, the *yajna*, with which Krishna is here identified. In the *Vedas* Brahman is represented as the power which sustains the sacrifice, and since the sacrifice is said to sustain the world, Brahman is seen to be the power which sustains the world. In the *Gita* (4.24) Brahman is said to be the sacrifice itself, the offerer, the thing offered and the act of offering. Here Krishna as the personal God is revealed as the one who offers sacrifice 'here in the body'. Krishna is identified with the Cosmic Person, from whose sacrifice the creation comes and by which it is sustained. One cannot help seeing how close this comes to the Christian concept of the sacrifice of Christ, which is an eternal sacrifice, offered by the eternal High-Priest and enacted once in time, 'here in the body' on Calvary, this being the power which sustains and redeems the world.

5. And he who at the end of his time leaves his body thinking of me, he in truth comes to my being: he in truth comes unto me.

If one is thinking of God at the end of one's life, one passes into the divine mode of being. In every religion the attitude of the mind at the time of death is considered of great importance, as it largely determines one's experience of life after death.

6. For on whomsoever one thinks at the last moment of life, unto him in truth he goes, through sympathy with his nature.

A strange phrase, *bhava*-bhavita, is used here. It means that he is made 'to grow into that nature'. It is as though this divine life has drawn us into itself. If we fix our mind on God, we are drawn into the divine life. What we worship exercises a powerful fascination over us and makes us grow into it so that in a sense we become it.

7. Think of me therefore at all times; remember thou me and fight. And with mind and reason on me thou shalt in truth come to me.

The aim is to focus the whole mind on God, on the Lord. The word *smara* means to remember, to bear in mind, and perhaps we should keep in mind the Greek *anamnesis*, a word which is used in the Christian Eucharist, "Do this in memory of me." This has been a key word in the Christian dialogue on the Eucharist. Many object to the word 'sacrifice' applied to the Eucharist, and still more to the term 'transubstantiation' with its peculiar scholastic associations, but everyone accepts the word *anamnesis* as found in the Gospel, "Do this in remembrance of me." It is understood that a remembrance in that sense is not just a mental function; it is a bringing into the present, a re-presenting, of what took place in the past.

The Jews have their paschal meal, the idea being that the deliverance from Egypt which took place in the past becomes present; through the paschal meal Jews of every generation share in the event of the past. Undoubtedly that was what Jesus had in mind when he instituted the Eucharist, 'in remembrance of me'. 'To remember' in this sense is to recall the past event in such a way that it becomes present to the believer. That is the understanding of this word 'remember' today, and perhaps this is also the meaning of Krishna's words, "Remember thou me and fight." Arjuna is still facing the battle. Previously the injunction was, "Do your duty, without attachment, offer it as a sacrifice." Now Krishna says, "Do it with your mind fixed on me, in devotion to me." This is the transformation which the *Gita* has introduced. A religion of law, of duty and sacrifice is transformed into a religion of love and self-surrender. This is the transformation which has to take place in every religion. There always has to be a movement from external law and commandment to interior spirit and grace. So here also the external fight in which Arjuna is engaged is being transformed into an internal warfare against passion and desire which involves the surrender of the heart and mind to God. The 'mind' and 'reason' are the *manas* and the heart, the inner intuitive mind or spirit is the *buddhi*. All the faculties which have been *yukta*, united in yoga, are to be fixed on the One, and then the soul will truly find God.

8. For if a man thinks of the Spirit Supreme with a mind that wanders not, because it has been trained in Yoga, he goes to that Spirit of Light.

The Spirit Supreme is the supreme divine Person, the *Purusha*, who is the supreme power of the Godhead, and all devotion is fixed on him. Detachment and yoga are there just the same but all is now focused on devotion to the personal God. Zaehner translates, "Let a man's thoughts be integrated by Yoga (*abhyasa yoga yuktena*) and by constant striving: let them not stray to anything else at all." The mind is fixed on this and on nothing else, so by meditating on the *paramam Purusham divyam*, the supreme divine Person, he comes to that Person.

9. He who remembers the Poet, the Creator, who rules all things from all time, smaller than the smallest atom, but upholding this vast universe, who shines like the sun beyond darkness, far far beyond human thought;

This is a beautiful passage. This *kavim puranam*, the ancient poet, comes in the *Upanishads*. He is the seer or *rishi*. The Indian had a much finer idea of the poet than the Greeks. Plato, though he regarded the poet as inspired, rejected him from the Republic because he told immoral stories of the gods. But in the Vedic tradition, the poet was the one who had vision; he was the one who saw and had knowledge. The *Vedas* are the poetic expression of this divine knowledge. So the creator himself is a poet. He is also "smaller than the smallest atom", and is the ordainer or *dhataram*, which signifies firmness and can be translated supporter, establisher, creator. He is of unthinkable form, *acintya-rupam*, literally 'whose form cannot be conceived'. Then there comes a reference to the *Shvetashvatara Upanishad*, "I know that great Person of the colour of the sun beyond the darkness; only by knowing

Him, one goes beyond death. There is no other way to go." This is one of the most beautiful expressions of faith in the personal God by which one goes beyond death. For a Christian, Christ is that supreme Person who has passed beyond death, and who, in the Resurrection, shines like the sun beyond the darkness.

10. And at the time of his departure is in union of love and the power of Yoga and, with a mind that wanders not, keeps the power of his life between his eye-brows, he goes to that Spirit Supreme, the Supreme Spirit of Light.

It is significant that the mind is controlled now not only by the power of yoga but by love. *Bhaktya yukta* means integrated by *bhakti*. "Keeps the power of life between his eyebrows." The point between the eyebrows is the *ajna chakra*, the sixth of the seven chakras or centres of psychic power. One of the methods of yoga is to concentrate all the powers of life, all the energy of one's being, at that point.

11. Hear now of that Path which the seers of the Veda call the Eternal, and which is reached by those who, in peace from earthly passions, live a life of holiness and strive for perfection.

The word for eternal is *aksharam* which, as we have seen, is 'the imperishable'. The term is used of both Brahman and the word OM. The Sanskrit for 'state' is *padam* which can also mean 'word', so that it could be translated the 'imperishable word', that is the OM. This is how the *Katha Upanishad* speaks of OM as the Word, "which all the Vedas glorify, all self-sacrifice expresses, all sacred studies and holy life speak." The word OM thus comes to be identified with the primordial Word, the supreme Reality.

12. If when a man leaves his earthly body he is in the silence of Yoga and, closing the doors of the soul, he keeps the mind in his heart, and places in the head the breath of life.

13. And remembering me he utters OM the eternal WORD of Brahman, he goes to the Path Supreme.

This is how one should approach death. One should close the body's gates, the gates of the senses, and "hold the mind within the heart", or as the Greek Fathers say, "Lead your thoughts from your mind into your heart." When a yogi dies he is said to enter *samadhi*. In other words, he has simply gone into the final state of meditation. That is how one should die. One should sit and meditate and withdraw the mind from the senses, then withdraw the inner mind from the movements of the mind, the *buddhi* from the *manas*. Finally one should withdraw into the inmost centre of one's being and then, as everything else drops off, one enters into that eternal *samadhi*.

There is a story which illustrates this in the life of Tapasve Maharaj who was a great ascetic. He surrendered his body in Bangalore in 1955 and the event was witnessed by a judge from Bangalore who later wrote his biography. This yogi had led an extremely ascetic existence and lived to be 185. He was born in 1770 and died in 1955. He lived in the Himalayas and when he was ninety years old he was getting very infirm; his teeth were falling out, his hearing and eyesight were failing and he could no longer walk upright. At this time he met a sadhu who taught him the secret of rejuvenation. He told him of a particular medicine, known as *kaya-kalpa* which is found in the Himalayas, and which, the sadhu said, he would prepare for him. The sadhu collected the medicine and instructed the yogi to build himself a little hut and put bedding there made of paddy straw. He then told the yogi that he must lie on this bed for ninety days and he would bring him daily a measure of the medicine he had prepared and a glass of milk. For 90 days the yogi remained in his hut, locked up in the dark without any companion at all except that once a day the sadhu brought the medicine and the milk and each day took his pulse and temperature. After six days the yogi became unconscious and remained so for over a fortnight while each day the sadhu checked the pulse and administered the medicine. After about twenty days the yogi revived. His eyesight recovered and his hair and his teeth came out and then gradually new hair and new teeth began to grow. As time went on he was gradually rejuvenated and when he came out he looked like a man of twenty with black hair and a sturdy frame. And so he began again his ascetic life. When again he became old and infirm he did this a second time and then again a third time. Each time he gained a certain degree of rejuvenation but the process became less and less effective. At last he felt his time had come to die so he gathered a number of people round him. At this stage he was seriously ill and had two wounds on his thighs so that he could not move his legs. For weeks he had been lying in bed, unable to move his legs and eventually he could not even sit up in bed. Apparently he was a large and heavy man and it took several people to hold him whenever he wanted to sit up. He could not speak for his voice had gone. He remained in this condition for several weeks and eventually, when the time came, he signalled to the people to put him on the floor. They laid him down and he signalled how many hours it would be before death would come – three, then two, then one. When the hour came to die, he suddenly began to move his legs and he lifted up his trunk without any assistance. Finally he sat up fully in the lotus posture. Then, though he had been unable to speak before, a tremendous OM came from the depths of his being and he surrendered his soul in that way, exactly as the *Gita* prescribes. That was witnessed by the judge and all his family and written down in 1955. "So that is the way to die! Remembering me, he utters OM, the eternal WORD of Brahman, he goes to the Path Supreme."

14. Those who in the devotion of Yoga rest all their soul ever on me, very soon come unto me.

15. And when those great spirits are in me, the Abode of joy supreme, they never return again to this world of human sorrow.

In the Hindu tradition the aim of life is to pass beyond *samsara*, beyond the whole world of time and change, and to enter the deathless state of Brahman, which, according to the *Gita*, is reached by devotion to the personal God.

16. For all the worlds pass away, even the world of Brahma, the Creator: they pass away and return. But he who comes unto me goes no more from death to death.

The Hindu view of time is cyclic. Everything comes forth from Brahman in the beginning and goes through all the stages of evolution and then returns to Brahman, only to come forth again when a new age begins.

17. They know that the vast day of Brahma, the god of creation, ever lasts a thousand ages; and that his night lasts also a thousand ages – they know in truth day and night.

These are the ages of Brahma, each composed of four *yugas* and supposed to last 4,320,000 years. We are said to be now in the middle of the *Kali yuga*. It is commonly believed that there are still many thousands of years to go before the *Kali yuga* ends, although some hold that we are nearing the end, when everything is to be dissolved in *pralaya* and a new age will begin.

18. When that day comes, all the visible creation arises from the Invisible; and all creation disappears into the Invisible when the night of darkness comes.

The 'invisible' is the Unmanifest, the *avyakta*. Here the meaning of *avyakta* is *mula prakriti*, the root nature or womb of nature from which everything comes. The *avyakta* is mentioned in the *Katha Upanishad*: "Beyond the senses is the mind, the *manas*; beyond the *manas* is the intellect, the *buddhi*; beyond the *buddhi* is the *Mahat*, the cosmic order, the cosmic intelligence; beyond the *Mahat* is the *avyakta*, the Unmanifest; beyond *avyakta* the Unmanifest, is *Purusha*, the Person. That is the highest goal." Looking at the process from the highest downwards, there is first Brahman, the original source from which everything comes, then Brahman divides, as it were, into *purusha* and *prakriti*. *Purusha* is the male or active principle, spirit, consciousness. *Prakriti* is nature, the feminine principle, the unconscious, the womb from which all creation comes, which is here called the Unmanifest. So there is on the one hand the Spirit, consciousness and the light of day, and on the other hand matter, the unconscious and the darkness of night. Those are the two principles, the male and female, *purusha* and *prakriti* from which the whole of creation comes into being and then dissolves again.

19. Thus the infinity of beings which live again and again all powerlessly disappear when the night of darkness comes; and they all return again at the rising of the day.

This is a cyclic view of time, in which everything goes in cycles based on the rhythm of nature: the rising and setting of the sun; the waxing and waning of the moon; the succession of spring, summer, autumn and winter, and then spring again; and birth, death and rebirth. So the whole cosmos, the wheel of time, *samsara*, goes in this circle. *Moksha* is the state of liberation from the whole wheel of time and from the cosmic process. It is to be altogether beyond. That is the final liberation.

20. But beyond this creation, visible and invisible, there is an Invisible, Higher, Eternal; and when all things pass away this remains for ever and ever.

The Samkhya doctrine which the *Gita* follows postulates, as we have seen, two principles. On the one hand there is the *Purusha*, the Person, which is also spirit and consciousness, and on the other hand there is *prakriti*, the unconscious, the unmanifest, which Mascaró calls 'the invisible'. So the *Gita* is saying that beyond the *avyakta*, the unmanifest womb of nature, there is another unmanifest which is the masculine principle, the *Purusha*. The idea of the unmanifest is that the whole of this cosmos, which is manifest to the senses and to the mind, comes forth from an unmanifest state, the state of potentiality. But beyond this darkness of the Unmanifest there is always the uncreated being, the *Purusha*. Everything comes from him. So beyond this unmanifest womb of nature is the Unmanifest Person, the *Purusha*, the Supreme. He remains while all comes into being and passes away.

21. This invisible is called the Everlasting and is the highest End supreme. Those who reach him never return. This is my supreme abode.

What Krishna is saying is that beyond the unmanifest aspect of nature is the Unmanifest Person and that Person is the imperishable, the eternal Brahman. This is the highest goal. As it is said in the *Katha Upanishad*, which is very close to this, "Beyond the Unmanifest is the Person – this is the highest state; beyond this there is nothing." That is the Supreme. If we want to put these into Christian terms one could say that the Father is the Source, the Origin, the *Nirguna Brahman*, Brahman without attributes, beyond everything. From the Father comes forth the Son, the Word. The Word is the unmanifest Person, the Supreme Person, beyond all creatures, uncreated, who is nevertheless the source of all creation. Nature, *prakriti*, is the *materia prima*, the 'prime matter' of Aristotle, the passive principle in creation. It is what may be called the 'potentiality' of all being. Outside God, as it were, there is a vast potentiality of being; it has no being in itself – it derives its being from God but it is a power, a capacity to be. It is not matter in the ordinary sense; it is that from which all matter comes. It is the 'chaos' of Genesis, the *tohu ve bohu*: "In the beginning God created the heaven and the earth, and the earth was without form and void" (Gen. 1:1-2). It is the emptiness, the darkness, the void, the chaos from which everything comes. This is *mula prakriti*, the unmanifest.

There is another aspect of this which may be mentioned. These potentialities of nature can be thought of as existing passively in the womb, in their seed condition, in the darkness of nature, but they can also be conceived as existing actively in God. All beings exist eternally in God, in their seed, as it were, in what St. Augustine called their *rationes seminales*. The Father begets the Word and in that Word all things are contained in their 'ideas', their 'seminal reasons'. That Word brings everything to birth through the *shakti*, the power of the Holy Spirit, in which all these powers of nature are contained, and which brings them forth in creation. *Mula prakriti*, the chaos, the darkness, the womb, is the created aspect of the uncreated power of the Holy Spirit.

22. This Spirit Supreme, Arjuna, is attained by an ever-living love. In him all things have their life, and from him all things have come.

Literally: "That highest person, the *purusha para*, is to be won by *bhakti* directed to none other" (Z). That is the whole point of *bhakti*. It must be centred on God alone and must not be directed to anyone or anything else. In him and by him this universe is literally 'spun out' like a spider spinning its web. This can be compared with St. Paul's conception of Christ as the Person, in whom all hings consist or 'hold together'. So that highest Person in whom all these things exist is the Word of God, the Supreme Person, the *Purushottama*. And he is to be attained by love, by *bhakti*.

23. Hear now of a time of light when Yogis go to eternal Life; and hear of a time of darkness when they return to death on earth.

The idea is that after death there are two paths. This is found in most traditions. It is very clear, for instance, in the *Tibetan Book of the Dead*. At death there is a path of light and if one has prepared during life for it, one goes by this path of light to the eternal. But if one has not prepared for it, then one goes by the path of darkness of the moon and eventually returns to the earth.

24. If they depart in the flame, the light, the day, the bright weeks of the moon and the months of increasing light of the sun, those who know Brahman go unto Brahman.

25. But if they depart in the smoke, the night, the dark weeks of the moon and the months of decreasing days of the sun, they enter the lunar light and return to the world of death.

The idea that those who die in the months when the light is increasing go to the world of light may be taken symbolically. Krishna Prem has an enlightening explanation of this. He says: "These times of the months and the years are not times at all; they are stages on the path that souls must tread. One is the bright path of consciousness, the path beyond, trodden by him who knows the Self, the Atman, in all. The other is the dark path of matter trodden by the ignorant. He who goes by the first climbs the steep inner path from flickering firelight to the sunshine of eternal day. Rising from light to light in every widening splendour, he treads the trackless swan's path, which is the goal. That is the path of the *hamsa*, the swan, who goes to the beyond. The other is the path of gloom and sorrow. Here the only light is that reflected by the moon of matter." The moon is always the element of change. The sun is the source of light, the moon reflects the light. The sun is constant and the moon is always changing. One is masculine and the other is feminine — and the feminine is always conceived as the principle of change.

Krishna Prem goes on to say: "The only light is that reflected in the moon of matter and the traveller in that pale radiance takes foes for friends losing himself in forms which are illusions, knowing not the Immortal, he goes from death to death."

26. These are the two paths that are for ever: the path of light and the path of darkness. The one leads to the land of never-returning: the other returns to sorrow.

So those are the two paths. If we want to give a Christian interpretation of it, we can say that the first is the path of eternal life, and the other is the path of purgatory. One who leaves this life with many attachments, unpurified, has to go through this moonlight, through this realm of semi-darkness, until gradually he passes into the realm of light.

27. The Yogi who knows these two paths lives nevermore in delusion. Therefore ever and for ever be thou one in Yoga, Arjuna.

28. There is a reward that comes from the Vedas, or from sacrifice, from an austere life or from holy gifts. But a far greater reward is attained by the Yogi who knows the truth of Light and darkness; he attains his Everlasting Home.

There are always these two ways. The way of the *Vedas*, of sacrifice, austerity and gifts, *dana*, is the lower path. It is the path of ritual religion where one looks for a reward and although the reward is in heaven one eventually returns to earth again, not having reached the Supreme. But the yogi is one who goes beyond all these things, who sees the inner light and also knows the darkness. He is able to discern between the darkness and the light. He attains the Everlasting, the *param sthanam*, the supreme state, the deathless state which consists in being one with Brahman, with God.

The Yoga of The Royal Science and The Royal Secret

Chapter 9 begins: "I will tell thee a supreme mystery," and it is always well to remember that the *Gita*, like the *Upanishads*, is revealing a mystery. In the case of the *Upanishads*, this comes out very clearly. For instance, in the *Katha Upanishad*, when the boy, Nachiketas descends to the underworld, the world of Yama, god of death, and through him learns the secrets of the world beyond. The meaning of that is that one has to pass through a kind of death before one can attain this knowledge. In Christianity this is the death of baptism, death in Christ. The knowledge gained in this way is initiatory. It is quite different from the mental or intellectual knowledge which one can acquire at college and in which one can get a degree. It is an interior wisdom which is gained by an interior death and it comes as a gift of God.

Speaking of this mysterious knowledge Krishna begins:

1. I will tell thee a supreme mystery, because thy soul has faith. It is vision and wisdom and when known thou shalt be free from sin.

More literally, "most secret and mysterious is this wisdom" (Z). There is *jnana*, the supreme wisdom which may be called unitive knowledge or intuitive wisdom, and there is *vijnana*, discriminative knowledge. As most people have only *vijnana*, they can only discriminate with their discursive reason and they do not attain to the *jnana*, the supreme knowledge. But once one has *jnana*, one can also have *vijnana*, discrimination. *Jnana* and *vijnana* go together. "And knowing this, you shall be free from sin, from evil" (Z).

2. It is the supreme mystery and wisdom and the purification supreme. Seen in a wonder of vision, it is a path of righteousness very easy to follow, leading to the highest End.

In this verse Krishna calls this knowledge *rajavidhya*, a science of kings or a royal knowledge, and *rajaguhya*, a royal secret, and *pavitra uttama*, a supreme purity or supreme purifier. This knowledge is royal, it is secret and it is purifying. Then he uses the term *pratyaksha*, which means known by direct experience, or intuitional. This is in contrast to rational or discursive knowledge, which is knowledge gained first through the senses, going from one point to another and then, by inference and logic, building up a system. Intuitive knowledge is quite different for it is a matter of seeing from within and grasping the whole, in all its inter-relationships, as a whole. For this reason it is also called unitive knowledge. This is the way in which we know ourselves. We do not have to learn about ourselves from outside but rather we have an intuitive inner awareness of ourselves and that intuitive awareness can grow into genuine self-knowledge.

The same principle applies with all other things. One can have a merely external knowledge of things and of the world around, or one can have an intuitive, inner awareness. I mentioned the lady at Findhorn in Scotland who, with this kind of intuitive, inner awareness, knows the spirits of the trees and plants. Intuitive knowledge is also righteous knowledge, *dharma*. *Dharma* is law, righteousness. Again, and this is important, such knowledge depends on the person's moral character. Scientific knowledge is different. One can be a very immoral person and still have great scientific or philosophical knowledge whereas intuitive wisdom can only be attained through moral perfection, through *dharma*. And yet it is *susukham*, very easy to carry out, very easy to practise. Once we have it, all our actions spring from that inner understanding, that intuitive wisdom, and this abides forever.

3. But those who have no faith in this Truth, come not unto me: they return to the cycles of life in death.

That is always the principle. Unless we can go beyond this world, beyond the outer appearances, beyond discriminative knowledge to discover the inner centre, the truth, the root of all, and unless we return continually to that centre, we are always caught up in the toils of nature. When we go beyond, we are set free, liberated.

4. All this visible universe comes from my invisible Being. All beings have their rest in me, but I have not my rest in them.

Here it is made very clear that Krishna is truly the creator God. Hinduism is often said to be pantheistic, and there is no doubt that the language used is often pantheistic. But here Krishna makes it clear that while the whole universe comes from him he does not depend on it in any way.

The same idea is found is St. Paul who says of Christ, "In him and through him and for him all things were created and in him all things subsist or stand together" (Col. 1.15-17). The idea is the same that the whole universe finds its centre and support in the cosmic Person, who is at once both transcendent and immanent. Now Krishna makes a very important distinction. "All things have their rest in me but I do not have my rest in them." In other words, they are completely under Krishna's control, but he is not under their control in any way. Then he goes on to refine even that.

5. And in truth they rest not in me: consider my sacred mystery. I am the source of all beings, I support them all, but I rest not in them.

To say that they "rest in me" might suggest that in some way they modify his nature but the *Gita* wants to show that the Creator is absolutely beyond the whole creation. "Behold my skill in works" (Z). The word which Mascaró translates 'sacred mystery' is yoga. We should remember that the word yoga has many kindred meanings and one of them is 'skill in action'. When one is integrated, *yukta*, (which is the root meaning of 'yoga'), one's actions are perfectly harmonious, perfectly right. The yoga of God is that action which flows from his person, from his *dharma*, from his law. That is the yoga of God.

This is one of the most remarkable expressions of creative power in Hindu literature. The tendency of Hindu mysticism is to stress rather that God (Brahman) is the ground of everything. Everything is in Brahman and eventually, it can be said, everything is Brahman; "all this world is Brahman" (*Chandogya Upanishad* 3:14).

To say, as the *Upanishad* does, that all is Brahman, is, on the surface at least, a pantheistic expression. But here in this passage, Krishna is extremely careful to explain how all things come totally from the Supreme. He is the one source. All things are pervaded by him, 'spun out' by him, and all things are completely controlled, supported by him; yet he is in no way dependent on them or affected by them. So this is a most important passage. It shows the proper idea of creation, that God is at once both totally transcendent and totally immanent in creation.

6. Even as the mighty winds rest in the vastness of the ethereal space, all beings have their rest in me. Know thou this truth.

The analogy of space naturally suggests itself, for space pervades everything but cannot be identified with anything.

7. At the end of the night of time all things return to my nature; and when the new day of time begins I bring them again into light.

That is the idea of the day and night of Brahman. The whole creation comes out from Brahman in the beginning; then at the end it is drawn back again. These are the systole and the dyastole, the breathing in and out of Brahman. When he breathes out, the whole creation comes forth; when he breathes in, the whole creation returns to him. This is the cyclic view of time and creation; it is what Mircea Eliade has called the 'myth of the eternal return'. But the goal is always to go beyond *samsara* altogether, beyond the days and the nights, to the eternal day.

8. Thus through my nature I bring forth all creation, and this rolls round in the circles of time.

The meaning here is that everything comes forth from nature, from *prakriti*, which elsewhere Krishna calls his 'lower nature'. "Hidden in nature which is mine own. I emanate again and again this multitude of beings necessarily by the force of nature" (B & D) is a somewhat different translation. It is a common idea that the phenomenal world comes forth from Brahman according to its own laws. The reason why creatures come forth again and again is because of their *karma*. There are actions which have not borne their fruit at the end of time. So they go back into the night of Brahman and then because the seeds of activity are still there, they come forth again. There is a force in nature which causes all beings to come into existence. It drives them on in their course, brings them back and then again drives them out again. This force is *karma*, the force of nature, and it is the cause of the world. But we find in the *Gita* another idea that, over and above *karma*, over and above nature, is the personal God and he by his grace is able to control the course of nature. We each have our own *karma*. We come into being because of inevitable laws and we have a particular nature because of these laws and are driven inevitably by that nature. But nevertheless, there is something in us which is free from these laws. The grace of God comes and releases us from the power of this *karma*.

All this is closely akin to the Christian idea of original sin. We are all born into this condition as the result of primordial sin, without being able to help it. From infancy we are conditioned by our heredity, by our environment, by all the forces around us, and our lives are largely shaped by all the forces of the unconscious. But there is in everybody a principle of freedom, very minute at first, like a grain of mustard seed, having the power to respond to the grace of God, and when this touches us, it is able to set us free from this law of *karma*, from the bondage of original sin. So in one sense we must do justice to the terrible power of *karma*, to the mechanical law. Aurobindo was one of the great sages of India who experienced very deeply the resistance of nature to every effort to get beyond its control. The ordinary yogi goes beyond nature and experiences freedom and joy, but Aurobindo maintained that that does not really answer the problem. One has not changed the world and the conditions of the world. Aurobindo was trying to bring the 'supermental' power, as he called it, the power from above, down into the soul, the *psyche*, and into the body, where the mechanical laws of nature are strongest. It was easy, he felt, to rise to Brahman and experience bliss, but to bring that power down into the body, in the face of all the resistance of nature, was a superhuman task. He was struggling with this to the end of his life, and his colleague, the Mother, continued the struggle after him. They had hoped to make the body immortal. They thought that the supermind, the divine consciousness, could descend and transform the soul and then, through the soul, transform the body, so that the body would be free from being determined by laws of nature. It was a profound intuition, to have grasped that the body is destined to be immortal.

What Aurobindo and the Mother were attempting to do is, according to Christian tradition, precisely what happened at the Resurrection of Jesus. The body of Jesus at that point was set free from all the determination of the laws of nature, of life and of the *psyche*. He opened a breach in the whole mechanism of nature and released a force which could set men free from death and eventually transform the whole creation.

9. But I am not bound by this vast work of creation. I am and I watch the drama of works.

Literally he says, "I look on and supervise" (Z). That is another key phrase. It is not that God, the Person, the *Purusha*, is merely a witness. The view of the Samkhya is that *Purusha* is the witness and that all action comes from *prakriti*, from Nature. The Spirit, consciousness, is inactive. As witness it watches the whole creation, while all the activity of nature comes from *prakriti*, from the feminine, from the mother. So nature is at work in the world and Spirit, consciousness, is looking on as the witness. Now in the *Gita*, a deeper tradition is developed. Krishna, the Lord, looks on and he supervises and eventually he controls. That is a much deeper view which is comes out in the next verse.

10. I watch and in its work of creation nature brings forth all that moves and moves not: and thus the revolutions of the world go round.

The translation of Besant and Das is more to the point here: "Under Me, as supervisor, Nature sends forth the moving and unmoving beings; because of this the universe revolves." God is not only the witness; he is the controller also. But there remains a tendency to suggest that Nature just proceeds on its own way. The yoga school of asceticism holds that the aim of life is to detach oneself from the body, from nature, from the whole curse of existence and to become the pure witness. The injunction is not to interfere, but rather, with complete indifference, to allow the processes of nature to take their course. The *Gita* goes right beyond this. It teaches not indifference but detachment. Being detached, it is possible to accept and to give meaning to what is happening. That, of course, is a far more profound understanding. But there is always a danger, which occurs also in Christianity, of a kind of spirituality which so detaches itself from the world that it is not concerned with this world at all and only seeks the kingdom of God above. But the concern of the *Gita*, as of deeper tradition in Christianity, is precisely to be detached from the world in the first place, in order to be able to guide and to control the world, which means bringing everything under the control of the Spirit.

11. But the fools of the world know not me when they see me in my own human body. They know not my Spirit supreme, the infinite God of this all.

The idea that nature is all-powerful is an illusion, because behind the whole course of nature is this eternal Being who is sustaining everything, and who pervades everything, and who is guiding everything to its destiny. It is ignorance which makes people think that they are simply subject to mechanical laws. Through that ignorance, "the foolish disregard me when clad in human semblance, ignorant of my supreme nature, the great Lord of beings" (B & D).

There is a scene in the Gospel when Jesus goes to Nazareth, his home town, and the people say, is not this the carpenter's son? Do we not know his brothers and sisters? They were unable to see behind that semblance of his human form to the great being, the Lord within.

12. Their hope is in vain, their works are in vain, their learning is vain, their thoughts are vain. They fall down to the nature of demons, towards the darkness of delusion of hell.

The *Gita*, like the Gospel, has a very definite understanding of the power of evil spirits. We may interpret them as forces of the unconscious, but they are none the less real. In the *Gita* the demoniacal nature is that of the Rakhashas and the Asuras, the evil powers, which are opposed to the *devas*, the powers of light.

If one is deceived by the mechanical laws of the universe into thinking that the material world is the one reality, one becomes subject to the world and then one becomes demonic. Monod, the French biologist, attempted to demonstrate from biology that the whole universe is simply an effect of chance and necessity, and nothing else. One can see the world like that, as simply obeying mechanical laws and evolving as the result of chance variations. That is a purely scientific view, the result of observing phenomena. But the scientific view ignores the reality behind the phenomena. Such a view is eventually demonic and becomes positively evil. It ignores the ultimate truth of things and fails to see the whole truth of reality. It is no accident that this view of the world has led to the pollution of earth and sky and sea and has produced weapons which can destroy all life on the planet. When a scientist abdicates his moral responsibility for his inventions and ignores the spiritual basis of the material world, he becomes subject to the forces of the unconscious in the human *psyche* and the psychic elements of the natural world, and so releases power of death and destruction.

13. But there are some great souls who know me: their refuge is my own divine nature. They love me with a oneness of love: they know that I am the source of all.

"The Mahatmas, partaking of my divine nature" (B & D) is a good translation. A *mahatma* is one who has realised his divine nature, the Atman, the Spirit in man. "They worship me (*bhajanti*) with devotional love and with unwavering mind." The mind must be fixed on God alone; only then is the love total and complete. "Then they know me as the imperishable source of being" (B & D). So this is the essential need, to see behind nature itself, behind the appearance of things, to the one Reality which is only known by faith and by the grace of God. It is this only which gives us insight into that which lies beyond.

14. They praise me with devotion, they praise me for ever and ever. Their vows are strong; their harmony is ever one; and they worship me with their love.

"Always singing my glory" (B & D). The word is *kirtayanto*, which refers to the *kirtan*. Along with the *bhajan*, the *kirtan* is the most popular form of worship, particularly in Northern India.

15. Others worship me, and work for me, with the sacrifice of spiritual vision. They worship me as One and as many, because they see all that is in me.

"Others sacrificing with the sacrifice of wisdom worship me as the one and the manifold everywhere present" (B & D). "With the sacrifice of wisdom": as always, wisdom is a sacrifice because wisdom always comes from God. Only when we sacrifice, that is, offer our mind to God, do we receive the illumination of wisdom. Sacrifice means that offering of the mind. "Worship me as One, yet manifold." This is a matter of fundamental importance. We come to the source of all beings, the One, and then we realise the many in the One and that is the goal. The impression is sometimes given that one should leave all the manifold phenomena of this world to arrive at a sort of abstract unity but that is not how it is. In the One, the supreme Brahman, all the diversity of matter and nature is contained, but in simplicity — not spread out in time and space. In Brahman all things are united and integrated in a unitive vision, so that the whole diversity of matter and nature is contained in the absolute simplicity of the One.

One often hears the question asked: In the ultimate state, is there One or are there many? Do all the individual souls disappear in that One? The answer is that they disappear as separate beings but they are rediscovered as distinct and yet one. And that is the ultimate goal. The distinctions remain. Everything in nature, even every grain of sand, is distinct in God. Every single being in its own distinct nature exists eternally in God. Each one of us is a unique individual eternally known and eternally realised in God. All the distinctions are contained in the absolute unity of the divine nature in which there are no differences, no oppositions, no conflicts of any kind. It is extremely difficult for us to grasp this. If we conceive of one, then it becomes abstract so we lose the sense of the many; if we think of the many, then we lose the sense of the One. But in God, the many are contained in the One and the One is manifest in the many.

This is an example of intuitive knowledge as opposed to discursive, discriminative knowledge. Ordinary knowledge is that in which we distinguish one thing from another and from which we build up logical systems. Unitive knowledge, on the other hand is intuitive. It grasps, apprehends, in a way which is a little like the intuition of a poet who has a unified vision of reality. Going further, there is a mystical intuition in which the whole multiplicity of being is experienced in its unity. That is the supreme intuitive knowledge. Now intuition in a poet, where it is imperfect and partial, is compatible with an immoral nature. There are many poets who are basically immoral although they may have wonderful intuitions. But in order to attain the final mystic knowledge, the whole being has to be integrated. Therefore it has to have moral perfection, to be morally integrated. That is why the two bases of yoga are *yama* and *niyama*, in other words, the moral law.

At this point, half way through the book and half way through Chapter 9, it would be appropriate to summarise what has been said so far. In chapters

9, 10, and 11 we are coming to the culmination of the *Gita.* The stages of development are there. The question was, how to reach the knowledge of Brahman, of Atman. In the *Upanishads* it is simply by way of *jnana,* by way of renunciation and self-realisation. That was generally understood to mean that one should not do any work, any *karma. Karma* binds one. Whatever work one does, good or bad, one is bound to the consequences. Therefore to reach true knowledge which is free from all limitation, one should renounce work. The *Bhagavad Gita* introduces another understanding which is that ordinary work, selfish work, binds one, whereas unselfish work, that is, work done without any attachment at all, so far from being binding, is a way of reaching God. So *karma* yoga is the way of work, in total detachment, total surrender and total sacrifice. Making a sacrifice of one's work by offering it to the Supreme is the means by which one attains to the Supreme. The *Gita* maintains that the householder, doing his duty in the spirit of love, detachment and surrender, can reach God, the Supreme, just as effectively, if not more so, than can the *sannyasi* who abstains from all work whatever.

Ramakrishna advocated the way of *bhakti.* He said that because this is the *Kali Yuga,* when people cannot easily attain *jnana,* they must follow the path of *bhakti,* devotion. So *karma,* unselfish action, is a way of reaching the Supreme; and *bhakti,* devotion to the personal God is another. That is the position of the *Gita* up to now.

Now, in Chapter 9, Krishna reveals himself as the God who is the source of all. We have seen that he says that "all things are in me," and yet he says, "I am not in them." He is the source of all, the support of all, but he is not affected by anything; he remains unattached and uncontaminated. He is the supreme Lord, the creator and the source, who sends everything forth. He, the one Supreme God sustains everything and controls it from within; he pervades it through and through and yet is not affected by any of it. All this is very profound and very true, but certain questions arise.

There are three basic questions and we shall see as we go on how, although answers are given, the questions in a sense remain. The first is, it is true that the universe comes from the Lord, that he sustains it, brings it back and sends it forth again and again, and if so has that universe any ultimate reality? It definitely has a certain reality but the question is, when one gets to the ultimate stage, does anything remain? The general view, held by most orthodox Hindus, and for instance by Ramakrishna, is that as long as you are in the present state of being, you will enjoy the universe and you can see God manifest in the universe. But when you go into *samadhi*, the ultimate state, it all disappears. The universe is only real as long as you retain your ego, as long as you live in this state of consciousness; in the end it is all *maya*. Now with that goes the question: When you get beyond, does the ego survive? Does any self remain? And Ramakrishna again says rather clearly that *bhakti* is your way to God, but you can only have *bhakti* as long as you have an ego. If your ego dies and you enter *samadhi*, there is no more *bhakti*; there is only absolute oneness. This leads to the third question. When the individual self disappears and only the One remains and there is no more love, no more *bhakti*, what of the reality of the personal God?

We are concerned here then with the qustion of the ultimate reality of the universe, the individual soul and the personal God. The *Gita* is insisting all the time, and all through this chapter, on the reality of the personal God and on his love. "Those who love me are dear to me and I am in them and they are in me, they can come to me, they will have eternal peace." But the question remains, is the personal God ultimately real? When one enters *samadhi*, does the person remain? There are differing views, but again, the prevailing view is that the personal aspect of God disappears. Ramakrishna speaks of God with form and without form. When he speaks of God with form he means not only another *avatara*, another appearance on earth, as of Krishna, Rama or anyone else; he means also the form of the Mother Goddess, the eternal Mother, and this again is just an appearance. As he said, it is like the foam on the water, it is just a thing that passes. And so God without form is the ultimate reality and as there is no *bhakta* and no *bhakti*, it is difficult to say that any person remains. It is an absolute beyond. That, I think, is the prevailing view and this is one of the main points on which the Hindu-Christian dialogue must take place. The usual Christian position is that in the ultimate state this universe remains, realised in the vision of God. The universe passes beyond its present state in time and space and beyond the present laws of matter and causality. That it passes there is no doubt, but is there not another state beyond, when one goes beyond the body and beyond the mind and realises the Spirit within? At that point one realises the whole creation in its ground, in its source and in its fulness. In the vision of God, all things are present. Every grain of sand, every plant and every tree, in all their stages of development; the waves on the sea, the drops of water in the river, all is present to God in an eternal oneness, not diffused in space and time, not changing and passing, but in its eternal reality. In the Word of God all is present. When one reaches heaven, the ultimate state, one enjoys all this world, for everything that is in it is present, without any of the flux, without the change, the suffering, the corruption and the death, which is in the present world.

That is precisely what is meant by the new creation, the new heaven and the new earth. This is the plentitude of reality when the material universe is transfigured, when it ceases to be subject to the present laws of matter, space and time, and is realised in God. It is the same also with an individual soul. As long as we retain an ego, in the ordinary sense, worshipping God in a dualistic sense, that is an imperfect state. When we reach union with God, when we reach the ultimate stage, does the individual remain? The Christian would say yes. We are persons within the person of Christ. In the mystical body of Christ, each person is a cell, as it we, and each one retains its uniqueness and yet again, though there are many persons in the one body, they all make one person. This is known as circumincession, where one is totally in the other. Jesus says, "As I am in the Father and the Father in Me, that they may be one in us" (John 17:21). That is, each one is fulfilled in himself, but going beyond himself, is fulfilled in the whole and going beyond the whole, is fulfilled in God, the *Purusha*, the Supreme Person. There is an absolute fullness there, so that each one is utterly fulfilled, yet also utterly transformed. He is no longer a little isolated person, separated as now, but all are fully realised, transcending all limitations, and knowing themselves through the One and in the One. Each is a unique person in the one Person.

And finally, in the Godhead itself, does the person remain? The idea of the Christian doctrine of the Trinity is precisely that in the ultimate Godhead, beyond words and thought, beyond all conception, there is communion; an intercommunion in knowledge and love. We cannot imagine or properly conceive it but we can suggest how it can be. The language of Jesus in the New Testament is "that they may be one, as Thou in Me and I in Thee, that they may be one in us." This is the circumincession, as it is called, of the Persons in the Trinity. The Father is in the Son, the Son is in the Father and the Father and Son are absolutely one in the Spirit, without duality. There is no difference in them at all. And yet there is relationship, relationship in perfect unity. Thus in the Godhead itself there is love. In the ultimate there is a communion of love, and participation in the mystical Body of Christ is participation in that communion of love.

We can see how this doctrine of the Trinity points towards the idea of total fulfillment in the intercommunion of persons in the Godhead, of persons within the Body of Christ, the supreme Person, and finally of the whole creation in a new mode of existence in this whole. In this sense Christ, as the supreme Person, fills the whole creation. As St. Paul says, "He ascended above to heaven so that he might fill all things with his presence" (Eph. 4:10). The whole creation is permeated by his presence and transfigured by it.

In contrast with this unitive vision, which is *jnana* or wisdom, is the merely rational view of the lower mind. The wisdom of the world is the wisdom of man, complete in himself. It is the wisdom of scientific man trying to control the universe. And that is the essence of sin. The fall of man in the Book of Genesis, with the eating of the tree of good and evil, is symbolic of this. It means that by reason, by science and technology, man becomes master of the universe. In doing so he excludes the idea of there being anything above him. Reason is supreme. That is the essence of sin. It is also the 'wisdom' of the twentieth century! In contrast to this, true wisdom is the recognition that beyond the human reason is the *buddhi*, the medium of the higher wisdom and the human mind has to submit itself to that. We are not the master any more for we surrender to that which is beyond us. It is then that a light comes from above and we are illuminated and transfigured by that light. This means self-surrender which is precisely the opposite of self-assertion. So wisdom is a sacrifice. We surrender ourself and then we find ourself in the true light of God. It is God's grace and grace is a gift. So that is the sacrifice of wisdom. Meister Eckhart has a good way of putting this. He says that there are three ways of knowing God. The first he calls morning knowledge, which is when one knows God in the world. One sees the world and realises God is in everything around. The second he calls evening knowledge, when one sees the world in God. Here one moves from the world as center and instead of seeing the world first and God in the world, one now sees God first and the whole world is taken up into God. The third is to see God Himself, going beyond the world.

When we compare this Christian vision with that of the *Gita*, there are both resemblences and differences. In the *Gita* Krishna declares that the whole universe is in him. The biblical tradition has little sense of God pervading the universe. The Jews were anxious to show God above the universe. He overturns the hills and makes the dry lands water and the water dry, and so on. He is always overwhelming nature. But the sense

that he is in the water, in the fire, in the world, is lacking. The transcendence
of God had to be grasped at that point in history, and they could not attend
to this immanent aspect. The immanent aspect, on the contrary, was
developed particularly in India, with the profound sense that God is pervading
everything. This immanent aspect is really a function of the Holy Spirit.
The old theology spoke of a special creation of the human soul; God created
all this world and then there had to be a special creation a sort of divine
intervention, when a human being appeared. On this theory not only the
first but every soul demands such a special intervention. That whole mode
of reasoning arises from the view that God is not immanent. Once we see
that the Holy Spirit is immanent in matter from the beginning of the creation
and that the Holy Spirit is bringing forth life from the earth, the grass and
the plants and so on, and that same Holy Spirit that is latent in matter
brings forth consciousness when the matter is sufficiently organised, then
those arguments are not only unnecessary but inappropriate. The soul comes
from God, but no special intervention is needed, for it is part of the plan
of God from the beginning that the Spirit should permeate matter and
gradually transform it. The human soul has to be more and more penetrated
by the Holy Spirit until it becomes totally transfigured and shares in the
life of God himself. It was hidden in matter, it comes forth in life, it emerges
further in consciousness, but it is only in divine consciousness, in the life
of grace, that the Holy Spirit fully manifests himself in us. There is no special
intervention or anything like that. It is all a unified whole.

So when Krishna says that he is in all what he means is that he is
immanent in everything. God is present in everything, causing its existence.
As St. Thomas himself says, God causes the existence of everything, sustains
everything in existence at every moment, and causes each thing to act. No
tree can emerge from the earth unless there is an actual activity of God
working in it, making it rise. God is active in all things all the time.

16.   For I am the sacrifice and the offering, the sacred gift and the sacred
      plant. I am the holy words, the holy food, the holy fire, and the offering
      that is made in the fire.

"I am the oblation, I am the sacrifice, I am the ancestral offering, I am
the sacred herb, I am the mantra, I am the sacred butter (the ghee), I am
the fire and the burnt offering" (B & D). The idea is that not only does
God receive the sacrifice but he is the sacrifice. He penetrated the whole

creation and the whole creation is offered to God and God himself is the offering, as was said of 'great Brahman' in the previous text, "Brahman is the offering offered to Brahman in the fire of Brahman." The One is manifest in the whole and the whole universe is the sacrifice of the One. This can be applied to the sacrifice of Christ. He is creating and redeeming the world, offering the whole creation and assuming it into himself. This is the offering of the mystical body of Christ. St. Augustine says that he is the head and we are the members, and in every Eucharist the head is offering himself in his members. It is a sacrifice of the mystical body of Christ in which the whole creation is contained.

17. I am the Father of this universe, and even the Source of the Father. I am the Mother of this universe, and the Creator of all. I am the Highest to be known, the Path of purification, the holy OM, the Three Vedas.

It is significant that in the Hindu tradition God is both Father and Mother. In Christianity the feminine aspect of God has never been properly realised.

18. I am the Way, and the Master who watches in silence; thy friend and thy shelter and thy abode of peace. I am the beginning and the middle and the end of all things: their seed of Eternity, their Treasure supreme.

"The Master who watches in silence" is literally "the support, the Lord, the witness." 'Support' can also be translated 'husband', so intimate is the relation of the Lord to his creation.

19. The heat of the sun comes from me, and I send and withhold the rain. I am life immortal and death, I am what is and I am what is not.

Notice that Krishna says that he is both life and death, what is and what is not. A Christian would say that God is life and being, but death and non-being are outside God. That is, they are not due to the action of God but to the defect of nature.

20. There are men who know the Three Vedas, who drink the Soma,

who are pure from sin. They worship and pray for heaven. They reach indeed the heaven of Indra, the king of the gods, and there they enjoy royal pleasures.

The Vedic religion relied on sacrifice with the object of reaching the state of heaven, *svarga*, where one gets the reward of one's good deeds. This was a religion of the law, similar to what the Torah is to the Jews. When one does one's duty, one gets the reward. The *Upanishads* and the Gita go beyond that, beyond duty and reward to realisation of God, which is also union with God in love. So anyone who follows the *Vedas*, anyone who is subject to the law, is still on a lower level of religion. There is always this distinction between a religion of the law and a religion of the Spirit.

"Knowers of the Three Vedas who drink the Soma wine." The Soma is an intoxicating drink which was taken at the Vedic sacrifice. It must have been made from some kind of psychedelic plant and those who drank it felt a kind of divine inspiration. It was also considered to be a purification from sin and a way to heaven or paradise, the *Indra-loka*, the heaven of Indra, King of the gods. Those who drink the Soma go to the world of the gods, the *devas*, but they do not go beyond.

21. They enjoy that vast world of heaven, but the reward of their work comes to an end: they return to the world of death. They follow the words of the Three Vedas, they lust for pleasures that pass away: in truth they attain pleasures that pass away.

Having enjoyed the spacious heaven world and having exhausted their good deeds" (B & D). Their good deeds have limited value and when they have had their reward, then they must return. Only the grace of God can take one beyond all these and give final liberation. "Following the virtues enjoined by the Three Vedas, desiring enjoyment, they obtain the transitory." Here is a very interesting phrase meaning literally that those who stick to the Three Vedas receive a reward that comes and goes, *gatagatam. Kamanam kama* is desire of desires, and desire is the root of all limitations. As long as one desires desire, one may get what one seeks, but one will exhaust these things also and so fall back on the wheel of *samsara*. Only when one goes beyond desire altogether is one set free. That is liberation.

22. But to those who adore me with a pure oneness of soul, to those who

are ever in harmony, I increase what they have and I give them what they have not.

Only those obtain all their desires who worship the transcendent Lord, who have gone beyond the ego and have become 'one with the One', because they have ceased to desire.

23. Even those who in faith worship other gods, because of their love they worship me, although not in the right way.

Even though people worship other gods, Krishna accepts their worship because of their good faith. They do not know the right way but still they worship me. This is a profound insight, that all true worship goes to the one Supreme Being, whatever may be the form which one worships. One can understand worship in a Hindu temple in this way. All the worship goes to the one Supreme Being; we unite ourselves in worship to the One under whatever form he may be represented. These are only the outer forms, while the faith and the worship of the devotee go to the One. Some may be stopping short at the mere outward form but one's worship can always go beyond, and one can take the *prasad* that is given at the sacrifice. God has blessed the offering and the gift, and he gives his blessing.

24. For I accept every sacrifice, and I am their Lord supreme. But they know not my pure being, and because of this they fall.

"I am the enjoyer of all sacrifices" (B & D). A Christian can understand this in the same sense that Christ receives all sacrifice. He is "a priest forever of the order of Melchizedeck" (Heb. 7.21). Melchizedeck was a pagan priest and Christ fulfills not only all Jewish sacrifices, but also all pagan sacrifices which were offered in faith from the beginning.

In this way Christ is understood as the enjoyer of all sacrifices in the Hindu temple. He is the One who respondes to the faith of the devotee. This is something which often comes out in dialogue, that all genuine faith, whatever its particular form, is always directed to the Absolute. It is a commitment to the ultimate. One's idea and image of the ultimate may be defective but the faith in one's heart is directed towards an ultimate. When a person worships for his own benefit and the good that he hopes to receive, that is an inferior worship, but genuine faith is always in an ultimate reality beyond the human. Even an atheist can have that ultimate faith. If a man is seeking social justice and love and truth with absolute conviction, his faith is in an ultimate and may be accepted by God.

25. For those who worship the gods go to the gods, and those who worship the fathers go to the fathers. Those who worship the lower spirits go to the lower spirits; but those who worship me come unto me.

The 'fathers' are the ancestors who were always included in ancient worship; in Christian tradition we recall the souls of the departed as well as the saints in our worship.

"The 'lower spirits' are the *stoicheia* of St. Paul, the elemental spirits of the universe which are present everywhere. "But those who worship me come unto me." This suggests that they do not all reach the goal. A person worshipping the gods can limit himself, in that his faith is a limited faith; he wants certain advantages, certain pleasures in this world or in the world to come, and he may seek to obtain them from the spirits of the dead or the elemental powers. It is a selfish desire and he gets his due, but those who go beyond their selfish desires, who have a real faith in an ultimate, they come to the One whichever the form they worship. And as to who it is who has real faith, who can judge?

Now here is a very famous verse, and it is very beautiful.

26. He who offers to me with devotion only a leaf, or a flower, or a fruit, or even a little water, this I accept from that yearning soul, because with a pure heart it was offered with love.

In every sacrifice it is not the thing offered which is important but the love and devotion which goes into the offering. One is reminded of the saying of Jesus, "He who gives a cup of water to one of these little ones, because he is a disciple, shall not lose his reward" (Matt. 10:42; Mark 9:41).

27. Whatever you do, or eat, or give, or offer in adoration, let it be an offering to me; and whatever you suffer, suffer it for me.

"Whatever you suffer" is not quite accurate. It is whatever *tapas* or penance you may perform. "Whatever austerity (*tapas*) you do, do it as an offering to me" (B & D). By themselves, eating and sacrificing and austerity have a limited value but when they are offered to God, then whatever we do, or eat, or drink, we do all for the glory of God (cf 1 Cor. 10:31).

28. Thus thou shalt be free from the bonds of Karma which yield fruits that are evil and good; and with thy soul one in renunciation thou shalt be free and come to me.

"Thus you will be liberated from the bonds of action" (B & D). Anything done selfishly binds us. If we eat for our own pleasure or simply for our own health, as most people do, we are bound by our eating, and we will reap the consequences of it. We may have good health but that is a very limited thing; it does not last. But if we make an offering of what we are eating, then we transcend this world altogether and our eating itself is a sacrament. Then we are freed, liberated by our action. "You will be liberated from the bonds of action which yield good and evil fruits" (B & D). Good fruits are really just as bad as evil because they are limited, they do not take one to God. There is no finality in them.

29. I am the same to all beings, and my love is ever the same; but those who worship me with devotion, they are in me and I am in them.

"I am the same to all beings; there is none hateful to me nor dear" (B & D). This is the divine indifference, which is accepted also in Christianity; as Jesus says in the Gospel. "Your heavenly Father sends rain on the just and the unjust" (Matt. 5.45). To God all people are equal in a sense. But Krishna goes on to say, "Those who worship me with devotion, they are in me and I in them." The word used is bhajanti, from the word bhakti which we translate as love or devotion but it also means 'to partake of', or 'to commune with'. So Zaehner translates: "Those who commune with me in love's devotion, those abide in me and I in them." While God is good equally to all, he has a special love for those who love him. This corresponds to the saying of Jesus in St. John's Gospel, "He who loves me will be loved of my Father and I will love him and manifest myself to him" (John. 14.21).

30. For even if the greatest sinner worships me with all his soul, he must be considered righteous, because of his righteous will.

"Even if the most sinful worship me with undivided heart, he too must be accounted righteous for he is rightly resolved" (B & D). So that even a sinful person, when he worships with an undivided heart, — that is, when he is converted — attains to this righteousness if his resolve is right. Zaehner comments, "The evil doer is changed by his love of God just as Mary Magdalen and most of the more attractive Christian saints were."

31. And he shall soon become pure and reach everlasting peace. For this is my word of promise, that he who loves me shall not perish.

"His soul becomes dharmic, and *dharma* is righteousness. He becomes righteous, in the righteousness of God." Zaehner recalls that this is exactly like Chapter 6, verse 30: "He who sees me everywhere and all in me, I am not lost to him nor is he lost to me."

32. For all those who come to me for shelter, however weak or humble or sinful they may be — women or Vaisyas or Sudras — they all reach the Path supreme.

In the strict Vedic tradition as it later developed, no woman or person of a lower caste could attain *moksha*. One had first to obtain birth as a man. But in the *bhakti* movement of devotion to a personal God, all this was changed and the *bhakti* cults opened themselves to women and to lower castes. Shankara said that you cannot attain final liberation until you get a male birth but the *Gita* offers *moksha* to all devout souls, whether male or female, of high or low caste. In most of the *bhakti* cults there are low caste people who are devotees and saints, but unfortunately they all tend to close in again and become once more a separate caste.

33. How much more the holy Brahmins and the royal saints who love me! Having come to this world of sorrow, which is transient, love thou me.

We notice here what is very strong in Ramakrishna. He wants everybody to love God and worship God but there tends to be a negative attitude to the world. There is no sense that by work, by serving, one is loving God in the world and changing the world through work in the world. This latter motivation has become so strong today that even the *Gita* is not fully satisfying to many people. It is the same in many contemporary Christian circles where it is held that an unworldly spirituality is inadequate and that one must serve God by working in the world. By that involvement one's love is more effective than if one retires from the world. Even a very deep and beautiful devotion may still be considered defective and incomplete unless there is also as real concern and awareness of the needs of the world.

34. Give me thy mind and give me thy heart, give me thy offerings and thy adoration; and thus with thy soul in harmony and making me thy goal supreme, thou shalt in truth come to me.

This last verse marks the culmination of bhakti. "Set your mind on me, be devoted to me, sacrifice to me, do your *namaskaras* to me." *Namaskara* means bowed, prostrated, but that is too weak; it is an act of adoration, a prostration before the Supreme Reality.

The Yoga of The Pervading Forms

The essential teaching of the *Gita* is that Krishna, the personal, incarnate God, is identified with Brahman, the Origin, the One Reality. Chapter 10 begins with this identification where, in the third sloka, Krishna identifies himself with the beginningless source of all, to know whom is to be transformed and liberated.

Krishna is speaking:

1. Hear again mighty Arjuna, hear the glory of my Word again. I speak for thy true good, because thy heart finds joy in me.

This glory is literally his 'highest Word', *parama vac.* It consists of the revelation of the personal God who is known only to those who find their joy in him.

2. The hosts of the gods know not my birth, nor the great seers on earth, for all the gods come from me, and all the great seers, all.

Even the 'gods', the highest intelligences, which in Christian tradition are known as the angels, and the 'seers', the wisest among men, cannot comprehend the supreme Being.

3. He who knows I am beginningless, unborn, the Lord of all the worlds, this mortal is free from delusion, and from all evils he is free.

The highest knowledge is of the 'beginningless, unborn Lord' which brings freedom from sin and delusion, that is, which transforms the person. "From all evils he is free" is a better translation than "freed from all their sins" (B & D). Papa does mean sin, but it also means evil and thus, as Zaehner says, "It means both the evil we do and the evil we suffer." It is the whole of evil, not simply sin.
Krishna then describes the qualities that come from him.

4. Intelligence, spiritual vision, victory over delusion, patient

5. forgiveness, truth, self-harmony, peacefulness, joys and sorrows, to be and not to be, fear and freedom from fear, harmlessness and non-violence, an ever-quietness, satisfaction, simple austerity, generosity, honour and dishonour: these are the conditions of mortals and they all arise from me.

Buddhi is intelligence; *jnana*, wisdom; *asammoha*, freedom from delusion; *ksama* is translated by Zaehner as long suffering but others translate as forgiveness; *satya*, truth; *dama*, restraint or self restraint; and *sama* which is from the same root as sameness and means equanimity or tranquility. Then *sukha* and *dubkha*, pleasure and pain; *bhava* and *abhava*, coming to be and ceasing to be; and fear and fearlessness, *bhaya* and *abaya*. Krishna is the source of all, both of positive and negative qualities. Then he goes on with the list: *ahimsa*, refusal to do harm; *samata*, which is the same as *sama*, equanimity; *tushti*, content; *tapas*, austerity, discipline; *dana*, gifts or charity; and *yasah* and *ayasah*, honour and dishonour.
"Such are the dispositions of the *bhuta*, or the creatures, and they all come from the Lord." The *Gita* is showing that the Lord is the source of everything; the whole creation and all human powers and capacities, all are present in Him.

6. The seven seers of times immemorial, and the four founders of the human race, being in me, came from my mind; and from them came this world of men.

Here we have a reference to the seven seers, the *sapta rishis*, and then the four Manus. Sri Krishna Prem gives an illuminating commentary on this. He says that the seven *rishis* are the seven great lights which represent the planes of being. There are said to be seven planes of being or consciousness. The word *rishi* means also a light or a ray and it is in this latter sense that the word has been used here. As so often, the ambiguity of the Sanskrit has been used to symbolise abstract thought in personal forms. The seven planes of being are represented by the seven *chakras*. The lowest level is the physical, the *muladhara chakra*; then comes the vital level, the *svadhistana*; then the navel, the *manipura*, which is the emotional level; then the heart, the *anahata*, the affective level; the throat, the *visuddha*, which is the source of speech, of song and communication; then the *ajna chakra*, the seat of the *buddhi* or intuitive mind; and finally the *sahasrara*, the thousand-petalled lotus, the supreme consciousness.

Another scheme is that of the Sankhya which begins with *purusha*, pure consciousness, the Unmanifest Self; then comes *prakriti*, unmanifest nature, nature as potentiality. Next is the *mahat*, the cosmic order, or cosmic consciousness; then the *buddhi* or intuitive mind; the *manas*, the rational mind; then the world of the senses, and finally the world of matter.

Krishna Prem interprets the seven seers and the four *manus* in this way:

> The seven great Lights are the planes of being. These seven Lights or planes are here divided into three main classes. First come the 'previous four', the four high levels of being (two of them 'unmanifest') beyond all individuation. These have been symbolised as four eternal, chaste ascetic youths, the four 'Kumaras', who refused to create offspring, preferring to remain in contemplation of the One. The truth behind this symbol is that these four planes are planes of unity in which the separate individualities have not yet been formed.
>
> Below these come the 'Manus', here the separate individuals (*jivas*), the 'points of view' within the all-seeing Light. From them, the age-enduring points issued 'this race of men', dying and being born on endless wheels of change.
>
> The Manus are the central or, as it were, neutral points of the whole manifold creation; on them as on a pivot all is balanced. The two higher levels (for we can leave aside the 'unmanifested' two as no part of the manifested cosmos) are mainly inward turned, so to speak, centripetal, and hence are symbolised as chaste ascetics. The lowest two, the changing worlds of beings, are outward turned or centrifugal in their tendency, while between both, as points of equilibrium, are

found 'The Manus', standing firmly in themselves. Of them, of 'through' them, come the changing beings, the sons of 'Manu' known as 'Manavas' (men).

This is a symbolic interpretation. The more general one is that the *manus* are the four races of man which correspond to the four *yugas*, the four ages — the golden, the silver, the bronze and the iron ages. The age in which we are living now is the iron age, very suitably represented as an iron age of industrialism.

7. He who knows my glory and power, he has the oneness of unwavering harmony. This is my truth.

My glory is my *vibhuti*. *Vibhuti* is the power of pervading everything. God pervades everything by his *vibhuti*, which corresponds with the 'glory' or manifestation of his power. The word for power here is 'yoga', of which Zaehner says, "God's yoga in the universe is like the yoga conducted by the 'buddhi', the 'soul' in man. It is the orderly integration of all things about their immortal centre. To take the analogy a stage further, it might be said that God's 'Far flung power' (Vibhuti) corresponds to the senses in man: He controls and integrates it into an orderly and unitary whole just as the soul co-ordinates and integrates the senses into and around the immortal self. This play on the word 'yoga' is not only exceedingly subtle, but also throws a flood of light on to the central philosophy of the Gita — the ultimate inseparablity of eternal being from existence in time, and the inter-dependence of man's integration of himself and the cosmic integration around him and in God."

8. I am the One source of all: the evolution of all comes from me. The wise think this and they worship me in adoration of love.

The word for love here is *bhava* which means simply being, but it is used here in the sense of affection. This is what Ramakrishna commonly experienced, the state below *samadhi*, complete absorption, but above the ordinary state of mind. It is a state of adoration. So Krishna says that those who know me as the source of all, they *bhajante*, devote themselves, they commune with me in *bhakti*, in love or devotion.

It is conspicuous that the early chapters were much more concerned with the yoga of work and how to reach that still state of Brahman, the *nirvana* of Brahman, where one is fully integrated and realises the Self. All those stages are valid: the yoga of work, the gradual integration of the being, the discovery of the self within and realising that self in inner harmony and perfect tranquility. But now we go beyond that to worship, love, rapture and ecstasy.

9. Their thoughts are on me, their life is in me, and they give light to each other. Forever they speak of my glory; and they find peace and joy.

Their thoughts are on me, *madgataprana*, literally their life has gone to me, and they are "enlightening one another", "they tell my story". The word here is *katha* and it refers to the kind of story which is very popular in villages all over India. People go around telling the story of the *Ramayana* or the *Puranas*. It is usually done with singing so that they tell the story, then they have a song illustrating it, and so on. One can hear this even now in many villages and some Christians have taken it up. There was one very talented Christian who composed the life of St. Anthony in this way. He would tell the story accompanied by musical instruments and then all the people would burst into song.

Katha kali is a form of this, popular in Kerala. The story is told in dance and there are no words. I attended a performance once in a village in Kerala where the drama went on all night from six in the evening to six in the morning. People came and went, others went to sleep but the dance went on. The actors' faces were painted in the form of a mask and the story was told by means of wonderfully elaborate gestures called *mudras*. It was all highly stylised, as were the costumes and the figures of the gods and demons. The main dance went on for a long time and then a little girl of about fourteen danced the story of Krishna. The story is that when he was a baby his uncle wanted to kill him so Krishna was put out to a nurse who put poison in her breast. Krishna drank the poison but it did not affect him and he went on to drink all her milk and then he began to drink all her blood. The girl was dancing this, holding the child at her breast and gradualy getting exhausted as her blood was all being sucked away until finally she collapsed. The child danced it superbly and it made a tremendous impression on me.

10. To those who are ever in harmony, and who worship me with their love, I give the Yoga of vision and with this they come to me.

To those who are always *yukta*, integrated, and *bhajatam*, devoted to me, I give the yoga of the *buddhi*, the inner mind, the intuitive mind. And they draw near to me, they come to me.

11. In my mercy I dwell in their hearts and I dispel their darkness of ignorance by the light of the lamp of wisdom.

I dispel the darkness, the ignorance, the *ajnana*, with the shining lamp of wisdom, *jnana*. And then a rather difficult phrase: "I dwell in their hearts." Literally, it is *atma bhava stho*, which means "abiding in the state of being peculiar to the Self" (Z). Besant and Das translate it as "dwelling within their Self", and that is probably the meaning.

Krishna the Lord dwells in the self of that person. That means that he is dwelling also in his own nature because in the inner self we are one with the self of the Lord. When we reach the deepest centre of being, we reach our centre in God, and God is in us and we are in God. That is the goal.

Arjuna now responds to Krishna:

12. Supreme Brahman, Light supreme, and supreme purification, Spirit divine eternal, unborn God from the beginning, omnipresent Lord of all.

Arjuna addresses Krishna as *param Brahma*, supreme Brahman. As we have said, there is in the earliest stage of the *Upanishads* the idea of Brahman, the absolute Supreme Being, from which everything comes, which pervades everything and to which everything returns. Brahman is the Ultimate Reality. This Ultimate Reality is seen also as the Atman, the source of consciousness, the source of personality in the person, and so each one of us in his deepest self is one with that Brahman. Now this Brahman, this Atman, is one with the Lord, the personal God, *Purusha*. So Arjuna calls him first *Param dhama* which means highest home, highest abode, and then supreme purity, *pavitram*. The word which Mascaró translates Spirit is *Purusha*. Purusha is the primeval Person who appears in the *Rig Veda* as the Cosmic Man, from whose sacrifice the whole creation comes into being. He himself is the Person in whom the whole creation stands, as it were, but at the same time he is also above the whole creation. So in the *Rig Veda* it says, "With one fourth he entered creation, three forths remained above in heaven". So this *Purusha* is the heavenly man.

This is very interesting from the Christian point of view as it is akin to the concept of the Son of Man who is also Son of God. Krishna is here conceived as this eternal *Purusha*, in whom the whole universe stands and who at the same time transcends it.

Diviyam adi-devam is literally the divine, primeval God. The word *adi* is used of the first person in line of descent. For instance, in the Shankara school all the heads of the school are called 'Shankaracharya' but the founder of the school, the original Shankara is referred to as '*Adi-Shankara*'. In the same way, *Adi*-devam is the primeval god, the god before the gods. *Ajam* means unborn and *vibhum*, pervading everything.

13. Thus all the seers praised thee; the seer divine Narada; Asita, Devala and Vyasa. And this is now thy revelation.

Vyasa is the supposed author of the *Mahabharata*, Narada is the great rishi to whom the Narada sutras were attributed. They are a supreme expression of the way of love.

14. I have faith in all thy words, because these words are words of truth, and neither the gods in heaven nor the demons in hell can grasp thy infinite vastness.

The gods and demons are the *devas* and the *danavas*. In every religious tradition there are always the good and the evil powers, known in Hinduism as the *devas* and the *asuras* or *danayas*, just as in the Christian tradition there are the good and the evil angels. The Hebrew prophets came to think of the gods of the heathens as demons, but at an earlier stage they were reckoned among the gods. In the Book of Job, Satan appears among the 'sons of God'. The Greek Fathers speak of the angels as presiding both over the world of nature and over the nations. Origen in particular, in the third century, speaks of all the nations having their good angels protecting them and also the bad angels who lead them into error. It is said that every human being also has a bad angel as well as a good one, one helping and one hindering all the time. This takes place in this psychic world, the world of the unconscious, which we very often ignore, but whether we acknowledge it or not we are all constantly exposed to its forces.

15. Only thy Spirit knows thy Spirit: only thou knowest thyself. Source of Being in all beings, God of gods, ruler of all.

Literally it is, "Thou thyself knowest thyself by thyself." This verse is addressed to the Supreme Person, *Purushottama*, the Supreme *Purusha*. He alone knows himself, for his being is itself pure consciousness. "Source of beings", literally 'one who causes beings to become'. In the sanctuary of the chapel in our ashram we have a quotation from the *Mahanarayana Upanishad*, which says, "You are alone the supreme being; there is no other Lord of the World," followed by the words Kurios Christus in Greek letters – the Lord Christ. Here in the *Gita* Krishna is identified with the Supreme Being, the "god of gods and ruler of the world". In Christian tradition this Person is identified with Christ.

16. Tell me in thy mercy of thy divine glory wherein thou art ever, and all the worlds are.

"Tell me of thy glory," that is, the *atma vibhuti*, "the pervading power of yourself by which you pervade all the world while yourself standing unchanged" (Z). The Lord remains ever unchanged while he pervades all the world.

17. For ever in meditation, how shall I ever know thee? And in what manifestations shall I think of thee, my Lord?

In the text Arjuna addresses Krishna as a Yogi because he controls the whole universe. The yogi controls himself, and Krishna, who is the Self of the whole creation, is the great Yogi controlling the universe. Arjuna asks how he is to know God and under what aspect should he think of him. This is always the problem – we cannot know God in himself; we have always to think of him under one aspect or another.

18. Speak to me again in full of thy power and of thy glory, for I am never tired, never, of hearing thy words of life.

Tell me again of this *yogam vibhutim*, this all-pervading power, for I can never have enough of hearing it.

Krishna responds to Arjuna's request and we have this wonderful description of his powers and of how he pervades the universe.

19. Listen and I shall reveal to thee some manifestations of my divine glory. Only the greatest, Arjuna, for there is no end to my infinite greatness.

20. I am the soul, prince victorious, which dwells in the heart of all things. I am the beginning, the middle, and the end of all that lives.

"I am self, established in the heart of all beings" (Z). That is the point. When one comes to the heart of any created thing, one comes to God. Take anything, a grain of sand for instance, and analyse it into molecules and atoms, protons and electrons, but at the end one comes to the source of being. The Lord is at the centre of every being, every grain of sand. The one Lord pervades the whole creation. In Christian terms the Holy Trinity is present in every grain of sand.

"I am the beginning, the middle and the end of all." This reminds one of the words of Jesus in the Revelation of St. John where Jesus says, "I am the alpha and the omega, the first and the last" (Rev. 1:8). Alpha and omega are the first and last letters of the Greek alphabet. The Lord comprehends all speech, all language, all meaning in himself.

21. Among the sons of light I am Vishnu, and of luminaries the radiant sun. I am the lord of the winds and storms, and of the lights in the night I am the moon.

Krishna now reveals himself in terms of the Vedic mythology. We must always remember that we can only speak of God in symbolic language and the Vedas are rich in such symbolism. "Among the sons of light I am Vishnu, and of luminaries, the radiant sun." The sons of light are the Adityas, *aditi* meaning the infinite, the primeval mother, and the Adityas are all her sons, the sons of God, we could say. Here Krishna speaks simply of Vishnu as one of the sons of light. Krishna is an incarnation of Vishnu, who in the course of time was raised to be the highest God. A little later in the *Gita* he speaks of Shiva as among the Rudras, while later Shiva also was recognised as the Supreme God. This shows how the myth undergoes a gradual evolution. "The winds and storms" are the Maruts, a group of storm gods associated with lightning and thunder which have little place in modern Hinduism.

22. Of the Vedas I am the Veda of songs, and I am Indra, the chief of the gods. Above man's senses I am the mind, and in all living beings I am the light of consciousness.

There are four *Vedas*, the *Rig*, the *Sama*, the *Yajur* and the *Atharva*. The *Sama Veda* is the one that is chanted at the sacrifice which Krishna proclaims to be the most excellent of all. "I am Indra amongst the gods." Indra was the king of the gods. In the *Vedas* he was supreme but in modern India he has no place at all. There are no temples dedicated to him. The Vedic gods have almost disappeared while Brahma, Vishnu and Shiva have become the three principal gods regarded as the creator, preserver and destroyer of the world. There is now only one temple of Brahma in the whole of India, at Pushkar in the north, while as for Vishnu and Shiva, almost every village in India has a Vishnu and a Shiva temple. In a Brahmin street there is often a Vishnu temple at one end and a Shiva temple at the other. It was at the time of the *Mahabharata* that Vishnu and Shiva came to be recognised as supreme.

"Of the senses I am the manas." The *manas*, the mind, is considered the sixth sense, the common sense. The five senses bring us information from the world around us, while the *manas* is the inner sense which co-ordinates all the evidence of the senses.

"Among *bhutas*", which Mascaró translates as 'all living beings', "I am the light of consciousness." That is the *cetana* from the root *cit*, the ordinary word for consciousness.

23. Among the terrible powers I am the god of destruction; and among monsters Vittesa, the lord of wealth. Of radiant spirits I am fire; and among high mountains the mountain of the gods.

Literally it is "among the Rudras I am Shiva." The Rudras is another name for the *asuras* or demons. In the *Vedas* Shiva is known as Rudra. He was originally a non-Vedic God. He was a god of the wilds and the forests. There are the gods who belong to the cosmic order and Vishnu particularly was the god of this world, often identified with the sun, who is the source of light. Shiva originally was the god of the wilds, the god of the graveyards and of darkness, a terrible deity who had to be propitiated. He was dark in colour, that is, he was identified with the non-Aryans. Then, since he was to be feared, he had to be propitiated and he was given names signifying kindness. Shiva means the auspicious. So this dark and terrible god came to be called Shiva, the auspicious, the kindly one, and gradually his nature was transformed. He was the destroyer, but he was the destroyer who also saves, redeems and recreates.

The meaning of these gods is that they are symbols, archetypes of the unconscious. They often had completely opposing characteristics but the opposites were all brought together into unity. The gods focus in themselves the whole creation with all its conflicting elements. Through meditating on them, people could relate themselves to all the conflicting forces in life. So Shiva is both terrible and infinitely loving and compassionate. In this he is like Kali who is the goddess of destruction but also the divine mother who is depicted as Shiva's spouse, his divine energy or Shakti.

"Among monsters I am Vittesa, the lord of wealth." Zaehner has a note on this, that "Kuvera, the king of the underworld, who very closely resembles the Greek god Pluto, is also Lord of wealth." The Vedic gods were akin to the Greek gods and share in a common Aryan inheritance. "Among the Vasus", a group of deities originally associated with Indra, "I am fire." In the *Upanishads* the Vasus are spoken of as earth, air, wind, fire, atmosphere, sky, moon and stars — Fire is one of them.

"Among high mountains, Mount Meru." Mount Meru is the mythical mountain which is really the symbol of the whole universe. It is identified with Mount Kailasa in the Himalayas. Mascaró translates this the "mountain of the gods" and it is like Mount Olympus for the Greeks. The mountain has always been an appropriate symbol of the abode of the gods. The mountain is the place where one can come nearest to God. The idea is that as one ascends one rises out of the dust and obscurity of the earth into the clear atmosphere. People feel this as they ascend an ordinary mountain; the mind becomes elevated, and one is nearer to the light. So the mountain is the symbol of the whole creation and the top of the mountain is the point where one reaches to heaven.

24. Of priests I am the divine priest Brihaspati, and among warriors Skanda, the god of war. Of lakes I am the vast ocean.

Skanda is a fascinating figure. He is the son of Shiva and is the lord of armies, as Yahweh in the Old Testament was called 'lord of hosts'. He is also identified with Murugan, a local Tamil god, young and beautiful, and most popular throughout Tamil Nadu.

25. Among great seers I am Bhrigu; and of words I am OM, the Word of Eternity. Of prayers I am the prayer of silence; and of things that move not I am the Himalayas.

The OM is the sacred syllable, the *pranava*, which signifies the supreme reality. It represents the vibration of energy from which the whole universe comes. There is the *anahata shabda*, the unheard sound from which comes the sound which is heard. OM is the sound through which we pass to the sound that cannot be heard, the word which is spoken which leads to the Word from which all words come.

"Of prayers, I am the prayer of silence." The reference here is to the *japa*, the silent prayer which is more potent than external prayer. That is a point which is often emphasised by Hindus. When they do a *puja* they perform the external rite, but strictly speaking, there is a *manasa puja* which is performed in the mind and only then is the external offering really effective. The inner offering is 'the silent prayer'. This also applies to *nama japa*, where the name of God can first be repeated aloud, then silently within and then it goes deep into the heart. It is this that is the prayer of the heart, the deepest prayer, the prayer of silence.

26. Of trees I am the tree of life, and of heavenly seers Narada. Among celestial musicians, Chitra-ratha; and among seers on earth, Kapila.

Mascaró translates it as, "I am the tree of life" but strictly, it is the *asvatta* tree, that is the holy fig tree, the banyan, which is the tree of enlightenment.

27. Of horses I am the horse of Indra, and of elephants his elephant Airavata. Among men I am king of men.

28. Of weapons I am the thunderbolt, and of cows the cow of wonder. Among creators I am the creator of love; and among serpents the serpent of Eternity.

"Of weapons I am the thunderbolt." The thunderbolt was the symbol of divine power. It is found in Greek mythology as the thunderbolt of Zeus, the symbol of divine justice, and in the Old Testament Yahweh was the God of thunder, who is described as "breaking in pieces the cedars and stripping the forest bare" (Ps. 28). In Tibetan Buddhism, this thunderbolt, the *vajra* is the force of spiritual power. The *vajra* is compared to a diamond and Tibetan buddhists speak of a 'diamond body' which is a body that has been transformed by the hidden power within.

"And of cows, the cow of wonder," that is what is called the Kamadhenu, the cow who grants all desires.

29.   Among the snakes of mystery I am Ananta, and of those born in the
       waters I am Varuna, their lord. Of the spirits of the fathers I am
       Aryaman, and of rulers Yama, the ruler of death.

"Amongst snakes of mystery I am Ananta." Ananta is the great serpent on which Vishnu rests. It means literally the 'infinite' and symbolises the infinite ocean of being.

"And of water dwellers I am Varuna." Varuna was one of the principal gods of the *Vedas* but has now disappeared. Some people think that his name is connected with Ouranos, the Greek heaven, the god of heaven, the sky, but he is also very much connected with the waters. Here he is considered the God of the waters.

"Of spirits of the Fathers" refers to the ancestors, the *pitras*. Each month every pious Hindu offers sacrifice to the *pitras*, the ancestors, the fathers. And of course, with the Chinese, ancestor worship was almost the basis of their religion. There is something very profound about the sense of belonging to the ancestors. In more primitive cultures, in Africa for instance, the people frequently dream of their ancestors or shades. In Africa the shades are considered as living in the village and it is very important for the people to perform the proper funeral rites so that the shades return to the right place and become the continuous protectors of the village. It is also important to perform particular sacrifices and other rites at appropriate times to retain the favour of the shades. The shades of the ancestors also appear in dreams. Confucius once said, "Something must be wrong with me. It is several months since I dreamt of the Emperor Chu." The Emperor Chu was a very holy emperor and to dream of him was a most auspicious event. This sense of the presence of the dead is something that we have largely lost. The meaning of all those masses for the dead which Catholics used to celebrate was connected with this for they formed a link with the past, with the dead. The dead are among the living; they are only in a different region of being.

"And of the rulers, I am Yama, the god of death." He is the judge, the inner judge. Yama really represents the inner Self which is the judge at the hour of death, and also the inner guide and initiator into spiritual life.

30. Of demons I am Prahlada their prince, and of all things that measure I am time. Of beasts I am the king of beasts, and of birds Vainateya who carries a god.

"Of demons I am Prahlada". The 'demons' here are the *daityas*, rather like the Titans among the Greeks, the enemies of the gods. Prahlada had a deep devotion to Vishnu and his father tried to kill him by every means but he always escaped and was eventually granted immortality. Prahlada is the archetypal devotee.

"And of all things that measure I am time." He is time and time can be a terrible thing bringing death and destruction, though it is also the source of a creative energy and achievement. God is present continuously. Every moment which is given us is a gift of God. He is present in every moment. The danger is that we tend to accept things as they appear. Now it is three o'clock, then it is four, then it is five — just a passage of time without significance. But we do not recall that God is coming into our lives in a particular way at three o'clock and in another way at four, another at five. Every moment of time is the coming of God into our lives. Everything is a coming of God. Every person we meet is a coming of God and every breath of wind a coming of God. God is manifest in everything.

"I am the king of beasts," that is the lion, and of birds, Vainateya or Garuda, the eagle.

31. Among things of purification I am the wind, and among warriors I am Rama, the hero supreme. Of fishes in the sea I am Makara the wonderful, and among all rivers the holy Ganges.

This Rama is not the hero of the great epic, the Ramayana, who is a model of righteousness (*dharma*), but Parasurama, Rama of the axe, a great warrior. "Of fishes in the sea, I am Makara," the shark, "and among all rivers, the holy Ganges." The Ganges is, of course, the holy river of India. It comes down from the Himalayas and brings life to all in the plains. Every Hindu desires to die by the Ganges, so that he may be purified by its waters.

32. I am the beginning and the middle and the end of all that is. Of all

knowledge I am the knowledge of the Soul. Of the many paths of reason I am the one that leads to Truth.

Of all knowledge I am the knowledge of the Self, the supreme knowledge. There is a knowledge of physics and chemistry, a knowledge of biology, and a knowledge of psychology and metaphysics, but all these are the lower levels of knowledge. The highest knowledge one can have is the knowledge of the Atman, the Spirit, the Self, and that cannot be had by any academic learning at all but only by Self-realization, by experience of the Spirit within. The highest knowledge is this experiential knowledge, this wisdom.

"Of the many paths of reason, I am the one that leads to truth." This seems to be a mistranslation. The correct translation is: "Among those who speak I am their speech." God speaks through us. We cannot speak without God. We cannot do anything by ourselves. Everything is the work of the one Spirit. The Lord is acting in you and in me. If I move my hand it is he who is moving my hand and I cannot move it without him.

33. Of sounds I am the first sound, A; of compounds I am coordination. I am time, never-ending time. I am the Creator who sees all.

"Of sounds, I am the first sound, A." This idea is found in the Tirukural, the Tamil classic which was composed about the first century AD, and consists of poetic couplets in the form of aphorisms. It is a book of wisdom akin to the book of Proverbs, and of special interest because the Tamil culture is quite different from the Vedic. It is very much more 'this-wordly' and is concerned with love and war rather than with God and the spiritual life. In the *Tirukurals* first chapter it says that as A is the first letter of the alphabet, so God is the first of all. But in the rest of the poem very little is said about God. It is concerned with the duties of the family and the state, and the last chapter is all about love. It is a 'this-wordly' morality which is rare in India. But it is true to the ancient Indian tradition which recognised four 'ends' of life: *kama*, love; *artha*, wealth; *dharma*, duty and *moksha*, liberation. The Tirukural deals with the first three but it does not touch on *moksha* which is the principal concern in the Hindu tradition. *Moksha* is liberation, the final state of being, beyond this world.

34. I am death that carries off all things, and I am the source of things

to come. Of feminine nouns I am Fame and Prosperity; Speech, Memory and Intelligence; Constancy and patient Forgiveness.

"I am death that carries off all things, and I am the source of things to come." This is a kind of negative aspect of God. God is manifested in this whole creation in every part of it and he is manifested in death no less than in life. But we have to discern exactly what that means. Akin to this is "I am the cleverness in the gambler's dice" (sloka 36), which probably refers to Yudhishthira and the famous game of dice in which he lost his throne and had to go into exile. This suggests that God is in the wicked as well as in the good, but this is probably not the intention there for if we look into it we see that it is rather the excellence in everything, the cleverness, the intelligence of the gambler that comes from God and not the vice.

This raises the problem of evil and the providence of God. We can put it in this way. The one light, the one Sun, is shining upon all creatures as into so many different mirrors, each reflecting that light according to its capacity. But there are defects in all nature and each created thing reflects the divine light in a very limited way. The divine being, the infinite, is limited in its effects by all these finite beings in which it shines. In the inanimate world there is no life, and the Spirit manifests as light and energy. When the earth is sufficiently evolved to produce life, then life emerges and the divine manifests as life on earth. When the living thing is sufficiently organised to produce the animal, then God manifests in sensation, in movement, in reproduction. And then when the animal life is sufficiently organised for human beings to appear, the divine manifests in the human soul and consciousness.

Obviously there are defects in all nature. All matter is limited and is subject to corruption and death, but this is due to the limitations of finite being, the limitations of the matter in which the divine life is manifested. All that is positive in nature, in the earth, in plant, in animal and man, comes from God; all that is negative is the defect of the created, of the finite being. The light is shining in the darkness and the darkness limits it. And then with the human being there appears sin, moral evil, and that makes a further difference. Whereas the plant and animal respond to the divine life instinctively and naturally and it produces its natural effects, in the human being there is an intelligence and a will and that intelligence can reflect the light but it can also refuse to accept the light. There is a freedom in the will. We can withdraw our will from the light and centre it on ourselves, or on the external world, and then we no longer reflect that light. Evil is simply the negative element in us which cannot affect the light in itself, and the more we open ourselves to virtue, to grace, the more that light shines in us and purifies us so that we become transparent to the light.

35. I am the Brihat songs of all songs in the Vedas. I am the Gayatri of all measures in verse. Of months I am the first of the year, and of the seasons the season of flowers.

The *Sama Veda*, the Veda of Songs, was considered the best of the Vedas, and the *Brihat Sama* was the best portion of that. "I am the Gayatri of all measures in verse." The Gayatri mantra is the most sacred verse mantra in the *Vedas*. In our ashram in India we chant it three times at the beginning of each prayer:

OM BHUR BHUVAS SVAHA
TAT SAVITUR *VARENYAM*
BARGO DEVASYA DHIMAHI
DHIYO YO NAH PRACHODAYAT

Savitri is a name for the sun, not merely the physical sun, but the sun as the source of life and of light. This Gayatri mantra is given to every Brahmin during his initiation at the Upanayana ceremony when he receives the sacred thread. From that time he is supposed to recite it regularly, one hundred and eight times at morning, noon and night. The Gayatri mantra can be translated: "Let us meditate on the splendour of that glorious light; may he illumine our mediation." It is asking for light in the mind, not merely for light from the sun.

"Of seasons I am the season of flowers"; that is the month of Margari which coresponds more or less with December and is a very holy month. The tradition is that in this month the unmarried girls are supposed to rise very early and to go around the village singing songs. In Tamil Nadu particularly they sing the songs of Andal, the woman poet, and those of Manika Vasahar addressed to God as a bridegroom, to whom they are the bride. It is a very sacred month for Hindus.

36. I am the cleverness in the gambler's dice. I am the beauty of all things beautiful. I am victory and the struggle for victory. I am the goodness of those who are good.

37. Of the children of Vrishni I am Krishna; and of the sons of Pandu I am Arjuna. Among Seers in silence I am Vyasa; and among poets the poet Usana.

Literally it is: 'of the children of Vrishni I am Vasudeva,' Krishna was said to be the son of Vasudeva, but was later identified with him. In the *Gita* he is identified with the one supreme Reality.

Vyasa is the legendary author of the *Mahabharata*, to whom the arrangement of the *Vedas* was also attributed, somewhat as Moses was considered the author of the Hebrew Torah.

38. I am the sceptre of the rulers of men; and I am the policy of those who seek victory. I am the silence of hidden mysteries; and I am the knowledge of those who know.

In these verses Krishna identifies himself with all that is good and beautiful in the world, as well as with the heroes of the *Mahabharata* and finally with the supreme knowledge of the *jnani*.

39. And know, Arjuna, that I am the seed of all things that are; and that no being that moves or moves not can ever be without me.

Having described his various particular manifestations, he identifies himself with the source of all. He is the creative power which rules and upholds the whole world.

40. There is no end of my divine greatness, Arjuna. What I have spoken here to thee shows only a small part of my Infinity.

And yet all that is manifest in this world and in the creative power of God is but a small portion of his greatness. God himself remains infinitely beyond all manifestations of his being.

41. Know that whatever is beautiful and good, whatever has glory and power is only a portion of my own radiance.

42. But of what help is it to know this diversity? Know that with one single fraction of my Being I pervade and support the Universe, and know that I AM.

That is the perspective. The whole vast universe, the stellar universe and the galaxies and this whole earth, is only a minute portion in which the Godhead is manifesting. It is like the famous incident in Julian of Norwich's *Revelations of Divine Love*, when she saw in her hand a little object the size of a hazel nut and when she asked what this was, she was told, "This is all that is." The whole creation is like this little hazel nut in the palm of one's hand.

It is important to keep this perspective because we tend to think that the universe is so vast, particularly in terms of modern astronomy. Pascal said that all the material universe is nothing compared to a single thought, and all the thoughts in the world are not the equivalent in value to a single act of charity. Those are the real values. Matter is the lowest level of reality; thought is a somewhat higher level and charity, love, or the Spirit, is the only real value in which everything is ultimately contained. We have exactly the reverse conception in our modern view where spirit is something infinitely remote and unreal, thought is very important, but matter is the supreme reality.

Chapter 11

The Yoga of the Vision of the Cosmic Form

In this chapter Krishna reveals his manifest form. In a sense this is very wonderful but let us not forget that it is only a kind of *maya*. Krishna is only manifesting what appears; the reality is always beyond the appearance and it is the reality that we are seeking. That is why, although Zaehner says that this chapter is the culmination of the *Gita*, Krishna Prem points out that it is not so at all. To know the manifest universe or God in the manifest universe is not the goal at all. We want to get beyond the manifest universe and to know God in himself. So this is a stage on the way, and an important stage which, as we shall see at the end of the chapter, brings some problems with it. For one thing, there is evil as well as good in the universe and how to relate the two is a difficult matter.

Arjuna begins by asking Krishna to reveal his glory.

1. In thy mercy thou hast told me the secret supreme of thy Spirit, and thy words have dispelled my delusion.

"Thy Spirit" is not quite accurate; the Sanskrit term is the *adhyatman*, which means the secret 'concerning the Self'. At the beginning of the *Gita* Arjuna is about to engage in the battle when Krishna comes to counsel him. The first thing Krishna says is that one must raise one's mind above the battle, the sphere of conflict in the world, and discover the Atman, the Self, the true reality which is beyond the sphere of conflict. Then it will be possible to face one's task in life.

2. I have heard in full from thee of the coming and going of beings, and also of thy infinite greatness.

"Thy infinite greatness" is *mahatmya*. This refers to the mahat, the great Self. There is the lower self, which consists of the physical world, the vital world and the mental world. Above this is the *mahat*, the great Self, or the cosmic order, but that is still the manifest world. Beyond that is the true Self, the *Paramatman*.

3. I have heard thy words of truth but my soul is yearning to see: to see thy form as God of this all.

It has been said that when people came to Ramikrishna they would ask, "Can you see God?" He would reply, "Yes, I have seen him many times." And then he would add, "You cannot see him with these eyes, of course." One must have what Krishna here calls the *divyam chakshuh*, the Divine Eye. It is through the *buddhi* that this divine illumination is received; but we must always remember that any form that can be seen, any vision, is immeasurably below God.

St. John of the Cross always warns that one should not be taken in by visions or by revelations. These are only manifestations and we have always to go beyond these to the truth. That is why we must not take too seriously this sphere of manifestation whether it is the physical world or whether it is the psychic world, the world of the angels and the gods or the occult. People are easily attracted by visions and revelations, but these are not the highest reality. The danger is that if we get involved in that level of reality, we may never get beyond it.

4. If thou thinkest, O my Lord, that it can be seen by me, show me, O God of Yoga, the glory of thine own Supreme Being.

Arjuna asks to see the divine form of Krishna. He calls him the Lord of Yoga. This Yoga is the power by which God manifests Himself in the universe. Arjuna asks for a vision of this presence of God in the world and is given a vision which, like all visions, belongs to the world of psychic

appearances. Such visions have their value, like that of Yahweh on Mount Sinai, but they still belong to the world of appearances.
Krishna now reveals his divine form.

5. By hundreds and then by thousands, behold, Arjuna, my manifold celestial forms of innumerable shapes and colours.

6. Behold the gods of the sun, and those of fire and light; the gods of storm and lightning, and the two luminous charioteers of heaven. Behold, descendant of Bharata, marvels never seen before.

These are the Adityas, Rudras, Asvins, and Maruts, figures of the ancient Vedic mythology, which represent the various cosmic powers.

7. See now the whole universe with all things that move and move not, and whatever thy soul may yearn to see. See it all as One in me.

It is very important to be able to see that there is unity in the whole cosmos. It does not matter how vast the stellar universe is; behind it, underlying it, there is a unity. It is an organic whole. Scientists today recognise that the universe is an inter-dependent whole. The same idea is to be found in the concept of the mystical body of Christ. Christ is the Lord who assumes human nature and reunites human nature in himself and in reuniting human nature, he reunites the whole cosmic order in himself. He becomes the Lord, the centre of the whole. This corresponds very closely with the idea in the *Gita*. All is one in the Lord.

The question of pantheism arises here. Pantheism identifies God with the universe and maintains that there is nothing beyond. God is the universe, and the universe is God. But here the *Gita* says God manifests a very small portion of his being in the universe and extends infinitely beyond. That is the Hindu view. It is not pantheism, but pantheism which means God in all. God is immanent in the whole of creation but is not identified with it. That is also Catholic doctrine. St. Thomas says that God is in all things by his power, his presence and his essence. He distinguishes first that he is present in all things by his power, because he creates all things and it is only by the power of God that anything exists at all. Then he says that it is not as though His power is exercised at a distance since there is no distance in God. He is in all things by his actual presence, activating everything, giving it being, structuring it and then actually moving it. Again, it is not as if he were present with a part of himself, because there are no parts in God. He is present in all things by his essence; the very being of God is present in everything, activating the whole universe.

8. But thou never canst see me with these thy mortal eyes: I will give thee divine sight. Behold my wonder and glory.

That is a very famous phrase, *divyam cakshuh*, a divine eye. That is the third eye, the divine eye which sees the truth. This is the eye which is symbolised by the *ajna chakra*, the point between the eyebrows, which is held to be the centre of this inner light. In Byzantine ikons this third eye can often be seen on the face of Christ, suggesting that this symbolism may have been widespread in the ancient world. It is also the meaning of the Gospel saying, "If thine eye be single, thy whole body shall be full of light" (Mat. 6.22).

Sanjaya, who is acting as a kind of narrator, now interjects to tell of the revelation of Krishna to Arjuna:

9. When Krishna, the God of Yoga, had thus spoken, O king, he appeared then to Arjuna in his supreme divine form.

10. And Arjuna saw in that form countless visions of wonder: eyes from innumerable faces, numerous celestial ornaments, numberless heavenly weapons.

11. Celestial garlands and vestures, forms anointed with heavenly perfumes. The Infinite Divinity was facing all sides, all marvels in him containing.

The imagery is that of the Hindu gods, of course. Many people find it a bit disconcerting to see representations of the gods with many arms and legs and heads, but what it is intended to convey is this divine energy, the *vibhuti* or power of pervading all things, emanating on all sides, manifesting itself in all directions. Once one is used to the symbolism, it is very meaningful.

The idea is that behind all the forms of the universe and of man, behind the eyes, the ears, the faces, the arms, the legs, is the One who is, the one Spirit who is active through all. He faces in all directions and is manifested in every person and in every thing.

We can relate this to St. Paul's conception of Christ as the Lord who has "ascended above the heavens", so that he "fills all things" (Eph. 4.10). The whole creation becomes the *pleroma*, "the fullness of him who fills all in all" (Eph. 1.22).

12. If the light of a thousand suns suddenly arose in the sky, that splendour might be compared to the radiance of the Supreme Spirit.

13. And Arjuna saw in that radiance the whole universe in its variety, standing in a vast unity in the body of the God of gods.

Ramanuja, in his commentary on the *Gita*, develops the idea that the whole universe is the body of God. God is, as it were, the Soul, the whole universe is his body and he is the *antaryamin*, the ruler within, the Spirit who guides everything within. Just as the soul is in the body directing the bodily functions, so the Lord is in the body and the soul of every existing being. He is the ruler within. Arjuna, with his 'divine sight', sees that the whole universe is the body of the Lord.

From a Christian point of view, we can say that God, in Christ, takes on a human body and, in that human body, he is united with the whole of humanity. Humanity becomes the mystical body of Christ and, since humanity is part of the cosmic order, the whole cosmos is taken into this Body of Christ. The Lord is the heart of the whole of creation in whom all things 'hold together' (Col. 1.17). So St. Paul can say that "in him all things were created in heaven and on earth" and "all things were created through him and for him" (Col. 1.15.16). This is very close to the doctrine of the *Gita*. The difference is that in the Hindu view the universe is the body of the Lord and is thus divine by nature, and it is ignorance that has made us lose that vision, whereas in the Christian view the universe becomes the body of the Lord by grace. He redeems creation in redeeming humanity and he restores it to communion with God, thus giving it a divine character. The whole creation becomes divine in Christ and that is the ultimate goal of creation.

14. Trembling with awe and wonder, Arjuna bowed his head, and joining his hands in adoration he thus spoke to his God.

Arjuna addresses Krishna humbly and with adoration:

15. I see in thee all the gods, O my God; and the infinity of the beings of thy creation. I see god Brahma on his throne of lotus, and all the seers and serpents of light.

Brahma, with a long 'a', is masculine and is the god Brahma who must always be distinguished from Brahman. Brahman is the neuter form and signifies the infinite absolute Being itself. Brahma is a mythological figure. The story is that Vishnu is lying on the serpent Ananta which is the infinite, and at the beginning of every era a lotus issues from the navel of Vishnu. Brahma is seated on the lotus and it is he who creates the whole world. So he is only a mythological figure. He is not worshipped in India today; as was mentioned before, there is only one temple of Brahma. The Godhead used to be represented as the *trimurti*; Brahma, Vishnu and Shiva, but now Brahma has disappeared and Vishnu and Shiva are considered as figures of the Supreme God.

16. All around I behold thy Infinity: the power of thy innumerable arms, the visions from thy innumerable eyes, the words from thy innumerable mouths, and the fire of life of thy innumerable bodies. Nowhere do I see a beginning or middle or end of thee, O God of all, Form Infinite.

This is the universal form of God, the *visvarupa* – God manifest in the universe.

17. I see the splendour of an infinite beauty which illumines the whole universe. It is thee! With thy crown and sceptre and circle. How difficult thou art to see! But I see thee: as fire, as the sun, blinding, incomprehensible.

Alain Daniélou in his *Hindu Polytheism* gives the following description (p. 153):

> "In each of his hands Vishnu holds one of his four attributes. In the usual image these are in a given order.
> 'In my (lower right) hand, which represents the revolving creative tendency, I hold the conch symbol of the five elements.'
> 'In the (upper right) hand, which represents the cohesive tendency, I hold the discus (shining like an) infant (Sun), symbol of the mind.'

'In the (upper left) hand, which represents the tendency towards dispersion and liberation, I hold the bow, symbol of the causal power of illusion (from which the universe rises) and the lotus, symbol of the moving universe.'

'In my (lower left) hand, which represents the notion of individual existence, is the mace, symbol of primeval knowledge (adya vidya).' [*Gopala-uttara-tadini Upanishad 55-57* (218)]".

Now we come to some very important verses, and to a more philosophical aspect of the matter.

18. Thou art the Imperishable, the highest End of knowledge, the support of this vast universe. Thou, the everlasting ruler of the law of righteousness, the Spirit who is and who was at the beginning.

"The highest End of Knowledge", literally the highest thing to be known, the *paramam veditavyam*. The whole universe is *kshara*, the perishable, and beyond the perishable is the *akshara*, the imperishable, which, in the *Gita*, is itself divided. There is a lower imperishable, which is the universe of thought, the intelligible universe, and above that is the Supreme who rules both the perishable and the imperishable and that is the Lord Krishna. So God is this higher imperishable, the highest goal of wisdom. What we are seeking is to go beyond both the perishable and the imperishable to the Supreme.

"You are the *para nidhana* ", which means the resting place, or 'treasure house', which is the proper meaning of *nidhana*. St. Paul says of Jesus, "In him are hidden all the treasures of wisdom and knowledge" (Col. 2.3). "You are the changeless one, the guardian of the eternal law" (Z). The *sanatana dharma. Dharma* is the law which governs the whole cosmos, the stars and the elements, as well as human nature.

The function of the king is always to conserve the *dharma*. That concept has been lost in the modern world. We have given up kings and now we have chief ministers to organise economic and political life. The old idea however was that the king, the raja, represented the eternal law and it was his duty to defend and preserve it. It is a great loss when this concept disappears. We need someone who is above the economic and political sphere, who stands both for the principle of continuity and for the eternal in man. The old rajas were very impressive figures and through the many ceremonies connected with them in their relation with the temple, the mind was continually refocussed on that which is above.

The "Spirit who is and was in the beginning" is the *sanatana Purusha*, the eternal *Purusha*. So far in the *Gita* we have encountered the *Purusha* (the Person or the Man) many times. In the Muslim tradition he is called the Perfect Man. He is the archetype from which the whole of humanity, the whole of creation comes. In the *Rig Veda* he appears as the primeval man, or primeval person, in whom the whole creation and all humanity is contained. We are all one in that person and in fact the whole of humanity was believed to be one person, one Adam. This is the *Adam Kadmon* of the Jewish tradition. *Adam* simply means 'man'. So God created Man and all humanity is contained in that Man. When Adam falls, humanity falls. Each one of us was in that Adam. According to St. Paul, Jesus Christ was the second Adam. The first Man falls into darkness, into sin, and is divided, disintegrated, but he, and the whole of humanity with him, is restored to unity by the second Adam, the new Man, who may be compared with the *Purusha*. Jesus always speaks of himself as the Son of Man. In both Hebrew and Aramaic the term 'Son of Man' is equivalent to 'Man'. Thus Christ is the eternal Man who restores man to his relationship with God. So this *sanatana Purusha*, this eternal Man, is the primeval Person. There is a mystical reality here to which we all belong, and the death and resurrection of Christ is the death of that first man and his resurrection, his recreation in the 'new man' of St. Paul. "You must put away the old man and put on the new man who is created after the image of God in holiness and truth" (Eph. 4.22 and 24). That is the second Adam, the *Purusha*.

19. I see thee without beginning, middle, or end; I behold thy infinite power, the power of thy innumerable arms. I see thine eyes as the sun and the moon. And I see thy face as a sacred fire that gives light and life to the whole universe in the splendour of a vast offering.

20. Heaven and earth and all the infinite spaces are filled with thy Spirit; and before the wonder of thy fearful majesty the three worlds tremble.

These three worlds are *divah*, the heavens, *prithvya*, the earth, and *antaram*, the atmosphere between. That is the whole created universe, beyond which is the Supreme. The three worlds may also be interpreted as the physical universe, the psychic universe and the spiritual universe. In much of modern thought, however, the three worlds become reduced to two or even one of these dimensions.

21. The hosts of the gods come to thee and, joining palms in awe and wonder, praise and adore. Sages and saints come to thee, and praise thee with songs of glory.

The sages and saints are seers or *rishis* and the *siddhas*, men that is who have reached perfection. They are all filled with awe. This brings out the 'terrible' aspect of God. Rudolf Otto, in his book *The Idea of the Holy*, showed how the 'holy' or the 'sacred' or the 'numinous' reveals itself as *mysterium tremendum et fascinans*. It is a 'mystery' which is 'tremendous' — it strikes terror into us. This aspect of God as 'terrible' is biblical; for instance in the book of Job, where Job says, "Let not his terror make me afraid" (Job 9.34). We tremble before this immensity; it is an uncanny fear, the fear of the unknown. At the same time, it is *fascinans*, fascinating; it draws and attracts us like a bridegroom drawing the bride.

22. The Rudras of destruction, the Vasus of fire, the Sadhyas of prayers, the Adityas of the sun; the lesser gods Visvedevas, the two Asvins, charioteers of heaven, the Maruts of winds and storms, the Ushmapas spirits of ancestors; the celestial choirs of Gandharvas, the Yakshas keepers of wealth, the demons of hell and the Siddhas who, on earth, reached perfection: they all behold thee with awe and wonder.

These are all mythological figures but they represent the spiritual powers of the universe, the cosmic powers, and also the spirits of the ancestors, and they all worship and adore this great form.

23. But the worlds also behold thy fearful mighty form, with many mouths and eyes, with many bellies, thighs and feet, frightening with terrible teeth: they tremble in fear, and I also tremble.

This is the terrible aspect of life which presents a great problem. How do we fit this aspect of the world into our concept of God? If God is the creator of all, if he is immanent in all and if in a sense, all is God, how can we account for all this horror and terror and fear and violence? How does that fit in? In the Temple of Elephanta outside Bombay, there is a

great three-headed figure of Shiva. The front face is solemn and benign
and represents his contemplative aspect. Of the other faces one represents
his gentle aspect, the other his terrible aspect. Thus Hinduism recognises
the multi aspect of God.

24.   When I see thy vast form, reaching the sky, burning with many colours,
with wide open mouths, with vast flaming eyes, my heart shakes in
terror: my power is gone and gone is my peace, O Vishnu!

It is very dangerous to ask to see God. In the Old Testament it is said
that no one can see God and live. This aspect is brought out particularly
in the Book of Job, where Yahweh reveals the wonder of his power in all
creation, Job is overwhelmed by the revelation and cries, "I had heard of
thee by the hearing of the ear, but now mine eye seeth thee and I repent
in dust ashes" (Job 42.5,6). When we 'realise' God, we surrender ourselves.
We can no longer pass judgement. This is the realisation of the terrible
aspect of God.

25.   Like the fire at the end of Time burns all in the last day, I see thy
vast mouths and thy terrible teeth. Where am I? Where is my shelter?
Have mercy on me, God of gods, Refuge Supreme of the world!

The dissolution of all things by fire at the end of time is depicted in
the Book of Revelation and, in the second letter of Peter which was written
at much the same time, it is said that "the day of the Lord will come like
a thief and the heavens will pass away with a loud noise and the elements
will be dissolved with fire and the earth and the works that are upon it
will be burned up" (2 Pet. 3.10). That is the Christian vision of the end.
The early Christians lived constantly in that expectation of the end of the
world when everything would be consumed by fire and then the new creation
would come into being. In many traditions there is a similar vision of the
destruction of the world before the final consummation.

In the Hindu conception of the "Ten Avatars of Vishnu" the last *avatara*
is Kalki. Kalki is to come at the end of the world when the world will
be destroyed and a new age will begin. I once saw a film in which this
was depicted most dramatically. The whole world was going up in flames,
towns and villages and hills, everything collapsing in the holocaust. Then
a terrible figure with a mask and an open mouth appeared and everything

began pouring into this great mouth, all the people, animals, trees; everything was being sucked in in an endless stream. It was the end of the world when everything goes back to its source. That is the destructive aspect of God.

26. The sons of Dhrita-rashtra, all of them, with other princes of this

27. earth, and Bhishma and Drona and great Karna, and also the greatest warriors of our host, all enter rushing into thy mouths, terror-inspiring with their fearful fangs. Some are caught between them, and their heads crushed into powder.

Arjuna now sees the end of all the heroes of the *Mahabharata* who were mentioned in the first book of the *Gita*; all the great warriors are seen rushing into the mouth of Krishna.

28. As roaring torrents of waters rush forward into the ocean, so do these heroes of our mortal world rush into thy flaming mouths.

29. And as moths swiftly rushing enter a burning flame and die, so all these men rush to thy fire, rush fast to their own destruction.

30. The flames of thy mouths devour all the worlds. Thy glory fills the whole universe. But how terrible thy splendours burn!

31. Reveal thyself to me! Who art thou in this form of terror? I adore thee, O God supreme: be gracious unto me. I yearn to know thee, who art from the beginning: for I understand not thy mysterious works.

This brings us back to the question, how is all this violence and destruction to be related to the concept to God? There is infinite glory and beauty and love and also infinite evil and violence and destruction at the same time. How do we reconcile these contradictory aspects? Krishna replies:

32. I am all-powerful Time which destroys all things, and I have come here to slay these men. Even if thou dost not fight, all the warriors facing thee shall die.

There is a terrible power in the universe which is destroying people all the time. We may or may not be the instruments of this but the destruction goes on. One can recall the example of the 1914-18 war. In one battle, at Ypres, 50,000 people were killed within two or three hours. Thousands of soldiers were thrown into the battle in the face of a barrage of artillery. Even more appalling, of course, is the effect of the atom bomb on Nagasaki. It is the case, then, that people are going over to the other world by the thousands.

33. Arise therefore! Win thy glory, conquer thine enemies, and enjoy thy kingdom. Through the fate of their Karma I have doomed them to die: be thou merely the means of my work.

34. Drona, Bhishma, Jayad-ratha and Karna, and other heroic warriors of this great war have already been slain by me: tremble not, fight and slay them. Thou shalt conquer thine enemies in battle.

This is the philosophy of the *Gita.* Everyone is bound by his *karma,* the actions of past lives. You have done your deeds in the past, you are acting now, and you are reaping the fruit of all these deeds. There is an inevitable law in the universe; you sin and then judgement comes upon you. This or that person may be the instrument of your judgement, but it is ultimately the judgement of God. Fight your battle – you are a *kshatriya,* a warrior, and your duty is to fight, to overcome the powers of evil, to conquer your enemies and enjoy your kingdom. This is the work of God.

The Bible has a somewhat different view. The biblical view is that God is the God of infinite justice and that all evil and destruction comes upon men because of their sins. All this is the judgement of God. St. John has a vision on the island of Patmos, full of all the imagery of the Old Testament as this is of the Vedas, and this is how he sees it: "Then I heard a loud voice from the temple telling the seven angels to go and pour out upon the earth the seven bowls of the wrath of God. The seventh angel poured out his bowl and a great voice came from the temple saying, 'It is done.' And there were flashes of lightning, loud noises, peals of thunder, great earthquakes which have never been since men were on the earth and the city was split in three parts and the cities of the nations fell, and God remembered Babylon to make her drain the fury of his wrath" (Rev. 16:1:17-19). That is a Jewish-Christian vision of the judgement and the end of the world. It is a judgement of a righteous God on the sins of the world. Yet I do not feel that we can accept the idea that all the evil and suffering in the world is a punishment for sins, because that is not how things actually happen. In a war or any other human or natural calamity the innocent suffer with the guilty. This point of view was voiced in the Old Testament in the book of Job. All Job's comforters came to him when he was suffering from boils all over his body and lying in misery on a heap of ashes, completely abandoned, and they said, "You must have sinned: it is the Lord who is punishing you." In this view, if you sin, you suffer; if you suffer, it is because you have sinned. In the Hindu tradition it is due to your *karma*, from your past life, and all this suffering is because you have sinned in a past life. But Job says: "I have not sinned. I have not deserved this at all", and at the end Yahweh justifies Job and not his so-called comforters. Simply to say that the wicked are punished and the good are rewarded is an over-simplication. It can be valid up to a point, but it is not the final truth. On the other hand, simply to say there are two aspects of God, his wrathful and his loving aspect, does not solve it either.

There is a terrible sort of blindness in nature in the way people suffer without apparent reason. This blindness seems to belong to nature herself. There is, as experiments in quantum physics have made clear, an element of indeterminacy, of sheer chance and unpredictability at the very heart of matter. The process of evolution consists in the gradual ordering and structuring of this original chaos, but the element of chance and unpredictability still remains. When we come to human existence, man has a free will and a capacity to order his life by reason, but in most people this capacity is very limited. We are all conditioned by heredity and environment, and by the forces of the unconscious which prevent our acting freely. Christian tradition attributes this to 'original sin', which is a sin or disorder in the very nature of man, while Hindu tradition attributes it to *karma*, the effects of actions in this and past lives. But in any case, the greater part of the evils and sufferings of life are due to the defects of nature and cannot be attributed to God. The most we can say is that God permits these things to happen; he has ordered nature in such a way that evil and suffering are inevitable but evil and suffering are not effects of the action of God. Both the Hindu and the Christian would say that the grace of God can enable us to overcome evil and suffering, and that God makes use of evil, including disease and death, as a means of drawing human persons to himself. In the case of very many people, it is only when struck down by disease or death that they turn to God.

For the Christian there still remains, however, the problem of hell. Is it possible to believe that a God of infinite love can allow the eternal sufferings of his creatures? St. Thomas Aquinas says that part of the joy of heaven would be that the just will rejoice in the just suffering and just punishment of the wicked, but that is a view that few would accept today. I think that we must recognise that this conception belongs to a particular image of the world. The 'Gehenna' of the Gospel, where the "worm dies not and the fire is not quenched", is a symbol which Jesus used to signify the disastrous effects of sin. Jesus was constantly using symbols which were intended to emphasise the reality of sin and evil and make it meaningful to his hearers; but to take that as a metaphysical statement of an absolute reality is another matter. I would like to suggest that ultimately evil is unreal. Only the real is, and evil is part of this whole world of *maya*, of becoming. Becoming is a state between unreality and reality with no finality. In the Hindu view, the world as it appears to us is *maya*. It appears in this way because we are ignorant; we are not seeing things as they are, but rather we are projecting everything from our own consciousness. If we introduce the concept of sin as the idea that something has gone wrong in the universe, not only with man but with the whole creation, then we can say that this 'ignorance' is due to sin. Cosmic evil is ascribed in the biblical tradition to the fall of the angels. It is fundamental in the biblical revelation that there is evil not only in man but in the whole cosmos. It is appropriate to speak of cosmic evil. Forces of destruction, of violence, of disintegration, are present in the universe and these forces are represented in the Biblical tradition as 'demons' or powers of evil, but they have no ultimate reality. Evil is not a real being, it is a shadow, a darkness, an absence, a negation. When we come to the truth, to the reality, to the One, to the final fulfillment, then the darkness will simply disappear, since there is no ultimate reality in sin or evil.

Sanjaya tells of Arjuna's response to Krishna's revelation of his glorious and awe-inspiring form:

35. When Arjuna heard the words of Krishna he folded his hands trembling; and with a faltering voice, and bowing in adoration, he spoke.

Arjuna, overwhelmed with awe, addresses Krishna:

36. It is right, O God, that people sing thy praises, and that they are glad and rejoice in thee. All evil spirits fly away in fear; but the hosts of the saints bow down before thee.

The 'evil spirits' here are the *rakshasas*; the 'hosts of the saints' are the *siddhas*, those who have reached perfection.

37. How could they not bow down in love and adoration, before thee, God of gods, Spirit Supreme? Thou creator of Brahma, the god of creation, thou infinite, eternal refuge of the world! Thou who art all that is, and all that is not, and all that is Beyond.

'Spirit Supreme is *mahatma*, which means 'great soul' and is a word that can be used of any holy man. It was used above all of Gandhi, as a supreme example of a *mahatma* in modern times.

'Creator of Brahma, the god of creation', is literally 'greater than Brahma'. Zaehner would like to believe that this means that Krishna, the personal God, is 'greater than Brahman'. But Brahman, alike in the *Gita* and the *Upanishads*, normally stands for the supreme reality, and it is better to take it here, as Mascaró does, as greater than Brahma the mythical god of creation.

Krishna is said to be all that is and all that is not, that is, all existence and all non-existence, and at the same time beyond both. This means that he transcends all dualities and yet is present in all.

38. Thou God from the beginning, God in man since man was. Thou Treasure supreme of this vast universe. Thou the one to be known and the Knower, the final resting place. Thou infinite Presence in whom all things are.

"God from the beginning" is the *adi-deva*, the primal god, and "God in man" is the *Purusha*, the cosmic Person.

God is both the 'Knower' and the 'one to be known', as it was said in the *Brihadanyaka Upanishad*, 'how can one know the Knower?' — to know the Knower is to share in his own Self-knowledge.

"Infinite Person in whom all things are" is literally 'infinite form by whom the universe is spread' (B & D) or 'spun out' (Z), *tatam*.

39. God of the winds and the waters, of fire and death! Lord of the solitary moon, the Creator, the Ancestor of all! Adoration to thee, a thousand adorations; and again and again unto thee adoration.

The winds and the waters are the gods Vayu and Varuna; fire and death are Agni and Yama. We must never forget that all the powers of nature are spiritual and not merely material beings. The 'creator' is Prajapati, the 'Lord of creatures', and the 'Ancestor of all' is literally the 'Great-grandfather'!

The word translated as 'adoration' is *namah*, which comes from a root meaning 'to prostrate'. *Namaste* said with hands folded is the normal greeting between people in India, signifying 'adoration to God in you'.

40. Adoration unto thee who art before me and behind me: adoration unto thee who art on all sides, God in all. All-powerful God of immeasurable might. Thou art the consummation of all: thou art all.

"Who art before me and behind me" is reminiscent of the famous hymn of St. Patrick celebrating "Christ before me, Christ behind me, Christ within me, Christ without me".

"Thou art the consummation of all: thou art all" finds an echo in the Hebrew tradition: "We may say many things, yet we shall not attain; and the sum of our words is, he is all" (Sir. 43.27).

41. If in careless presumption, or even in friendliness, I said 'Krishna! Son of Yadu! My friend!', this I did unconscious of thy greatness.

42. And if in irreverence I was disrespectful — when alone or with others — and made jest of thee at games, or resting, or at a feast, forgive me in thy mercy, O thou immeasurable!

Arjuna remembers how he had lived with Krishna as a friend and boon-companion without recognising who or what he was. We find the same thing in the Gospel when Jesus goes to Nazareth, his own home, and is not recognised as different from anyone else.

43. Father of all. Master Supreme. Power supreme in all the worlds. Who is like thee? Who is beyond thee?

Krishna is described as the 'Father' of the world and the great 'guru'. In the prophecy of Isaiah the Messiah is described as the "wonderful counsellor, mighty God, everlasting Father, Prince of Peace" (Is. 9.6). This is parallel in many respects to the conception of Krishna, as the incarnate God.

44. I bow before thee, I prostrate in adoration; and I beg thy grace, O glorious Lord! As a father to his son, as a friend to his friend, as a lover to his beloved, be gracious unto me, O God.

In Hindu tradition there are said to be five ways of relating to God; as a servant to a Lord, as a son to a father, as a friend to a friend, as a lover to the beloved, and also as a parent to his child, as is found in devotion to the baby Krishna and the child Jesus.

45. In a vision I have seen what no man has seen before: I rejoice in exultation, and yet my heart trembles with fear. Have mercy upon me, Lord of gods, Refuge of the whole universe: show me again thy human form.

Arjuna experiences both joy and fear, and this element of fear or awe should always be present in one's relationship with God. Love without fear is sentimental, fear without love is just terrible.

46. I yearn to see thee again with thy crown and sceptre and circle. Show thyself to me again in thine own four-armed form, thou of arms infinite, Infinite Form.

Arjuna has seen the supreme form of Krishna which is too sublime to be contemplated for long and he wants now to see him in his more familiar form. In a similar way most Christians prefer to contemplate the human form of Jesus in the Gospels rather than the gloried Christ as depicted in the great Byzantine mosaics.

Krishna accedes to Arjuna's request:

47. By my grace and my wondrous power I have shown to thee, Arjuna, this form supreme made of light, which is the Infinite, the All: mine own form from the beginning, never seen by man before.

"By my grace and wondrous power" is literally 'by my *atma-yoga*', the 'yoga' or active power of my Self, my Spirit. This supreme form of Krishna is said to be 'made of light', *tejomayam*, universal, infinite and primeval. One might compare this vision of Krishna with that of Jesus at the transfiguration when "his face shone like the sun and his garments became white as light"

(Matt. 17.2) or that of the Book of Revelation when "his face was like the sun shining in full strenth" (Rev. 1.16). One may also compare it with the vision of Yahweh on Mount Sinai when "the glory of the Lord was like a devouring fire on top of the mount" (Ex. 24.17) and to the vsion of Ezekiel when the Lord appears seated on a throne, and there was "the appearance of fire and brightness all around him" (Ezek. 1.27).

48. Neither Vedas, nor sacrifices, nor studies, nor benefactions, nor rituals, nor fearful austerities can give the vision of my Form Supreme. Thou alone hast seen this Form, thou the greatest of the Kurus.

The *Katha Upanishad* says in a similar way, "Not by the Vedas, not by the intellect, not by much learning is the Atman to be known. He whom the Atman chooses, by him the Atman is attained." The knowledge of God comes only through the grace of God.

49. Thou hast seen the tremendous form of my greatness, but fear not, and be not bewildered. Free from fear and with a glad heart see my friendly form again.

Sanjaya takes up the narrative:

50. Thus spoke Vasudeva to Arjuna, and revealed himself in his human form. The God of all gave peace to his fears and showed himself in his peaceful beauty.

Arjuna responds to the beautiful familiar form of Krishna:

51. When I see thy gentle human face, Krishna, I return to my own nature, and my heart has peace.

Krishna resumes his natural, peaceful form, that form of beauty which has enraptured so many Hindus, from Chaitanya who used to go into an ecstasy at the very thought of Krishna, to his follower Vishnu Prabhupada who in modern times has organised the Hare Krishna movement centred on devotion to Krishna.

Krishna concludes:

52. Thou hast seen now face to face my form divine so hard to see: for even the gods in heaven ever long to see what thou hast seen.

53. Not by the Vedas, or an austere life, or gifts to the poor, or ritual offerings can I be seen as thou hast seen me.

54. Only by love can men see me, and know me, and come unto me.

Krishna repeats again that it is only by love that man can come to see and know him. It remains true in every mystical tradition that love is the only way to knowledge and union with God. Some traditions, like that of Shankara and Hindu Advaita, and of Thomas Aquinas in Christian traiditon, emphasise the aspect of knowledge; yet the great advaitins like Shankara himeslf, and Ramana Maharshi, wrote poetry of ecstatic beauty in praise of the personal God; others, like Ramanuja of the Vaishnava tradition and St. Bonaventure and the Franciscans in the Christian tradition, emphasise the path of love. But in the ultimate state one goes beyond all such distinctions and realises being in the fullness of truth alone.

55. He who works for me, who loves me, whose End Supreme I am, free from attachment to all things, and with love for all creation, he in truth comes to me.

Krishna here adds to the ways of love and of knowledge, *bhakti* and *jnana*, the way of *karma*, works done in a spirit of detachment. Finally he adds "love for all creation", though literally it is "freedom from hatred for or enmity towards all creatures". This somewhat weakens the force of the words, but in all genuine mystical experience there is a profound concern for the world as a whole, often implicit rather than explicit.

Chapter 12

The Yoga of Devotion

This chapter opens with the great question concerning the immanent and the transcendent, the personal and the impersonal aspects of God. There are two views on this. The common Christian view which Zaehner puts forward is that the personal God is above the impersonal Brahman. Among Hindus, the advaitins say on the contrary that the impersonal Brahman is above the personal God, the latter being merely a manifestation of the transcendent One. The view which I hold and which I think is that of the *Gita* is that the personal and impersonal are simply two aspects of the one Reality, which is beyond our comprehension. At times one may experience God as the immutable, the eternal, the One, and at other times one may experience him as Lord and Saviour in a relationship of love.

Arjuna asks:

1. Those who in oneness worship thee as God immanent in all; and those who worship the Transcendent, the Imperishable − Of those, who are the best Yogis?

Krishna explains:

2. Those who set their hearts on me and ever in love worship me, and who have unshakable faith, those I hold as the best Yogis.

In a sense the *Gita* was written to balance the view of the *Upanishads* which insists on the realization of Brahman as the supreme Absolute and pays less attention to the personal aspect of the Godhead. One purpose of the *Gita* is to show that this personal aspect of Brahman is supremely important and that it is known by faith and love. That is why Christians are particularly attracted to it. Faith, shraddha, and love, *bhakti*, are the ways by which we come to know God in a personal way.

3. But those who worship the Imperishable, the Infinite, Transcendent unmanifested; the Omnipresent, the Beyond all thought, the Immutable, the Neverchanging, the Ever One;

Krishna makes no distinction; each is equally valid. Those who set their heart on him and worship him in faith and in love "are the best yogis", but equally those who worship the imperishable reach his very Self. The word for imperishable is *aksharam*. The *kshara*, the perishable, is all this material world and also all that in this human world is subject to corruption, while the imperishable is all that is beyond change and decay. But above this 'imperishable' the *Gita* recognizes a higher 'imperishable'. There is an intelligence in man and in nature, which can be called the imperishable, but the supreme personal God is the imperishable beyond; he is the Absolute. Here Krishna identifies this imperishable with his 'very self'. It is also called the infinite, or rather the ineffable, *anirdesyam*, and the *avyaktam*, the unmanifest. The visible world, and even the invisible world of angels and gods, belongs to the manifest, the created world. But beyond the created world is what is called the unmanifest. It is also called omnipresent, literally 'moving everywhere', unthinkable, *acintyam*, 'rock-seated', *kutastham*, immutable and firm, going back to the description of the Supreme Spirit in Chapter 2.25. Krishna declares that those who worship this infinite, imperishable One, attain to his 'very self'. This makes it clear against Zaehner that there is no real difference between the personal God and the impersonal Godhead.

4. Who have all the powers of their soul in harmony, and the same loving mind for all; who find joy in the good of all beings — they reach in truth my very self.

But they also need to have their souls in harmony and to have loving minds to all. Thus love is an essential condition of union with God, whether he is conceived as the Absolute One or the personal God.

5. Yet greater is the toil of those whose minds are set on the Transcendent, for the path of the Transcendent is hard for mortals to attain.

Krishna maintains that the path of the transcendent is the more difficult way. For most people the way of devotion to a personal God is the normal form of religion. This is evident in Christianity, but even in Buddhism with its strictly impersonal character, the Mahayana or Great Way, introduced the idea of the bodhisattva, the figure of the compassionate Buddha who becomes an object of devotion.

6. But they for whom I am the End Supreme, who surrender all their works to

7. me, and who with pure love meditate on me and adore me − these I very soon deliver from the ocean of death and life-in-death, because they have set their heart on me.

For the *Gita* the way of devotion to Krishna as the manifestation of the personal God is the way that soon brings deliverance which those who follow the ascetic way have to seek over many years.

8. Set thy heart on me alone, and given to me thy understanding: thou shalt in truth live in me hereafter.

So Krishna calls for surrender to him alone, the offering of both the mind and the heart which leads to 'living in him'. There is an exact parallel to this in St. John's Gospel where Jesus says that if anyone loves him, he will come to dwell in him (John 14:23).

Perfect contemplation is to see all the created universe in the One and the One in the whole created universe. Nothing is lost. It is a mistake to think that when we go beyond this world to the One, we lose this world or that when we see God in this world we lose the One. The whole creation is in God and God is in the whole creation. In Christian terms the whole creation is in the 'Word'. When God utters his Word, he utters the whole creation from the beginning to the end of time. All is present in that one Word and fully present in it.

It should be noted that the same distinction between the personal God and the transcendent Godhead is to be found in Christian tradition. While the Bible, both in the Old and the New Testament, normally speaks of God in personal terms, a later tradition found especially in Dionysius the Areopagite under Neo-Platonic influence speaks of going beyond all names and forms and all words and thoughts, and encountering the supreme Godhead, which is 'unutterable, ineffable, beyond mind, beyond life, beyond seeing' (Dionysius, *Divine Names*, 2.10). This one, ineffable being is manifested in the whole creation and in every person, but there is an element in creation and in human nature which resists the manifestation of God. It can be called sin or it can be called ignorance. There is a defect in human nature and also in the universe. There is a cosmic sin, the sin of the angels, that is, of the cosmic powers. So the divine is not fully manifested in the universe. There is something opposing the divine. There is a darkness, a shadow across the divine. And then when we human beings enter into this darkness, this shadow, we encounter sin and ignorance as the darkness which hides the One from us. Our present human state is a state of sin, a state in which this body is going to die and decay and in which the soul is going to be separated from the body. That state of sin and ignorance is *maya*. Redemption consists in being set free from this sin and this ignorance and being restored to the original state. In that original state, each human being and everything in the creation is a perfect image of God, a perfect mirror of the One. That is the resurrection of the body when our whole being, our body and our soul will be transformed. Instead of this gross body which will disintegrate, and this psychic organism which, in so far as it depends on the body, will also disintegrate, the body and soul are totally united in the One, the Spirit, the Self, the Atman, and we experience God in total unity. The resurrection of body and soul in the Spirit was the original purpose of creation. In that state the one Spirit is manifesting himself at every level of being without any darkness or ignorance, suffering or death.

9. But if thou art unable to rest thy mind on me, then seek to reach me by the practice of Yoga concentration.

That is *abhyasa*-yogena, by practice of yoga. Many people have not this insight, this wisdom, nor have they this devotion, but one can practice yoga by controlling the body and the breath, thus achieving equilibrium, and then going on to control the mind and keeping it free from all distracting thoughts and desires and bringing it into harmony. So that is a preliminary practice which almost everybody can do. Some find that they are helped by physical exercise, others do not need it. There are many different ways of controlling the mind. Simply observing the breath or focussing the mind on one point is one way. All these different methods can be used if one has not yet reached that state of wisdom and devotion.

10. If thou art not able to practice concentration, consecrate all thy work to me. By merely doing actions in my service thou shalt attain perfection.

This is *karma* yoga. "By doing actions in my service you shall obtain perfection"; that is the other great way of the *Gita*. All the first six books of the *Gita* were concerned with *karma* yoga. Again there are differing views. In the strict advaitic view, one should not do any work, any *karma*, any ritualistic work or any practical work, the only way to attain God is by knowledge. But in the view of the *Gita*, the householder doing his *dharma*, his duty, working in God's service and offering his work to God, is able to be united in God, no less than the yogi or the ascetic.

So that is the other way, the way of devoted service and of course, today, that is what most people are drawn to. Some people are drawn to yoga, but almost everybody feels the call to service of some sort. Unselfish, devoted service is the most practical way to God that exists. It can also be the most effective. One can take the example of Mother Theresa or any of those innumerable people working in religious orders. Theirs is a practical way of finding God, though it has its limitations as we saw and can become an obstacle if one simply gives oneself to work. But work done out of love for God, in the service of one's neighbour, is always effective. That was the way of Mahatma Gandhi. He once said, "My one object in life is to obtain *moksha*, liberation, and if I thought I could attain it by going to a cave in the Himalayas, I would go there straight away, but I believe that I can find God in my neighbour, particularly in my suffering fellow countrymen, therefore I devote my life to them in order that I may find God." That is the way of *Karma* yoga.

11. And if even this thou art not able to do, then take refuge in devotion to me and surrender to me the fruit of all thy work — with the selfless devotion of a humble heart.

That was the first message of the *Gita* — to do work without seeking its fruit. Do the work, whatever has to be done, and leave the results to God. The great danger of work is that the ego seeks satisfaction in it. If we give up the satisfaction of the ego and simply do the work, because it is our *dharma*, our duty, then such work brings liberation. This was Krishna's first guidance to Arjuna; you are a *kshatriya*, you have to fight in this war, this is your *dharma*, therefore do your duty, seek no reward from it and then that work will not bind you at all, it will lead to me. So those are the various methods he suggests.

12. For concentration is better than mere practice, and meditation is better than concentration; but higher than meditation is surrender in love of the fruit of one's actions, for on surrender follows peace.

"Better is concentration than mere practice." I think that this is a good translation, the word simply is *jnana* which means knowledge, primarily, but it seems that it means here that concentration of the mind in knowledge is better than mere yoga practice. Better than simply concentrating the mind is the state of *dhyana*, when the mind dwells on the object of meditation and the mind is filled with that object. It is like an even flow of oil, the mind is in a state of even flow. So that is a better state still, but "higher than meditation is surrender in love of the fruit of one's actions, for from surrender follows peace." The meaning of this seems to be that total self-surrender in love brings one to God more effectively than any other method. So that is the path of the *Gita* and that is the path which many follow. Such self-surrender to God is the most fundamental way and anybody can practice it. A mother with twelve children trying to earn her living by coolie work can still surrender to God, to the will of God. To accept the will of God in everything that comes, in total self-surrender is the most perfect way and the most universal. It is not that there is a lower way which everybody can practice and a higher way for a few. The commonest, most universal way is the most profound. The others are special ways. And this is also the difference between the layman and the religious. It is not that the religious has found a better way. For the laymen to do the will of God in his state, wherever it is, in total self-surrender is the perfect way. A religious man adopts certain methods, which can help him to make that surrender but it is not necessarily a better way. The religious who does not achieve his goal of self-surrender is far worse than the layman or the devotee who has made a real surrender.

13. The man who has a good will for all, who is friendly and has
    compassion; who has no thoughts of 'I' or 'mine', whose peace is the
    same in pleasures and sorrows, and who is forgiving

Krishna says, "The man who has good will for all," which is literally
"who has no ill will for anyone," and "who is friendly and has compassion."
The two words used here, *maitra*, friendliness, and *karuna*, compassion,
are terms from Buddhism designating the two of the principal Buddhist
virtues. Zaehner speaks of *maitra* and *karuna* as the virtues with which the
Buddhist monk "suffuses the whole universe" while abandoning the thought
of 'I' and 'mine'. The *Gita* has absorbed many elements of Buddhist
understanding, integrating them into the main lines of its teaching. In this
verse the person who is friendly and has compassion is to have no thought
of 'I' or 'mine'. Here again we must make a distinction. When I think of
myself as separate in any way from others or from God, then that is sin,
that is maya, that is illusion – the ego separated from God and from the
rest of the world. But when I know myself in that One, and in a living
relation with all others, it is not *maya* at all. It is fulfillment. The ultimate
fulfillment is not to lose one's true self but to discover one's true self living
in harmony with all other selves and with the one source of all, the one
Atman who is present, manifesting himself in all these selves.

"Whose peace is the same in pleasures and sorrows." That sameness
in good or evil is often emphasised and it means that whatever happens
one is not to be disturbed. And also, "Who is forgiving" or long-suffering,
kshami. Kshami is a very beautiful virtue, like the 'long-suffering' of St. Paul
(cf. Col. 3.12).

14. This Yogi of union, ever full of my joy, whose soul is in harmony
    and whose determination is strong; whose mind and inner vision are
    set on me – this man loves me, and he is dear to me.

His mind and soul are surrendered to me. "Let him worship me with
love and then I will love him" (Z). This is an important teaching of the
Gita. It is not simply that the soul loves God and is devoted to him, but
that God loves the soul. One may get the idea that one is ascending above
the mind and the *buddhi*, reaching beyond and going into a sort of void,
but actually as one reaches that point, one meets the descending movement

of love which is coming down through the whole universe; at that point one encounters this love, the self-giving love of God.

That is the supreme experience, when the love of the soul for God meets the love of God for the soul. We often think that we are loving God and are trying to reach him, when in fact it is God who is loving us and drawing us towards himself. So this movement of grace and love meets us.

15. He whose peace is not shaken by others, and before whom other people find peace, beyond excitement and anger and fear — he is dear to me.

Literally, "from whom the people do not shrink and who does not shrink from them" (Z). This is a great characteristic of the yogi. He is fearless and therefore others have no fear of him. Animals have no fear of the yogi, as in the experience of the Desert Fathers. The lion or the snake will come to the yogi without fear. It is psychologically true that the reason why animals attack us is because we are afraid. We exude vibrations of fear which affect the animal. But when we have perfect fearlessness, nothing is afraid of us.

"Who is free from exaltation, anger and fear" (Z). The word for exaltation can be translated 'excitement', and anger and fear are among the three basic passions. Almost our whole life is dominated by those three basic passions of desire, anger and fear. It starts from infancy. A baby has this desire for its own pleasure, for warmth and love from its mother and when it realises that the love is not being given, and it is not getting its milk, or attention, or whatever it is that it wants, then it begins to be angry and afraid. That is the basic human drama. Everyone of us from the age of one day has experienced this love or lack of love, this anger and this fear. There can be repressed anger which goes back even to the moment of birth, and this can be terrible. It is said that coming out of the womb is often a terrifying experience and some poeple never get over it. I remember one young man came to us who had had an exceptionally difficult birth, his mother having taken about a week to deliver him. All his life it had seemed to him that he was not wanted and he had felt rejected from the word go. In time and in spite of all sorts of complexes, he eventually came through to a wonderful experience of God, a marvellous release. These kind of emotions, then, are deeply rooted in us and we reap the consequences all our life, but at the same time, we are not determined by them. We are conditioned but our conditioning can be overcome by God's grace. The mystery of grace is that even the worst anger and fear can be healed and transformed into creative forces for love.

16. He who is free from vain expectations, who is pure, who is wise and knows what to do, who in inner peace watches both sides, who shakes not, who works for God and not for himself – this man loves me, and he is dear to me.

So many people spend their time, with vain expectations, hopeful for improbable things that never come. For "who is pure and wise," Zaehner has 'skilled'; 'expert' is perhaps the best word. Yoga is skill in action and the wise man is the one who is skilled in that way. He knows what to do. 'Skill' in this sense is the art of seeing what ought to be done in a given situation. Some people in very difficult situations can immediately see what ought to be done in a practical way. There is also a deeper psychological discernment as to how to treat a given situation or the persons involved, which is 'skill in action' or 'skillful action', another concept, incidentally, from Buddhist understanding. Skillful action comes from purity of heart: "who is pure and wise and knows what to do." Mascaró's translation: "who works for God and not for himself" is too free. Zaehner says: "who gives up all selfish enterprises" and another translation is: "renouncing every undertaking" (B & D). I think that Zaehner is correct, for the meaning is not that a person gives up all work, but rather that he renounces any selfish undertaking. We must always understand that. The *Gita* often speaks of being free from all desire when it means all selfish desire.

17. He who feels neither excitement nor repulsion, who complains not and lusts not for things; who is beyond good and evil, and who has love – he is dear to me.

"He who feels neither excitement nor repulsion" or, 'who neither hates nor exults'(Z). That again is the virtue of equanimity when one is neither opposed to people nor excessively attracted. One keeps a balance and harmony within. And then a phrase which Mascaró translates as, "who is beyond good and evil." I think that is very deceptive. The clause is better translated: "who puts away both the pleasant and the unpleasant things" (Z). It is not a case of moral good and evil at all. It is simply a matter of the contraries in life, the pleasant and the unpleasant, and the point is to accept all equally. It is a very deceptive view to think that one can go beyond good and evil in the moral sense.

18. The man whose love is the same for his enemies or his friends, whose soul is the same in honour or disgrace, who is beyond heat or cold or pleasure or pain, who is free from the chains of attachments;

"The man whose love is the same for his enemies and his friends." Christians often think of the Gospel teaching, "love your enemies, do good to those who hate you," as something specifically Christian but it is really universal. It is present in Buddhism and it is equally strong here.

'Attachment' is a key word. Attachment is selfish desire. The soul is at the centre in its living relation with God, with the Supreme, and it has the world around it. It can enjoy the world and all the pleasures of the senses and values of human relationship, but without any attachment. The only attachment is to the Lord within. Then one attains the perfect state. But normally we get attached to people, to things, to work, above all to the ego and this is what is fragmenting us. This attachment is sin.

Detachment, therefore, has to apply at every level. It is necessary to be detached, as the Gospel says, from father and mother, from wife and children, from everything we have. Total detachment is the condition of total love. It is not a sort of puritan asceticism; it is total detachment from the self, total surrender to God and therefore a total love for others. It is a total compassion and understanding. That is the aim.

19. Who is balanced in blame and in praise, whose soul is silent, who is happy with whatever he has, whose home is not in this world, and who has love — this man is dear to me.

"Whose soul is silent" means not merely absence of words but silence of the mind. "Who is happy with whatever he has, whose home is not in this world." This applies equally to the Christian and the Hindu. Neither has a home in this world; we have here no abiding city. That is what is meant by detachment from the world. And again, it does not mean that we cannot enjoy the world. We have not settled down and become rooted in the world but we are able to experience it and enjoy it without clinging, aware that we are passing through and on. That is the ideal of the *sannyasi*;

he has no settled abode. This was also the condition of the Israelites in the desert. God led them out of Egypt into the desert and in the desert, as Jeremiah said, Israel was "holiness to the Lord", because they were completely detached, journeying through the desert. They had no home, no fixed abode. Israel always considered that this was the perfect state. The Feast of Tabernacles, on which the transfiguration occurred, was precisely the time in every year when the Israelites went to live in tents for a week to remind themselves of the time when they were pilgrims in the desert.

In South India there is a pilgrimage to a place called Sabarimala. It is a pilgrimage to the forest and hundreds of thousands of people go there every year. The deep meaning of this is that people need to go back from time to time to the forest, to the wilds, where they were before they belonged to a settled civilisation with a home and a city. We need to recall the freedom of the forest. Some time each year, at least, we should go out from our fixed abode, leaving our possessions and everything to which we are attached, and become free to wander or to settle in some very quiet place, to be free for some time like the *sannyasi.*

"Whose home is not in this world," and Krishna adds, "who has love." We must always distinguish the kind of stoic attitude of a person who despises and rejects the world from that of the person who is full of love but is also totally detached.

20. But even dearer to me are those who have faith and love and who have me as their End Supreme: those who hear my words of Truth, and who come to the waters of Everlasting Life.

Mascaró's translation, "the waters of Everlasting Life", is too reminiscent of biblical language. Literally it is the *amrita* or 'nectar of righteousness'. In this passage we have in a nutshell the main teaching of the *Gita.* The method in the *Gita* is to keep going over the same themes, not simply going from one thing to another. It introduces a theme, then it takes it up again and develops it much like musical score, later bringing in another theme and developing that before returning to the first theme again. In the eighteenth chapter it brings the whole to completion by recalling all the basic themes. So again and again one finds that the whole is present in a particular part.

Chapter 13

The Yoga of the Distinction Between the Field and the Knower of the Field

We come now to the thirteenth chapter and the *jnana marga*. The first six chapters concerned the *karma marga*, the next six the *bhakti marga*, and now the last six chapters on *jnana*, the way of knowledge. We begin with a verse which is omitted in Mascaró's version. Arjuna asks Krishna:

> What is nature? What is the Person (Purusha)? What is the field and the knower of the field? What is knowledge; what is that which should be known? (Z).

These are fundamental questions. We need to know what exactly is this reality that we are exploring. Nature and person, *prakriti* and *purusha*, are familiar terms. They are now interpreted in terms of the "field" and the "knower of the field", terms which are reminiscent of modern physics. Krishna replies:

1. This body, Arjuna, is called the field. He who knows this is called the knower of the field.

The field is the whole world of nature, or what contemporary physics calls a 'field of energies'. The spirit is the knower, it is the principle of consciousness which pervades this field.

2. Know that I am the knower in all the fields of my creation; and that the wisdom which sees the field and the knower of the field is true wisdom.

This is the key: there is ultimately only one knower, one Self, one *Purusha*, that is manifesting in the whole creation. All humanity and every human consciousness is a reflection of this one consciousness. Shankara uses the illustration of the one sun shining in many pools of water. There is one sun, one light manifesting itself in innumerable pools of water, like innumerable mirrors. Each mirror reflects the sun and the other mirrors so there is a continuous interplay. The essential point is that there is one knower in all these fields. Behind my body is my soul, the *manas*, the mind. Into this mind, through the *buddhi*, the intelligence, the light of the Atman is shining. All my action comes from the knower within. In the *Upanishads* it is asked, "Who shall know the knower?" We imagine that we know this and do that, but in actual fact our knowledge is always a reflection of this light of knowledge which comes to us from above. The great illusion is to think that "I" know this, "I" think this, "I" do this, whereas really it is the One who is thinking and knowing and acting in me.

Wisdom is the realization of the one Spirit in all. The centre of consciousness then passes from the ego, the *ahankara* or I-consciousness, to the Self, the Spirit within, who is the real centre of our being. When we see everything in the light of the Spirit, we see the truth; when we see everything in the light of the ego, we are the victims of error and illusion.

"Know that I am the knower of the field in every field." Each one of us is a field of energy and consciousness in which the Lord is the knower, and in whose consciousness each one of us participates. That is the only true knowledge.

3. Hear from me briefly what the field is and how it is, what its changes are and whence each one comes; who is the knower and what is his power.

We tend to think of the body as solid matter, of particular shape and size, but we know that even from a scientific point of view this is illusory. The body is made up of innumerable cells, and the cells are made up of innumerable molecules and atoms, all of which are forms of energy. Our body is in fact a focus of energies. This is the fundamental Buddhist understanding of the nature of the body. For the Buddhist there is no fixed being; the body is simply the coming together of elements, of energies, which produce this appearance. Our senses give it this particular form. We reflect these particular vibrations of energy through our senses, and project the appearance of the world around us. Each one of us is a focus of these energies. But beyond these forms and vibrations of energy is the one *Atman*. He is manifesting Himself in all these vibrations and building up the whole creation from atoms and molecules and living cells, from plant and animal and human forms.

The experience of having a solid body, then, is an illusion. "Oh that this too, too solid flesh would melt," said Hamlet. But the flesh is not solid at all. It is continually dissolving. It is said that in seven years not a single atom in the body remains the same; the body is building up and dissolving all the time. When we die it is simply a final dissolution. Dissolution is nothing to be worried about; it has been going on all the time. Our real being is not involved in this process of coming and going; the Spirit within, the *Atman* within, is not affected by death. So that is the nature of the body; it is the field in which this process of change and transformation takes place.

4. This has been sung by seers of the *Vedas* in many musical measures of verse; and in great words about Brahman, words of faith and full of truth.

The phrase 'words about Brahman' is *Brahma Sutra*, which is the name of a famous text on the doctrine of Vedanta. There are three foundations of the Vedanta. The Source of all wisdom is said to be the *Vedas*, which are *shruti*, that is, revealed wisdom. The *Upanishads* are called Vedanta, the end of the *Vedas*, the last portion and the fulfillment of the *Vedas*. Then the word Vedanta came to be applied also to the various systems of philosophy based not only on the *Upanishads* but also upon the *Bhagavad Gita* which is really a continuation of the whole movement of the *Upanishads*, and on the *Brahma Sutras* as well. The *Brahma Sutras* of Badarayana may have been composed some time after the *Gita*, but these systems of philosophy, like *Yoga* and *Sankhya*, though they were formally organised about the third or fourth century A.D., had their beginnings long before. Probably some *Brahma Sutras*, aphorisms about Brahman, already existed when the *Gita* was written.

5. The five elements, the thought of 'I', consciousness, subconsciousness, the five powers of feeling and the five of action, the one mind over them, the five fields of sense perception;

This verse describes the structure of the universe according to the Sankhya philosophy. First the gross elements, earth, air, water, fire, and ether; then the structure of the mind, the 'sense of I', *ahankara,* the intellect, *buddhi,* and the unmanifest which could well be translated as the 'unconscious' in the Jungian sense. Then there are the eleven senses, that is, the five senses or organs of perception, and the five organs of actions, together with the *manas* or common sense, and finally the objects of sense perception.

6. Desire, aversion, pleasure, pain, the power of mental unification, intelligence, and courage: this is the field and its modifications.

Now we have several verses which describe the nature of wisdom or the subjective aspect of reality. It begins with the basic passions, love, hate, pleasure and pain. Then comes an interesting word, *samghatas.* It means literally 'aggregate'. Besant and Das translate it 'organism', meaning the body. Mascaró says 'power of mental unification', following Shankara who takes it to mean the 'bringing together of the bodily senses'.

7. Humbleness, sincerity, harmlessness, forgiveness, uprightness, devotion to the spiritual master, purity, steadiness, self-harmony;

We come to the qualities that lead to wisdom. These virtues are universal; they are found alike in Hinduism, Buddhism, Islam and Christianity. The first one is best translated 'humility' but it means literally 'unhaughtiness', *amanitvam.* The second is *adambhitvam* which is 'unpretentiousness' or 'sincerity'. Then 'harmlessness', *ahimsa:* that is the virtue which Gandhi made the basis of his life and philosophy, but it is fundamental also for a *sannyasi.* It is said that a *sannyasi* is not afraid of anyone and no one is afraid of him. It is not simply negative in the sense of 'not killing', but it is a whole attitude of mind involving freedom from aggression. Then there is *kshanti,* 'forgiveness', 'forbearance' or 'tolerance'. This is central to St. Paul's list of virtues in the letter to the Colossians, with which this whole passage can be compared (Col. 3.12,13). Next there is 'uprightness and devotion to the teacher, the guru'. That is considered a truly fundamental virtue in India. The primary virtue is devotion to the mother and the father, and then to the guru and teacher and traditionally every Indian child was trained in this attitude of reverence. Then *saucha*, 'purity of heart' or 'cleanliness of mind and body' is one of the *yamas* or disciplines of the yoga of Patanjali. Next comes 'steadfastness' and finally 'self-control'.

8. Freedom from the lust of the senses, absence of the thought of 'I', perception of the sorrows of birth, death, old age, disease, and suffering;

These are the more negative virtues. First, detachment from the objects of the senses; that is the stage in yoga called *pratyahara*. It does not mean suppression of the senses, but the opposite. When we suppress our senses we remain attached to them and they continue to affect us consciously. When we are detached, we are absolutely free; we can use our senses, enjoy food and drink and all created things, but we are detached, not bound by them in any way. The next virtue is *anahankara*, that is, 'without egoism or self-centeredness', which is the essence of sin. Then there is 'insight into birth, death, disease, old age and pain'. This is an excellent example of Buddhist terminology. The Buddha's teaching is essentially moral and this came to influence the whole Vedantic tradition. The Buddha's great insight was into sickness, old age, and death as the basic conditions of human life. The story is that he was a prince who was kept in his father's palace and was never allowed to see any evil or suffering. One day he went out and saw a sick man and he asked what this was. He was told that it was sickness which came to everybody in time. Again he went out and saw an old man, and was told that old age comes to us all, and finally he saw a dead man being carried out to his last rites, and he realized that these things were inescapable; that this was a universal law. There is another story of his sending a woman, whose child had died, to every house in a village to ask if there was one house where no one had ever died, and she found no such house. This is a universal law and yet we always tend to ignore it. But the Buddha faced the negative aspect of life and, in facing it, came to realize the ultimate meaning of life, which is beyond suffering and death.

9. Freedom from the chains of attachments, even from a selfish attachment to one's children, wife, or home; an ever-present evenness of mind in pleasant or unpleasant events;

This is put very strongly in the Gospel, where it is said, unless a man hate his father and his mother and his wife and his children, and all that he has, he cannot be the disciple of the Lord (Luke 14.26). This does not mean hatred in the ordinary sense but a radical detachment from everyone and everything. The idea is to be fundamentally detached and then we can love people unselfishly, devotedly and totally; but when we are attached, there is always a selfish element in our love. The mother's love for the child, the husband's love for the wife, is normally somewhat selfish and attached. As Kabir says in his poems, love and detachment should go together. Those who are perfectly detached are able to preserve a perfect equilibrium, 'constant equal-mindedness', *sama-chitta*.

10. A single oneness of pure love, of never-straying love for me; retiring to solitary places, and avoiding the noisy multitudes;

The *Gita* introduces *bhakti*, or devotion to the personal God, as an essential element in the pursuit of wisdom, together with the more traditional separation from the world. Separation from the world is nevertheless important. Everybody needs at times to retire to a solitary place, to be alone in the silence of nature, mountains, hills, and forests. This is not escape, it is a way to recover oneself. When one is pressed with people all the time, one cannot be oneself.

This theme of the solitary place or desert is found, as we have seen, in the history of Israel. The people of Israel went into the desert to find God. In the same way Moses went into the desert and encountered God in the burning bush. Elijah too went out into the desert and met with God on Mount Horeb. John the Baptist prepared the way for Jesus by retiring to the wilderness, and Jesus, before beginning his ministry, was driven by the Spirit into the desert. After his conversion, St. Paul did not go straight away to preach the Gospel, but went to the desert of Arabia for three years to meditate. Then again with the Fathers of the desert, there was the whole movement of withdrawal to the desert from the cities of the Roman empire. There is a dual movement of life such that involvement needs to be balanced by withdrawal. Everybody needs to be able to be alone. There are so many devices in our society which serve as distractions so that one cannot become aware of the Self. One of the important needs today is the creation of small centres of quiet, whether in a town or in the country, where people can experience silence and solitude.

"Avoiding the noisy multitude" is a good expression because it is not simply avoiding people altogether. The translation, "absence of enjoyment in the company of men" (B & D), is misleading because the meaning is not that one should not enjoy oneself in company, but rather that one does not want to be overwhelmed by "the noisy multitudes". Wanting to have people around and noise going on means one wants to be distracted; one does not want to be oneself. Of course, the ideal is that when this inner awareness of the Self is reached, one should be able to go out and interact with people without being disturbed. It is then possible to relate to others while preserving that inner integrity. These are the virtues of the wise man.

11. A constant yearning to know the inner Spirit, and a vision of Truth which gives liberation: this is true wisdom leading to vision. All against this is ignorance.

"Constant yearning to know the inner Spirit" is *adhyatman jnana*, knowledge of the Self. The knowledge of the senses and of the mind is always limited but if we know the inner Spirit, the point of union with God, we have supreme knowledge.

"A vision of truth which gives liberation" more literally means "constant attention to the wisdom which appertains to self" (Z), a *tattva jnana darshana*. *Darshana* is the word used to describe all the early systems of philosophy. These include the *Nyaya* and *Vaisheshika*, that is logic and cosmology; then the *Sankhya* and *Yoga*, that is metaphysics and practical philosophy; and finally *Mimansa*, the interpretation of the *Vedas*, and *Vedanta* which is the doctrine of ultimate reality. These are the six *darshanas*, points of view, or visions of reality.

It is *Vedanta* which is intended to lead to the Supreme knowledge, "the vision of truth which gives liberation." Without the knowledge of the inner self all knowledge is ignorance. It is unrelated to the truth itself. Scientific knowledge by itself is also ignorance because it is simply knowing a part. It is simply an empty knowledge unless it is related to the Supreme. There is a significant movement among scientists today to relate scientific knowledge to the knowledge of the *Atman*, the Reality behind the whole cosmos and all sensory and psychological experience.

Knowledge of science or philosophy will never give one immortality. Wisdom is a knowledge of experience, not a so-called objective knowledge which is really only a partial knowledge. Wisdom is the knowledge which involves our inner being and transforms us. If we know the Self we become the Self. This is wisdom; this is knowledge of Brahman.

12. Now I shall tell thee of the End of wisdom. When a man knows this he goes beyond death. It is Brahman, beginningless, supreme: beyond what is and beyond what is not.

"Now I shall tell thee of the End of wisdom," or rather, that which is to be known, the *jneya*, and "knowing which man goes beyond death." This is the supreme knowledge which brings immortality. And what is this knowledge? "It is Brahman, beginningless, supreme, which is neither being nor not being" (Z). Brahman, the Supreme, is beyond being and not being; this is the *Nirguna Brahman*, the absolute Supreme beyond everything, the source of all and that is what has to be known. This one Supreme manifests in the whole creation. This is the picture we must keep always in mind. We must try to fix it in our minds, the absolutely transcendent One beyond, nameless, formless, absolute, which we call God because we cannot name it. This One is manifested in the whole creation, in the earth, the sky, the sea, in man, in animal, in plant; everything is a manifestation of the One supreme.

If we want to put this in Christian terms we can say that Brahman is God. God the Father is the source, the origin of all; and God speaks his Word and the whole creation is the expression of the Word of God, the manifestation of God. Each thing is a word, a word in the one Word.

Now we get a series of texts which are taken from the *Upanishads*. Of course, the *Bhagavad Gita* builds on the *Upanishads* throughout.

13. His hands and feet are everywhere, he has heads and mounts everywhere; he sees all, he hears all. He is in all, and he is.

The one person, the one *Purusha*, the one reality, is manifested in all creation, in every person, in every thing, and all human beings are, as it were, his hands, his feet, his heads. He is in you and me; he is acting through our hands and feet, our heads and our mouths. All these are his members, as it were. In the Christian tradition there is the understanding that the universe is the body of Christ. Christ has assumed the whole creation in himself and he now acts in and through the whole creation. Christ is present in every human being. Similarly, Buddhists speak of the Buddha nature in every man. Behind our bodily nature and behind our psychic nature we each have that inner Spirit and that inner Spirit is the Christ within, the *Atman* within. He is eternally active, and to realise that is salvation. When we realise, 'I am not this body, I am not this soul, I am this inner Spirit living and active and breathing in me', then we attain wisdom. Wisdom is knowing that this One is speaking in us and acting in us, whereas ignorance is when we think 'I am the doer' and forget about the Spirit altogether.

Now the obvious question is, if this Brahman, the Lord, is manifest in the whole creation, does that mean that he is subject to it? If he is in the earth, then is he suffering all the effects of being in the earth? Or if he is in a human being, is he suffering from all the defects of my mind, my will, my senses? No, he is in all the senses but he is not affected by them at all. His light shines in my senses but he himself is not affected. The model always is the sun. The sun is shedding its light on the whole world and all the earth and everything is receiving that light, but the sun is not affected by it. The light is shining through all these different colors, in all these different forms and is received in all these different materials. They are all different but all are manifesting the one Light.

14. The Light of consciousness comes to him through infinite powers of perception and yet he is above all these powers. He is beyond all, and yet he supports all. He is beyond the world of matter, and yet he has joy in this world.

The one Light of consciousness is manifest in the consciousness of each one of us and shines through it and yet is not affected by it. "Devoid of all senses, it yet sheds light on all their qualities" (Z). The Spirit has no senses himself but he shines through our senses. He is unattached. That is why the great virtue is detachment. We have to detach ourselves from the senses, from the feelings and particularly from the mind, because God himself is completely unattached in the midst of all. Being unattached, he is unaffected. He is detached and yet he supports the whole creation. "Free from nature's constituents, he yet experiences them" (Z). The constituents are the *gunas*, darkness, fire and light which are part of *prakriti*, nature. The Lord manifests in them but he is free from them; he is beyond the *gunas*.

When we are speaking of the Lord, it is the Lord in us and we have to be one with him and experience as he does. We have to be in the senses, in the body and yet not attached in any way.

15. He is invisible: he cannot be seen. He is far and he is near, he moves and he moves not, he is within all and he is outside all.

This is a quotation from the *Isa Upanishad* which is here using paradoxes. God is infinitely beyond us and yet infinitely near. He is, as St. Augustine said in a wonderful phrase, *Summior summo meo intimior intimo meo*, "higher than my highest being and more intimate than my inmost self". He is at once both immanent and transcendent. Paradoxically again, "he moves and he moves not". He is the mover, everything moves, acts, works, behaves, through his presence, through his power and yet he himself remains unmoved, the 'unmoved mover'. We cannot grasp this vision a a whole, we have to conceive it by means of these contradictory notions. We have to think of God as infinitely beyond all that is and yet as immanent in every particle of matter. Totally immanent and totally transcendent. All this is completely Christian; there is no difference here between the Christian and Hindu view.

He moves in the sense that everything is moved by him for, it is through his activity that the whole creation moves, and yet he is utterly unmoved in himself. And again, this is how we ought to be. We ought to be unmoved in the midst of all motion. The wise man, the *jnani*, is totally unmoved. He is fixed in Brahman and therefore, though he acts, he is not disturbed by any action. This is the model. It does not refer to some far away God up there; it is God in each one of us. He is within all, he is outside all. And now a further consideration.

16.   He is ONE in all, but it seems as if he were many. He supports all beings: from him comes destruction, and from him comes creation.

"He is ONE in all, but it seems as if he were many." Here again the same principle is evident. God is one but as he is manifesting in all the multiplicity of creatures, he appears to be many: he appears as a tree, as the earth, as the sky, as you and as me. Or as I suggested before, the one Spirit is received in a different way in each person and in each thing, according to its capacity. Each inorganic object receives the power of the Spirit but it does not receive life. The living being receives the power and the life but it does not receive consciousness. The human being receives the power, the life, and consciousness — but only a limited mental human consciousness. The whole purpose of creation is that the human being should develop his capacity until he receives the fullness of divine consciousness into himself. That is our goal: to develop beyond our human consciousness with its limitations to the divine consciousness when we become aware of the Lord within and we think with him, speak with him and act with him. Then we are realised souls. That is our goal, to be one with the One who appears as many.

Then the text says, "from him comes destruction and from him comes creation." God is the creator, the preserver and the destroyer. He creates the world, he preserves it, but he is also the source of corruption, of death. Every creature is born and dies and life is the cause of death. Every death is the beginning of life, it is the rhythm of nature and our own death is equally the beginning of a new life. So God is in death inasmuch as he wills death in nature no less than life. Life and death are the rhythm of nature and eventually we have to pass beyond both life and death because God is beyond both.

17.   He is the Light of all lights which shines beyond all darkness. It is vision, the end of vision, to be reached by vision, dwelling in the heart of all.

This is reminiscent of the *Shvetashvatara Upanishad*: "The sun does not shine there neither the moon nor the stars, much less any earthly fire. By his light all these are illumined and his radiance illumines all creation."

The one light is shining through all these things and they have no light in themselves. There is a story in the *Kena Upanishad* which brings it out very well. The three gods, Indra, the king of the gods, Vayu, the wind, and Agni, the fire, met together after obtaining a victory in battle. They attributed to themselves what they had achieved and did not realise that they were all dependent on Brahman. So Brahman appeared to them in a strange form and they went to ask who and what this was. First Agni, the fire, went and Brahman asked him, "Who are you?" And he said, "I am the fire, I can burn up anything on earth," so Brahman took a piece of straw and said, "Burn that." Agni tried and tried but he could not burn it. So he went back and said, "I don't know who this being is." Then Vayu, the wind, came and Brahman said, "Who are you?" And he said, "I am the wind, I can blow anything on this earth." So Brahman took a straw and said, "Blow that away." Vayu blew and blew but he could not move it at all, so he retired saying that he could not find who this being was. Then Indra, the king of the gods, approached Brahman, but as he got near, Brahman disappeared, and then a heavenly being appeared saying that this was Brahman, and that it was through him that they had obtained the victory and not through their own powers.

All the powers of nature depend on the one supreme God and do not act of themselves at all. The wind and the fire and the earth are all dependent on the power of Brahman and not on their own power.

It is the same with human beings; no one does anything of his own power. When Pilate asked Jesus at his trial, "Do you know that I have power to release you and power to put you to death?", Jesus replied, "You would have no power over me if it had not been given to you from on high"(John 19.10,11). Nothing comes except what is given from on high. "It is vision, the end of vision, to be reached by vision, dwelling in the hearts of all." This 'vision' is literally knowledge, *jnana*, and *jneya* is the thing to be known. *Jnana gamyam* is that which leads to knowledge. What we are really trying to do is to discover the Lord in this way, dwelling in the hearts of all.

18. I have told you briefly what is the field, what is wisdom, and what is the End of man's vision. When a man knows this he enters into my Being.

Krishna explains that he has now made clear what is the 'field' of knowledge and what is the nature of this knowledge when it leads to enlightenment.

We now go back to the Sankhya division of nature and spirit.

19. Know that *Prakriti*, Nature, and *Purusha*, Spirit, are both without beginning, and that temporal changes and Gunas, conditions, come all from nature.

There is the eternal reality: *Purusha*, which is really the eternal Word of God from which all knowledge comes, and nature, *prakriti*, is the potentiality of all beings from which everything comes. The Word of God, the light, shines in that darkness, the womb of nature, and from it draws forth the whole creation.

20. Nature is the source of all material things: the maker, the means of making, and the thing made. Spirit is the source of all consciousness which feels pleasure and feels pain.

Nature is said to be *karya*, *karana*, and *kartritve*, the cause, the effect and the activity. *Prakriti* embraces all that we mean by the object of science;

all the laws of cause and effect which science studies are the laws of *prakriti*. Wisdom consists in realising that these laws are quite valid in themselves and that they operate according to their own principles but that there is something beyond; there is a consciousness, a spirit, which is beyond nature. The great mistake so many scientists make is that they study the phenomena of nature, of *prakriti*, and they think that this is reality, but they forget they are exercising a consciousness which is actually involved in all that they are seeing and knowing. What is implied in Einstein's discovery that all observations are relative to the observer is that the scientist is simply observing and cognizing what his consciousness presents to him. There is no such thing as matter without consciousness. *Prakriti* is matter, *purusha* is consciousness, and they cannot be separated.

21. The spirit of man when in nature feels the ever-changing conditions of nature. When he binds himself to things ever-changing, a good or evil fate whirls him round through life-in-death.

The best way to understand this is to recall the division of spirit, soul and body. The soul is placed between the Spirit, *purusha*, the source of consciousness, and *prakriti*, nature, the body. The soul is a mirror of the Spirit, *purusha*, and if the soul turns towards *purusha*, it is illumined by it and it is set free; but if it involves itself in matter, in the body, in nature and turns away from the light of the spirit, of consciousness, then it is whirled around by the forces of nature. This is the whole problem of freedom and necessity. If we subject ourselves to the forces of nature, of the body, of physical causality and of psychological causality, then we are subject to *samsara*, to the wheel of time and to endless frustration. Only when we separate ourselves from nature, from matter, and attain to pure consciousness do we free ourselves. So either we have to discover this freedom in the spirit, or we are being swept along by the forces of nature or the unconscious.

Put in those terms there are three levels. There is first the unconscious, which is all the forces of nature, physical and psychological, working in us. Then there is the region of mental consciousness; and further above there is super-consciousness, the transcendent Spirit. Everything depends on whether we allow ourselves to be the play of the forces of the unconscious, which are driving us, or whether we are able to detach ourselves from that, and allow ourselves to be moved and activated by the Spirit, the pure consciousness beyond. We are always between the super-conscious and the unconscious: either we are subject to one or the other. The one is freedom and immortality, and the other is death and destruction. That is the choice. "He binds himself to ever-changing things." If a person allows himself to be taken up by the senses, the passions, the imagination, and ordinary mental activity, then "a good or evil fate whirls him round through life-in-death." A more literal translation is: "He comes to birth in good or evil wombs" (Z). The understanding about rebirth is that as one becomes attached to nature, to matter, to the body and the passions, one is caught in the wheel of time, until one learns to free oneself from it. But above this whole mechanism of nature is the Spirit Supreme, the *Purusha*.

22. But the Spirit Supreme in man is beyond fate. He watches, gives blessing, bears all, feels all. He is called the Lord Supreme and the Supreme Soul.

If one submits to nature, one is caught in the wheel of fate. But the Spirit in man is beyond fate. He watches and permits, surveys and approves, supports and experiences. This mighty Lord is *Maheshvara*, the Great Lord, and the *Paramatman* or *Purushottama*, the highest Person. This Supreme Lord is within us and he watches and surveys and supports the world, but he is not involved in it. What we have to do is to identify with the Spirit within so that we also are able to watch, to observe and to support, but not to get involved and carried away.

23. He who knows in truth this Spirit and knows nature with its changing conditions, wherever this man may be he is no more whirled round by fate.

"He is no more whirled round by fate" is literally, "he shall not be born again." Perhaps it is the same thing, for to be born again is to be subject to fate. At any rate, the essential meaning of it is clear: if one knows the Supreme Spirit dwelling within, and if one recognises nature and its conditions working all around, then one can be set free from this fate. But if one submits oneself to nature and the world, then one is subject to its conditions.

How do we separate ourselves from nature and its conditions? How do we get this freedom? He mentions three ways.

24. Some by the yoga of meditation, and by the grace of the Spirit, see the Spirit in themselves; some by the yoga of the vision of Truth; and others by the yoga of work.

A better translation is, "Some by meditation, by *dhyana*, behold the Self in the Self by the Self" (B & D). That is contemplation. When we withdraw beyond the senses, beyond the mind, to our inner person, we discover that indwelling Self. It is by the Self that we know the Self. We cannot know ourselves by the ordinary rational consciousness. We have to go beyond the rational consciousness to the intuitive awareness. It is a unified knowledge: knowing the Self, in the Self, by the Self. It is the difference between intuitive knowledge which is unitive, bringing our whole being into unity, and discursive knowledge which goes from one person to another, from one thing to another. The latter is our ordinary way of knowing; the former is this withdrawing into the *buddhi*, into the inner centre, and uniting all the faculties in one. Then we know the Self by the Self in the Self. And that Self is the *Paramatman* within, the Supreme Spirit within. At that point we are united with the One. We should keep in mind the illustration of the light shining in the mirror. When the mirror is clouded, we do not see the light. When the mirror is clear, in meditation, then the light shines in and we are simply aware of the light within, we are transparent to the light. Then we know the Self in the Self by the Self. This is what in Christian terminology is called contemplation.

The next way which is mentioned is that of ordinary meditation, or *Sankhya yoga*, which Mascaró translates as the 'vision of truth'. By *Sankhya yoga* is meant what is called *Buddhi yoga*, the yoga of wisdom, or *Raja yoga*, which consists of four stages: *pratyahara*, the withdrawing from the objects of the senses, recollection; *dharana*, concentration; *dhyana*, meditation; and *samadhi*, absorption into the One.

The third way is *karma yoga*, the yoga of action. One can transcend the ego by devoting oneself to the good of others. For many people that is the most natural and normal way. The question is how to get beyond the ego, and the answer given is either through contemplation or by ordinary meditation or by selfless service. *Bhakti*, or simple surrender, is not mentioned here, though it is one of the main themes of the *Gita*. These are the different ways to God; some people are drawn more to one and some to another. *Karma yoga* is the simplest way of losing oneself and finding God in one's neighbor.

25. And yet there are others who do not know, but they hear from others
and adore. They also cross beyond death, because of their devotion
to words of Truth.

Shrutva means hearing, "adhering to what they have heard" (B & D).
Many people live by faith. They are unable to meditate and they cannot
even do much unselfish work, but on the authority of others they believe,
and because of their faith they are saved. Simple faith can sometimes carry
one beyond all these other things. Simple faith in God can be the greatest
way of union. This is again typical of every religion: the great mass of the
followers have faith without having much experience; they believe, and
through that faith they are saved.

26. Whatever is born, Arjuna, whether it moves or it moves not, know
that it comes from the union of the field and the knower of the field.

This verse refers back to the first verse of the chapter where Arjuna
asked, "What is nature? What is the Person? What is the field and the knower
of the field?" Krishna is answering this. He has shown us what nature and
the person are. Now he goes back to the field and the knower of the field.
The field is *prakriti*, nature, the whole object of consciousness; and the knower
is the subject, that is, the Spirit, *purusha*, within. Everything that is born,
whether it moves or moves not comes from the union of *purusha* and *prakriti*,
the field and the knower of the field.

27. He who sees that the Lord of all is ever the same in all that is, immortal
in the field of mortality — he sees the truth.

This is Truth; to see behind all the perishing phenomena of nature,
the unchanging Person, the Being who is within all. That is the wisdom
and that is immortality.

28. And when a man sees that the God in himself is the same God in
all that is, he hurts not himself by hurting others: then he goes indeed
to the highest Path.

That is the basic Hindu understanding, that the one Lord, the one Self, is the same in every human being. If I hurt another I am hurting myself. There is only one Self in all. Every time we hurt somebody else, we hurt ourselves. This is seen in the Christian doctrine of the mystical body of Christ, of which St. Paul says, "We though many, are one body in Christ and individually members of one another" (Rom. 12.5). We are all members of one another and we are all members of the one body of the Lord. We cannot hurt anybody else without hurting ourselves. This is what is meant by 'seeing Christ in another'. Christ is in every human being, and to respect every human being is to respect Christ, the Lord, in him. And to hurt that human being is to hurt Christ in him. Jesus said, "As you did it to the least of my brethren you did it to me" (Matt. 25.40). That is fundamental, and it is common to Hindu, Christian and Buddhist teaching.

29. He who sees that all work, everywhere, is only the work of nature; and that the Spirit watches this work — he sees the truth.

The original idea of *purusha* and *prakriti* was that all activity comes from nature, and that *purusha*, consciousness, is simply the observer, the witness. It is not really involved in the work at all; it appears to be, and so we have to separate *purusha*, consciousness, from nature, and reach that state of freedom. The *Gita* takes this a step further, identifying *purusha* with the Lord, and holding that although, strictly speaking, the Lord does not act in nature, he is witnessing and supporting all the activity of nature. So in a sense God is present in all nature in its structure and activity, without being affected by it. To be able to discern the action of God in every event in our lives is real wisdom and that is the goal. We normally attribute most events to chance. If it rains, we say it is because clouds formed and were blown this way, but we should be able to discern behind the rain, that God is the cause of the rain. It is He who is causing all the laws of nature which govern the clouds and the rain. Similarly, if somebody gets angry with us, we think it is because his character is like that, but we should discern also that it is because God has given him that nature, that character, that freedom. So there is a cause behind everything and that cause is the presence of God. There is a book which has influenced many people called *Abandonment to Divine Providence*, by J.P. de Caussade, a Jesuit in the eighteenth century. He has only one idea in the whole book, but he develops it in a very impressive way, and that is that sanctity consists in responding to the will of God at every moment of one's life. The will of God comes to us at every moment through everything that happens to us. If we see the will of God in everything and respond to it, then we are perfectly one with God. But we need to be able to discern the action of God in every tiny detail of life. Normally we are simply blind to it. If something very dramatic happens, if, for instance, contrary to all expectations, somebody is cured of an illness, we may respond by saying that this is the work of God. But the fact that God is doing everything, all the time, continuously escapes us. And yet to realise that is wisdom, that is *viveka*, discrimination between the real and the unreal; to see the action of God in the whole manifest world, from moment to moment.

30.　When a man sees that the infinity of various beings is abiding in the ONE, and is an evolution from the ONE, then he becomes one with Brahman.

　　More literally, "When a man sees that all the diversity of contingent beings are *eka-stham*, abiding in the One, standing in the One". We see everything separately; we see every person and all things separately and we deal with them separately. But to discern that they are all standing in the One, and that the One is present and acting in them, that is wisdom. The whole creation is coming forth from God at every moment. God does not create the world and then leave it; He is behind everything that happens from moment to moment. When we recognise that, when we realise this presence of God acting in our lives at every point, then we become one with Brahman. Conversely, when we ignore that, then we become One with matter, with nature, and we are swept about by all the forces of nature.

31.　Beginningless and free from changing conditions, imperishable in the Spirit Supreme. Though he is in the body, not his is the work of the body, and he is pure from the imperfection of all work.

　　The one Supreme Spirit is in you and in me; the Word of God, the Spirit of God, is beginningless and free from all changing conditions, and is imperishable. But He is in the body; *sharirastho*, literally, He stands in the body. It is He who enables us to act, but we are responsible for the action which we take. This is a delicate point, this point where the light shines into the mirror. Everything in a sense comes from the light, but nevertheless, the imperfections of the mirror distort the light and color it. That is where things go wrong with each one of us. The one Light is shining in each one, but each of us, with his imperfections, dissipates and distorts the light. But just as the sun is not affected by anything that happens to the light, so the Lord is not affected by our distortions, our selfishness, our sin.

32. Just as the omnipresent ether is pure because intangible, so the Spirit dwelling in matter is pure from the touch of matter.

At one time scientists believed that behind all the elements there was an invisible ether. The Sanskrit word is *akasha* and, since we do not believe in 'ether' anymore, the best translation is 'space'. All matter is in space, and space pervades it all; so the Spirit is present in everything, in all matter, but is invisible and immaterial. It cannot be seen; it can only be 'known'. The Spirit is everywhere in the body, within but unaffected by it. ·

33. And even as one sun gives light to all things in this world, so the Lord of the field gives light to all his field.

That is the best illustration. The sun illumines the whole world and so the Lord of the field, the *Kshetri* literally the 'owner of the field', illumines the whole field. The light of God is shining through the whole creation, through everyone, and is the source of all.

34. Those who with the eye of inner vision see the distinction between the field and the knower of the field, and see the liberation of spirit from matter, they go into the Supreme.

This is what one has to see: the distinction between the field and the knower, matter and consciousness. And when we discern that and see how the Spirit is free of matter and is not determined, then we can unite ourselves with that Spirit and we are no longer affected by matter and by the laws of nature. To do this is to be set free; this is *moksha*, liberation.

Chapter 14

The Yoga of the Three Gunas

This chapter is concerned with the exposition of the three *gunas* and their effects. The three *gunas* — *sattva*, *rajas* and *tamas* — are the constituents of nature and they, in their characteristic ways, determine the whole of samsaric existence. The 'supreme wisdom' referred to in the first *sloka* is not so much the teaching about the *gunas* as such, for this would hardly be the highest wisdom. Rather, it is the secret, or mystery, that it is only by becoming one with Brahman, with God, that we are liberated from the conditioning power of the *gunas*. Only then are we able to see *samsara* and the *gunas* for what they are, and to pass beyond them.

Krishna is speaking:

1. I will reveal again a supreme wisdom, of all wisdom the highest: sages who have known it have gone hence to supreme perfection.

2. Taking refuge in this wisdom they have become part of me: they are not reborn at the time of creation, and they are not destroyed at the time of dissolution.

"Taking refuge in this wisdom they have become part of me." *Mama sadharmyam agatah*, "They go to my mode of existence." The goal is to share in the divine mode of existence. "They are not reborn at the time of creation and they are not destroyed at the time of dissolution." There is always this wheel of *samsara* moving through birth and death and then there is also the *pralaya* when the whole creation goes back into Brahman and then it comes forth again. *Moksha* is the deliverance from the wheel of *samsara*, the ability to go beyond, to the One Supreme.

3. In the vastness of my Nature I place the seed of things to come; and from this union comes the birth of all beings.

This *shloka* describes the process of creation and an alternative translation is "Great Brahman is to me a womb (*yoni*) and in it I plant the seed; from this derives the origin of all creatures" (Z).

This is a very unusual use of the word *Brahman*. Generally it is used to denote the Supreme Being. However, as we have seen, it can be used at various levels. The *Shvetashvatara Upanishad*, for instance, says that in Brahman there is a triad. There is nature, the soul and the Lord, and together these three constitute Brahman. So Brahman is in a sense the universality of all, and nature, the soul and the Lord are all parts of this one. Brahman can be used as the *Parambrahman*, the Supreme beyond everything, or it can be used as the source of everything, the *Saguna Brahman*, or, as in this case, it can be used of *mula prakriti*, the womb of nature from which all creatures come. Here it seems to be used in the sense of *mula prakriti*, the womb of nature.

4. Wherever a being may be born, Arjuna, know that my Nature is his mother and that I am the Father who gave him life.

Or: "In whatever wombs mortals are produced, Arjuna, great Brahman is their womb and I their generating father" (B & D). Here again the phrase *Mahat Brahman* is used for that which is normally called *mula prakriti*, the womb of creation, in which Krishna, the personal God, plants the seed of life. This is the base of all the sexual imagery in Hinduism which often shocks people. It is usually depicted by the *lingam* and the *yoni*. The whole creation is the union of the masculine and feminine principles and this is present everywhere in creation, in the earth, and in human beings. It is a fundamental principle and it is only a kind of puritanism which prevents people from seeing it; there is nothing objectionable about it at all. In Hinduism, as in all ancient traditions, sex is essentially holy and is referred to as a holy mystery. Marriage in Christianity is also holy, which is why it is considered a sacrament. It is only in a very materialistic civilization that sex becomes unholy, profane, or simply an object of pleasure. Essentially sex is holy and as St. Paul says, the union of the husband and the wife is a symbol of the union of Christ and the Church,' of God and the soul (Eph. 5.32). The Song of Songs in the Old Testament is at one level a love poem, but the marriage of the male and female is seen to represent the marriage of God with his people, God and the soul. The Song of Songs has served as the basis of the sexual symbolism in Christian mysticism from the time of Origen and St. Gregory of Nyssa, to St. Bernard, and finally St. John of the Cross. So this is what is behind all the sexual imagery and we should understand and accept *purusha* and *prakriti*, the male and female principles, as the source of all.

5. SATTVA, RAJAS, TAMAS − light, fire and darkness − are the three constituents of nature. They appear to limit in finite bodies the liberty of their infinite Spirit.

These three constituents of nature are the three *gunas* with which this chapter is concerned. Literally *guna* means a strand, and nature is conceived as woven of these three strands. They hold together, and constitute, the whole of *prakriti*, nature. The three strands, *sattva*, *rajas*, and *tamas* are best translated, as by Mascaró, "light, fire and darkness." *Sattva* is light and when the light of *Purusha* shines into the darkness *sattva* is the first effect of it; that is the radiance of the light. This applies both in the cosmos and in man. Wherever there is light and radiance in nature it is the effect of *sattva* and where there is purity, intelligence, and goodness in man, this also is *sattva*. *Sattva* is the first manifestation, and from *sattva* one descends to *rajas*.

Rajas is fire; it is energy and passion. It is said that the divine light shines out and manifests in all the different spheres of consciousness. Each one of us is like a mirror in which this light shines. In the *buddhi* of each person this light is shining. At that point the One becomes many and the one light is divided among the many separate consciousnesses. Once it becomes individualized in us, it receives the force of what is called *pravritti*. *Pravritti* is the force which drives one out, as opposed to that of *nivritti* which is that same force returning to the source. *Rajas* is the energy of courage and battle, ambition and work. It is the outward force in both man and nature. The light descends and divides, as it were, and these forces come into play.

They are the forces of nature. Violence and conflict in the world come from the force of *rajas*. It is the source of conflict but of course all these forces have both a positive and a negative side. *Rajas* has its own value as energy and power.

Thirdly, there is *tamas*, darkness, dullness, sloth and inertia. This is where the light rushing out becomes solidified, becomes earth, becomes matter. It is the lowest level to which the light descends. The *Gita* tends to speak of *tamas* as the bad element but obviously there is a good side to *tamas*. We all need the three elements in our nature. We need *sattva*, light, intelligence, goodness, and we need energy which is force and power to act, and we also need to be earthed, grounded, to have a solid base. Many people suffer from an insufficient proportion of *tamas*. They are working all from the head and not based on the earth at all. So tamas does have a positive value, but of course it is a force which drives down more than anything else. That is why it is described as negative.

An alternative way of translating this *shloka* is: "These are the three constituents sprung from nature which bind the embodied self in the body though the Self itself is changeless" (Z). This refers to the *dehinam*, the embodied One. The individual self comes forth from the Supreme and the Self is embodied in the body, and becomes bound to the body. *Tamas, rajas*, and *sattva* are the forces which bind the embodied self. Mascaró translates, "They appear to limit in finite bodies the liberty of the Infinite Spirit." It is right to say "they appear to" because in reality the Spirit is not affected by the *gunas*, for it is beyond them. In appearance and in our experience, the One is limited, is bound. It is *maya* or *karma* which binds us to the three *gunas*.

6. Of these Sattva, because it is pure and it gives light and is the health of life, binds to earthly happiness and to lower knowledge.

The *sattva guna* is the one which is superior. Nevertheless it binds one to pleasure or happiness. Every created thing is a bondage if one seeks to make attaining it an end in itself. This applies not only to material good but also to spiritual good which can be more binding than anything else in the end. Attachment to spiritual goods can be the most binding force. Such attachment prevents one from going to God himself. One stops at a lesser, created good and this is the danger of *sattva*. Many intelligent and good people can be terribly limited by their intelligence and goodness.

The word *jnanasangena* which Mascaró translates as 'lower knowledge', means rather all knowledge: the whole sphere of knowledge and wisdom which is so tempting and attractive. The better the thing, the more it can bind. However this is not the Supreme wisdom for that goes beyond the *gunas*.

7. Rajas is of the nature of passion, the source of thirst and attachment. It binds the soul of man to action.

The word used is *trishna*, a Buddhist word which means 'clinging to life'. It is the thirst which binds one to his world. It binds the soul to action – *karma*. This is what most people suffer from today; the urge to work, to do, to act. The Western world in general is under the influence of *rajas*, the energy of action; the 'work ethic', as it is called. One is bound by good works just as much as by bad. Good works bind when the ego enters into them, but if the work is done freely from the Spirit within then it is a wholly different matter.

People who are so full of virtuous energy, seeking to improve the world, are often being dominated by their egos and are simply under the control of *rajas* – the forces of nature. They are no longer free but rather are controlled by these forces. That is why people with the best will in the world can do such terrible things. This applies to all the great revolutions like the French Revolution with its motto of 'liberty, equality and fraternity'. So often these high ideals lead to such tragic results because *rajas* gets into the process and people are driven to obliterate anyone who opposes them. Their opponents end up in concentration camps – or are 'liquidated'. All this is the effect of *rajas* in its negative aspect of blind force and passion.

8. Tamas, which is born of ignorance, darkens the soul of all men. It binds them to sleepy dullness, and then they do not watch and then they do not work.

Ignorance, *ajnana*, is the key word here, for just as *jnana*, wisdom, is the effect of *sattva*, ignorance is the effect of *tamas*. Ignorance, of course, is used in a wide sense; it means primal ignorance, the ignorance of Reality, of Truth, of the One. *Tamas* manifests itself when the mind is clouded by ignorance and we are weighed down by the body, and that leads to indolence and sloth. This is a purely negative view of *tamas*. We should always remember that *tamas* has also a positive character of being 'down to earth.'

9. Sattva binds to happiness; Rajas to action; Tamas, over-clouding wisdom, binds to lack of vigilance.

Sattva binds to happiness. Everyone is seeking happiness, for it is something desirable, something good in itself; yet, because it is limited, it still binds one. Passion, *rajas*, binds to action, *karma*; and *tamas* stifles and obscures wisdom and attaches one to heedlessness. We all suffer from *tamas* when we are feeling depressed and dull, or when we wake up in the morning with a headache. This is *tamas* working in our nature.

10. Sometimes Sattva may prevail over Rajas and Tamas, at others Rajas over Tamas and Sattva, and at others Tamas over Sattva and Rajas.

So we are all being subjected to these forces. One day *sattva* can be strong in us and the others subdued, and the next day *sattva* is overcome by *rajas*, and then again both are overcome by *tamas*.

Sometimes these *gunas* are translated by 'moods' since they are the equivalent of the moods by which we are often dominated. Sometimes the mood is light and wonderful and then suddenly for no apparent reason depression takes over and everything becomes sad and gloomy, which is *tamas*. Or we get an urge to go out and do something, which is *rajas*. We are always moving between these three *gunas* and the goal is to get beyond all three of them.

11. When the light of wisdom shines from the portals of the body's dwelling, then we know that Sattva is in power.

The "portals of the body's dwelling" are the senses. Where *sattva* prevails, then the whole body is lighted up. As it says in the Gospel, "If thine eye (the eye of wisdom) be single, thy whole body shall be full of light" (Matt. 6.22).

12. Greed, busy activity, many undertakings, unrest, the lust of desire — these arise when Rajas increases.

When *rajas* increases then the result is greed. *Pravritti* is this irrational force which drives one out, committing oneself to work and many undertakings, and *asamah* is being upset, restless, always changing. This is the effect of *rajas* upsetting one's equilibrium. *Spriha* is translated by Zaehner as ambition, which is the typical effect of *rajas*. The *rajasic* person is highly ambitious, someone who likes to do many things and get on in the world. All this has value but has great limitations also.

13. Darkness, inertia, negligence, delusion – these appear when Tamas prevails.

With *tamas, apravritti*, the opposite of *pravritti*, occurs. Instead of being urged to action, slothfulness takes over. The ideal is to have neither one nor the other, but to be centered in the Self within and so to be free to act or not to act. But here the person is being driven either by outgoing impulses and ambition, or by sloth and indolence. In each case, it is the unconscious, which is part of the forces of nature, which is acting. This darkness, *apravritti*, is unwillingness to act; it is heedlessness. These are the effects of *tamas*. One could go a long way by noting every day how the different gunas prevail day by day, and hour by hour. Such observation can provide quite an index of one's character.

14. If the soul meets death when Sattva prevails, then it goes to the pure regions of those who are seeking Truth.

Great importance is attached to the state of mind in which one leaves the world. That is why many people are afraid of sudden death. But in reality, it is not so much the attitude of mind prevailing at the moment of death that matters, as the habitual tendency of the mind towards light and truth or towards darkness and death.

15. If a man meets death in a state of Rajas, he is reborn amongst those who are bound by their restless activity; and if he dies in Tamas he is reborn in the wombs of the irrational.

The more ancient tradition about rebirth was that one could pass from human birth to animal and even to lower forms of existence, just as one could also pass to the world of the gods and then return again. This brings out the fact that we are all members of a cosmic whole which embraces many states of consciousness, and we all bear within ourselves not only the past experiences of the human race but also the course of cosmic evolution. Our bodies are linked with the first living cells and with the first atoms which came from the original explosion of matter.

16. Any work when it is well done bears the pure harmony of Sattva; but when done in Rajas it brings pain, and when done in Tamas it brings ignorance.

The fruit of a good action is *nirmala*, without stain, pure. The fruit of *rajas* is *duhkha*, sorrow and pain. And the fruit of *tamas* is ignorance, *ajnana*, darkness of the mind.

17. From Sattva arises wisdom, from Rajas greed, from Tamas negligence, delusion and ignorance.

18. Those who are in Sattva climb the path that leads on high, those who are in Rajas follows the level path, those who are in Tamas sink downwards on the lower path.

It is noticeable that *rajas* and *tamas* are always conceived in negative terms, *sattva* alone being given positive value. A more balanced view would see that the energy of *rajas* and the firmness and solidity of *tamas* are both necessary for a balanced life. Over-emphasis on *sattva* in certain schools of Hinduism could well be a sign of neglect of the material aspect of life, as Sri Aurobindo maintained.

19. When the man of vision sees that the powers of nature are the only actors of this vast drama, and he beholds THAT which is beyond the powers of nature then he comes into my Being.

This perception is *viveka*, discernment, which comes when we realize that we are being driven by the forces of nature. We imagine that we are doing things because we want to, but really it is the forces of nature working inside which are governing us all the time. We have to rise above the *gunas* and realize that the real source of our being is not in our nature; it is not in the body with its feelings and passions, and it is not even in our minds. The mind, the feelings, and the body are all constituents of nature and the real source from which everything comes is the Spirit, the *Atman* within. When we realize that which is beyond the power of nature, then we are free. The soul is between *Purusha*, the *Atman*, the Spirit, and nature, *prakriti*, with the three *gunas*. Either we incline towards nature and let ourselves be governed by these forces or we awake to the Spirit within and allow that Spirit to move, guide and act on our lives. The one is freedom and the other is bondage. Most people believe they are free when they follow their *gunas*, when they follow their will and inclinations, but this is only a surrendering to the forces of nature. Only when we turn back and discover the Self is there any real freedom.

20. And when he goes beyond the three conditions of nature which constitute his mortal body then, free from birth, old age, and death, and sorrow, he enters into Immortality.

He receives the *amrita*, the drink of immortality. Zaehner points out that in the teaching of the Buddha, birth, death, and old age are all sufferings and he quotes the saying: " 'What is the noble truth about suffering?' and the Buddha replies, 'Birth is suffering, old age is suffering, death is suffering.' " That is the great insight of the Buddha; all this world, separate from the One Reality, is suffering. When we accept this world as it is, on its own appearance, and allow ourselves to be subject to it, then birth, death and old age are all suffering.

The cinema is a perfect illustration of this. The lights go out and we are completely absorbed in the drama, forgetting our own selves, our own lives, and everything else, and just living that drama. Then the lights go on and we realize that the whole thing was only a story and a show that we were seeing.

We live in this imaginary world without realizing the Eternal One, who is there all the time behind it all. We take all this for the Ultimate Reality. It has a reality and is meaningful but only in the light of the Ultimate Reality. When we mistake the appearance for the reality then we are in *maya*. When we wake to the Reality, the world does not lose its meaning − it recovers its meaning. All our life and actions are meaningful when consciously related to the transcendent One. Life is real, not in itself, but in relation to the One. That is the meaning of going beyond the *gunas* and being freed from the sufferings of old age and death.

Arjuna asks:

21. How is the man known who has gone beyond the three powers of nature? What is his path, and how does he transcend the three?

And Krishna replies:

22. He who hates not light, nor busy activity, nor even darkness, when
they are near, neither longs for them when they are far;

The aim is not simply to repudiate all this world of appearances. It
is to be able to observe it, to be the witness of all that goes on around,
to be aware of it and sensitive to it, but not to be dominated by it. It is
the law of detachment.

23. Who unperturbed by changing conditions sits apart and watches and
says 'the powers of nature go round', and remains firm and shakes not;

This is detachment. When we are able to observe ourselves becoming
attached to the activity of the mind, or to the activity of works, or to our
outgoing activity, or to the body, and, having observed, to detach ourselves
from all that, then we are free.

Nearly all Buddhist discipline is based on this constant awareness which
is called mindfulness. To be aware when thinking and when acting, when
eating or drinking, is to be free from attachment. But we tend to be
completely absorbed by what is going on, and that is the whole difference.
We can be as active as we like, but when we retain this simple awareness
it keeps us free from atachment to our activity. If we observe our different
moods we become free of them. If we realize that we are being moved
by this mood and that mood, then we are no longer dominated.

24. Who dwells in his inner self, and is the same in pleasure and pain;
to whom gold or stones or earth are one, and what is pleasing or
displeasing leave him in peace; who is beyond both praise and blame,
and whose mind is steady and quiet;

This is the mark of a wise man. He is the same in pleasure and pain;
and that is extremely difficult. We get excited by pleasure and are averse
to pain. 'To whom gold or stones or earth are one'. Ramakrishna, as we
observed before, used to take some earth in one hand and gold in the other
and try to imagine that they were the same. The fascination of money is
immeasurable. Often one can be talking to people quite calmly about many
things when something comes up about money and the whole mood changes.

Suddenly everyone becomes excited. We need to learn to look also on money evenly and not get disturbed by it.

25. Who is the same in honour or disgrace, and has the same love for enemies or friends, who surrenders all selfish undertakings – this man has gone beyond the three.

This is much more difficult. We all tend to be attached to people whom we like and who like us, and inevitably we are averted from people whom we do not like and who do not like us. It does not mean that we may never dislike any person; temperamentally we may be opposed to them and they may irritate us, but we can have a perfectly equal love for them. We can serve them and do every good for them just as much as for someone to whom we are attracted. Love is the same for all, but likes and dislikes belong to our temperament. St. Thomas was once asked if one should love father and mother more than other people and he answered that it is not exactly more, but differently. We should have a different love for father and mother, for wife and children, for friends and for enemies. The one love is for all but it is modified by the different persons. A person who is simply indifferent and cannot see the difference between a friend and a foe, or a mother and a child is obviously not human. We have to have our human feelings, yet they are all to be controlled and under the direction of this universal love.

We can get the impression, if we are not careful, that the *Gita* recommends doing nothing and being indifferent to everybody. It is not that we do not see the difference between earth and gold but it is a matter of our attitude; we are not attracted by the one or averted from the other. As we know that the Spirit is One although it is manifold in all its operations, so we should be one in ourselves and thus be able to act in all these manifold ways without disturbing that inner unity.

26. And he who with never-failing love adores me and works for me, he passes beyond the three powers and can be one with Brahman, the ONE.

In the *Gita* it is the love for Krishna, the personal God, which controls all other loves and leads to perfect unity.

27. For I am the abode of Brahman, the never-failing fountain of everlasting life. The law of righteousness is my law; and my joy is infinite joy.

Zaehner translates this as, "I am the base supporting Brahman", the *Brahmano pratistha*, but his attempt to show that Krishna is above Brahman is based on a misunderstanding. The relation between Brahman and the personal God may be illustrated by the ideal of circumincession within the Trinity. The Father is in the Son, and the Son is in the Father, but the Father is not superior to the Son. They are distinct and yet they are one. Krishna is in Brahman and Brahman is in him. They are different aspects of the One. "The law of righteousness is my law." The word in the text is *dharma*, which is the law of the universe, of the whole creation, the law of man and the law of every individual human being: *dharma* is our duty in life.

The idea is that we are all involved in these forces of nature which are working around us and within us all the time. Yet we have in us the capacity to go beyond, to transcend the *tamas*, the *rajas* and the *sattva*; to experience the presence of the One within, and in going beyond we become one with the Lord. We become Brahman, *Brahma-bhuta*. We are not our true self when we are being dominated by all these forces. That is what is meant by Self-realization. Ordinarily we are being driven by the psychological forces around and we do not know who we are or what we stand for. When we free ourselves from these forces we discover our identity, our true Self who is One with the Self of the universe. Our only true Self is our Self in God.

Chapter 15

The Yoga of the Highest Spirit

In this chapter Krishna reveals how he, the Lord, the Highest Spirit, is present in the human soul and in the whole physical universe, pervading and sustaining all things. Particularly important here is the teaching that the Highest Spirit, the Spirit Supreme, is not only beyond the perishable but is also beyond the imperishable. In this the *Gita* marks an advance on all but the later *Upanishads* (cf. the introduction to Chapter 8).

Krishna begins by speaking of the great cosmic tree:

1. There is a tree, the tree of Transmigration, the Asvattha tree everlasting.
   Its roots are above in the Highest, and its branches are here below.
   Its leaves are sacred songs, and he who knows them knows the Vedas.

This tree of transmigration is the tree of *samsara*, the world of becoming. The tree is a great symbol in mythology. Normally, it has its roots in the earth and ascends to heaven, but this tree has its roots above, a symbol which is derived from the *Rig Veda*. Zaehner quotes:

> "In the bottomless abyss King Varuna
> By the power of his pure will, upholds aloft
> The cosmic tree's high crown. There stands below
> The branches and above the roots. Within us
> May the banners of his light be firmly set."

That is the image taken from the *Rig Veda*. The idea is that the whole creation comes forth from Brahman above and spreads out below. This can be taken as an image of the brain. The whole structure of the body comes from the brain which sends out its branches in the form of the nervous system. In the *Vedas* the intelligible worlds of the gods and angels come forth first from Brahman, and then the material world which is its manifestation.

2. Its branches spread from earth to heaven, and the powers of nature give them life. Its buds are the pleasures of the senses. Far down below, its roots stretch into the world of men, binding a mortal through selfish actions.

"Its branches spread from earth to heaven and the powers of nature give them life." This translation is not quite accurate. The text says, "Downwards and upwards spread the branches", and the meaning is that the branches come down and root themselves, and then also spread up, like the banyan tree. The tree comes down from above and as it descends it gets rooted in us. Then we become bound within this great wheel of *samsara*.

3.-4. Men do not see the changing form of that tree, nor its beginning, nor its end, nor where its roots are. But let the wise see, and with the strong sword of dispassion let him cut this strong-rooted tree, and seek that path wherefrom those who go never return. Such a man can say: "I go for refuge to that Eternal Spirit from whom the stream of creation came at the beginning."

As we have seen, the one way of getting out of this whole cosmic *maya*, this *samsara*, is through detachment, *asanga*. There has to be detachment from the senses and the mind, and then awakening to the reality beyond. This same tree is also mentioned in the *Katha Upanishad*. In it all the worlds are established; beyond it none can pass. Then in the *Shvetashvatara Upanishad* it says, "Beyond him, there is nothing whatever, no one is more minute than he, no one more vast, like a sturdy tree firm fixed in heaven he stands; the One, the Person, who fills this whole universe."

The cosmic Person, *Purusha*, in whom this whole universe exists, is symbolised by this cosmic tree. Zaehner has an interesting quotation from the *Mahabharata*, "From the seed of the Unmanifest grows up the tree of

Brahman, mighty, primordial; its trunk, the *buddhi*, the soul; its shoots the *ahankara*, the ego; its inmost recesses, the senses; boughs, the gross elements; and the boughs that tally with them, their several parts. Always in leaf, always in flower, producing fair fruits and foul, the means of life of all contingent beings, the primordial tree of Brahman stands. Cut it down, chop it up with wisdom."

What it means is that things appear to us as permanent, as absolute, but by *viveka*, discrimination, we recognize that all this is a reflection of the One beyond. When we see it as a reflection of the One, then it has reality, but when we mistake it for the real, that is *maya* and we are involved in *avidya*, in ignorance.

"I go for refuge to that Eternal Spirit from whom this stream of creation came at the beginning." The "Eternal Spirit" is the 'Primeval Person', the *Adhyam Purusham*. This is the cosmic Person of the *Rig Veda* who is an archetype of the whole universe. From him flows the energy or the primordial power which is called *pravritti*. *Pravritti* is the energy which flows into the world; so from Brahman flows forth eternally the creative power which creates *samsara*, this world of change. The return journey is *nivritti*, which is going back through the senses and the mind and returning to the One.

5. Because the man of pure vision, without pride or delusion, in liberty from the chains of attachments, with his soul ever in his inner Spirit, all selfish desires gone, and free from the two contraries known as pleasure and pain, goes to the abode of Eternity.

To be free from *samsara* we must be free from pride and *moha*, delusion; that is, we must be free from being deceived by appearances. Released from all the dualities of pleasure and pain, we then can go to the *avyayam padam*, the eternal path or goal.

6. There the sun shines not, nor the moon gives light, nor fire burns, for the Light of my glory is there. Those who reach that abode return no more.

The first part of this *shloka* is found in several *Upanishads*. The second part is more literally, "Those who go there return no more; that is my supreme abode." This passage is similar to the Revelation of St. John: "I saw no sun there, nor moon; for the glory of God is its light, and its lamp is the Lamb" (Rev. 21.23). When we reach the source of light, there all created lights are eclipsed.

The tree is the tree of the world, of becoming, of change, of *samsara.* By detachment one frees oneself from this *maya,* this bondage, and one goes beyond to the world of light, where one experiences the Eternal Reality, the One.

7. A spark of my eternal Spirit becomes in this world a living soul; and this draws around its centre the five senses and the mind resting in nature.

"An eternal portion of my own Self, transformed in the world of life into a living spirit (*jivatman*), draws around itself the senses of which the mind is the sixth, clothed in matter" (B & D). The word *amsha* which Mascaró translates as "a spark" is rendered by Zaehner, "a minute part of me".

Zaehner quotes Shankara: "The *jiva* is a particle of the divine substance imprisoned in material nature which when thus ensouled is called *jiva bhuta prakriti,* living nature." Shankara asked, "How can the Absolute, which is by definition partless, have a minute part of itself divided?" He answered, "It is like the reflection of the sun in water; remove the water and the reflection disappears into the sun which alone is real. It is like space or ether in a jar; remove the jar and the continuity of the space or ether is again restored."

The first illustration is the best. As the sun shines in the water, so the one Light is shining in each *jiva.* This reflection can be called a part, but it does not divide the light which remains undivided in itself. Ramanuja says that Brahman is modified by all the *jivas* and souls, but that is inadequate because it suggests that Brahman undergoes a change. Shankara always insisted that Brahman cannot change – but it can manifest like the sun in water. The one Spirit manifests itself in all these different *jivas,* souls, and the senses gather around them with the mind, and that constitutes our individual nature. At the point of the *buddhi,* the light from above shines into each one of us. It is in the *buddhi* that the One appears to be divided into the many. It is the point which reflects this eternal light, which is then divided up by the *manas,* the mind, and the *indriyas,* the senses.

8. When the Lord of the body arrives, and when he departs and wanders

on, he takes them over with him, as the wind takes perfumes from their places of sleep.

More literally, "When the Lord acquires a body, and when he abandons it, he seizes these (the mind and the senses), and goes with them, as the wind takes fragrances from their place" (B & D). This is strong support for saying that it is the Lord who is the transmigrator. It is not the individual soul that migrates; it is the Lord. The One spirit is manifesting himself in all these individual consciousnesses; and he enters into your consciousness and mine through the *buddhi*, and he takes a *manas*, a mind, and senses. That is why we say that when I act and when I think, it is the Lord that is acting and thinking in me. When I die, the Lord takes back my senses and my mind and my *buddhi* into himself, and from the Lord again comes forth another being, but it is not me. I have returned to the Lord. What I have done in the world will affect what comes again into existence here but I cannot call that myself. There is the one Self who is manifesting in all these selves. I come from my parents, and various physical and psychological characteristics come down to me through my ancestors. On the theory of individual rebirth, I am being reborn again and again. A deeper view is that the one Self is manifesting in all my ancestors and when coming to birth in me, he is bringing all the experiences of my past ancestors. That accounts for the Buddhist understanding of the reincarnation of the Dalai Lama and other important Lamas. The Lord is manifesting in different races and different peoples, and in Tibet there is this manifestation of the Lord, which goes through certain channels. It is not that the individual Dalai Lama is being reborn again and again; the Lord is manifesting himself in the Dalai Lama and bringing with him the experience of the Dalai Lamas of the past. And so the Lord is reborn again and again in the succession of Dalai Lamas.

It must be remembered that Buddhists do not believe in an individual soul. They hold that there are only different physical and psychological elements, *skandhas*, which come together, and are continually changing. This aggregate of *skandhas* is what is perceived as an individual self. At the moment of death all these elements have come into a certain order, or structure, and that goes on; not the individual soul precisely, but these tendencies in one's nature go on to another birth. That expresses very nearly the same point of view. The Lord who has taken a particular nature and has lived his life in it, reassumes those elements into himself and all that is left unfulfilled in that nature goes on to be manifested in another birth. It is the Lord who is transmigrating. That makes sense from a Christian point of view. One can say that Christ is, as it were, incarnate in every human being; the whole of humanity is the Body of Christ. That Body is built up of all these cells of individual human beings. Sin enters into the Body and disrupts it, and in the Incarnation the Lord assumes the Body of humanity, all these cells, all these individual lives, into himself and restores them to their unity in the Self.

I think that this is worth reflecting on; otherwise from a Christian point of view transmigration is not meaningful. To say that the individual, when he dies, is not going to meet Christ, or to enter into eternal life, and that he is going to be reborn in this world, is contrary to the Christian view. But I think the text here really supports the Christian understanding. Zaehner, following Shankara, asserts that the word *Iswara*, which usually means 'The Lord', can here only mean the individual soul; but this is to give the word *Iswara* a totally different meaning. It is the Lord who is transmigrating, not the individual soul.

9. And he watches over the mind and its senses — ear, eye, touch, and taste, and smell — and his consciousness enjoys their world.

The Spirit, the *Atman*, enters into each individual and takes to himself the senses and the mind and enjoys himself in this world. But he is not affected by this experience because he is completely detached. He experiences it but it does not change his nature. So we each have in us an individual soul which is experiencing and which is suffering, and we also have the Eternal Spirit within us, presiding over us, working in us, and seeking to free us from our sin and from our limitation, and to bring us back to fulfillment.

10. When he departs, or when he stays, and with the powers of his nature enjoys life, those in delusion see him not, but he who has the eye of wisdom sees.

"The deluded do not perceive when he departs or stays (meaning in death or in life) swayed by the *gunas*. But those who have the eye of wisdom see" (B & D). That is the *jnana cakshu*, the single eye that sees the inner self. That is what is called the third eye, which is symbolically located in the centre of the forehead. The ordinary person sees with the mind and

the senses, but the man of wisdom sees that the mind and senses are all
rooted in the *Atman*, the Spirit Supreme. One has to have the eye of wisdom
to see behind the person to the Christ within him.

"When he departs or when he stays"; when a person dies and the soul
has apparently disappeared, and we think that the poor man is dead, the
reality is that the spirit has withdrawn from that gross body, which is going
to dissolve, and the soul has ceased to function through reason and
imagination and memory. But all the powers of the body and the soul have
been assumed into the Spirit. That is why the death of a holy man in India
is called a *samadhi*. In *samadhi* all the powers of the soul are drawn into
the centre of the Spirit which is in God. So at death we simply pass beyond
the world of appearances into the reality of our being, in the Self. We see
ourself in the Lord and the Lord in ourself; and that is the Last Judgement.

11.   Seekers of union ever striving, see him dwelling in their own hearts;
      but those who are not pure and have not wisdom, though they strive,
      never see him.

That would apply after death. If we have been purified then the light
shines in us and we know the Lord and enter into him. If we are unpurified,
then the fire of purgatory has to purify us before we are capable of receiving
that life and entering into it.

We come now to a new development – the Lord is present in the
human soul, as the *Atman* illuminating the minds and the senses. He is
also present in the whole physical universe.

12.   The splendour of light that comes from the sun and which illumines
      the whole universe, the soft light of the moon, the brightness of fire
      – know that they all come from me.

It was said before, "The sun does not shine there nor the moon nor
earthly fire," because one has gone beyond the manifestations to the source.
Now it is the other way around. From that source streams out the light
which shines in the sun and the moon and the stars and the fire. This may
be compared to the Christian doctrine, "In him was light and the light was
light of men and the light shines in the darkness" (John 1.4,5). The divine
light is shining into the darkness, into *prakriti*, the womb of nature, and
that light gives life to the whole earth. It is the inner light of the soul.

13. I come into the earth and with life-giving love I support all things
    on earth. And I become the scent and taste of the sacred plant Soma,
    which is the wandering moon.

"Permeating the soil, I support all beings with my vital energy" (B &
D). That is, with my *ojas*, which is the interior energy. It is said that, in
yoga, vital energy is concentrated in the *muladhara chakra* at the base of
the spine. It generates terrific heat in the form of vital energy, this *ojas*,
which rises through the seven *chakras* and becomes a source of illumination
in the mind. To awaken the *ojas* in oneself is an important stage in yoga.
It is not unlike the libido of Freud, in a way, but a libido not limited to
sex, the energy of which is centered in only one of the *chakras*. It is a life-
force penetrating the *chakras* and permeating the whole being.

"Becoming the moon plant (soma) I, the very sap of life, cause all healing
herbs to grow" (Z). This *soma* was the juice which was pressed out from
a plant like marijuana or the peyote of the American Indians. It was one
of the hallucinogenic drugs, and in Vedic tradition the drinking of the *soma*
was an essential part of the Vedic sacrifice. Wonderful poems were written
on the ecstasy induced by the *soma*. The *soma* is the sap of life which depends
on the moon. The moon was considered to be the source of the *soma*, because
it was believed that the moon had a profound influence on the growth of
plants. Some say that one should always plant at the waxing of the moon.
Most country people think that. The vital power is supposed to be in the
moon and then the moon draws it up in the plants.

14. I become the fire of life which is in all things that breathe; and in
    union with the breath that flows in and flows out I burn the four
    kinds of food.

This is the verse which is often chanted as grace after meals. The Lord
is manifesting in the sun and the moon, he is manifesting in the fire, in
the earth, he is manifesting in the sap in the trees, and he is manifest in
our bodies with the vital energy which digests the food. Only the Lord
can digest our food.

That is why one has to pray when one eats. One can get violent
indigestion if the Lord is not helping to digest the food. This is perfectly
true. When people are distracted all the time, doing telephone calls and
so on while they eat, they may well get indigestion and stomach ulcers.

But if we allow the Lord to digest the food within us and surrender to him, then we will have a perfect digestion. The 'four kinds of food' can be interpreted to mean food composed of the four elements, earth, air, fire and water. But it has been held that three of the kinds of food are the material food and the fourth is spiritual.

15. And I am in the heart of all. With me come memory and wisdom, and without me they depart. I am the knower and the knowledge of the Vedas, and the creator of their end, the Vedanta.

"And I am in the heart of all." The *Gita* makes this point again and again, the Lord is seated in the heart. This can be related to the Christian doctrine of the Sacred Heart. The heart is considered the centre of the personality, the place of the indwelling presence of God. It is in the heart of Christ that this indwelling presence of God is most clearly manifested. Through love we ourselves have to discover this Christ dwelling in our hearts and ourselves dwelling in the heart of Christ. "With me come memory and wisdom and without me they depart." The word *apohanam* means 'dispelling'. Zaehner suggests that it means "the dispelling of doubts". Krishna Prem says, "from Him comes also absence and loss of memory or knowledge." He explains that it is only by limitation of the all-pervading knowledge, by shutting out the images of the future which form the other half of 'memory' and which are equally present to his gaze, that the movement of life is made to flow in a given direction. The Lord is shining into our hearts and he is the fullness of knowledge, but when he enters into us he takes on the limitations of our minds; he only remembers from the past what we remember and he only sees in the future what we conceive. The one infinite takes on the limitations of the finite. That is also true of the incarnation. Jesus in his inner being is one with the Father and can see all things, but he chooses to take upon himself the limitations of human nature, of the *buddhi,* of the *manas,* and the *indriyas,* the senses. He can only know through his Jewish backgkround, through the Jewish language and through the memories of the Jewish Bible. So he takes on himself all these limitations of a human individual. That is why he said of the end of the world that that day no man knows, not even the Son, but only the Father. He takes on the limitations of the human mind. He does not know the future. Of course, with us it is much more limited but that is the limitation the Lord takes upon himself when he enters the body and assumes its limitations.

"I am the knower and the knowledge of the *Vedas* and the creator of their end, the Vedanta." The *Upanishads* come at the end of the *Vedas*. They are the last portion and in a sense, the supreme portion of the *Vedas*, and are therefore called 'Vedanta', *anta* meaning 'end'. The idea is that the *Vedas* are an expression of that supreme knowledge which enters into this world of time and space and accepts those limitations. It is the one eternal wisdom manifesting himself in Sanskrit terms and the culture of the Sanskrit world, as in the Bible he manifests in the culture of the Jews and in the Koran in the culture of the Arabs. The One Knower, revealing himself in all these different conditions, comes down to you and me with our particular limitations.

16. There are two spirits in this universe, the perishable and the imperishable. The perishable is all things in creation. The imperishable is that which moves out.

17. But the highest spirit is another: it is called the Spirit Supreme. He is the God of Eternity who pervading all sustains all.

Now we come to a very interesting matter. Zaehner seems to have had a very good insight here. The *Gita* says that there are two *Purushas* in the universe, the perishable, the *kshara*, and the imperishable, the *akshara*. "The perishable is all things in creation. The imperishable is that which moves not." But beyond these two persons is the *Purushottaman*, the supreme Person, who manifests himself in these different levels. In himself he is the imperishable Supreme, beyond all. When the mind withdraws in meditation beyond all movements of the *manas* and, concentrating in the *buddhi*, is fixed and still, then it becomes aware of the cosmic unity. Now this is the point which Zaehner brings out and I think it is very important. In the earlier stage of the *Upanishads* no distinction was made between the three levels of manifestation. There was only the perishable and then the imperishable. So in the *Shvetashvatara Upanishad* there are two birds on the tree. One eats the fruit and the other looks on. The first is the *jivatman*, the other, uninvolved, is the *paramatman*. But here a further distinction is made. There are three levels, not two. The self manifests first on the level of the body, then in the soul, and the *mahat*, the cosmic order, the angelic order, the order of light. The *Gita* is saying that there are two *Purushas*, persons, the perishable, which is the world of nature, of becoming, and

the imperishable, which is the world of spirit, the unchanging, the intelligible
world. But beyond these the *Gita* recognises another, the highest Spirit,
beyond the imperishable. It is the *Puroshottoman*, the Supreme Person, the
highest Self who pervades and sustains all, the changeless Lord.

People often confuse the state of stillness, of quiet, the state of oneness
with the final state of the Absolute. *Samadhi* may be no more than this
cosmic consciousness. One has gone beyond the mental consciousness, and
realised the unity of the whole creation; one is at one with the whole, one
realises the One pervading all, one is standing above everything in a pure
state of bliss and it seems that is all; and very often people stop there. But
now the *Gita* says that beyond that is the Lord himself. The Lord is beyond
the *kutastho*, the 'still-point'. He is beyond this cosmic order altogether. He
pervades all and sustains but he is beyond all.

If we stop at the imperishable we get the idea that we leave the sense
world behind and go into the state of *samadhi*, the state of pure intelligence
and pure bliss, and we have forgotten about the world altogether. But in
the understanding of the *Gita* we go beyond that stage and we realise the
Supreme Person. We realise that He is active in the whole creation, in every
person and everything. That is also the Christian vision. One has to go beyond
both the sensible and the intelligible world, beyond even the 'still state' of
Brahman, and discover the personal God, who is 'known by love', who
reveals himself to those who open themselves to his love. When one comes
to the Lord beyond, one is open to all humanity. And then one is free!
But when one reaches *Purushottoma*, the supreme Person, then one is at
his disposal and one can do anything, including work in the world. That
is the Christian view of *sannyasa*. We go through *samadhi*, the experience
of oneness, to the total surrender to the Lord, and then, because he is a
personal God and because he is love, he takes us to himself and sets us
free to do whatever he wills us to do in the world. So that is the true sannyasi
who has attained the state of pure love and also pure abandonment and
availability for everyone and everything.

There is the same distinction in Buddhism between the *pratyeka* Buddha
who seeks enlightenment for himself alone and enters *nirvana* and the
bodhisattva who refuses to enter *nirvana* until all souls have been saved. So
also the Christian goes beyond the passive state of contemplation to the
experience of the Trinity, when he knows himself in Christ as Son of the
Father and experiences the power of the Spirit which moves him to the
service of love.

18. Because I am beyond the perishable, and even beyond the imperishable, in this world and in the Vedas I am known as the Spirit Supreme.

19. He who with a clear vision sees me as the Spirit Supreme he knows all there is to be known, and he adores me with all his soul.

Vedantic philosophers often talk as though when one reaches the supreme state there is no longer a Lord to adore, there is no worship, there is no love left. One simply is that One and this is considered to be the supreme state. But that is only a particular level of consciousness. If we go beyond that level, there is activity, there is love, there is adoration. We come back to the origin, in a sense. We become like a little child, but with the wisdom which comes from total fulfillment.

This has to be understood in the light of the Christian tradition of contemplative life. Those who reject the contemplative tradition remain at the lower level of faith and activity, which is very good in its way, but is far from perfect. The division is often made between the active life and the state of those who have reached this higher state of *samadhi*, of contemplation. But there is a higher state still, which goes beyond both and fulfills both. One can be a contemplative, in perfect stillness, and at the same time fully active. Jesus was the perfect example of that. Many Christians interpret Jesus in the New Testament simply as a man going about doing good, helping people and always busy and active, and they do not realise that he had gone beyond. In his six weeks in the desert and in the depths of his being he was enjoying pure *samadhi*. He was a pure contemplative, always abiding with the Father as the source of his being, and always seeing what the Father does as the source of his action. He is in that state of transcendent awareness in which he is one with the Father, and at the same time perfectly natural and human. That is why, in the case of the Gospels, the three Synoptics Gospels have to be corrected by the Fourth Gospel. St. John profoundly grasped the depth of the inner life of Christ, and was able to see his whole life and work in the light of this inner experience.

This state is known in Hinduism as *sahaja samadhi*, the state in which the yogi has gone beyond all forms of asceticism, of *sadhana*, and is able to live and act with perfect naturalness. Of this Ramana Maharshi in our day is the supreme example.

20. I have revealed to thee the most secret doctrine, Arjuna. He who sees
it has seen light, and his task in this world is done.

The Besant and Das translation put it nicely: "Having known this (let
him who has heard) be illuminated". The word is *buddhiman*, his *buddhi*
has been enlightened. It can be translated: "Then he will be an enlightened
man. And his task in this world is done." This is the state of the Buddha,
the Enlightened One.

Chapter 16

The Yoga of the Division Between the Divine and the Daemoniacal Power

This is an important chapter as it raises the question of good and evil. We have constantly referred to *purusha* and *prakriti*; *purusha* is light, spirit, consciousness, while *prakriti* is the receptive principle, the mother, the darkness of the womb.

There are two movements in nature, one is the movement from the light to the darkness; the light streams out into the darkness, the spirit is manifesting itself in the womb of nature in an outgoing movement. God is manifesting himself in nature and in matter. The light is manifested in the darkness and the darkness receives the light. The whole universe is constructed through this meeting of light and darkness. So one movement is *pravritti*; light streaming out and creating all the forms of nature right down to the material base, and the other is *nivritti*, a turning back in the opposite direction. It is a return to the light, a movement of the whole creation back to its source in the light. Krishna Prem's commentary on this is very interesting. There is nothing wrong, intrinsically, with this outward movement. The movement of creation comes forth from God and becomes involved in matter. That was the original intention of the creation, that the light should be manifested in the darkness. This material world is not evil at all. Its forces can become oppressive and destructive but in themselves they are willed by God. So we must not simply equate *pravritti* with evil and darkness and *nivritti* with light and goodness. This makes a very interesting problem of morality. The suggestion is given by Krishna Prem that something which is perfectly right at one stage of a person's development and at one stage in the development of the universe, becomes the reverse at a later stage. This is well illustrated in the case of a child. The child has first of all to grow and have a strong body and at that stage the child must eat and drink and enjoy himself. When a child appears greedy, it is not a fault; it shows that he is healthy and that he is growing. The first seven years of a child's life are largely years of physical and emotional development. Then from about seven to fourteen the child has to develop an ego, a self; to discover himself or herself, to realise his difference from others, to acquire the capacity to act, to go out, to achieve. At this stage it is natural to become aggressive. It is not bad when a boy is naughty and is always fighting. People may say that he is a bad boy or that he is mischievous, but they are also very pleased because it means he is growing up. It is at the next stage that he has to learn to control his bodily activities and to control his passions and desires. That is when the evil begins, when an ego refuses to grow and to transcend its selfish desires.

We have to develop this nature, these energies and enthusiasms, but as we grow up we have to learn to control them, to bring them into relation with a deeper aspect of the personality, that is, with the level of the spirit. This is where sin comes in. It might be all right for the child and for the growing boy to be very self-assertive and aggressive, but when, as a young man, he continues to be so and to indulge his passions, which may lead to violence and crime, he is carrying over what was appropriate at an earlier stage into a later stage when he should be changing. In the same way, when he is only interested in food and drink and having a good time, he is simply remaining on the level of the child's need to eat and grow, when he should be going beyond it. So this is the real problem: that people are all at different levels of evolution. This is not only children but grown people, and it applies to the history of the race.

Early on in evolution the chief concern was for physical well-being, the need being to become established in nature. Primitive man therefore was concerned with hunting, fishing and agriculture, and with generally developing the physical aspects of life. At this stage the spiritual life came through attachment to nature, to work, to activities of the physical kind. It was the age of the Earth Mother. Then as man grew and evolved, there came the heroic age. Every culture has an heroic age in which the hero or warrior is the ideal. In that stage of evolution the hero is the model, as we see for instance in the *Iliad* and the *Mahabharata*. This is the time when the *rajasic* power is dominant and man is following the fiery dynamic aspect of nature, where he is powerful and courageous and is fighting for justice. And then the difficult point comes, when the civilisation, the culture, grows beyond that and is trying to go beyond war and violence and passion and to develop a deeper spiritual awareness. So also individual people are on these different levels. When development is taking place there is often a conflict going on and therefore it is difficult to make a moral assessment. A person may be very greedy and selfish but at his stage of evolution, it may be the best that he can do. Another may be very aggressive and violent, but he is going through that stage. On the other hand, there are people who are too spiritual. They have not gone through the earlier stages and they are always seeking divine things but without enough base in nature. Without a well-developed self-identity, their spirituality becomes vague and unrealistic.

Now where does sin begin? The law is that one must follow the movement of the Spirit. The one Spirit is active in all this and when the Spirit leads us to develop our body and our physical powers, then we are right to do so. But then the same Spirit is beginning to lead us beyond, and when we begin to resist it, the way is open for the demonic element to come in. It is evil because we are resisting the movement of the Spirit. That is why the only law of morality is to follow the guidance of the Spirit. Each one has to find out what the Spirit is saying to him at each stage of his development.

It is the problem of the Old and the New Testament. In the Old Testament there is continuous evolution. First of all there was the agricultural stage when the festivals were concerned with sowing and harvesting. This was followed by the warrior age when the people of Israel had to conquer their enemies and Yahweh was seen as the Lord of Hosts leading his people into the promised land and overcoming all their enemies. At this stage it was quite right for Israel to think of God as the Lord of Hosts and to look forward to a conquering Messiah. Then Israel went through the crisis of the exile and all the suffering involved in that, and a new spirit began to emerge. The idea grew up of an interior religion and an interior law, a law "written in the heart", when the evil to be overcome was seen to be the evil in the heart. When Jesus came, the conflict between the external law and the internal law came to a head. This principle works through all human experience. When a child is young, one has to make rules for him: he must learn to obey them. Then he has got to come to the time when he realises the meaning of the law; he begins to respond to it in his own way and to interiorise the law. Finally he has to go beyond the law, when he is simply surrendering to the Spirit, and fulfills the law by the power of the Spirit within.

In India the same process of growth can be seen. The early gods of the *Vedas* gradually disappeared. Indra was the god of the heroic age, of thunder and rain; he was the warrior and leader of the hosts like Yahweh. By the time of the *Upanishads*, the people had gone beyond that stage. So Indra and those other gods simply disappeared. Vishnu and Shiva came to the fore as the figure of the Supreme God. Shiva was originally a dark god, the god of the dark forces outside, living in the graveyards and in the mountains — a fearful figure. Then as the people developed, Shiva began to be absorbed into the Aryan pantheon and to be regarded as the Kindly One, as his name implies, and finally he came to be seen as the God of Love.

When we reach the *Bhagavad Gita* we can see this process of change taking place. The *Gita* is at the intermediate stage. It is passing from the concept of external war to that of the interior conflict. Krishna tells Arjuna: "You are a *kshatriya;* you must fight; it is your *dharma*, your duty. In doing that you are fulfilling the law of the Spirit." But at the same time the teaching of the *Gita* is always going beyond that. Zaehner shows how that conflict was present in the *Mahabharata*. The ordinary morality was that one should conquer the enemy in battle, and then become a great king and govern the people. In the *Mahabharata* the evil forces, the Kauravas, were attacking the Pandavas, who were in the right. It was a duty to conquer them in battle, but Yuddhistra, the head of the Pandavas, realises that ultimately everybody will kill everybody else and the whole thing will be a disaster. He realises that this kind of morality is not enough. He is not unlike Mahatma Gandhi; he goes beyond the whole morality of war. We have the same problem today. In the past war was considered heroic and to fight for one's country was a duty which everybody recognised and the Church blessed. Now we have reached the stage of evolution when more and more people realise that it is no longer so and that we have to go beyond war. Our morality is changing. That is a major problem in the Church today. Morality is changing. We are getting beyond a certain stage and evolving into a higher one, and again only the law of the Spirit can teach us what is the right course. So that is the background to Chapter 16.

As we will see, the main emphasis of the chapter is on non-violence, love and goodness, the virtues of the spiritual man, while the evil person is shown to be the one who gives way to his passions and desires and who rejects the law of the Spirit.

1. Freedom from fear, purity of heart, constancy in sacred learning and contemplation, generosity, self-harmony, adoration, study of the scriptures, austerity, righteousness;

Krishna describes "the treasures of the man who is born for heaven". In the Hindu tradition the forces of good and evil are called the *devas* and the *asuras*. The *devas* are the gods, the shining ones, which are the powers of light. The *asuras* are the powers of darkness, the demonic forces. We can see in this a curious example of the change of roles in the ancient tradition. In the Persian religion the *asuras* were the gods, the powers of good, but in the Hindu tradition the *asuras* became the demons and the *devas* were the beings opposed to them.

Among the 'heavenly' virtues there is first fearlessness, *abhaya*, which is a great virtue and is characteristic of the man who has conquered his passions. *Sattva samshuddhir* is almost exactly 'purity of heart', one of the 'beatitudes' of the Sermon on the Mount. Then comes steadfastness in *jnana yoga*, the yoga of wisdom and discernment. Then *dana* which literally means 'gift' and is expressed in the practice of hospitality. In India this is still a living tradition; wherever you go people will receive you into their homes and offer you a meal. *Dama* means self-control, self-restraint, *yajna*, sacrifice, and then *svadhyaya*, which comes to mean study of the scriptures but actually it means self-study, knowledge of the self, which is attained by the study of the scriptures. Then *tapas*, asceticism, the word for every kind of spiritual discipline, and *arjavam*, righteousness.

2. Non-violence, truth, freedom from anger, renunciation, serenity, aversion to fault-finding, sympathy for all beings, peace from greedy cravings, gentleness, modesty, steadiness;

It is striking evidence of the similarity of all moral teaching that this might well be a list of Christian virtues. *Ahimsa*, non-violence; *satya*, truth; *akrodha*, freedom from anger and *tyaga* which is one of the words for renunciation. *Sannyasa* is a much deeper, more profound form of self-surrender while *tyaga* is just to renounce things. Peace, *shanti*, is a great virtue reflected in the Beatitude 'blessed are the peace-makers'. *Apaishuna* means aversion to fault-finding or freedom from malice and *daya* is compassion. It is one of the main virtues in Buddhism to be compassionate to all living beings, not just human beings; *daya* includes being concerned for the whole of nature. *Aloluptva* means freedom from greed; Besant and Das translate it as 'uncovetousness'. Then follow gentleness, modesty and steadiness or absence of fickleness. One may compare these virtues with the list of the fruits of the Spirit in St. Paul: "Love, joy, peace, patience, kindness, goodness, faithfulness, gentleness, self-control" (Gal. 5.22,23).

3. Energy, forgiveness, fortitude, purity, a good will, freedom from pride — these are the treasures of the man who is born for heaven.

Tejas is energy or vigour or splendour, and *ksama* means both endurance, the bearing of all things and the forbearance of forgiveness. *Dhriti* is fortitude and *saucha*, purity. For "not treacherous or arrogant" Besant and Das give "absence of envy or pride".

These are the virtues, the divine qualities, the *daiva*, belonging to the *devas*, the principles of light. These are the treasures of the man who is born for heaven, the world of the *devas*. There follows the list of vices or daemonic qualities.

4. Deceitfulness, insolence and self-conceit, anger and harshness and ignorance — these belong to a man who is born for hell.

One may compare this with a similar list of the 'works of the flesh' in St. Paul: "enmity, strife, jealousy, anger, selfishness, dissension" (Gal. 5.20).

5. The virtues of heaven are for liberation but the sins of hell are the chains of the soul. Grieve not, Arjuna, for heaven is thy final end.

6. There are two natures in his world: the one is of heaven, the other of hell. The heavenly nature has been explained; hear now of the evil of hell.

"Twofold is this living creation, the *daivas* and the *asuras*, the divine and the daemonic" (B & D). I prefer the word daemonic because it is less moral than devilish. The word *daemon* in Greek means spirit and it could be a good spirit or an evil spirit. For instance, Socrates had a 'daemon' which told him whenever he was doing anything wrong. It was like his conscience and he said that in all his life he had never disobeyed this daemon. When he was put on trial and in prison, his friends all wanted him to escape, but he said that his daemon would not let him evade the law.

So there we have a clear example of a good spirit. But in Christian times, all these daemons, these spirits, were classed as evil and so the word daemon came to mean a devil which in both Greek and English is quite different. The word *diabolos* in Greek means a slanderer, one who causes division. But the daemon was not anything of the sort. I think that this use of *diabolos* for *daemon* was one of the great mistakes of the Church in the Roman Empire. The whole pagan religion was considered devilish and the good spirits were consequently not recognised. It is only today that the Church has begun to recognise just to that there are good spirits as well as evil ones in the pagan world – in African religion, for instance, and in tribal religion in general.

7. Evil men know not what should be done or what should not be done. Purity is not in their hearts, nor good conduct, nor truth.

The daemonic people do not know either "what shall be done nor what shall not be done". Another translation is, "Daemoniacal men know neither right activity nor right abstinence (B & D). *Pravritti* is the outgoing force of work and activity and *nivritti* the coming back to God or to inner life. These daemonic people do not know either of them. It is not that they are not active people but they have neither purity, morality, nor truth. They do not know what should be done. And then there is a very significant description of the daemonic person which is typical of the unbeliever in every age.

8. They say: 'This world has no truth, no moral foundation, no God. There is no law of creation: what is the cause of birth but lust?'

Asatya means there is no truth in it, and "no moral foundation" is *apratishtham*. Thirdly, there is no *Isvara*, no God. Then there is a rather difficult phrase, *aparaspara-sambbutham* which Mascaró translates: "There is no law of creation." A more literal translation is, "it is brought about by mutual union, caused by lust and nothing else" (B & D).

Many people think that all that is required is to believe in God and in the moral law. Now what was said above is relevant here. Morality is not as simple as people would like to think. It would make things much easier if there were clear and definite moral laws — so that one could say this is right and that is wrong, and also if people could be divided into sheep and goats so that it was easy to say which was which. But in fact morality is tremendously involved. What is really the right thing to do in a given situation can only be known by spiritual discernment. We may have general laws, general moral principles, but the application of those principles to our own peculiar situation needs practical judgement, an inner guide, and the discernment of the spirit. That is why no laws are absolute. There can never be a system of absolute laws because laws are general and reality is particular. A general principle may have to be broken in a concrete situation. This was one of the problems raised by the conduct of Jesus in the Gospels. Often he would break the letter of the law and appeal to its underlying spirit. Thus he could say, "The Sabbath (or any legal observance) is made for man, not man for the Sabbath."

So what we are discovering is that everybody is called to exercise his moral responsibility all the time. According to St. Thomas, God is the eternal law, and the Holy Spirit is the principle of the eternal law. But once we try to translate the eternal law into temporal categories then we get particular, positive laws and these depend on particular circumstances.

In one sense, however, there is an absolute law. The absolute law consists in correspondence with the eternal order. We are called to know the eternal Reality, beyond all words, beyond all concepts, beyond all philosophical and theological systems and only when we know that Truth beyond words, are we conformed to reality. Equally in morality, we are called to obey the eternal principle of goodness, of truth, of love and of grace. These are all names for that principle which is at work in all our lives and in the whole of creation, and when we obey that living principle, the eternal law, then we are in the truth, then we are in love. But when this eternal law is translated into human laws and regulations it always has an ambivalent character. It is never final. That is why no dogma and no morality is ever final. Dogma and morality both operate as a sign, an indication, of an ultimate which is beyond. The only ultimate law is love. To translate love into practice, we need guidelines and directives, but again we so often mistake the directives and guidelines for the absolute. So we can never substitute any human system or human pattern for the absolute law and the absolute truth.

9. Firm is this belief, these men of dead souls, of truly little intelligence, undertake their work of evil: they are the enemies of this fair world, working for its destruction.

The actual phrase for 'dead souls' is *nastatmano*, that is, people who destroy their souls. They are *alpa buddhyah*, the *buddhi* has become feeble and ineffective.

10. They torture their soul with insatiable desires and full of deceit, insolence, and pride, they hold fast their dark ideas, and they carry on their impure work.

Kama is this lust, this desire, this passion which carries everything away, as we saw in the second chapter. That is what makes men do evil even against their will. "And full of deceit, insolence and pride" is translated by Zaehner, "hypocrisy, pride and frenzy".

11. Thus they are beset with innumerable cares which last long, all their life, until death. Their highest aim is sensual enjoyment, and they firmly think that this is all.

The more we give way to desire and passion, the more anxious and worried we become. If we are anxious about our life, we give way to worry and anxiety. Zaehner translates here "unmeasured care, right up to the time of death".

Bhoga is enjoyment. The *bhogi* is the one who is enjoying himself in everything, "convinced that this is all", and the yogi is the one who renounces selfish enjoyment. So many think that this kind of enjoyment is all there is. They are obsessed with the pleasures of this world. Thinking that this is the only world we have, they say, "Let us enjoy ourselves now; there is not going to be anything else." This is a great illusion.

12. They are bound by hundreds of vain hopes. Anger and lust is their refuge; and they strive by unjust means to amass wealth for their own cravings.

Desire for pleasure makes such people want to strive for their own satisfaction and anger follows when their desires are frustrated. Another

great problem is the amassing of wealth. Never before have people all over
the world been able to acquire so many things and so much wealth. One
hears of African politicians, for instance, who build and live in magnificent
palaces while their people starve, and here in India the same thing happens.
This can be daemonic. People may be possessed and driven by the forces
of acquisitiveness and gain so that they cannot stop themselves. Now we
have a picture of how this type of person speaks to himself.

13. 'I have gained this today, and I shall attain this desire. This wealth
is mine, and that shall also be mine.'

14. 'I have slain that enemy, and others also shall I slay. I am a Lord,
I enjoy life, I am successful, powerful and happy.'

Ishvaro'ham means "I am the Lord" or "I am God". This is really trying
to make oneself a God, as though the world had been created for your
enjoyment, whereas true happiness consists in transcending the ego with
its selfish desires and finding God within.

15. 'I am wealthy and of noble birth: who else is there like me? I shall
pay for religious rituals, I shall make benefactions, I shall enjoy myself.'
Thus they say in their darkness of delusion.

"I shall pay for religious rituals." This, of course, is a characteristic of
the world of the *Gita*. The modern man would not dream of such a thing.
He is free from all religion. In those days, there was no question of leaving
religion out and a great show was made of religious rituals.
    "And then I shall give alms." Giving of alms was a popular custom but,
like every good thing, it can become evil. Giving of alms is good but, as
Jesus showed in regard to the offering in the temple at Jerusalem, the rich
were giving of their wealth, but a poor widow came and gave all that she
had. For the rich this giving of alms was just a show but for the widow
it was a genuine sacrifice.

16. Led astray by many wrong thoughts, entangled in the net of delusion,
enchained to the pleasures of their cravings, they fall down into a foul
hell.

"Led astray by wrong thoughts." *Aneka* is literally "not one". When the *citta*, the mind, is one, *eka*, then we are in the truth, but when the mind is *aneka* we lose the one and we are wandering about among the many. Then we are in delusion. "Caught up in delusion's net" (Z). *Moha-jala* is this net of *moha* or delusion. "Obsessed by the satisfaction of their lusts" (Z) is a good translation, *kama-bhogeshu* being the enjoyment of lust.

17. In their haughtiness of vainglory, drunk with the pride of their wealth, they offer their wrong sacrifices for ostentation, against divine law.

This was a religious society in which there is always the great danger that the sacrifices are made for worldly purposes, that is, just to make a show and not according to prescribed law. That still happens today in India, where vast sums of 'black' money are offered in the temples. Many modern reformers are working to reduce the amount of money and things wasted in useless ceremonies and sacrifices.

18. In their chains of selfishness and arrogance, of violence and anger and lust, these malignant men hate me: they hate me in themselves and in others.

"In their chains of selfishness and arrogance". This arrogance, *ahankara*, is ego sense, the sense of 'I'. "These men hate me dwelling in themselves and in others." This is the great teaching of the *Gita*, of course. God is dwelling in every man, dwelling in one's own self. When we reverence God in ourselves, we reverence Him in the other, and when we pursue our own lusts and desires then we hate this God who is both within us and in the world around. We become deluded like that and then God becomes the enemy, the one standing behind us, the one saying 'No' to all we do. Sometimes when we have a false idea of God as one who is denying all pleasures, this is an illusory God, but what can also be happening is that we are hearing the voice of conscience. As we go against our deeper self, it becomes our accuser all the time. And so the further we are carried, the more we hate that voice in ourself and the more we hate it when we encounter it in others. The more we are deluded in ourself, the more we project our delusion onto others and the more everybody else appears evil. It is like the story of the man who had three sons and he sent them out to inquire into the state of the world. The first was a gentle and good person and he went around everywhere and came back saying everyone was very good. The second son was a bad young man and he came back and said he could not find one good man, everyone was very bad. The third one was more balanced and when he investigated he found good and evil everywhere. It is quite true that we see people in our own image. We project our image onto others.

19.   In the vast cycles of life and death I inexorably hurl them down to destruction: these the lowest of men, cruel and evil, whose soul is hate.

"These haters, evil, pitiless, vilest among men, I ever throw them down into daemoniacal wombs," to use the more literal translation of Besant and Das. It probably means they are born again. In the view of the *Gita*, our evil deeds pursue us in another life and we go into an evil womb: we are born with an evil nature. Of course, one can say that as a result of heredity some people are born with a propensity to evil.

20.   Reborn in a lower life, in darkness birth after birth, they come not to me, Arjuna; but they go down the path of hell.

Or, "they tread the lowest way" (Z). Zaehner raises the question of whether they ever get out of the lower way and I think, in the Hindu tradition, one always escapes in the end. There is no everlasting hell in either the Hindu or the Buddhist tradition. They may go down to the lowest level but there is always something which can call them and bring them back. Everybody eventually is saved. On the other hand, we have the problem of hell in the Christian tradition. Perhaps we can put it in this way. The purpose of creation was to bring matter through life into conciousness and, in man, this matter, this life, this consciousness has been opened up to God, to the light, to truth and love. We only really fulfill ourselves when we discover the true person in ourselves. We are not fully persons as human beings until we have found ourselves in God and God in us. This ego we have is not a person; it is still a slave to our appetites, desires and passions. If one does not become that true person and find God, it seems to me one dissolves, one is not a person, one is simply a part of nature and one goes back into nature. I do not know whether we can hold that view. The body dissolves into matter and the soul into all the psychological forces around it, which one has been obeying all one's life. One is just a sport of all these forces and one remains such. The person has not become a self, a true being. And that is loss of God. Hell is essentially the loss of God.

I think for most Hindus and Buddhists and for many Christians, the idea of eternal punishment is difficult to accept. But, of course, we must be careful how we think about that, because when we think of eternity, we tend to think of an endless time. But eternity is not an extension in time, but a timeless state. Hell, however it may be conceived, is not in time; it is a state beyond time.

In one of C.S. Lewis's books, *The Great Divorce*, the scene begins in hell; then it goes into a sort of purgatory where people come down from heaven to try to help the people in purgatory. There is one wonderful scene where a man who is always boasting and always pretending to be other than he is, meets an angel who tries to get him to say something sincere. But the man is divided. There is a little man who remains silent, and he is chained to a big man who does all the talking, and the more he talks, the taller he gets, while the little man is gradually reduced to nothing. He gets smaller and smaller while the other man goes on talking and talking until at last there is just a lot of noise coming out. There is nobody there at all.

21. Three are the gates to this hell, the death of the soul: the gate of lust, the gate of wrath, and gate of greed. Let a man shun the three.

More literally, "Triple are the gates of hell which are destructive of self" (Z). *Nashanam atmanah* is "destructive of the self" and it means you are no longer a self, you are nothing. You have lost yourself, you have lost your soul.

22. When a man is free from these three doors of darkness, he does what is good for his soul, and then he enters the Path Supreme.

23. But the man who rejects the words of the Scriptures and follows the impulse of desire attains neither his perfection, nor joy, nor the Path Supreme.

Zaehner says, and he may be right, that Krishna really came to establish the *dharma* which is the law of the four classes, the *varnas*, and because of this the Scriptures, the *shastras*, were of great importance, as the law was to the Jews. Later on the *shastras* can become a great obstacle in that people cling to the law, to the caste system, for instance, and lose the deeper meaning of life. But at this stage the *shastras* are still regarded as a rule of life.

24. Let the Scriptures be therefore thy authority as to what is right and
    what is not right. Know the words of the Scriptures, and do in this
    life the work to be done.

Besant and Das say, "determining what ought to be done and what
ought not to be done". I think the *Gita* is taking a position between the
two points of view. It is to some extent holding on to a law because people
need some laws to tell them what they must do and what they must not
do. If they obey those laws, they will find salvation. But the *Gita* is moving
to the higher point of view which sees the Spirit, the Self, as the ultimate
law of life, and all particular laws and customs as depending on the law
of the Spirit. That is exactly the position of St. Thomas Aquinas. He says
that the difference between the Old and New Testament is that the Old
Testament is the law written on stone tablets, an external ordinance which
had to be obeyed, whereas the New Testament is the law written in the heart.

Chapter 17

The Yoga of The Three Fold Faith

At the end of the previous chapter it was said that the man who rejects
the words of the scriptures, who follows the impulse of desire, does not
attain either perfection and joy, or the Path Supreme. "Let the scriptures
therefore be your authority as to what is right and what is not right." The
scriptures are the *shastras*, of course. "Know the words of the *shastras* and
do in this life the work to be done." This is the view of orthodox religion,
but the question remains, who is to interpret the scriptures? In Chapter
2, Krishna had given a deeper view, when he said: 'when the mind that
may be wandering in this contradictions of many scriptures, shall rest in
divine contemplation, then the goal of yoga is thine'. (2.53). Ultimately,
it is only contemplation, the knowledge of the self which can give liberation.
Arjuna asks:

1. Those who forsake the law of the Scriptures and yet offer sacrifice
    full of faith — What is their condition, Krishna? Is it of Sattva, Rajas,
    or Tamas — of light, of fire or of darkness?

This raises the question of faith. It is more meaningful to look at it
in terms of the scheme of first the senses, then the *manas*, the mind, which
works through the senses; next the *buddhi*, the point where we receive the
light from above, and finally the *Atman*, the Supreme, who is shining into
the *buddhi*. The light of the *Atman* shines into the *buddhi*, into the intelligence,

and then it is reflected in the *manas*. Faith is really the reflection of this light of the *Atman*, the Supreme, in the *manas*, the rational mind. Wisdom or knowledge (*jnana*) is when we rise above the *manas*, above all these images and concepts and awaken to truth itself through the *buddhi*, the intelligence. This makes it easier to grasp what faith is and also helps to see why there can be such tremendous diversities of faith. Faith is reflected through the *manas*, which is the mind working through the senses and the feelings, and therefore through the whole cultural environment. This means that the same light of truth can shine in this man and that man, yet each will see it and interpret it and understand it in terms of his own culture. The one light of truth, the one reality, is shining through the whole of creation, through the whole of humanity and through every different culture. Thus the one light of truth is broken up. A good image of this is to think of the one light and the many colours, where each culture is like a colour which reflects, as it were, a certain aspect of the one light. This applies to all peoples; to primitive African tribal culture, Australian aborigines, the American Indians, the tribal people in India and Asia. The same light of truth is reflected in different measures, in different degrees, in all these different cultures and cultural complexes with their rituals, sacrifices, prayers, dance, songs, music and worship. With time these complex smaller groups form into the wider religions and then into the world religions: Christianity, Buddhism, Islam, Hinduism. The same one light is shining in each and each one is receiving the truth in its own way. It is very important to see that the one light of truth is shining into every human being through the *buddhi* and into the *manas* and the senses. It is broken up at all these different levels. But each is in contact with the truth. There is no human being to whom the truth, or God and grace in religious terms is not coming in some way. It comes to him through the cultural complex in which he is living, through the images, the modes of thought, the ways of expression, the style of life and so on. Faith is the awakening to the light of truth in our own minds. It is never simply that we believe somebody; that is only the initial stage. Faith proper is always an illumination of the mind from the Supreme.

The rest of the chapter is Krishna's teaching in reply to Arjuna's question.

2. The faith of men, born of their nature, is of three kinds: of light, of fire and of darkness. Hear now of these.

3. The faith of a man follows his nature, Arjuna. Man is made of faith: as his faith is so he is.

A man is what his faith is because the one light is shining through to each person, and what everybody is seeking, whether they know it or not, is God. One may seek God through drink or through power or through sex or through philosophy or through science, but as a human being one is seeking that truth or that ultimate experience. It is the dynamism of our nature. A man may think that he is an atheist and conceptually he may be an atheist, but the urge to the absolute, to truth itself, to God, is in his nature, and an atheist may be very near to God. He may be seeking the one reality while conceptually he has rejected all images and concepts of God preferring to call himself an atheist. We are what we believe and that applies to any level of existence.

Everybody lives by faith. That is why despair is the worst thing, for to despair is to lose the meaning of life. So Krishna says, "the faith of a man follows his nature, man is made of faith: as his faith is, so he is." And that, of course, applies on every level. If we have a true faith, if we are really illumined from above and receive this true light into our heart, then we are conformed to the truth. Faith is actual participation in the divine truth. That was St. Thomas' idea when he said that faith is the *semen gloriae*, the seed of glory. Already the same light which will illumine us in heaven in fullness is present by faith. It may be a tiny spark, but it is a spark from the eternal. So faith links us to the absolute.

4. Men of light worship the gods of Light; men of fire worship the gods of power and wealth; men of darkness worship ghosts and spirits of night.

The idea is that *sattvic* people worship the gods of Light, the powers of light, truth and goodness. *Rajasic* people worship power and wealth. As for *tamasic* people, Krishna Prem suggests that they are in love with death and so attached to ghosts and spirits. Probably what the *Gita* intends here are the sorcerers that one finds in many small villages in India, who are in contact with occult powers and can work evil through these powers. Krishna suggests that those who practise extreme austerity and do violence to themselves are also *tamasic*. The *Gita* represents the central tradition of Hinduism which is opposed to extreme austerities much less than to sensual indulgence.

5.-6. There are men selfish and false who moved by their lusts and passions perform terrible austerities not ordained by sacred books: fools who torture the powers of life in their bodies and me who dwells in them. Know that their mind is darkness.

Extreme asceticism is always regarded as a vice, not a virtue. It is true that there are holy men who are very ascetic. Among the Christian monks in the Egyptian desert there were some extreme ascetics who were nevertheless very holy men, and among Hindu yogis there are some who torture their bodies and yet have real devotion to God. But mere torturing of the body is not a virtue and is normally a vice. A modern psychologist would say this kind of thing is due to unconscious motivations such as repressed sex or anger. Another translation reads, "tormenting the aggregated elements forming the body" (B & D). That is near to St. Paul's *stoicheia*, the elemental powers of the universe, present in the body. By torturing their bodies, Krishna says, such people torture me, who dwells in them. God dwells within the body and when one is torturing the body, one is not reverencing God in the body. This is very important in yoga and in the whole Indian spiritual tradition. It always takes the middle way. There is a famous saying in the *Gita*: "Yoga is not for him who eats too much or for him who eats too little or for him who sleeps too much or for him who sleeps too little."(6.16) It is always a matter of balance, of harmony, integration of the body, the senses, the feelings, the mind, and the will. Yoga is a total integration and any violence is against the principles of yoga. Even in Hatha yoga one should not strain the muscles at all; rather one gradually relaxes as one allows oneself to be transformed through patient effort.

7. Hear now of three kinds of food, the three kinds of sacrifice, the three kinds of harmony, and the three kinds of gifts.

8. Men who are pure like food which is pure: which gives health, mental power, strength and long life: which has taste, is soothing and nourishing, and which makes glad the heart of men.

There are *sattvic* foods which produce "strength, health, joy and cheerfulness" (B & D). These foods are "delicious and bland" (B & D); bland means oily, rich in oil. This is typically Indian where everything is cooked with oil. But actually it goes much deeper than this. The question of *sattvic* food is very important in yoga. It is always said that our mind is deeply affected by the food we eat. It is almost true to say that we are what we eat. That is why for a yogi the tradition is that he should only eat *sattvic*, that is vegetarian, food.

9. Men of Rajas like food of Rajas: acid and sharp, and salty and dry, and which brings heaviness and sickness and pain.

Then there is *rajasic* food, food that gives energy. There is a famous story of Mahatma Gandhi which tells how, when he was a boy, he wanted to drive the British out of India, and decided that he must eat meat and grow strong. So he and his friends started to eat meat. It only lasted a week, as they all became ill, but his idea was that *rajasic* food would make him strong and aggressive. So a yogi eats *sattvic* food, that is, a vegetarian diet with milk and curds but no meat. Meat is considered to be *rajasic*. From a mere economic point of view, they say that if Americans would give up eating meat the whole world could be fed. It takes ten times as much vegetable matter to produce meat than if one eats it in the vegetable form.

Rajasic foods according to the *Gita* are those which are pungent, cooked often with plenty of chillies, "sour and salty and too hot, pungent, dry and burning which produce pain and grief and sickness" (B & D). These are what the *rajasic* man loves. That is more common in tropical countries, where all food tends to be highly spiced. This is also an excellent description of the snacks served in cocktail bars in the West.

10. Men of darkness eat food which is stale and tasteless, which is rotten and left overnight, impure, unfit for holy offerings.

We notice again that *rajasic* and *tamasic* foods are conceived in entirely negative terms. But one can also speak of *rajasic* foods, like meat, which give energy and strength, and *tamasic* foods, like all starchy foods, which give heat and also a certain physical energy.

11. A sacrifice is pure when it is an offering of adoration in harmony with the holy law, with no expectation of a reward, and with the heart saying 'it is my duty'.

This is the right manner of sacrifice. It is offered without desire for fruits. The fundamental teaching of the *Bhagavad Gita* is that one works without seeking a reward. One does it because it is right and one makes the offering to God. We should remember that sacrifice was considered the fundamental duty of all men. It is a very profound idea that the whole universe is based on sacrifice and that man puts himself in tune with the universe when he offers sacrifice. The whole Vedic religion is centered around the Vedic sacrifice, and of course for Christians the whole creation centres around the sacrifice of Christ.

12. But a sacrifice that is done for the sake of a reward, or for the sake of vainglory is an impure sacrifice of Rajas.

Although it may not necessarily be wrong to try to obtain something from God by sacrifice, when it is done with an exclusively selfish motive, and for self-glorification, then it is rajasic.

13. And a sacrifice done against the holy law, without faith, and sacred words, and the gifts of food, and the due offering, is a sacrifice of darkness.

This would presumably be a sacrifice without any religious or moral motive, a kind of masochism.

14. Reverence for the gods of Light, for the twice born, for the teachers of the Spirit and for the wise; and also purity, righteousness, chastity and non-violence: this is the harmony of the body.

Mascaró translates *tapas* as 'harmony', but it is really self-control, discipline. The term *tapas* is difficult to translate since there is no exact equivalent in English. *Tapas* can mean a physical discipline or a mental discipline, and above all it can be a spiritual discipline. Here the sense is rather that of spiritual discipline although it is the *tapas* of the body. Krishna speaks of the reverence paid to the gods, the *devas* and to the *divyas*, the twice-born. The three higher castes, Brahmins, ksatriyas, and vaisyas are called 'twice born'. When they receive the sacred thread, they are born again to the life of the spirit. This is still found especially with the Brahmin today, when at the Upanayana ceremony the Brahmin boy receives the thread and is said to be born again. That is why there was great reverence for the Brahmin; he is the one who studies the *Vedas* and who has knowledge of God, and whose business it is to bring the knowledge of God to men.

The *Gita* speaks also of reverence for the guru and the wise man, the *jnani*. This is still very strong among Hindus today, this great reverence for the guru, the teacher, the *jnani*, the wise man. A *sannyasi*, or Indian monk, is one who is dedicated to God and therefore reverence for the *sannyasi* is reverence for God. For a *sannyasi* to come into a house is like God coming into that house.

I remember when I was travelling once from Benares to Calcutta there was a Hindu gentleman sitting opposite me and we began to talk. I explained I was a Christian priest and monk but he just took me for a *sannyasi* and therefore someone who had to be treated with great respect. So he brought me all my food and coffee all through the journey and when we arrived in Calcutta, he introduced me to a friend, a doctor, who took me in his car to his house and all the family came and 'took the dust of my feet', that is, bowed down to touch my feet. For a *sannyasi* to come into their house is a blessing from God. And for them, as Hindus, the fact that I was a Christian did not matter. Whether one is a Christian or a Buddhist, a guru or a *jnani* represents God; the presence of God is there and it is to that presence that reverence is paid.

Brahmacharya is what we translate as chastity but it is much more. It is the whole process of seeking God, literally 'moving in Brahman'. *Ahimsa* is non-violence, not harming anybody which of course also means much more; it implies a reverence for all life. So this is the true *tapas* of the body.

15. Words which give peace, words which are good and beautiful and true, and also the reading of sacred books: this the harmony of words.

This is literally the *tapas* of speech.

16. Quietness of mind, silence, self-harmony, loving- kindness, and a pure heart: this is the harmony of the mind.

Silence is *mauna* and *mauna* is of great importance in Hinduism. All *sannyasis* who are serious have periods of *mauna*. Gandhiji used to have his day of silence every Monday. A *sannyasi* who came to our ashram recently was taking three years of *mauna*. A *muni* may listen to people and he may write, but he must not speak. Abhishiktananda, one of the founders of our ashram, had frequent periods of *mauna* in his life and his French disciple who was living in the Himalayas had taken a vow of silence for ten years.

17. This threefold harmony is called pure when it is practised with supreme faith with no desire for a reward and with oneness of soul.

18. But false austerity, for the sake of reputation, honour and reverence is impure: it belongs to Rajas and is unstable and uncertain.

19. When self-control is self-torture, due to dullness of the mind, or when it aims at hurting another, then self-control is of darkness.

It is interesting that a careful distinction is made between different types of *tapas*. Not all asceticism is good. When it is motivated by faith without egoism or ambition, it can be good. But asceticism which is self-centred and motivated by exhibitionism, and still more, that which is sadistic and aims at causing harm to others by the psychic powers attained, is positively evil.

The idea is very strongly held that if one practises *tapas* one can help others but also harm them. There is a strong belief that a yogi has terrible powers and people are often very much afraid of a *sadhu* if he comes into a house. Nobody dares to contradict him in any way or he may curse the house and then disaster will result. So that is an example of *tamasic* asceticism.

Then the text goes on to *dana*, to gifts. As I have mentioned before, *dana* is alms-giving. It is one of the great Hindu virtues and still very much practised.

20. A gift is pure when it is given from the heart to the right person at the right time and at the right place, and when we expect nothing in return.

21. But when it is given expecting something in return, or for the sake of a future reward, or when it is given unwillingly, the gift is of Rajas, impure.

22. And a gift given to the wrong person, at the wrong time and the wrong place, or a gift which comes not from the heart, and is given with proud contempt, is a gift of darkness.

It is very interesting how different gifts can be. We all know how one of the great problems in India when one is travelling by bus is when so many people come begging; should one give or should one not give and if one does give, in what spirit should it be done? Some people say do not give at all since it only encourages people to beg, but then one feels very hard-hearted. On the other hand, to throw something at somebody is hardly better. And yet to take a serious interest in the person is often impossible. So it is a matter of doing one's best in each situation. If one has the opportunity during an encounter, one can perhaps give something as well as showing one's personal concern, but in the long term some means has to be found to help people in a more serious way by undertaking positive social action.

Now we come to the concluding part which is more interesting.

23. OM, TAT, SAT. Each one of these three words is one word for Brahman, from whom came in the beginning the Brahmins, the Vedas and the Sacrifice.

These are words which point to the Absolute. It does seems that the original meaning of OM is the same as 'Amen' in the Judaeo-Christian tradition. It is a form of affirmation. St. Paul said of Christ, "all the promises of God find their Yes in Him. That is why we utter the Amen through Him to the glory of God" (2 Cor. 1.20). Amen is saying yes, in affirmation; it is saying 'yes' to God. Then again it has a deeper meaning. In the East there is a distinction between the OM which is sound and the OM which is silent. The OM which is sound comes forth from the OM which is silent. The same idea is found in the Christian tradition, in the understanding that the Word came forth from the silence of the Father. This comes, for instance, in St. Ignatius of Antioch who speaks of "the Word which was spoken from the silence of the Father". The OM itself is beyond sound. In the *Maitri Upanishad* it says, "There are two ways of contemplation of Brahman: in sound and in silence. The sound of Brahman is OM. With OM we go to the End: the silence of Brahman. The End is immortality, union and peace." So when one pronounces the word OM one is going through the sound to the soundless reality.

And then there is the beautiful passage in the *Katha Upanishad*: "I will tell you the Word that all the *Vedas* glorify, all self-sacrifice expresses, all sacred studies and holy life seek. That Word is OM. That Word is the everlasting Brahman: that Word is the highest End. When that sacred Word is known, all longings are fulfilled. It is the supreme means of salvation:

it is the help supreme. When that great Word is known, one is great in the heaven of Brahman."

So OM signifies the Absolute, the one Reality. That is why it is generally accepted among many Christians today. There is no particular sectarian significance about it. We find OM also used in Buddhism, Jainism and other religions. Also, there are other meanings found in it. The three syllables, A+U+M, are supposed to include all sound, and therefore all words and all meaning, like the alpha and omega, the first and last letters of the Greek alphabet, to which Jesus is compared in the Book of Revelation. OM is 'the' word, the Word of God which includes all sounds, all words, all meaning. Then again it is said to represent the three *Vedas*, the three times, past, present and future and what is beyond the three states of human consciousness. The syllable A represents the waking state of external consciousness, U represents the dream state of internal consciousness, and M represents the state of deep sleep when one goes beyond words and beyond images. OM itself represents, and indeed is, the fourth state, *turiya*, the state of pure unity, which is the final state of being.

As we come out into manifestation, we see duality and multiplicity, but when we go back to the One, we go back to non-duality. So the OM is a sign of oneness, signifying the one source from which everything comes.

24.   Therefore with the word OM the lovers of Brahman begin all work of sacrifice, gift or self-harmony, done according to the Scriptures.

That is still the custom. Any sacred action begins with OM and it is used at the beginning of every prayer. It is a way of affirming the presence of God.

25.   And with the word TAT, and with renunciation of all reward, this same work of sacrifice, gift or self-harmony is being done by those seekers of Infinite Liberty.

The word TAT means simply 'that'. The Supreme Reality cannot be named; that is a most important understanding, both in the Christian and in other religious traditions. God cannot be named. In the Hebrew tradition Yahweh asks, why do you ask what is my name? And even when he reveals to Moses the name Yahweh, 'I am', 'I am' is not really a name. The nearest we can come to naming God is to say "He is", as is said also in the *Katha Upanishad*. In the *Vedic* tradition, all the gods are names and forms of the

One who has no name. So we have to pass through all the forms of manifestation until we come to the source, the One beyond. In order to point to this reality, we use the simplest word we can find. We say 'That', TAT. There is a famous example in the *Chandogya Upanishad* where the father is instructing his son on the nature of reality and gives various illustrations. The one I like best is this:

> 'Bring me a fruit from this banyan tree.'
> 'Here it is, father.'
> 'Break it.'
> 'It is broken, Sir.'
> 'What do you see in it?'
> 'Very small seeds, Sir.'
> 'Break one of them, my son.'
> 'It is broken, Sir.'
> 'What do you see in it?'
> 'Nothing at all, Sir.'

Then his father spoke to him: 'My son, from the very essence in the seed which you cannot see comes in truth this vast banyan tree. Believe me, my son, an invisible and subtle essence is the Spirit of the whole universe. That is Reality. That is Atman. THOU ART THAT.' TAT TVAM ASI.

TAT means 'that' or 'that one', 'that nameless one', 'that Supreme'. TAT is one of the mystical utterances. It is the sign of the going beyond, the mark of the nameless One which we can only point to as TAT – That. There is a very good illustration of how this works. It is said that all words are like fingers pointing at the moon. If we look at the finger, the word, we are missing the thing, because the word is pointing beyond itself. TAT is pointing to the beyond. Krishna Prem interprets this in a meaningful way. He says, "With OM, the acts of sacrifice and discipline that constitute the treading of the Path are begun, that is to say, the attainment of the true Self, though in its separated individual form, is the task of consciousness in the first stage. The next stage, marked by what we have seen to be the typically *sattvic* characteristic of abandonment of all desire for fruit, is the bringing about of the union of that individual Self with the unindividuated *buddhi*, the cognitive aspect of the *Mahat Atman*, the one great Life. This stage is referred to by the word TAT, because it is through union with the Light Ocean of the *buddhi* that true knowledge of TAT, the transcendent

Reality, is gained. The last stage is symbolised by SAT, which stands for Being, Goodness, Reality. This stage is the attainment of Brahman."

26. SAT is what is good and what is true: when therefore a work is well done the end of that work is SAT.

SAT is simply the word for being and ASAT is not being or non-being. We recall the *Katha Upanishad* which says, "How can he be known, except by one who says, 'He is'." That is the best way in which we can speak of God. So also St. Thomas says, God has no name but the nearest one can come to a name is Being, because being is the most universal concept one can form.

27. Constant faithfulness in sacrifice, gift, or self-harmony is SAT; and also all work consecrated to Brahman.

Self-harmony again is *tapas*, which may perhaps be better translated here as spiritual discipline.

28. But work done without faith is ASAT, is nothing: sacrifice, gift, or self-harmony done without faith are nothing, both in this world and in the world to come.

It is important to see that faith is made the basis of all action. Sacrifice and alms-giving and asceticism are of no value without faith. This is very near to St. Paul's doctrine of justification by faith.

Chapter 18

The Yoga of Liberation by Renunciation

This final chapter is again concerned with the question of the relationship between *sannyasa*, renunciation, and working for the world. The question is the very practical one of how to relate contemplation and action. That was one of the main themes in the earlier chapters and now it is taken up again. This chapter begins with a distinction which has not been found before, between *sannyasa* and *tyaga*. *Tyaga* is best translated as surrender. Arjuna asks:

1. Speak to me, Krishna, of the essence of renunciation, and of the essence of surrender.

And Krishna replies:

2. The renunciation of selfish works is called renunciation; but the surrender of the reward of all work is called surrender.

The distinction here is between renunciation of selfish work, that is, all work which is dictated by the ego, the lower self, and surrender of the reward of work, even though its motive may be unselfish.

This can be compared to the ideal of the *bodhisattva* in Buddhism. In the earlier Buddhism the accent is on the search for *nirvana*, freedom. One follows the Noble Eightfold Path to reach this final *nirvana* and then one passes beyond. The *bodhisattva* of the later Mahayana tradition made a vow not to enter *nirvana* and receive the reward of his works until all sentient beings had been saved. The ideal here is that after renouncing the world, one returns to the world in service. This is the ideal of the *Gita*, and that is why Mahatma Gandhi took it as his bible. The aim is to renounce all reward for one's work and to work for the benefit of the world.

3. Some say that there should be renunciation of action — since action disturbs contemplation; but others say that works of sacrifice, gift and self-harmony should not be renounced.

This has been a problem both in the Christian and the Hindu tradition. Pure contemplation is very difficult if one is leading an active life. Therefore, they say, give up the active life for pure contemplation. But the ideal which the *Gita* and the Gospels put before us is the renunciation of the self so as to enter the state of contemplation and knowledge of God and then to allow one's action to flow forth from contemplation.

The types of good works are *yajna, dana,* and *tapas. Yajna* is mainly religious sacrifice, but it can be taken in a wider sense. *Dana* is alms-giving, and *tapas* is self-discipline, self-control.

4. Hear my truth about the surrender of works, Arjuna. Surrender, O best of men, is of three kinds.

5. Works of sacrifice, gift, and self-harmony should not be abandoned, but should indeed be performed; for these are works of purification.

6. But even these works, Arjuna, should be done in the freedom of a pure offering, and without expectation of a reward. This is my final word.

Even spiritual works should be done in the spirit of *tyaga,* of surrender of all reward. This is a main theme of the *Gita*: to do our work out of love of God and as service to the world without seeking any reward.

7. It is not right to leave undone the holy work which ought to be done. Such a surrender of action would be a delusion of darkness.

Many used to believe that even religious actions should be abandoned, and even now there is a tradition of the *sannyasi* who abandons all work altogether. A *sannyasi* is not supposed to perform any ritual action, and he is not supposed to do any work in an ashram; that should be done by the devotees. He should be simply meditating, uniting with God. That is one way of life but the *Gita* is opposed to that. The *Gita* supports the ideal of contemplation and surrender to the Self, in order to act unselfishly. "To leave undone a holy work which ought to be done would be a delusion of darkness".

8. And he who abandons his duty because he has fear of pain, his surrender is of Rajas, impure, and in truth he has no reward.

9. But he who does holy work, Arjuna, because it ought to be done, and surrenders selfishness and thought of reward, his work is pure, and is peace.

If a work is done simply because it should be done, and is enjoined by the scripture, and all attachment and all thought of reward is given up, then that is a *sattvic*, or pure, surrender. The highest work is *sattvic*; *rajasic* work is impure, and *tamasic* is altogether gross. We do not do a thing because we like it or not do a thing because we do not like it. Whether it is pleasurable or painful, we must accept it as the will of God and as our duty.

10. This man sees and has no doubts: he surrenders, he is pure and has peace. Work, pleasant or painful, is for him joy.

11. For there is no man on earth who can fully renounce living work, but he who renounces the reward of his work is in truth a man of renunciation.

No embodied being can completely relinquish action. Repeatedly the *Gita* says that we cannot actually do nothing. We have to breathe and breathing is work to some extent. Eating is work. It is an illusion to think that we can do nothing. The *Gita* is here summarising what has been taught from the beginning. No one can fully renounce work, but he who renounces the reward is the true *sannyasi*. We cannot renounce work but we can renounce the self. If we renounce the self then we can do any work we like because it will not bind us.

12. When work is done for a reward, the work brings pleasure, or pain, or both, in its time; but when a man does work in Eternity, then Eternity is his reward.

Mascaró's translation is rather free. The meaning is that the fruit of work is good or evil or mixed if we work without renunciation; but if we renounce the fruit we are not affected by the results of our work at all.

13. Know now from me, Arjuna, the five causes of all actions as given in the Sankhya wisdom, wherein is found the end of all works.

14. The body, the lower 'I am', the means of perception, the means of action, and Fate. These are the five.

Sankhya is the earliest Indian system of philosophy which underlies the whole of the *Gita*. It describes all the elements of the universe and the functions of the human soul. In the present text the five causes of all actions are described as the 'material base', the *adhishthanam*, that is the body. Next is the *karta*, the agent, the doer of the work, and then 'material causes', the organs of perception. Then come the *prithakcesta*, best translated as the diverse kinds of energies, the means of action. The fifth cause is *daivam*, fate, or perhaps one could translate it, 'the will of God' (*deva*). There is a very strong idea in Hinduism that we are conditioned by our past, by the past of humanity as a whole, and by the whole situation in which we are working. All these factors come into any action.

15. Whatever a man does, good or bad, in thought, word or deed, has these five sources of action.

16. If one thinks that his infinite Spirit does the finite work which nature does, he is a man of clouded vision and he does not see the truth.

This can mean two things. If a man thinks that he is doing the action, and that the action does not come from the Spirit of God beyond, then he is deluded. Or it can mean that he who thinks that the Infinite Spirit is involved in the action is deluded. It is rather a complex question. There are three levels in all human action: physical, psychological and spiritual. The body and the mind are engaged in all, but behind them both is the *Atman*, the Spirit, and ultimately every action comes from the Spirit of God. When we imagine that 'I' am doing this, thinking that I alone am the author, we are deceiving ourselves because we are totally dependent on God for all our activity. Therefore one interpretation is that he who thinks that 'I am the doer' and forgets that he is dependent on God is deluded. But another aspect is that we can understand that God (*Atman*, Spirit,) is involved in all these actions, but then go on to think that if we do a bad action God is not only involved but is responsible. That is equally illusory. God is the first cause and is beyond all and although He works through all, He is not responsible for evil. We are responsible for the evil we do, sincere evil is the effect of a free will.

17. He who is free from the chains of selfishness, and whose mind is free from any ill-will, even if he kills all these warriors he kills them not and he is free.

There is a suggestion in Hinduism that if a man is a *jnani*, a knower, who has gone beyond the body and the mind and reached the inner spirit, then he may reach such a state of freedom that he is not responsible for anything he may do. This is a very dangerous doctrine and is not generally accepted. It is in fact a misinterpretation. What the text means is that if the spirit is free from the chains of selfishness and has rid itself of egoism, and if the mind is free from any ill will, then no evil can be conceived. The action will come from the Spirit within and that cannot be evil. But there is the suggestion in the *Gita*, as elsewhere, that Arjuna is being told, "You are a warrior, you are fighting in this battle; it is your duty to kill these people and you must not worry about it. It will not be you who is killing them; it will be the body that is killing them, not you yourself." That is very deceptive. What one finds in the *Gita*, as in all this tradition, is that there are different currents of the thought which are not always clearly distinguished. On the whole the *Gita* has gone beyond these contradictions. Zaehner is among those who maintain that the doctrine of the *Gita* is that killing only takes place on the phenomenal plane, not on the absolute. There is a danger in Hinduism of saying that no action in this world has any ultimate significance whether it is good or evil. This is a correlate of the view that the world is simply a world of phenomena, change and multiplicity, which is passing away all the time and has no ultimate reality. The need is to go beyond the whole world of phenomena and realise the one absolute Truth. Then one is totally free. But that is only one aspect of the *Gita* and on the whole the text is against that view. The true view of the *Gita* is that when we reach the level of the Spirit, we find that it is the Lord himself who is in us and is acting through us, and that we must unite ourselves with the Lord to fulfill his purpose in the world. This comes nearer to a Christian point of view.

18. In the idea of a work there is the knower, the knowing and the known. When the idea is work there is the doer, the doing and the thing done.

19. The knowing, the doer and the thing done are said in the science of the 'Gunas' to be of three kinds, according to their qualities. Hear of these three.

20. When one sees Eternity in things that pass away and Infinity in finite things, then one has pure knowledge.

Mascaró is little free, but he brings out the full sense of it. Zaehner, who is much more literal, translates, "That kind of knowledge by which one sees one mode of being, changeless, undivided in all contingent beings, divided as they are is goodness, (that is, *sattvic*) knowledge. Be sure of this."
One of the great intuitions of the *Gita* is that everything that happens in this world ultimately has its source in the one Eternal Reality beyond. As the text says, "One sees eternity in things that pass away and infinity in finite things." Behind all time and space there is the Infinite and the Eternal, and wisdom consists in seeing beyond the temporal and spatial to this Eternal Reality present everywhere in everything. Ignorance is when one takes the temporal, spatial phenomenon for the ultimate reality. This is what we all tend to do. We look around and see the earth and the trees and the sky, and we see each other and our own bodies – and we stop there. All these are phenomena, appearances that come to us through our senses. The sense phenomena are reflected in the mind and we arrive at a particular view of the phenomenal world. Wisdom is to see that beyond you and me and the earth, the One Reality, God, is present, in everyone and everything, in every moment, in every situation. The ideal of the *Gita* and the *Upanishads*

is thus to see beyond the phenomena to the Eternal Reality at every moment of one's life.

21. But if one merely sees the diversity of things with their divisions and limitations then one has impure knowledge.

That is what most people do, seeing the diversity and failing to see the unity. They see a tree and it is a tree and nothing else. They see a person and it is a person and nothing else. They do not relate the tree to the whole cosmos of which it is a part; they do not relate that person to the whole of humanity of which each one is part. They do not relate the tree and humanity to the whole cycle of nature and evolution which has been going on from the beginning of time and which is moving towards an end. They do not see things as a whole; they see them in part.

In a very real sense all evil comes from seeing the parts and not the whole. I am I, and you are you and we come into conflict when we do not recognise our dependence on one another in the unity of the whole. I often think of the illustration of the relation between light and colour. There is one light and in that light all colours are contained. But when the colours come out of the light, red, blue, green violet, orange, they all appear quite different and opposite; they even clash. Yet they are all manifestations of the one light.

When we see only the difference, when we see only red and blue and green without relating them to the light, we are in the world of duality, the world of opposition, violence, of conflict, indeed of all evil.

When we see ourselves as separate persons, separate from others, separate from the world, separate from God, that is the essence of sin. When we see ourselves and the world and everything in its total dependence on the One Truth, the One Reality, the Word of God, then we are in the truth.

22. And if one selfishly sees a thing as if it were everything, independent of the ONE and the many, then one is in the darkness of ignorance.

The *rajasic* man sees different things as opposed to one another, but the *tamasic* man sees one thing as if it were everything. He is completely obsessed with one thing. It may be money, it may be drink, it may be sex, it may be work. That is disastrous; it is a total reversal of the truth. Instead of seeing the One in everything, such people see each thing in isolation

as if it were all. They make a god of money, or work, or of pleasure. That
is the lowest level.

23. When work is done as sacred work, unselfishly, with a peaceful mind,
     without lust or hate, with no desire for reward, then the work is pure.

A sacred work is strictly one that is ordained by the scriptures, but
it can be applied to any work done without attachment. The work that
binds is work done with attachment to people or to things or to institutions,
and we nearly always act from attachment. To be detached from oneself,
from people, from things, and to act with a completely pure motive is
extremely difficult but that is the only proper work. As the Gospel says,
we have to be totally detached from father and mother and wife and children
and lands and whatever we have. Then we can love totally. All love which
is attached is a selfish love. A mother's love or a husband's love or that
of nuns working perhaps for some good cause, will normally contain an
element of selfishness. But when one is detached, one is completely free
from all self-motive and one loves that person for him or herself as God's
own creation; and that is perfect love. The love of God is totally detached.
He is not attached to any of us; he is completely detached and loves us
totally as a result.

It is equally wrong to be either averted from or attached to somebody
or something. We have to be totally detached and then we are able to deal
with the person, the thing, or the situation with calmness, with a peaceful
mind and with right understanding.

24. But when work is done with selfish desire, or feeling it is an effort,
     or thinking it is a sacrifice, then the work is impure.

When one feels that 'I am the doer', one is immediately pleased with
oneself or disappointed in oneself. On the other hand, when one realises
that God is the doer and that we are His instruments, the whole perspective
changes. Notice that to think that one is making a sacrifice is itself a mark
of impurity.

25. And that work which is done with a confused mind, without
     considering what may follow, or one's own powers, or the harm done
     to others, or one's own loss, is work of darkness.

26. A man free from the chains of selfish attachments, free from his lower 'I am', who has determination and perseverance, and whose inner peace is beyond victory or defeat — such a man has pure *sattva*.

That is, when we do our work unselfishly, in the spirit of surrender, we are not disturbed by success or failure. That, as we have seen before, is the test of unselfish work.

27. But a man who is a slave of his passions, who works for selfish ends, who is greedy, violent and impure, and who is moved by pleasure and pain, is a man of impure Rajas.

28. And a man without self-harmony, vulgar, arrogant and deceitful; malicious, indolent and despondent, and also procrastinating, is a man of the darkness of Tamas.

It is quite useful to examine oneself and to see all one's actions in the light of whether they are *sattvic*, *rajasic* or *tamasic*. We all have the three qualities in us, even the *tamasic* tendencies. Indolence, despondency, and procrastination afflict most people from time to time. We cannot get rid of these three *gunas*; they have to be harmonized. The *tamasic* and *rajasic* aspects must be under complete control and the *sattvic* quality must permeate everything.

Sattva is purity, intelligence, and clarity, and when that is in control it guides the *rajas*, the energy, the force, which gives us the drive to do our work. *Tamas* is inertia, but it is also a firmness, a solidity, in the sense of being 'down to earth'. So each has its place.

29. Hear now fully and in detail the threefold division of wisdom and steadiness, according to the three Gunas.

The word for wisdom is *buddhi*. This is a word with which we are very familiar, and 'reason' is perhaps the best translation here, but *buddhi* has two levels. There is the level of reason, discrimination, judgement of right and wrong, and so on, and then there is the higher *buddhi* which is the intuitive faculty through which we are able to perceive God and truth and eternal Reality. Here the text is dealing with the discriminating reason.

30. There is a wisdom which knows when to go and when to return, what is to be done and what is not be done, what is fear and what is courage, what is bondage and what is liberation — that is pure wisdom.

That kind of discrimination is really fundamental. It is what St. Thomas Aquinas called prudence, which teaches one what to do and what not to do, not merely in general, but in particular situations.

What is fear and what is courage? It is very easy to be mistaken. Fear can lead to cowardice, but courage can lead to presumption. The fundamental need is to have discrimination whereby we can discern the middle way.

31. Impure wisdom has no clear vision of what is right and what is wrong, what should be done and what should not be done.

32. And there is a wisdom obscured in darkness when wrong is thought to be right, and when things are thought to be that which they are not.

That is the lowest level. Seeing all things in a perverted way is the wisdom of *tamas*.

33. When in the yoga of holy contemplation the movements of the mind and of the breath of life are in a harmony of peace, there is steadiness, and that steadiness is pure.

The word for steadiness is *dhritya*. The root *dhr* occurs also in *dharma*. *Dharma* is the law which governs the universe and *dharma* is duty; it is the law, or that which is solidly based. Yoga is the state in which the breath is controlled and the mind no longer wanders, but is firmly established in the law, the harmony of the universe.

34. But that steadiness which, with a desire for rewards, attaches itself to wealth, pleasure, and even religious ritual, is a steadiness of passion, impure.

These are the three ends of life in the Hindu tradition: *kama, artha* and *dharma*. The fourth is *moksha*. *Kama* is pleasure and it is recognised that pleasure is one of the proper ends of life. Happiness and enjoyment are perfectly legitimate. Of course, they can also be illegitimate. *Artha* is wealth, and the pursuit of wealth is also considered necessary for the business of living. *Dharma* is the law which controls the pursuit of pleasure and wealth. One meaning of *dharma* is 'duty', but it is more than that. It is the law of the universe as a whole, which is what St. Thomas called the *lex eterna*, the eternal law, and it is that law manifested in human life and in human society. In India there is the law of caste. One's *dharma* is one's state of life, or in Christian terms, 'the state of life in which it has pleased God to call you'. In India if one is a Brahmin, one's duty is sacrifice and the study of the *Vedas*, whereas the duties of a *kshatriya* are to fight, and to govern and rule. The duty of the *vaisya* is to work as a farmer or a merchant, and the duty of the *shudra* is to serve. This is one's *dharma*, one's whole duty in life. So these are the three ends of life – *kama, artha,* and *dharma*. When they are pursued with a desire for reward, they are impure. When we seek pleasure for ourselves, when we seek wealth for ourselves and when we do our duty for selfish ends because it will make us respected, then the work is impure.

35. And that steadiness whereby a fool does not surrender laziness, fear, self-pity, depression and lust, is indeed a steadiness of darkness.

36. Hear now, great Arjuna, of the three kinds of pleasure. There is the pleasure of following that right path which leads to the end of all pain.

37. What seems at first a cup of sorrow is found in the end immortal wine. That pleasure is pure: it is the joy which arises from a clear vision of the Spirit.

Often things appear difficult and painful, but when we accept them, they become a source of joy. That is a pleasure that is good and that comes from the Spirit, a gift of God.

38. But the pleasure which comes from the craving of the senses with the objects of their desire, which seems at first a drink of sweetness but is found in the end a cup of poison, is the pleasure of passion, impure.

The fundamental teaching of the Bible is that the path of virtue seems difficult at first, but afterwards it brings rejoicing and the path of evil seems very attractive at first and pleasurable but it ends in sorrow. As it is said in the Gospel, "Narrow is the gate and straight the way that leads to life, and broad is the gate and easy the way that leads to destruction" (Matt. 7.13,14).

39. And that pleasure which both in the beginning and in the end is only a delusion of the soul, which comes from the dullness of sleep, laziness or carelessness, is the pleasure of darkness.

40. There is nothing on earth or in heaven which is free from these three powers of Nature.

So that is the doctrine. All this is included in the basic doctrine, which goes all through the *Gita*, of the two sources of all reality, *purusha*, spirit, consciousness, and *prakriti*, nature, matter. The whole creation comes from a union of *purusha* and *prakriti*. The light shines in the darkness, the light comes into this womb of nature and brings forth the whole creation. The whole of nature is governed by these three constituents: light, fire and darkness. If the light prevails, goodness prevails; if fire predominates, violence prevails; and if *tamas*, darkness, prevails, everything sinks down to death and darkness.

41. The works of Brahmins, Kshatriyas, Vaisyas and Shudras are different, in harmony with the three powers of their born nature.

The four classes, *varnas*, are now related to the three *gunas*. It is probably true to say that the intention of the *Gita* was to reinstate the *varnas* as the basis of the order of society. One can say that at this time Hindu society was being given its structure. It is a very interesting period. After the Vedic period which ends about 500 BC we have the epic period between 500 BC and 500 AD. Those thousand years constitute the formative period of Hindu society. There are many conflicting elements and different philosophies in which the *Gita* has a central place. It was then that the laws of Manu were codified and the four castes established. But it is better not to use the word 'caste'. In Sanskrit the term is *varna* which means colour. 'Class' is perhaps the best translation because there are only four *varnas* but there are hundreds of castes, different trades and different religious groups each having their own caste. The four *varnas* are really based on colour and this was perfectly intentional. The Aryan invaders were fair-skinned and to preserve their own colour they introduced the three higher classes of *Brahmins, kshatriyas* and *vaisyas,* while the dark-skinned Dravidians were classed as *sudras,* the latter being the workers. In a way there is a sort of universal character in this structure. Many Hindus today will say that they do not want the caste system as it is, but they say the basis was sound. In every human society there are these four orders. Similar structure was very evident in, for instance, the feudal society in Europe. In India there is the *Brahmin* who is concerned with God, religion, divine revelation and sacrifice, like the priestly caste in the Middle Ages in Europe. Then there is the *kshatriya,* the warrior, the ruler, the governor, like the nobles in medieval Europe. Then the *vaisya,* who is not only the merchant but also the landowning farmer, the producer. Fourthly, there is the worker, the *shudra,* collectively comprising the labouring class which is corresponds with the self in medieval society.

One can say the Brahmin priest is *sattvic.* He belongs to the order of light, intelligence, clarity and vision. The warrior is *rajasic,* a man of energy, courage, force, and so on. Then the *vaisya* comes in between; he has to have the energy of the warrior but he is somewhat more *tamasic.* Finally there is the worker, the labourer, the *shudra,* who belongs to the earth and who, like the earth, is solid and basic to society.

42. The works of a Brahmin are peace; self-harmony, austerity and purity; loving-forgiveness and righteousness; vision and wisdom and faith.

These are virtues, which have been referred to frequently throughout the *Gita. Sama* is peace, or more accurately serenity or sameness. *Dama* is self-restraint and *tapas,* asceticism, self-control, discipline. *Sauca* means purity, *kshanta* is long suffering or forbearance, and *arjavam* is uprightness. Then *jnana* is higher wisdom and *vijnana* is discriminative knowledge or understanding. Lastly there is religious faith. These are the virtues of a Brahmin.

Now this is what a Brahmin ought to be. In the course of history all these orders became hereditary, but even today it is often said that a man is not really a Brahmin unless he has these virtues. Many Hindus who defend the caste system today say a Brahmin is not so by birth; he has to be a Brahmin by nature.

Zaehner quotes an excerpt from the *Dhammapada* of the Buddha, which

I always like: "I call not a man a Brahmin because he was born from a certain family or mother, for he may be proud and he may be wealthy. The man who is free from possessions and free from desires — him I call a Brahmin."

So those are the virtues of the Brahmin. There is a tendency today to think that equality means that everybody has to be the same, whereas in a normal society there is inevitably differentiation. Mahatma Gandhi defended the caste system, but he said there should be no discrimination. A sweeper is equal to a lawyer or a doctor; each has a function in society, and each should be given proper respect. In our day everybody wants to be a clerical worker, not a manual worker, and that makes for an unbalanced society. In the same way no one wants to allow for differences of culture. Everybody has to have the same level of culture, but this is not possible. What happens in practice is that the general level of culture declines. It still remains a problem how to extend education to all and yet preserve differences of culture and distinctive ways of life.

43. These are the works of a Kshatriya: a heroic mind, inner fire, constancy, resourcefulness, courage in battle, generosity and noble leadership.

These are the typical virtues of the 'nobleman', the warrior of the heroic age, the Knight of the Middle Ages. Winston Churchill was a particularly good example in modern times.

44. Trade, agriculture and the rearing of cattle is the work of a Vaisya. And the work of the Shudra is service.

Trade and agriculture are the basis of any normal society and the agricultural worker, the peasant, though he may be *tamasic* in character, is yet the support of the whole community. The substitution of machinery for the farm worker only de-humanises society. Gandhi rightly saw the need to restore the self-supporting village community as the basis of the social order.

45. They all attain perfection when they find joy in their work. Hear how a man attains perfection and finds joy in his work.

People are happy when they find joy in their work and very few people today are happy for that reason. Work is something they have to do; they get through it and then enjoy themselves by doing something else. But that is a very imperfect mode of existence. The really happy existence is that of the person who is happy in his or her work. Now Krishna explains how to find joy in one's work.

46. A man attains perfection when his work is worship of God, from whom all things come and who is in all.

More literally, "By dedicating the work that is proper (to his caste) to him who is the source of the activity of all beings, by whom this whole universe was spun, a man attains perfection and success" (Z). When we do our work as work in God, we find God is working in us and all the different works are different modes of the divine action. This is exactly the teaching of St. Paul who says, "There are varieties of working, but it is the same God who inspires them all in everyone" (I Cor. 12.6). When we accept our own *dharma*, our work, and accept it as the work of God, then we find happiness in it. I think that is one of the reasons why people in the villages of India are comparatively happy. They may have a miserable life by modern standards, but it is fixed. They know where they are. They have their work to do and they take pleasure in their work and consequently find peace. I am always asking why, when one goes to a village, one finds such an atmosphere of joy. In many respects there is unhappiness but the general atmosphere is one of joy. I think it is because the people accept their situation. They do not worry about it or want it to be different, nor do they particularly want to improve their standard of life. The village people know they cannot change much and they accept that it comes from God. This leads to devotion to God in that they realise that God is present in their lives. That seems to be the source of happiness, and that is precisely what most people have lost today. They do not feel that their life is from God or that their work is His work. To most people the whole thing is simply chance and it is their job improve it if they can. On the other hand, if one's whole life and one's work are seen as coming from God, then one can discover this deep joy in life. The next *shloka* is interesting — yet few today would agree with it.

47. Greater is thine own work, even if this be humble, than the work of another, even if this be great. When a man does the work God gives him, no sin can touch this man.

There are dangers in this, which is really a defence of the caste system. One is born to a certain status, a certain way of life, as a carpenter, a mason, a washerman, a lawyer, a Brahmin or whatever it may be, and that comes from God and one does that *dharma*, that work. It is far better to do one's own work than to do what is apparently a better work of someone else. This was also the old Christian teaching, "To earn one's own living in that state of life in which it has pleased God to call you". Stay where you are and do your work there. That was the old tradition. Obviously there is a danger in it. It becomes too static and it can lead to great abuses. But I think we have gone to the opposite extreme. Nobody wants to keep to the state in which he was called; each person wants to move up. I think one must seek a balance in all these things. There can be a system more fluid than the old hereditary one, in which there is a general order of society and different degrees and different functions which are commonly accepted, without the divisions being rigidly fixed. That, I think, brings the greatest happiness. The most stable cultures in the world were the great mediaeval cultures of India, China, Islam and Europe from 500 AD to 1500 AD. In Europe, for instance, there was a more or less stable culture which was based on agriculture and different kinds of craftsmanship, yet it had the capacity for continual growth within it. There were schools and universities coming up with the beginning of the study of medicine and science, and culminating in the study of philosophy and theology. It was an ordered society and people felt confidence in the basic structure of society. Things often went wrong, to be sure. There were tragedies and disasters, natural and human, taking place, but the order was accepted. This was the *dharma.* But today it is the reverse. Many good things are happening and there are wonderful jobs and opportunities, for instance to study, but people are dissatisfied with the general state of society.

In the past, society was based on the right principles and, however much things might go wrong, the people felt a certain security. But now, however good things are and however well one does, somehow the whole thing is out of joint. So, "better your own work, your own *dharma*, than the *dharma* of somebody else."

48. And a man should not abandon his work, even if he cannot achieve it in full perfection; because in all work there may be imperfection, even as in all fire there is smoke.

Merely because they cannot achieve perfection in their work, people become discontented. They do something and then discover some imperfection; it is not altogether satisfactory and they become discouraged. But every human work is imperfect and none gives complete satisfaction. One has to put up with that "even as in all fire there is smoke." One cannot find perfection in this world. We come next to the whole question of human perfection, and the basis of the society in which we are to live. But how does one reach perfection in that society?

49. When a man has his reason in freedom from bondage, and his soul is in harmony, beyond desires, then renunciation leads him to a region supreme which is beyond earthly action.

50. Hear now how he then reaches Brahman, the highest vision of Light.

51. When the vision of reason is clear, and in steadiness the soul is in harmony; when the world of sound and other senses is gone, and the spirit has risen above passion and hate;

52. When a man dwells in the solitude of silence, and meditation and contemplation are ever with him; when too much food does not disturb his health, and his thoughts and words and body are in peace; when freedom from passion is his constant will;

53. And his selfishness and violence and pride are gone; when lust and anger and greediness are no more, and he is free from the thought 'this is mine'; then this man has risen on the mountain of the Highest: he is worthy to be one with Brahman, with God.

54. He is one with Brahman, with God, and beyond grief and desire his soul is in peace. His love is one for all creation, and he has supreme love for me.

We have here a summary of the basic teaching of the *Gita* on the path of union with God. When we have freed ourselves from the passions, from the senses, from the mind, and all its changes, and from the thought of an 'I' and a 'mine', then we reach this inner peace, this *shanti*, then we become

Brahman. We become one with God. The point where the human meets the divine is the *buddhi* and when we enter into that point we enter into the awareness of Brahman, of the eternal, everywhere and in everything. It is a part of our own being. That is *Brahma-vidhya. Brahma-bhuta* is the other phase; the individual becomes Brahman, becomes God. He is one with Brahman, with God; he no longer grieves and no longer feels desire. By desire is meant a passionate desire; it is one of two extremes. We are usually either depressed and grieving over something or passionately desiring, wanting something. When we have freed ourselves from that, we become *sama*, which means sameness. "He is the same to all creatures, to all beings and above all he is *madbhaktim*, devoted to me, the Lord." "His love is one for all creation and he has supreme love for me." That is the goal. So the *Gita* is leading the disciple up step by step. One frees oneself from all the encumbrances of the body, of the soul, of the mind and, opening oneself to the divine, to inner peace, one surrenders oneself to the Lord. This is the final stage: self-surrender.

55. By love he knows me in truth, who I am and what I am and when he knows me in truth he enters into my Being.

"By love he knows me in truth." This love leads to knowledge. In Christian doctrine true knowledge of God is always 'love-knowledge', or as St. Paul puts it, "the knowledge of the love of God which surpasses knowledge" (Eph.3.19). This is the precise nature of mystical knowledge. When we enter into this depth, this peace, this awareness of Brahman, we discover our inmost Self. At the point of the *buddhi* we encounter the *Atman*, the inner Self. We enter into communion with Brahman, with the Reality, the Eternal everywhere, in everything, and within that Brahman, at the heart of that Brahman, we find the Lord, the personal God. This is the path of self-knowledge, leading to the knowledge of God in all things and finally to the knowledge of the personal being of God. Love, *bhakti*, is an essential element in this knowledge. That is the ultimate goal. At this stage we become one with the personal God. This is exactly the teaching of St. John's gospel. "If a man love me, he will keep my word, and my Father will love him and we will come to him and make our abode with him" (John 14.23). And again, "He who abides in me and I in him, he it is who will bear much fruit" (John 15.5).

56. In whatever work he does he can take refuge in me, and he attains then by my grace the imperishable home of Eternity.

Another translation reads, "though ever performing all actions" (B & D). It is noteworthy that here the *Gita* has completely rejected the idea that one must give up action. We can do all our actions but we do them in this attitude of self-surrender; everything is then done by grace. What the *Gita* is affirming all the time is not that we simply give up all work and enter into a pure state of contemplation, but that, having surrendered all selfish work and the self altogether, we enter into the state of union with God and then we are free to do all work, whatever it is. We can find total freedom in everything because we have reached the state of total communion.

57. Offer in thy heart all thy works to me, and see me as the End of thy love, take refuge in the yoga of reason, and ever rest thy soul in me.

We come now to the climax of the *Gita's* teaching on the love of God. This is the way of *bhakti*; the whole mind is fixed on God all the time and one surrenders everything to Him and does everything as an offering to Him. It is a total self-surrender.

58. If thy soul finds rest in me, thou shalt overcome all dangers by my grace; but if thy thoughts are on thyself, and thou wilt not listen, thou shalt perish.

Prasad means grace and the *Gita* maintains that by self-surrender the whole work of man becomes the work of God, whereas if we remain centered on the ego, the *ahankara*, we are lost.

Krishna now turns Arjuna back to the original question of fighting in the battle:

59. If thou wilt not fight thy battle of life because in selfishness thou art afraid of the battle, thy resolution is in vain: nature will compel thee.

This is very interesting. The point is that if one is relying on the ego and thinking, "I will not fight", one will resolve in vain because one will

have to do it. I think what it means here is this: there are three principles
in the universe, the first two being *Purusha*, the Spirit Supreme, which is
working in everything, and *prakriti*, nature or matter, through which the
Supreme is working. The third principle, between *Purusha* and *prakriti*, is
the *jivatman*, the individual soul. Our error is to think that the individual
soul is doing everything, but in reality, the *Purusha*, the Supreme, is working
through. So either we surrender ourself to God and He will do everything
in us and through us, or else we will simply be surrendered to *prakriti* and
we will do everything by the compulsion of nature. So we have to choose;
there is no such thing as pure freedom. Many people today imagine they
are free to do whatever they like. That is pure illusion. One either does
the will of God, surrendering oneself to Him or one is driven by the
compulsion of nature, by one's own unconscious, and by the forces of the
world around. A man like Hitler thinks that he is being very strong and
powerful, but in actual fact he is simply being driven by the powers of nature
which are released in him. All such people are being driven by the
unconscious. They are not great men at all; they are men who have allowed
prakriti to take possession of them.

60. Because thou art in the bondage of Karma, of the forces of thine own
     past life; and that which thou, in thy delusion, with a good will dost
     not want to do, unwillingly thou shalt have to do.

61. God dwells in the heart of all beings, Arjuna: thy God dwells in thy
     heart. And his power of wonder moves all things — puppets in a play
     of shadows — whirling them onwards on the stream of time.

It can be said that such people are driven by nature, but it can also
be said that it is God who is working in them. God works through His
maya, his power of wonder, as Mascaró calls it, and the whole creation
is dominated by this *maya*. As long as we take this world to be the reality
itself, we are under the illusion of *maya*. When we see through *maya*, we
realise that it is God who works through all things.

62. Go to him for thy salvation with all thy soul, victorious man. By His
     grace thou shalt obtain the peace supreme, thy home of Eternity.

Notice that the *Gita* here uses the third person to refer to God, though a little later on it returns to the first person. It is God who is in the heart of everything, whirling it round. So that is the counsel, surrender to God; go beyond all the play of nature, the *maya*; put your whole trust in God and by His grace you will attain this peace supreme, the home of eternity.

63. I have given thee words of vision and wisdom more secret than hidden mysteries. Ponder them in the silence of thy soul, and then in freedom do thy will.

"More secret than all else that is secret" (B & D). It is a very strong phrase, *guhyad guhyataram*, more secret than the secret. The *guha* is the cave of the heart, the most secret place which contains the supreme secret of life.

64. Hear again my Word supreme, the deepest secret of silence. Because I love thee well, I will speak to thee words of salvation.

The climax of the *Gita's* teaching on the love of God is the recognition that God loves us. *Ishtah* means beloved. In Hinduism there is the practice of worshipping what is called an *ishta devata*; every Hindu chooses one particular form of God which he worships and that is called his *ishta devata*, the God of his choice. So Krishna says, you are *ishta*, you are my choice, beloved of me. Now in the next verse he brings it to a climax.

65. Give thy mind to me, and give me thy heart, and thy sacrifice, and thy adoration. This is my Word of promise: thou shalt in truth come to me, for thou art dear to me.

The Sanskrit phrases are very striking — *manmana, mad-bhakto, mad-yaji, mam namaskuru*, that is, me-minded, me-devoted, to me-sacrificed, me-worshipping.

Namaskara is literally to prostrate. When we greet somebody in India we say "Namaskara", that is, we greet God in the person. One prostrates before the person as before God. But Krishna now reveals the other aspect of this surrender to God: God gives his love to men. Zaehner emphasises that this is the culmination of the Hindu religion — not only that we love God, but that God loves us. In the same way the culmination of Christian revelation is: "In this is love, not that we loved God but that he loved us"

(John 4.10). At this point Hindu and Christian meet. We should look on
the *Gita* as a revelation, analogous to that of the Gospel. There is a gradual
movement in the *Upanishads* of man seeking God, discovering himself,
discovering Brahman. Then there is an awakening of this *bhakti*, this devotion,
this love, by which man surrenders himself to God. Then that *bhakti* leads
to the knowledge that we are loved by God. That is the culmination of
revelation: it is not merely that we love God, but that He loves us. That
is what is revealed in the *Gita*.

66.   Leave all things behind, and come to me for thy salvation. I will make
      thee free from the bondage of sins. Fear no more.

"Leave all things behind, come to me for thy salvation" is literally "give
up all *dharmas*". This is exactly what St. Paul means by the 'law'. *Dharma*
is the law. This is a call to go beyond the law, to enter into a state of grace.
Give up the *dharma*, give up the law and any human contrivance or effort,
and accept this gift from me. So give up all *dharmas*, turn to me as your
only refuge. I will deliver you from all evils. Have no fear, do not be afraid,
"I will make thee free from the bondage of sin", he says. The word is *papa*,
which is the ordinary word for sin. It is remarkable how close to Christian
revelation this comes.

67.   These things must never be spoken to one who lacks self-discipline
      or who has no love, or who does not want to hear or who argues
      against me.

It is said that one should not give this doctrine to everyone
indiscriminately or it will be abused. If one tells a person give up all *dharmas* and surrender to God, he will give up the law completely and do what
he likes. St. Augustine said, "Love and do what you will". If we love truly,
then we can do what we like. But if we mistake our own will for love,
then we are lost. "This should never be spoken to one who lacks self-
discipline," that is, one without *tapas*. Do not preach the Gospel to everybody.
One should only preach the Gospel to those who are ready for it, when
they are ready to receive it. When people for instance, put up on the railway
station a billboard, "God so loved the world", it makes a mockery of religion.

68.   But he who will teach this secret doctrine to those who have love
for me, and who himself has supreme love, he in truth shall come unto me.

Not only to receive this doctrine but to give it to others is the highest virtue, if others are ready to receive it.

69. For there can be no man among men who does greater work for me, nor can there be a man on earth who is dearer to me than he is.

To spread the love of God is the highest thing one can possibly do. "No man can render me more pleasing service than a man like this nor shall any man on earth be more beloved by me than he is" (Z). Here Krishna uses the word *priya* meaning dear or beloved.

70. He who learns in contemplation the holy words of our discourse, the light of his vision is his adoration. This is my truth.

"He who shall study this sacred dialogue of ours, by him I shall be worshipped with the sacrifice of wisdom, such is my mind" (B & D). *Yajna* is a sacrifice and *jnana yajna* is a sacrifice of wisdom. If we study the *Gita* in this way, out of love and devotion, this is to offer a sacrifice of wisdom, which is to say that our very reading of the *Gita* becomes an act of worship, a sacrificial act. That is all important. It should never be read simply academically. It has to be read in such a way as to awaken love and give the experience of the indwelling presence of God.

71. And he who only hears but has faith, and in his heart he has no doubts, he also attains liberation and the worlds of joy of righteous men.

Even if one does not have the knowledge of these things, but has love, that is enough. A Swami told me a rather amusing story about a scholar who was giving a lecture on the *Gita* in Sanskrit and the audience one by one became bored. They all walked out until eventually only one old man was left sitting in the front and he seemed quite enraptured. So the lecturer felt that at least he was appreciated by one man and at the end he went up to him and said, "I'm glad to know you appreciated my talk." "I wasn't listening to your talk at all," was the reply. So the lecturer said, "But you were showing such rapt attention." "Ah," said the old man, "but I saw Krishna in front of you and I was worshipping Krishna. I wasn't listening to your talk." So it is not really a learned exposition that is needed but rather to enable the reader to realise the presence of God.

72. Hast thou heard these words, Arjuna, in the silent communion of thy
     soul? Has the darkness of thy delusion been dispelled by thine inner
     Light?

This is rather a fanciful translation. Krishna's question is really, "Has
this been heard by thee with one-pointed mind"? (B & D). That is important.
Ekagrata means one-pointedness and one-pointedness arises when the mind
is concentrated in the *buddhi*, the pure intelligence, and one reaches the
inner knowledge. "Has your delusion, caused by unwisdom, been destroyed?"
(B & D). Arjuna had this *ajnana*, ignorance, and he felt that he could not
fight in the battle, but now he has seen the truth and his confusion has
been dispelled.
     Arjuna's final response to Krishna is:

73. By thy grace I remember my Light, and now gone is my delusion.
     My doubts are no more, my faith is firm; and now I can say 'Thy
     will be done'.

Or: "Destroyed is my delusion. I have gained knowledge through thy
grace, O immutable One, I am firm; my doubts have fled; I will do thy
bidding" (B & D). This is the conclusion. All Arjuna's doubts and fears have
been overcome and he is able to fight but — and this is the crucial point
— to do so in another spirit altogether.
     Sanjaya relates the final *shlokas*:

74. Thus I heard these words of glory between Arjuna and the God of
     all, and they fill my soul with awe and wonder.

75. By the grace of the poet Vyasa I heard these words of secret silence.
     I heard the mystery of Yoga, taught by Krishna the Master himself.

76. I remember, O king, I remember the words of holy wonder between
     Krishna and Arjuna, and again and again my soul feels joy.

77. And I remember, I ever remember, that vision of glory of the God
     of all, and again and again joy fills my soul.

78. Wherever is Krishna, the End of Yoga, wherever is Arjuna who masters

the bow, there is beauty and victory, and joy and all righteousness. This is my faith.

No one knows who wrote the *Gita*. It was ascribed, with the whole of the *Mahabharata* to Vyasa, just as all the books of the Jewish law were ascribed to Moses. But at some point an inspired poet must have arisen who composed this 'song' and inserted it in the *Gita*. It is truly a work to fill the soul with awe and wonder. To read it with devotion is to be purified within and to leave the mystery of Yoga, of the integration of the human person and its union with the personal God. For a Christian this is a wonderful confirmation of the revelation of God's love contained in the Gospel.

Glossary

Words which appear in *The Merriam-Webster Third New International Dictionary of the English Language* (1981) have been printed without italics. As well as being consistent with the usage in the *Commentary*, this gives an indication of the way Sanskrit terms are being accepted into the English Language.

acintya: inconceivable
aditi: infinite
advaita: non-duality
ahankara: ego, the sense of 'I'
ahimsa: non-violence
akshara: the imperishable
amrita: immortality
asanga: detachment
atman: the Self, God within; one's own reality
avatara: incarnate form of God
avidya: ignorance
avyakta: the unmanifest
bhakti: devotion, love
bhuta: a being, creature
brahmabhuta: becoming one with God

Brahman: the supreme reality, the ground of being
brahmavid: one who knows God
buddhi: the mind as functioning beyond discursive thought as in concentration, meditation and contemplation
chakra: one of the seven energy centers of the body
dama: inner control, self-restraint
deva: a god
dharma: law, duty; the cosmic law
dhyana: meditation
dubkha: unsatisfactoriness, suffering, sorrow
dvandva: duality
ekagrata: one-pointed
gunas: the (three) constituents of nature
indriyas: the senses
ishvara: the Lord
jiva: the individual soul
jivanmukta: one who has attained liberation in this life
jnana: wisdom, unitive knowledge
kama: desire
karma: work, action, ritual
karuna: compassion
krodha: anger
kshara: perishable
kshatriya: warrior
kutastho: the 'still point'
lila: play
lingam: symbolic representation of the formless God
loka: world
mahat: the Great Self, the level of consciousness in which the buddhi is transcended
manas: the reasoning or discursive mind
marga: path
maya: creative power; the created world, the world of appearance
moha: delusion
moksha: liberation
mukta: free, liberated
nirguna brahman: Brahman (God) without attributes
nirmala: without stain, pure

nirvana: the final state of being, beyond change and becoming
nivritti: movement of return, through the senses and the mind, to the One
papa: evil
paramatman: Supreme Self
pitri: father, ancestor
prakriti: nature, primal matter; the feminine principle
prasad: grace
prasanna: tranquil, transparent
pratyahara: detachment from objects of sense
pratyaksha: knowing by direct experience
pravritti: movement from the One to the many, flowing into the world
purusha: man; spirit; the masculine principle; the supreme personal God
rajas: fire, passion, activity (one of the three *gunas*)
sadhana: spiritual practice
sadhu: person dedicated to seeking holiness
saguna brahman: Brahman (God) without attributes
samadhi: pure awareness; concentration of ego, mind and senses into the self
samatva: equanimity
samsara: cyclic existence; birth, life and death
sanatana: eternal
sattva: goodness, purity, light (one of the three *gunas*)
shanti: peace
shudra: worker, labourer
tamas: darkness, dullness, sloth (one of the three *gunas*)
tapas: austerity, rigorous spiritual practice
tejas: splendour
trishna: clinging
turiya: the 'fourth state' (the others being waking consciousness, dreaming
    and dreamless sleep)
tyaga: surrender
vijnana: discriminative knowledge
viveka: discernment
vritti: movements of the mind
yajna: sacrifice
yoga: practice of spiritual discipline; the means whereby integration and union
    are attained
yuga: an age of the world (e.g., we are at present in the Kali Yuga)
yukta: one who is integrated